Advances in Old Age Psychiatry: Chromosomes to Community Care

Advances in
Old Age Psychiatry
Chromosomes to Community Care

Edited by

CLIVE HOLMES and ROBERT HOWARD

Section of Old Age Psychiatry, Institute of Psychiatry, London, UK

WRIGHTSON BIOMEDICAL PUBLISHING LTD
Petersfield, UK and Bristol, PA, USA

Editorial Office:

Wrightson Biomedical Publishing Ltd
Ash Barn House, Winchester Road, Stroud,
Petersfield, Hampshire GU32 3PN, UK
Telephone: 01730 265647
Fax: 01730 260368

British Library Cataloguing in Publication Data

Advances in old age psychiatry : chromosomes to community
   care
   1. Geriatric psychiatry 2. Aged – Mental health
   I. Holmes, Clive II. Howard, Robert, 1961–
   618.9'7'689

Library of Congress Cataloging in Publication Data

Advances in old age psychiatry : chromosomes to community care /.
   edited by Clive Holmes and Robert Howard.
       p. cm.
   Includes bibliographical references and index.
   ISBN 1-871816-34-3 (hard cover)
   1. Geriatric psychiatry. I. Holmes, Clive, 1960– . II. Howard,
Robert, 1961– .
   [DNLM: 1. Mental Disorders–in old age. 2. Mental Disorders–
therapy. 3. Geriatric Psychiatry–methods. WT 150 A2445 1997]
   618.97'689–dc21
   DNLM/DLC
   For Library of Congress   96-52925
                                    CIP

ISBN 1 871816 34 3

Composition by Scribe Design, Gillingham, Kent
Printed in Great Britain by Biddles Ltd, Guildford.

Contents

Contributors

Melanie Abas, *Section of Old Age Psychiatry, Institute of Psychiatry, De Crespigny Park, London SE5 8AF, UK*

Mark Ardern, *Department of Psychiatry of Old Age, St Charles' Hospital, Ladbroke Grove, London W10 6DZ, UK*

Robert Baldwin, *Department of Psychiatry for the Elderly, Psychiatry Directorate, Central Manchester Healthcare Trust, Oxford Road, Manchester M13 9WL, UK*

Martin Blanchard, *Department of Old Age Psychiatry, Royal Free Hospital, Pond Street, London NW3 1YD, UK*

Dan Blazer, *Department of Psychiatry and Behavioural Sciences, Duke University School of Medicine, Durham, NC 27710, USA*

Jorge A. Cervilla, *Section of Old Age Psychiatry, Institute of Psychiatry, De Crespigny Park, London SE5 8AF, UK*

Colm Cooney, *Department of Old Age Psychiatry, Carew House, St Vincent's Hospital, Elm Park, Dublin 4, Republic of Ireland*

Ashok Devasenapathy, *Department of Clinical Neurological Sciences, University of Western Ontario, London, London, Ontario N6A 5A5, Canada*

Vladimir Hachinski, *Department of Clinical Neurological Sciences, University of Western Ontario, London, Ontario N6A 5A5, Canada*

Clive Holmes, *Section of Old Age Psychiatry, Institute of Psychiatry, De Crespigny Park, London SE5 8AF, UK*

Robert Howard, *Section of Old Age Psychiatry, Institute of Psychiatry, De Crespigny Park, London SE5 8AF, UK*

Rob Jones, *Department of Health Care of the Elderly, University of Nottingham Medical School, Nottingham NG7 2UH, UK*

Cornelius L.E. Katona, *Department of Psychiatry, University College London Medical School, Wolfson Building, Riding House Street, London W1N 8AA, UK*

James Lindesay, *Department of Psychiatry for the Elderly, University of Leicester, Leicester General Hospital, Leicester LE5 4PW, UK*

Simon Lovestone, *Section of Old Age Psychiatry, Institute of Psychiatry, De Crespigny Park, London SE5 8AF, UK*

Ian G. McKeith, *Department of Old Age Psychiatry, Institute for the Health of the Elderly, Newcastle General Hospital, Westgate Road, Newcastle upon Tyne NE4 6BE, UK*

Anthony H. Mann, *Section of Old Age Psychiatry, Institute of Psychiatry, De Crespigny Park, London SE5 8AF, UK*

David M.A. Mann, *Department of Pathological Sciences, Division of Molecular Pathology, University of Manchester, Oxford Road, Manchester M13 9PT, UK*

Elaine Murphy, *Psychiatric Services Research and Development, United Medical and Dental Schools, Guy's Hospital, London SE1 9RT, UK*

Brice Pitt, *Department of Mental Health of the Elderly, St Charles' Hospital, Ladbroke Grove, London W10 6DZ, UK*

Martin J. Prince, *Section of Old Age Psychiatry, Institute of Psychiatry, De Crespigny Park, London SE5 8AF, UK*

Andrew W. Procter, *Department of Psychiatry, Manchester Royal Infirmary, Oxford Road, Manchester M13 9BX, UK*

Marcus Richards, *MRC National Survey of Health and Development, Department of Epidemiology and Public Health, University College London Medical School, 1–19 Torrington Place, London WC1E 6BT, UK*

David Wilkinson, *Department of Old Age Psychiatry, Elderly Mental Health Services, Western Community Hospital, Walnut Grove, Milbrook, Southampton SO16 4XE, UK*

Steven H. Zarit, *The Gerontology Center, The Pennsylvania State University, Henderson S–105, University Park, PA 16802, USA*

Preface

The aim of this book is to bring together in one volume recent developments in a number of diverse areas within old age psychiatry. As old age psychiatrists we are fortunate in that exciting and rapid progress is being made in all fields but unfortunate in that it can be difficult to keep abreast of such developments. There is thus a clear need for an up-to-date summary of the field which condenses recent findings into an easily digested form. The format of the book is essentially similar to that of a short course held at the Institute of Psychiatry in July, 1996, with approximately equal divisions between the dementias and functional disorders and between physical and psychological management approaches. These divisions are meant to reflect the day-to-day clinical practice of workers in the field and to emphasize the primary aim of this book as a guide to what is likely to affect clinical practice in the next few years. Contributors were carefully chosen for international eminence in their fields together with individual renown as teachers and we thank them heartily for their good natured and prompt chapter delivery. Lee Wilding, Margaret Derrick and Marian Ryde have our lasting gratitude for their work with us on the short courses. Lastly, thanks to our publisher, Judy Wrightson, who we would recommend to all putative book authors and editors who seek, as we did, a painless journey along the road to book production.

CLIVE HOLMES and ROBERT HOWARD
November 1996

I

Dementia Risk Factors

Advances in Old Age Psychiatry: Chromosomes to Community Care
Edited by C. Holmes and R. Howard
© 1997 Wrightson Biomedical Publishing Ltd

1

The Epidemiology of Alzheimer's Disease

JORGE A. CERVILLA, MARTIN J. PRINCE AND ANTHONY H. MANN
Section of Old Age Psychiatry, Institute of Psychiatry, London, UK

The world's elderly population is currently undergoing an unprecedented expansion. It has been predicted that during the last 20 years of the century the elderly population will have increased by 29.4% in developed countries and by 77% in developing countries (United Nations, 1979). It is expected that by the year 2000 the number of persons aged 65 and over will be about 423 million, nearly half of whom will live in developing countries (WHO, 1993). This will increase the absolute number of persons suffering from Alzheimer's disease (AD) and other types of dementia, as it has been shown that the risk of dementia increases exponentially with increasing age (Jorm *et al.*, 1987).

DEFINITION AND DIAGNOSIS

Dementia has been defined as a syndrome that includes an acquired global impairment of memory and other cognitive functions in the absence of clouding of consciousness (Lishman, 1987). Most of the currently accepted nosological systems also include within their diagnostic criteria evidence of gradual progression, the presence of functional limitations and exclusion of other primary psychiatric disorders. Therefore, the diagnosis of AD is frequently reached as much by a process of exclusion as of inclusion.

Several problems remain in diagnosing dementia. First, it is not agreed that dementia is a clear nosological category. Brayne and Calloway (1988) have proposed a theory of a continuum between normal ageing and dementia on the basis of the unimodal and smooth distribution of cognitive and behavioural scales scores in community populations. They suggested that, instead of asking 'Does this person have dementia?', we should ask 'How much dementia does he have?' Thus, normal ageing changes and cognitive impairment are considered to be a spectrum of impairments along which the subject can pass before acquiring a diagnosis of AD.

In keeping with this theory, O'Connor (1992) proposed a distinction between dementing and demented subjects. ICD-10 has now included a new category of mild cognitive impairment which does not amount to dementia but which may indicate incipient stages of a dementing process. Katzman *et al.* (1989) reported that 22% of 'normal' elderly volunteers who made eight errors on a cognitive test became demented within the following five years as opposed to just 1% of those who only made one error.

A contrasting view is given by those who propose clear-cut categories of dementia and its subtypes. It has been frequently argued that cross-sectional studies may provide a biased 'picture' of the disease and that this can explain the 'continuum' distribution of cognitive disorders. However, when cohorts are studied following a longitudinal design the division between cases of dementia and non-cases may prove to be sharper than in cross-sectional designs. Research studies have used standardized diagnostic criteria to increase comparability as well as to improve diagnostic accuracy. Most of the currently used diagnostic systems (ICD–10, DSM–IV, NINCDS–ADRDA) require evidence of both decline in cognitive function and functional limitations in order to allow diagnosis of AD.

Dementia is a clinical diagnosis based on demonstrable impairment in memory, and at least one other cognitive domain, together with evidence of progressive functional and behavioural impairment. Reliable diagnosis therefore requires at least three components: (1) cognitive testing, (2) clinical interview, (3) informant history. Additionally, (4) blood tests, and (5) CT (computerized tomography) or MRI (magnetic resonance imaging) scan may be required to identify secondary dementias.

ASSESSMENT MEASURES

Epidemiology researchers have tended to use one of two approaches to detect dementia in community surveys.

One-stage screening uses a comprehensive instrument such as CAMDEX or GMS/AGECAT with HAS. The CAMDEX (Roth *et al.*, 1986) is a standardized interview with structured questions about physical and mental state, personal and family histories, and the onset and course of illness. It also includes an informant-based interview. The CAMDEX takes some 60 minutes plus an extra 20 minutes for the informant interview. It includes a section used for cognitive assessment of subjects (the CAMCOG) from which the Mini-Mental State Examination score (see below) can also be calculated. Its authors reported a very high inter-rater reliability and claim that its main advantage is in being sensitive (92%) and specific (96%) in identifying cases of organic disorder and depressive states and in their differential diagnoses.

The Geriatric Mental State or GMS (Copeland et al., 1986) is a comprehensive interview for the diagnosis of dementia (and functional disorders) that has gained international acceptance, being in use in longitudinal studies worldwide. It has been translated into many languages. The GMS includes an informant-based interview, the HAS, that collects a collateral history in standard form. The GMS has shown high levels of inter-rater reliability and test–retest reliability. It is not as capable of the precise identification of focal cognitive dysfunction as the CAMDEX. However, its main advantages are its wider focus on nonorganic disorders and the fact that it is linked to the AGECAT, a computer algorithm that generates ICD-10 diagnoses from the GMS responses.

Two-stage screening uses a brief, sensitive cognitive test followed by a more comprehensive and specific dementia-diagnostic package for those who 'fail' the initial screen. A consensus has been reached internationally on the use of the Mini-Mental State Examination (MMSE) (Folstein et al., 1975) as the first-stage instrument followed by either CAMDEX or GMS/HAS and CAMCOG as the second-stage definitive dementia-diagnosis instruments.

The MMSE has attained current acceptance as it has been shown to be adequately sensitive and specific against the criterion of a clinical diagnosis of dementia. Reported sensitivities and specificities include 100%/84% (Kay et al., 1985); 83%/87% (Brayne and Calloway, 1988); 94%/85% (Roth et al., 1986); and 87%/82% (Anthony et al., 1982). The cut-off points used were in each case 23/24. Kay et al. (1985) reported a moderate predictive power for mild cases of dementia which could be improved to 89% sensitivity and 84% specificity using a cut-off point of 24/25. Two other community surveys report positive predictive values ((PPVs) of 69% (Fratiglioni et al., 1991) (over 75 year old subjects) and 49% (O'Connor et al., 1989) (over 65 year old subjects). The MMSE therefore seems a reliable and valid instrument for the detection of mild, moderate and severe cases of dementia in the community. Its use in the Epidemiologic Catchment Area Study (ECA) (Folstein et al., 1991), the Framingham cohort (Bachman et al., 1992) and the current Medical Research Council (MRC) Multi-Centre Study of Cognitive Function and Ageing (MRC-CFAS) will provide further validative and normative population data.

Briefer cognitive tests have been used as initial screening tests for dementia, but with generally less satisfactory results than have been obtained with the MMSE. The 10-item Mental States Quotient (MSQ) and the 10-item Information/Orientation (I/O) subscale of the Comprehensive Assessment of Performance of the Elderly (CAPE) have both been criticized (Brayne and Calloway, 1988; O'Connor et al., 1989) on the grounds that they failed to identify early, mild cases of dementia. Reported sensitivity and specificity are 90%/88% for the I/O CAPE (Morgan *et al.*, 1987) and a PPV for the MSQ of 82–92% (Cooper and Bickel, 1984).

One interesting possibility is the Short Blessed (Katzman *et al.*, 1983), variously known as the Blessed Orientation-Memory-Concentration, the Abbreviated Mental Test Score (AMTS) or Short Blessed Test (SBT). This is a 6-item abbreviation of the 26-item Blessed Information-Memory-Concentration scale. Item errors are given integer weights to reconstruct the original Blessed I-M-C scale. The Short Blessed has been widely used in the USA, and is currently recommended by the Royal College of General Practitioners (RCGP) for cognitive screening of the over-75s in the UK. The original Blessed I-M-C scale was reported to give 80% sensitivity with 96% specificity against a diagnosis of dementia (Kay *et al.*, 1977) in a community sample, and has been reported to correlate highly with the MMSE (Villardita and Lomeo, 1992). When the discriminating power of the Short Blessed, and the longer Blessed I-M-C and the SPMSQ were compared, all three were found equally to 'discern the presence and severity of dementia' (Davis *et al.*, 1990). In one (small) study (Gurland *et al.*, 1992) of the diagnosis of dementia in USA Black, Hispanic and White subjects the Short Blessed matched the predictive power of the SPMSQ and actually exceeded that of the MMSE.

Finally, one alternative option for screening in research studies is the Telephone Interview for Cognitive Status (TICS) (Brandt *et al.*, 1988). The TICS allows assessment of cognitive function of subjects who are unable to be interviewed in person and has been proposed as a way of solving the research problem of completing longitudinal studies of cognitive function with geographically scattered subjects. The TICS has been found to be reliable and accurate in discerning between cases and controls and correlated highly with performance on MMSE.

PREVALENCE STUDIES

Disease prevalence refers to the number of people of a defined population that have the disease at a given time divided by the total number of people at risk. There have been many reported prevalence studies of AD since the 1950s, but direct comparison between studies has only been possible since researchers started to use standardized assessment instruments and operationalized diagnostic criteria. Additional difficulties have been the absence of age and sex standardization across studies and the differences in response rates across studies. Another source of variation is that some studies include, and others exclude, subjects living in residential homes. Yet, as pointed out by O'Connor (1992), subjects living in residential care should not be excluded from epidemiological studies of AD that aim to provide a total 'head count' as he found that as many as 12% of mildly demented and 40% of moderately/severely demented subjects were found to be in a long-stay ward or residential homes.

Preston (1986) found that prevalence rates for dementia lay within relatively narrow bands after analysing the results of several rigorous epidemiological studies in a regression analysis. An integrative analysis by Jorm *et al.* (1987) reported that the prevalence of dementia approximately doubled for every five years' increase in age in subjects aged between 60 and 90. His analysis failed to show any sex difference in the prevalence rates of dementia but suggested a trend for higher rates of AD in rural rather than urban areas, and for the prevalence of AD to be higher than that of vascular dementia in Europe and North America while the reverse was found in Japan and Russia. However, this meta-analysis can be criticized for the inclusion of studies of unequal merit and differences in diagnostic and assessment procedures between studies.

In another integrative analysis by Hoffman *et al.* (1991) the prevalence of dementia ranged from 1.4% in those aged 60–64 to 32.2% in the older group aged 89–94. Age-specific prevalence rates for dementia from this EURODEM (European Concerted Action) study are shown in Table 1.

Controversy remains as to whether, if we all lived long enough, we would all eventually develop dementia. Prevalence studies are of limited help in resolving this issue as prevalence is a product of incidence and survival time. Thus, even if the incidence of AD were high in the oldest old, the prevalence rate of AD in this group might not appear high because of the short life expectancy. The ongoing incidence studies under the auspices of EURODEM may help to resolve this issue.

INCIDENCE STUDIES

Disease incidence can be defined as the number of new cases in the population at risk during a defined time period, usually a year. There are fewer incidence studies of AD than prevalence studies. Furthermore, some of the published studies refer to a broader concept of dementia rather than AD alone. Among the studies concentrating on the incidence of AD, considerable differences in assessment, sampling method and diagnostic criteria again make it difficult to draw definite conclusions about the real incidence of AD. Future studies, such as those included in the EURODEM initiative, may help to establish the incidence of AD in Europe.

In spite of these difficulties it seems clear that the incidence of AD increases steeply after the age of 60, but it is unclear whether it plateaus or even decreases in the older old (Henderson, 1994). Rocca and Amaducci

Table 1. Age-specific prevalence (%) of dementia all types in both sexes.[a]

Population	30–59	60–64	65–69	70–74	75–79	80–84	85–89	90–94	95–99
Federal Republic of Germany									
Mannheim			3.2 (5/516)[b]	2.8 (13/464)[b]	7.3 (19/260)[b]	9.2 (16/174)[b]	18.1 (15/83)[b]	66.7 (6/9)[b]	
Finland									
Total country	0.2 (8/5 466)	1.2 (8/651)	2.3 (16/696)	5.4 (30/554)	9.0 (32/354)	16.7 (33/198)	19.4 (12/62)	12.5 (2/16)	0.0 (0/3)
Italy									
Appignano		0.9 (2/228)	0.0 (0/131)	3.6 (6/169)	8.1 (11/135)	17.6 (12/68)	40.0 (16/40)	14.3 (1/7)	
The Netherlands									
Amsterdam/Rotterdam			0.9 (1/110)	1.5 (2/135)	3.8 (4/104)	6.0 (5/83)	22.8 (13/57)	58.6 (10/18)	0.0 (0/1)
The Netherlands									
Leiden							22.6 (120/530)	35.4 (58/164)	41.2 (14/34)
Norway									
Oslo					9.2[c]	18.3[c]	26.4[c]		
Spain									
Zaragoza	0.0 (0/971)	0.5 (1/191)	0.0 (0/85)	5.3 (5/94)	3.6 (3/84)	16.3 (7/43)	8.7 (2/23)	25.0 (1/4)	0.0 (0/1)
Sweden									
Lund			1.7 (3/177)	4.8 (6/126)	7.9 (6/76)	17.8 (8/45)	15.8 (3/19)	27.3 (3/11)	0.0 (0/1)
United Kingdom									
Cambridge					4.3 (45/1 037)	11.8 (93/786)	18.0 (64/356)	32.7 (35/107)	32.0 (8/25)
United Kingdom									
Liverpool			0.9 (3/343)	2.6 (8/309)	5.7 (13/228)	8.6 (10/116)	17.9 (10/56)	11.1 (2/18)	
United Kingdom									
London			2.0 (4/198)	4.1 (7/172)	5.9 (11/185)	18.4 (21/114)	33.3 (18/54)	25.0 (3/12)	50.0 (2/4)
Average[d]	0.1 (8/6 547)	1.0 (11/1 070)	1.4 (25/1 740)	4.1 (64/1 559)	5.7 (125/2 203)	13.0 (189/1 453)	21.6 (258/1 197)	32.2 (115/357)	34.7 (24/69)

[a] Numbers in brackets indicate the actual numerator and denominator figures.
[b] Prevalence estimates were weighted according to the sampling procedure: the denominator reported is computed by dividing the observed number of cases by the weighted prevalence.
[c] Prevalence estimates were weighted according to sampling procedures; actual numerator and denominator figures are not required.
[d] Weighted average of studies with prevalence estimate covering the whole age class (Federal Republic of Germany and Norway were excluded).
Source: From Hoffman et al., 1991.

Table 2. Incidence studies of Alzheimer's disease (AD) and dementia.

Authors	Sample size	Diagnosis	Country	Age	Annual incidence (per 1000)
Bachman et al. (1990)	2 117	AD	USA	75+	M = 10 F = 12
Kolmen et al. (1988)	25 284	AD	USA	60–69 70–79 80+	1.4 6.4 20.5
Nilsson (1984)	460	AD	Sweden	70–79	7.0
Rorsman et al. (1986)	2 550	Dementia	Denmark	70–79 80+	15.0 34.0
Copeland et al. (1992)	–	Dementia	UK	65+	9.2
Boothby et al. (1993)	705	Dementia	UK	65–69 70–79 80+	8.0 22.0 39.0
Treves et al. (1986)	–	Presenile AD	Israel	40–60	0.002

(1991) provided a useful age-specific analysis of incidence. Some studies have reported a higher incidence of AD among women (Åkesson, 1969; Hagnell et al., 1983) but others did not replicate this finding (Bachman et al., 1990). Table 2 summarizes published findings of incidence studies of AD.

RISK FACTOR STUDIES

Early epidemiological studies of dementia were designed to estimate prevalence rates. Aetiological investigations followed shortly afterwards. The principal design has been the case–control study of which over 20 have been carried out over the last three decades. In a case–control study, there is initial ascertainment of subjects with the disease (cases) and without the disease (controls), with a retrospective search for risk factors to compare the two groups. The main advantages of case–control studies are that they are relatively inexpensive, quick and easy to complete and they can allow analysis of association between the disease and many different potential risk factors or exposure. However, a major problem in using a retrospective design is that studies can be affected by multiple bias, such as observer, selection or recall bias. Direction of causality cannot be identified, that is, whether the putative risk factor causes the disease or vice versa. Prevalence bias may be an important source of flaws in the published dementia studies. The use of prevalence cases may mean that factors which predict survival rather than risk for developing the disease are identified. In case–control studies cases of AD are often excluded if they have a concomitant symptom or disease that is considered an exclusion criterion for access to the cases group, while it is often not an exclusion criterion for the control group, hampering proper comparison between groups. For instance, AD cases are often excluded if they have concurrent cardiovascular disease at the time of the study while the same does not apply in the control group. It should be ensured that controls have followed the same selection criteria as cases or spurious findings may emerge. Most of the risk factor studies reported to date have had a case–control design and their results should be interpreted with caution for this reason.

Current large-scale studies, such as MRC-CFAS and EURODEM projects, will be an improvement as they use a prospective design to detect incident cases. Such studies will be less prone to bias as cases are detected as they arise from two groups of initially healthy individuals which vary only in that one group is exposed to the risk factor while the other is not exposed at all. This design allows direct calculation of the relative risk (RR), i.e. the incidence in those exposed to the potential risk factor divided by that of those not exposed. These prospective studies are usually expensive, lengthy, and require large numbers of subjects. Close surveillance of subjects is required to identify the onset of disease and loss to follow-up may bias the results of the investigation. Until these studies are published we have to work with the results obtained from case–control studies. Table 3 summarizes the findings from a meta-analysis performed by the EURODEM group on 12 previous case–control studies (van Duijn et al., 1991). The following are some of the currently accepted risk factors for dementia.

Demographic

All epidemiological studies have shown that increasing age is a robust risk factor. As mentioned earlier, the prevalence of dementia doubles every 5.1 years (Jorm et al., 1987) but doubts remain as to what happens in the oldest old population. Age is, in fact, a number that reflects the passage of time which can be seen as a proxy for: (1) more time for genes to express themselves; (2) increasingly impaired cell 'maintenance'; (3) more time to meet exposures or more time for exposures to accumulate, any of which can be relevant for the onset of AD.

Rocca et al. (1991) suggested an association between AD and increased maternal age, although their re-analysis was based on four incomplete studies. Both old (40+) and young (–20) maternal ages have been found by different studies to increase the risk for subsequent AD, but the EURODEM meta-analysis of these studies concluded that the increased risks reported were minimal and did not reach statistical significance (van Duijn and Hoffman, 1992). Increased prevalence rates of AD among women, even after taking age into account, have been reported (Rocca et al., 1991).

Table 3. Risk factors for AD (modified from EURODEM studies, 1991).

Risk factor	Relative risk (95% CI)
Family history of dementia	3.5 (2.6–4.6)
Family history of Down's syndrome	2.7 (1.2–5.7)
Family history of Parkinson's disease	2.4 (1.0–5.8)
Hypothyroidism	2.3 (1.0–5.4)
Head trauma	1.8 (1.3–2.7)
	F = 0.9 (0.4–1.7)
	M = 2.7 (1.6–4.4)
Depression	1.9 (1.1–3.3)
Maternal age	(15–19 years) = 1.5 (0.8–3)
	(40+) = 1.7 (1.0–2.9)
Epilepsy	1.6[a]
Herpes zoster/simplex	1.15[a]
Alcohol	1[a]
Smoking (ever smoked)	0.8[a]

[a] Ninety-five per cent confidence intervals for relative risk value include 1, i.e. the association may be due to chance.

Individual attributes

The EURODEM meta-analysis (van Duijn et al., 1991) corroborated findings from previous studies that had reported increased frequency of AD in subjects with first-degree relatives suffering from either AD, Parkinson's disease or Down's syndrome.

Some studies have reported an association between previous history of psychiatric disease, depression in particular, and AD (French et al., 1985; Broe et al., 1990). This has been corroborated by the EURODEM study (Jorm et al., 1991) but only for late-onset AD. Furthermore, several studies have shown that the association between cognitive impairment and depression may be confounded by the presence of functional limitations, suggesting that such limitations may have relevance to the aetiology of both depression and dementia (Fuhrer et al., 1992; Cervilla et al., 1996).

A study by Weinreb (1985) reported an increased frequency of ulnar loops in the fingerprint patterns of AD patients when compared with controls. However, these findings have not been replicated by subsequent studies (Jorm, 1990). This latter study suggested that the left hemisphere of left-handed people may be more susceptible to dysfunction and the authors reviewed several studies that had found an association between left-handedness and AD.

Snowdon et al. (1996) followed a cohort of 93 American nuns who had written their autobiographies earlier at the average age of 22 on entry to the convent. This prose was used to measure linguistic ability quantified as idea density and grammatical density. Several of the nuns were then investigated in late life; both neuropsychological and neuropathological data were gathered. The authors found that an early life rating of low linguistic ability was a strong predictor of poor cognitive function and Alzheimer's disease. Low linguistic ability also predicted death associated with AD confirmed by high density of neurofibrillary tangles at post mortem.

Genetic factors

A genetic contribution to the aetiology of AD has long been recognized (Sjogren et al., 1952). In general, up to a half of probands have an affected relative, with 15–35% of probands having an affected first-degree relative in the family (Heston et al., 1981; Kay, 1986; Fitch, 1988). A useful distinction for genetic studies of AD has been that of early-onset familial AD (EOFAD) and late-onset familial AD (LOFAD). This is justified, to a degree, as early-onset AD has been claimed to be associated with a much greater risk for relatives, a characteristic inherited age of onset, and a greater severity of pathology.

EOFAD has been related to mutations in chromosome 21, in which there is an alteration involved in Down's syndrome, a syndrome known to carry a higher risk for developing EOFAD. St George-Hyslop et al. (1987) found two probes within chromosome 21 to be linked to familial AD. Later it was found that the gene coding for the senile plaque amyloid A4 protein was also located in chromosome 21 (Goldgaber et al., 1987). A later study reported evidence of linkage with chromosome 21 markers for EOFAD but not for LOFAD (St George-Hyslop et al., 1990). However, it soon became apparent that mutations in the A4 gene in chromosome 21 accounted only for a small proportion (less than 10%) of EOFAD.

Genetic heterogeneity of causation was suggested by the finding that markers of the long arm of chromosome 14 were linked to EOFAD families not linked to the mutations of the APP gene in chromosome 21 (St George-Hyslop et al., 1992; van Broechoven et al., 1992). Recently, a gene mutation for the presenilin-1 gene (located in chromosome 14) has been reported in those families that were earlier found to be linked to chromosome 14 markers (Sherrington et al., 1995). An additional candidate gene for EOFAD has recently been isolated in chromosome 1 by Levy–Lehad (1995). This gene is similar to the presenilin-1 gene and has been named presenilin-2 gene.

Study of genetic factors for LOFAD has proved to be more complex, mainly because of early death problems, as subjects with the putative gene conferring risk for LOFAD may die from a different cause before they reach the age of increased susceptibility. Martin et al. (1990) first reported a chromosomal 19 location for some later-onset families. The importance of a locus on chromosome 19 was corroborated by reports of an association between increased number of alleles ε4 of apolipoprotein E and an increased risk for LOFAD (Corder et al., 1993). A biological model for the explanation of this association has been suggested in that those subjects with the apolipoprotein E ε4 alleles may be less capable of maintaining long-term survival of neurones (Anderton, 1995). However, although the risk to individual carriers of the two ε4 alleles is much higher than than that of those subjects with only one or no ε4 alleles, the percentage of people with one ε4 allele is higher than that of people with two alleles (Kuusisto et al., 1994). These authors found that, in a study of 980 people aged between 69 and 78, 652 had no ε4 alleles, of whom 19 (2.9%) developed AD; 277 had just one ε4 allele, of whom 21 (7.6%) developed the disease; and only 28 subjects were homozygous for the ε4 allele, of whom six (21.4%) developed AD. Therefore, in terms of population-attributable risk (the proportion of new cases arising in a population that are attributable to the exposure), the presence of just one ε4 allele may be more relevant than that of two ε4 alleles.

In spite of increasing evidence of a genetic contribution to AD, it seems likely that AD is a polygenic multifactorial disorder in which some major gene effects may be found but where environmental influences and modulatory effects may be of central importance. Furthermore, as pointed out by Rocca and Amaducci (1991), caution should be taken in assuming that family history necessarily reflects a genetic mode of transmission.

CARDIOVASCULAR RISK FACTORS

The recent findings of a blood–brain barrier dysfunction (Mattila et al., 1994) and of an excessive cerebral microvascular pathology (Buee et al., 1994) in AD cases may provide a plausible biological model for a potential implication of blood vessel abnormalities in the pathogenesis of AD. This biological research may be supported by the increasing evidence that vascular risk factors and atherosclerosis may act as risk factors for cognitive impairment and dementia (Prince, 1995). In a large community sample of 4791 subjects, Breteler et al. (1994) investigated the cross-sectional association between atherosclerosis disease and cognitive function. They found that subjects with evidence of peripheral arterial disease, evidence of plaques in the internal carotid arteries detected by Doppler ultrasound, or electrocardiogram (ECG) evidence of past myocardial infarction, showed more impaired MMSE scores compared with subjects not so exposed. They concluded that their findings were 'compatible with the view that atherosclerotic disease accounts for considerable cognitive impairment in the general population'.

These findings are supported by those of Prince et al. (1994) who found that statistically significant decline of cognitive function measured by the

Paired Associate Learning Test was associated with ECG evidence of ischaemia among their 1545 elderly, hypertensive sample. Several cross-sectional and longitudinal studies have shown that hypertensives seem to perform less well than normotensives on some, but not all, cognitive tasks (Waldstein *et al.*, 1991; Sands and Meredith, 1992; Elias *et al.*, 1993).

Prince *et al.* (1994) also demonstrated positive associations at the border of statistical significance between AD and a variety of vascular risk factors, such as smoking, hypertension and ECG ischaemia. However, Graves *et al.* (1991) have suggested an inverse relationship between smoking and AD, reporting a statistically significant trend for a decreasing odds ratio, with an increasing number of pack-years smoking exposure ($p = 0.0003$). However, this meta-analysis can be criticized on a number of grounds: first, none of the studies included had a sufficient sample size to allow sufficient power on their own to detect an effect of the size reported by the meta-analysis study (odds ratio (OR) = 0.8); secondly, most of the studies had a low response rate and have a potential for selection bias as the samples were usually recruited from specialist hospital clinics; thirdly, the studies analysed used prevalent cases and were strikingly heterogenous (especially for age of onset). Finally, confounders were not adequately considered as smoking is a risk factor for many lethal diseases which may cause the death of subjects before they enter the age group where susceptibility is more pronounced (e.g. Apo E ε4 in LOFAD, see above).

Some of the recent findings in this area may prove to be a challenge for the traditional division between AD and vascular dementia, with evidence that vascular risk factors are of relevance in AD itself.

EXPOSURES DURING LIFE

Neuritic plaques and tangles are known to contain aluminium. Researchers thus became interested in the study of exposure to aluminium in patients with AD, an interest supported by the finding that dementia was more frequent in those with high levels of blood aluminium following renal dialysis. Although studies did report an association between exposure to aluminium in water, antacids or antiperspirants and AD, a review of the evidence by Doll (1993) concluded that previous studies had not ruled out the possibility of confounding. Thus although aluminium was neurotoxic it could not be claimed as a cause of AD. As part of the EURODEM study, Graves *et al.* (1991) found no evidence of an association between solvents and lead and AD but recommended prospective studies before conclusions were reached.

Excessive consumption of alcohol has been reported by Saunders *et al.* (1991) to be associated with dementia (not necessarily AD). Graves *et al.*

(1991) and Katzman *et al.* (1989) failed to demonstrate any increase in risk of AD at any level of alcohol intake.

Murray *et al.* (1970) found an association between analgesic abuse and dementia. However, subsequent studies failed to replicate this association. Several studies have now reported that intake of nonsteroidal anti-inflammatory drugs (NSAIDs), like aspirin, are negatively associated with the risk of developing AD (McGeer *et al.*, 1990; Rich *et al.*, 1995). This may be explained by the control exerted by NSAIDs over excessive inflammatory response in the brain, or by their ability to buffer brain free radicals (Rogers *et al.*, 1988; Udassin *et al.*, 1991). However, it must be remembered that these conditions come from case–control studies and that confounding may be a potential problem, as AD patients may be less likely to be prescribed NSAIDs because of both higher risk of contraindications or because they are less likely to complain of pain.

The EURODEM meta-analysis also considered the risk conferred by head trauma followed by loss of consciousness that had occurred more than one year before the onset of dementia. The pooled odds ratio was 1.8 (1.3–2.7) and this association was stronger for males than for females.

Previous studies have reported an association between lower education and AD that holds across different cultures (Weissman, 1985; Zhang *et al.*, 1990). However, Fratiglioni *et al.* (1991) have concluded that differential MMSE cut-off points for different educational levels or adjustment techniques for education are not universally applicable. Katzman (1993) has suggested a biological hypothesis for these findings, postulating that subjects with a higher level of education have increased synaptic density and therefore increased 'brain reserve'. This may lead to test failure to detect cognitive impairment so that the diagnosis needs to be supported by evidence of decline in social and functional capabilities, assessed on an individual basis. This view has been supported by the finding that subjects with AD who had a previous high level of education showed a significantly greater cerebral blood flow than severity-matched AD patients with a lower level of education (Stern *et al.*, 1992).

CONCLUSIONS

Research into Alzheimer's disease has two broad themes – the search for cause (why do certain individuals succumb and others of the same age do not?) and the search for mechanism (how does it come about, what is going on in the brain to cause the clinical syndrome?). These approaches *should* rather be complementary and, in theory, the former should lead to strategies for prevention and the latter to treatments. Epidemiological research addresses the former and much has been achieved despite limitations from data drawn from prevalent samples, and more should be illuminated from the results of the large-scale multicentre prospective studies under way.

However, it might be that it is timely for researchers in all areas to question current conceptualizations of Alzheimer's disease and this twin-track approach to research. The following suggestions are put forward for debate.

First, Alzheimer's disease, perhaps because it is an eponymous term, is conceptualized as distinct from other forms of dementia, particularly from vascular dementia and currently Lewy body dementia. Much taxonomic energy has gone into drawing up operational criteria for each of these types to clarify and solidify the distinctions. Should we persist in this categorical approach, or would a multiaxial system fit better? The latter would require a clinician to rate each case of dementia for the presence of typical Alzheimer features, for evidence of cardiovascular disease and risk factors, and for features of Lewy body dementia rather than to choose between them. There is enough evidence from epidemiological research (Livingston et al., 1990), where hierarchical categorical classification in the field can provide difficulties, and from pathological studies, where as many mixed- as single-pathology diagnoses are described to support such a change (Holmes, 1996). To this must be added the growing evidence that vascular risk factors may have a role to play in the onset of typical Alzheimer's disease. The advantage of a multiaxial approach would be the inclusion in case–control studies or drug trials of all cases of dementia in which some Alzheimer pathology was thought to be present, rather than, as at present, only the subgroup in which there appears to be a single pathology.

Secondly, is it helpful to continue with the world 'disease' attached to Alzheimer's rather than syndrome or process? What unites these patients is a pathological process and a fairly (but not absolutely) predictable clinical picture. The causes of this pathological process are likely to be multifactorial with an interplay of genetic and environmental factors varying for each individual. The equivalent for the liver would not be Wilson's disease, but cirrhosis.

Thirdly, can we continue with the twin-track approach to research? As more genetic studies in psychiatry are published it seems clear that more is under genetic control than formerly thought. Some component of what might be considered environmental exposure (family-rearing style, experience of life events) is under genetic control (McGuffin et al., 1988). We can create our own environment. Genes, too, can act through their effect on temperament, intelligence or even linguistic abilities as modifiers of the chances of an exposure causing a disease. In both situations, therefore, genes are confounders, as they influence both exposure and disease. Thus epidemiological research from now on should include, at a minimum, a genetic component, so that appropriate material can be collected for later gene analysis. Better still would be to develop genetically sensitive designs in which siblings or other family members are included in the research sample. One or more genes are perhaps responsible for promoting the pathological process, whereas adverse exposures perhaps act to reduce brain reserve, thereby bringing forward manifestations of the clinical syndrome. When both of these are quantified together, a useful model may emerge that allows current research strands to be joined.

REFERENCES

Åkesson, H.O. (1969). A population study of senile and arteriosclerotic psychoses. *Hum Hered* **19**, 546–566.

Anderton, B. (1995). Apolipoprotein E-ε4 and Alzheimer's disease. *Alzheimer's Rev* **5**, 97–101.

Anthony, J.C., LeResche, L., Niaz, U., von Korff, M.R. and Folstein, M.F. (1982). Limits of the Mini-Mental State as a screening test for dementia and delirium among hospital patients. *Psychol Med* **12**, 397–408.

Bachman, D.L. *et al.* (1990). Sexual differences in incidence and prevalence of Alzheimer's disease: the Framingham study. *Neurology* **40** (suppl 1): 176.

Bachman, D.L., Wolf, P.A., Linn, R. *et al.* (1992). Prevalence of dementia and probable senile dementia of the Alzheimer type in the Framingham study. *Neurology* **42**, 115–119.

Boothby, H., Blizard, R., Livingston, G. and Mann, A. (1993). The Gospel Oak Study Stage III: the incidence of dementia. *Psychol Med* **23**.

Brandt, J., Spencer, M. and Folstein, M. (1988). The telephone interview for cognitive status. *Neuropsychiatr Neuropsychol Behav Neurol* **1**, 111–117.

Brayne, C. and Calloway, P. (1988). Normal ageing, impaired cognitive function, and senile dementia of the Alzheimer's type: a continuum? *Lancet* **i**, 1265–1267.

Breteler, M.M., van Swieten, J.C., Bots, M.L. *et al.* (1994). Cerebral white matter lesions, vascular risk factors, and cognitive function in a population-based study: the Rotterdam Study. *Neurology* **44**, 1246–1252.

Broe, L. *et al.* (1990). A case–control study of Alzheimer's disease in Australia. *Neurology* **40**, 698–707.

Buee, L., Hof, P.R., Bouras, C. *et al.* (1994). Pathological alterations of the cerebral microvasculature in Alzheimer's disease and related disorders. *Acta Neuropathol* **57**, 469–480.

Cervilla, J.A., Lopez-Ibor, M.I., Matinez-Raga, J. and Prince, M.J. (1996). Depression y deterior cognitivo: un estudio transversal de comorbilidad. *Actas Luso-Espanol Neurol Psiquiatra Ciencias Afines* (in press).

Cooper, B. and Bickel, H. (1984). Population screening and the early detection of dementing disorders in old age: a review. *Psychol Med* **14**, 81–95.

Copeland, J.R.M., Dewey, M.E. and Griffith-Jones, H.M. (1986). A computerised psychiatric diagnostic system and case nomenclature for elderly subjects: GMS and AGECAT. *Psychol Med* **16**, 89–99.

Copeland, J.M.R., Davidson, I.A., Dewey, M.E. *et al.* (1992). Alzheimer's disease, other dementias, depression and pseudodementia: prevalence, incidence and three year outcome in Liverpool. *Br J Psychiatry* **161**, 230–239.

Corder, E.H., Saunders, A.M., Strittmatter, W.J. *et al.* (1993). Gene dose of apolipoprotein E type 4 allele and the risk of Alzheimer's disease in late onset families. *Science* **261**, 921–923.

Davis, P.B., Morris, J.C. and Grant, E. (1990). Brief screening tests versus clinical staging in senile dementia of the Alzheimer's type. *J Am Geriatr Soc* **38**, 129–135.

Doll, R. (1993). Review: Alzheimer's disease and environmental aluminium. *Age Ageing* **22**, 138–153.

Elias, M.F., Wolf P.A., D'Agostino, R.B., Cobb, J. and White, L.R. (1993). Untreated blood pressure is inversely related to cognitive functioning: the Framingham Study. *Am J Epidemiol* **138**, 353–364.

Fitch, N. (1988). The inheritance of Alzheimer's disease: a new interpretation. *Ann Neurol* **23**, 14–19.

Folstein, M.F., Folstein, S.E. and McHugh, P.R. (1975). 'Mini-mental State': a practical method for grading the cognitive state of patients for the clinician. *J Psychiatr Res* **12**, 189–198.

Folstein, M.F., Bassett, S.S., Anthony, J.C., Romanoski, A.J. and Nestadt, G.R. (1991). Dementia: case ascertainment in a community survey. *J Gerontol* **46**, M132–M138.

Fratiglioni, L., Grut, M., Forsell, Y. *et al.* (1991). Prevalence of Alzheimer's disease and other dementias in an elderly urban population: relationship with age, sex, and education. *Neurology* **41**, 1886–1892.

French, L.R., Schuman, L.M., Mortimer, J.A. *et al.* (1985). A case-control study of dementia of Alzheimer's type. *Am J Epidemiol* **121**, 414–421.

Fuhrer, R., Antonucci, T.C., Gagnon, M., Dartigues, J.F., Barberger Gateau, P. and Alperovitch, A. (1992). Depressive symptomatology and cognitive functioning: an epidemiological survey in an elderly community sample in France. *Psychol Med* **22**, 159–172.

Goldgaber, D., Lerman, M.I., McBride, O.W., Saffiotti, U. and Gajdusek, D.C. (1987). Characterization and chromosomal localization of a cDNA encoding brain amyloid of Alzheimer's disease. *Science* **235**, 877–880.

Graves, A.B., van Duijn, C.M., Chandra, V. *et al.* (1991). Alcohol and tobacco consumption as risk factors for Alzheimer's disease: A collaborative re-analysis of case–control studies. EURODEM Risk Factors Research Group. *Int J Epidemiol* **20** (suppl 2), S48–S57.

Gurland, B.J., Wilder, D.E., Cross, P., Teresi, J. and Barrett, V.W. (1992). Screening scales for dementia: toward reconciliation of conflicting cross-cultural findings. *Int J Geriatr Psychiatr* **7**, 105–113.

Hagnell, O., Lanke, J., Rorsman, B., Ohman, R. and Ojesjo, L. (1983). Current trends in the incidence of senile and multi-infarct dementia. A prospective study of a total population followed over 25 years; the Lundby study. *Arch Psychiatr Nervenkr* **233**, 423–438.

Hagnell, O. *et al.* (1991). Senile dementia of the Alzheimer's type in the Lundby study. *Eur Arch Psychiatry* **241**, 159–164.

Henderson, J. (1994). *Epidemiology of mental Disorders and Psychosocial Problems: Dementia*. World Health Organization, Geneva.

Heston, L.L. *et al.* (1981). Dementia of the Alzheimer type: clinical genetics, natural history, and associated conditions. *Arch Gen Psychiatry* **38**, 1085–1090.

Hoffman, A., Rocca, W.A. *et al.* (1991). The prevalence of dementia in Europe: a collaborative study of 1980–1990 findings. *Int J Epidemiol* **20**, 736–748.

Holmes, C. (1996). The Camberwell dementia care register. *Int J Geriatr Psychiatry* **11**, 369–375.

Jorm, A.F. (1990). *The Epidemiology of Alzheimer's Disease and Related Disorders*. Chapman and Hall, London.

Jorm, A.F., Korten, A.E. and Henderson, A.S. (1987). The prevalence of dementia: a quantitative integration of the literature. *Acta Psychiatr Scand* **76**, 465–479.

Jorm, A.F., van Duijn, C.M., Chandra, V. *et al.* (1991). Psychiatric history and related exposures as risk factors for Alzheimer's disease: a collaborative re-analysis of case–control studies. EURODEM Risk Factors Research Group. *Int J Epidemiol* **20** (suppl 2), S43–S47.

Katzman, R. (1993). Education and the prevalence of dementia and Alzheimer's disease. *Neurology* **43**, 13–20.

Katzman, R., Aronson, M., Fuld, P. *et al.* (1989). Development of dementing illnesses in an 80-year-old volunteer cohort. *Ann Neurol* **25**, 317–324.

Katzman, R., Brown, T., Fuld, P., Peck, A., Schechter, R. and Schimmel, H. (1983). Validation of a short orientation-memory-concentration test of cognitive impairment. *Am J Psychiatry* **140**, 734–739.

Kay, D.W.K. (1986). The genetics of Alzheimer's disease. *Br Med Bull* **42**, 19–23.

Kay, D.W., Britton, P.G., Bergmann, K. and Foster, E.M. (1977). Cognitive function and length of survival in elderly subjects living at home. *Aust NZ J Psychiatry* **11**, 113–117.

Kay, D.W., Henderson, A.S., Scott, R., Wilson, J., Rickwood, D. and Grayson, D.A. (1985). Dementia and depression among the elderly living in the Hobart community: the effect of the diagnostic criteria on the prevalence rates. *Psychol Med* **15**, 771–788.

Kolmen, E., Chandra, V. and Schoenberg, B.S. (1988). Trends in incidence of dementing illness in Rochester, Minnesota, in three quinquennial periods, 1960–1974. *Neurology* **38**: 975–980.

Kuusisto, J., Koivisto, K., Kervinen, K. *et al.* (1994). Association of apolipoprotein E phenotypes with late onset Alzheimer's disease: population-based study. *BMJ* **309**, 636–638.

Levy-Lehad, E. (1995). A familial Alzheimer's disease locus on chromosome 1. *Science* **269**: 970–977.

Lishman, D. (1987). *Organic Psychiatry* (2nd edition). Blackwell, London.

Livingston, G., Sax, K., Willison, J., Blizard, B. and Mann, A. (1990). The Gospel Oak Study Stage II: the diagnosis of dementia in the community. *Psychol Med* **20**, 137–146.

Martin, G.M. *et al.* (1990). Dominant susceptibility genes. *Nature* **347**, 124.

Mattila, K.M., Pirtilla, T., Blennow, K., Wallin, A., Viitanen, M. and Frey, H. (1994). Altered blood–brain barrier function in Alzheimer's disease? *Acta Neurol Scand* **89**, 192–198.

McGeer, P.L., McGeer, E., Rogers, J. and Sibley, J. (1990). Anti-inflammatory drugs and Alzheimer's disease [Letter]. *Lancet* **335**, 1037.

McGuffin, P., Katz, R. and Bebbington, P. (1988). The Camberwell Collaborative Depression Study. III. Depression and adversity in the relatives of depressed probands. *Br J Psychiatry* **152**, 775–782.

Morgan, K., Dallosso, H.M., Arie, T., Byrne, E., Jones, R. and Waite, J. (1987). Mental health and psychological well-being among the old and the very old living at home. *Br J Psychiatry* **150**, 801–807.

Murray, R.M., Timbury, G.C. and Linton, A.L. (1970). Analgesic abuse in psychiatric patients. *Lancet* **1**, 1303.

Nilsson, L.V. (1984). Incidence of severe dementia in an urban sample followed from 70 to 79 years of age. *Acta Psychiatr Scand* **69**: 519–527.

O'Connor, D.W. (1992). Current questions in epidemiology of dementia. In: Arie, T. (Ed.), *Recent Advances in Psychogeriatrics*. Churchill Livingstone, London, pp. 173–185.

O'Connor, D.W., Pollitt, P.A., Hyde, J.B. *et al.* (1989). The prevalence of dementia as measured by the Cambridge Mental Disorders of the Elderly Examination. *Acta Psychiatr Scand* **79**, 190–198.

Preston, G.A. (1986). Dementia in elderly adults: prevalence and institutionalization. *J Gerontol* **41**, 261–267.

Prince, M.J. (1995). Vascular risk factors and atherosclerosis as risk factors for cognitive decline and dementia. *J Psychosom Res* **39**, 525–530.

Prince, M.J., Cullen, M.C. and Mann, A.H. (1994). Risk factors for Alzheimer's disease and dementia: a case–control study based on the MRC Elderly Hypertension Trial. *Neurology* **44**, 97–104.

Rich, J.B., Rasmusson, D.X., Folstein, M.F., Carson, K.A., Kawas, C. and Brandt, J. (1995). Nonsteroidal anti-inflammatory drugs in Alzheimer's disease. *Neurology* **45**, 51–55.

Rocca, W.A. and Amaducci, L. (1991). Epidemiology of Alzheimer's disease. In: Anderson, D.W. (Ed.), *Neuroepidemiology: a Tribute to Bruce Schoenberg*. CRC Press, Boca Raton, FL, pp. 55–96.

Rocca, W.A. *et al.* (1991). Maternal age and Alzheimer's disease: a collaborative reanalysis of case–control studies. *Int J Epidemiol* **20**, S21–S27.

Rogers, J., Luber-Narod, J., Styren, S.D. and Civin, W.H. (1988). Expression of immune system-associated antigens by cells of the human nervous system: relationship to the pathology of Alzheimer's disease. *Neurobiol Aging* **9**, 339–349.

Rorsman, B., Hagnell, O. and Lanke, J. (1986). Prevalence and incidence of senile and multi infarct dementia in the Lundby study: a comparison between the time periods 1947–1957 and 1957–1972. *Neuropsychobiology* **15**, 122–129.

Roth, M., Tym, E., Mountjoy, C.Q. *et al.* (1986). CAMDEX. A standardized instrument for the diagnosis of mental disorder in the elderly with special reference to the early detection of dementia. *Br J Psychiatry* **149**, 698–709.

Sands, L.P. and Meredith, W. (1992). Blood pressure and intellectual functioning in late midlife. *J Gerontol* **47**, P81–P84.

Saunders, P.A. *et al.* (1991). Heavy drinking as a risk factor for depression and dementia in elderly men. Findings from the Liverpool Longitudinal Community Study. *Br J Psychiatry* **159**, 213–216.

Sherrington, R., Rogaev, E.I., Liang, Y. *et al.* (1995). Cloning of a gene bearing missense mutations in early-onset familial Alzheimer's disease. *Nature* **375**, 754–760.

Sjogren, T. *et al.* (1952). Morbus Alzheimer and Morbus Pick. A genetical, clinical and patho-anatomical study. *Acta Pathol Scand Suppl* **82**.

Snowdon, D.A., Kemper, S.J., Mortimer, J.A., Greiner, L.H., Wekstein, D.R. and Markesbery, W.R. (1996). Linguistic ability in early life and cognitive function and Alzheimer's disease in late life. Findings from the nun study. *JAMA* **275**, 528–532.

St George-Hyslop, P. *et al.* (1987). The genetic defect causing familial Alzheimer's disease maps on chromosome 21. *Science* **235**, 880–890.

St George-Hyslop, P., Haines, J.L., Farrer, L.A. *et al.* (1990). Genetic linkage studies suggest that Alzheimer's disease is not a single homogeneous disorder. FAD Collaborative Study Group. *Nature* **347**, 194–197.

St George-Hyslop, P., Haines, J., Rogaev, E. *et al.* (1992). Genetic evidence for a novel familial Alzheimer's disease locus on chromosome 14. *Nat Genet* **2**, 330–334.

Stern, R.G., Mohs, R.C., Bierer, L.M. *et al.* (1992). Deterioration on the Blessed test in Alzheimer's disease: longitudinal data and their implications for clinical trials and identification of subtypes. *Psychiatry Res* **42**, 101–110.

Treves, T. *et al.* (1986). Presenile dementia in Israel. *Arch Neurol* **43**, 26–29.

Udassin, R., Ariel, I., Haskel, Y., Kitrossky, N. and Chevion, M. (1991). Salicylate as an *in vivo* free radical trap: studies on ischemic insult to the rat intestine. *Free Radic Biol Med* **10**, 1–6.

United Nations (1979). *Age and Sex Composition by Country 1960–2000*. New York, United Nations.

van Duijn, C.M., Stijnen, T. and Hofman, A. (1991). Risk factors for Alzheimer's disease: overview of the EURODEM collaborative re-analysis of case–control studies. *Int J Epidemiol* **20** (suppl 2), S4–S12.

van Duijn, C.M. and Hoffman, A. (1992). Risk factors for Alzheimer's disease: the EURODEM collaborative re-analysis of case–control studies. *Neuroepidemiology* **11** (suppl 1), 1–122.

van Broechoven, C. *et al.* (1992). Mapping of a gene predisposing to early onset Alzheimer's disease to chromosome 14q 24.3. *Nat Genet* **2**, 335–338.

Villardita, C. and Lomeo, C. (1992). Alzheimer's disease: correlational analysis of three screening tests and three behavioural scales. *Acta Neurol Scand* **86**, 603–608.

Waldstein, S.R., Ryan, C.M. and Manuck, S.B. (1991). Learning and memory function in men with untreated blood pressure elevation. *J Consult Clin Psychol* **59**, 513–517.

Weinreb, H.J. (1985). Fingerprint patterns in Alzheimer's disease. *Arch Neurol* **42**, 50–54.

Weissman, G.K. (1985). A model of collaborative education: planning and implementing a collaborative program. NLN Publ 99–103.

WHO (1978). *Mental Disorders: Glossary and Guide to their Classification in Accordance with the Ninth Revision of the International Classification of Diseases (ICD-9)*. World Health Organization, Geneva.

WHO (1993). *Implementation of the Global Strategy for Health for All by the Year 2000, Second Evaluation; and Eighth Report on the World Health Situation.* World Health Organization, Geneva.

Zhang, M. *et al.* (1990). The prevalence of dementia and Alzheimer's disease in Shanghai, China: impact of age, gender, and education. *Ann Neurol* **27**, 428–437.

Advances in Old Age Psychiatry: Chromosomes to Community Care
Edited by C. Holmes and R. Howard
© 1997 Wrightson Biomedical Publishing Ltd

2

Cross-Cultural Studies of Dementia

MARCUS RICHARDS

*MRC National Survey of Health and Development, Department of Epidemiology
and Public Health, University College London Medical School, London, UK*

INTRODUCTION

The detection and management of dementia across diverse societies around the world have received relatively little attention, even though this disorder is associated with considerable disability and suffering. This chapter will attempt to describe the complex issues that surround the detection and management of dementia in a cross-cultural setting. The consideration of any construct from different perspectives and in different contexts inevitably leads to questions about the nature of that construct, and the possibility of ethnic differences in risk for dementia is potentially of great importance for distinguishing genetic from environmental causes. This chapter will therefore explore some of the ways in which cross-cultural studies can challenge and enrich our conception of dementia.

The Diagnostic and Statistical Manual of Mental Disorders, fourth edition, (DSM–IV) (American Psychiatric Association, 1994) and the *International Classification of Diseases*, tenth revision, (ICD–10) (World Health Organization, 1992) criteria for dementia require the demonstration of cognitive impairment of sufficient severity to interfere with activities of daily living. However, the assessment of both cognitive function and functional capacity provides a formidable challenge for cross-cultural research; most formal tests of cognitive function are culture-dependent. Ideally, if the assessment of cognitive function is to be undertaken in a cross-cultural setting, test items should have comparable meaning, familiarity and salience across cultures. Appropriate tests should be chosen or developed for use in populations containing a large proportion of people who cannot read or write, such as those of rural areas in many developing countries. Such assessment should also be grounded in a proper understanding of the experience and expectations that different cultures bring to the test situation. Furthermore, societies vary in the degree to which they place functional responsibilities upon their elders. In many industrialized societies it is common for older people to continue to face challenges routinely met by younger adults, such as domestic maintenance and financial management. In such cultures, an older person who is having difficulty with such activities is typically labelled as functionally impaired and is relatively easy to identify. Yet what of rural developing cultures that place few functional responsibilities upon their elders? It is also important to consider the extent to which different cultures label the symptoms of dementia pathological or normal for old age (Chandra, 1995). It could be argued that absence of a tendency to 'pathologize' disability only hinders identification of dementia in its early stages and that dementia will be readily detected once it is sufficiently severe to cause behavioural disturbance. However, mortality associated with dementia is high in such rural communities. Consequently, the later stage of more symptomatic dementia is not always reached (Chandra, 1995).

Chandra et al. (1994) summarize other methodological problems encountered during cross-cultural research. One example is the high prevalence of coexisting physical morbidity, such as sensory impairment and arthritis, in some countries that can mask functional disability resulting from cognitive decline. Other problems include the underreporting of dementia and difficulty in obtaining medical records, absence of well–defined study populations with adequate numbers of elderly people, and limited qualified personnel to detect dementia. With these methodological problems in mind, we now review cross-cultural studies of the prevalence of and risk factors for dementia.

CROSS-CULTURAL STUDIES OF DEMENTIA PREVALENCE

Populations of African origin

In 1992 Osuntokun and colleagues from the University of Ibadan, Nigeria, claimed that 'no authenticated case of AD [Alzheimer's disease] has been reported in an indigenous black African' (Osuntokun et al., 1992, p. 353). This statement was based on door to door prevalence studies in the Ibadan region, consecutive admissions to the University College Hospital, Ibadan, over a period of 30 years, and one post-mortem series. In fact, more recent work by Hendrie et al. (1995a) has documented cases of Alzheimer's disease in this region, although its prevalence still appears to be lower than among African Americans. These authors compared prevalence rates of dementia among residents aged 65 and older in two communities: Yorubas from a region of Ibadan, Nigeria (n = 2494), and African Americans from the community (n = 2212) and from nursing homes (n = 106) in Indianapolis, Indiana, USA. It should be noted in this context that most African Americans are of West African origin, although it has been estimated that the European admixture within the African American population is as high as 25%. Hendrie *et al.* used a two–stage (screening and assessment) design and developed an inter–site training programme to standardize case–finding procedure. Based on DSM-IIIR and ICD–10 criteria, 2.29% of the Ibadan sample and 4.82% of the Indianapolis community sample were classified as having dementia. The figure for Indianapolis rose to 8.24% when the nursing-home sample was added. Figures for Alzheimer's disease were 1.41% for Ibadan and 3.69% (community sample) and 6.24% (total) for the Indianapolis sample. There are several possible reasons for this lower rate of dementia in Nigeria.

First, in spite of rigorous cross-site standardization, diagnostic criteria developed in the USA or Western Europe may not be easily adaptable for the study region in Nigeria which, as the authors point out, is considerably less industrialized than that in Indianapolis. Secondly, it may be that selective mortality in Nigerians with dementia is high, thus reducing the likelihood of detecting cases at a single point in time. Incidence studies are necessary to resolve this difficulty. Thirdly, although Osuntokun *et al.* (1992) do not address the question of whether the symptoms of dementia in old age are labelled normal or pathological within Nigerian culture, it is possible that cases of dementia were concealed from investigators because of social stigma attached to this syndrome. However, in the Ibadan–Indianapolis study, Hendrie *et al.* (1995a) note that very ill subjects in Nigeria may have been especially motivated to participate in the study in order to obtain medical services. Fourthly, the possibility remains that black African populations are genuinely at low risk for dementia. In support of this possibility, Osuntokun *et al.* (1994) reported significantly lower rates of A4–amyloid deposition in a consecutive series of post-mortem brains of nondemented patients from Ibadan, compared with an equivalent series from Melbourne, Australia. It is not clear whether this putative low risk has an environmental locus or is the result of ethnic differences in biological (e.g. genetic, cardiovascular) disposition, or is an interaction between these two factors.

In contrast, African Americans appear to be at a higher risk of dementia. Indeed, two population-based studies found a higher prevalence of dementia among African Americans than among white Americans. In the first of these, Schoenberg *et al.* (1985) screened 8925 residents aged 40 and older of Copiah County, Mississippi, for severe dementia. Of these, 39.1% were African American. The age-adjusted prevalence rate for severe dementia was 817 per 100 000 for Whites and 987.2 per 100 000 for African Americans.

Heyman *et al.* (1991) compiled a stratified random sample of 83 African American and 81 White community residents aged 65 and older from the Piedmont region of North Carolina. A total of 26 residents were found to be demented, yielding a dementia prevalence of 16% for African Americans and 3.05% for Whites. The prevalence of both Alzheimer's disease and mixed or multi-infarct dementia was higher in African Americans.

Table 1. Selected population–based prevalence studies of dementia in different cultures.

Authors	Study region	Sample	Dementia prevalence
Zhang *et al.*, 1990	Shanghai, China	5 055 aged 65+	4.6%
Hendrie *et al.*, 1995a	Ibadan, Nigeria	2 494 Yorubas aged 65+	2.29%
Hendrie *et al.*, 1995b	Indianapolis, IN, USA	2 212 African Americans aged 65+	4.8%
Schoenberg *et al.*, 1985	Copiah County, MS, USA	3 490 African Americans aged 40+	987.2 per 100 000
Schoenberg *et al.*, 1985	Copiah County, MS, USA	5 364 White Americans aged 40+	817 per 100 000
Heyman *et al.*, 1991	Piedmont, NC, USA	83 African Americans aged 65+	16%
Heyman *et al.*, 1991	Piedmont, NC, USA	81 White Americans aged 65+	3.05%

Populations of Asian origin

Studies of dementia and cognitive impairment in the Asian continent are of particular interest because the proportion of the population aged 65 and older in this region is undergoing rapid growth. Yet several studies conducted in China have reported a low prevalence of dementia, ranging from 0.46% to 1.86% (reviewed by Zhang *et al.*, 1990). Li *et al.* (1989), in a survey of 1331 community residents of Beijing, reported a similar dementia prevalence of 1.82% for subjects aged 65 and older. Zhang *et al.* (1990) argue that differences in population structure, in survey methodology and in the application of diagnostic criteria account for this effect. In their own study of 5055 older community residents of Shanghai, these authors standardized their application of DSM-IIIR and NINCDS–ADRDA dementia criteria (National Institute for Neurological, Communicable Diseases and Stroke–Alzheimer's Disease and Related Disorders Association; McKhann *et al.*, 1984) to current practice in the USA. Using a two-phase survey methodology, a dementia prevalence of 4.6% was reported for subjects aged 65 and older. This figure is comparable with that for Western European and North American countries. As well as standardization of diagnostic procedure, two important differences between this and previous studies in China were the use of a more comprehensive clinical assessment of dementia and the use of a screening cut-point to identify cognitive impairment in Phase 1 of the survey that was adjusted for level of education.

Populations of European origin

It is often assumed that differences within the European community in educational attainment, familiarity with formal cognitive tests and conceptions of normality regarding cognitive and functional capacity in the elderly, are smaller than those of analogous developing communities. In this regard, a meta-analysis found no significant difference in the prevalence of dementia across Finland, Italy, Spain, Sweden and the UK (Hofman *et al.*, 1991). In contrast, Treves *et al.* (1986) compiled a register of all cases of presenile dementia based on data for every patient discharged with a neurological diagnosis from all hospitals in Israel between 1974 and 1978. These authors found a significantly higher prevalence of dementia in Israelis of European or American origin (2.9 per 100 000) than in Israelis of Asian or African origin (1.4 per 100 000), although there was no difference in survival rate between these two groups. However, Treves *et al.* (1986) point out that they were unable to rule out the possibility of underascertainment of African–Asian cases, due to families failing to recognize dementia or to their taking over the care of sufferers.

RISK FACTORS FOR DEMENTIA

One potential gain of cross-cultural prevalence and incidence studies of dementia is the provision of insights into dementia aetiology. As Osuntokun *et al.* (1992) point out, the identification of ethnic groups with significantly different prevalence rates of dementia could enhance the search for dementia risk factors. Furthermore, the comparison of communities in different environments and at different stages of economic development, but within the same ethnic group, may enable the differentiation of environmental from genetic risk factors. A meta-analysis by the EURODEM Risk Factors Research Group (van Duijn *et al.*, 1991) revealed a number of significant risk factors for AD. These are: a family history of dementia, Parkinson's disease or Down's syndrome; head trauma with loss of consciousness; a history of hypothyroidism; and a history of depression. In addition, having ever smoked emerged as a protective factor. Unfortunately, no data are available on cross-cultural comparisons of these risk factors.

In line with recent reports (e.g. American Heart Association, 1995) however, Heyman *et al.* (1991) found that African Americans were more likely than Whites to have had a history of stroke, hypertension and diabetes. This raises the question of ethnic differences in risk for vascular-related dementia. Some clues to these differences have come from clinical studies. Still *et al.* (1990) compiled a case register of patients diagnosed with dementia in South Carolina since April 1988. These authors reported that, although the proportion of African Americans did not exceed one-third of South Carolina's population, African Americans accounted for 44.3% of all dementia cases. Furthermore, although there was no difference between African Americans and Whites in the proportion of Alzheimer's and multi-infarct dementia cases, the frequency of alcoholic dementia was higher among African Americans. Autopsy studies report conflicting results, however. Miller et al. (1984) found no difference between African Americans and Whites in the neuritic plaque and neurofibrillary tangle count in the temporal regions of 199 consecutive post-mortem brains. De la Monte et al. (1989) studied 144 histologically confirmed cases of dementia among 6000 consecutive post-mortem brains. These authors reported an equal proportion of African American and Whites among the dementia cases. African Americans, however, had a higher proportion of multi-infarct and alcohol-related dementia. Whites, on the other hand, had a higher proportion of classical AD pathology and dementia associated with Parkinson's disease. However, the difficulties in extrapolating clinical data to the population at large are well known. In the case of mild AD, for example, African Americans may be less likely than Whites to come to the attention of a clinician and will therefore be underrepresented in clinical series. On the other hand, De la Monte and colleagues' finding of a higher proportion of cerebrovascular lesions among African American patients is consistent with population-based studies showing a higher frequency of cardiovascular risk factors in this ethnic group (Heyman et al., 1991).

We should also note a report by Osuntokun et al. (1995), arising from the Ibadan–Indianapolis study, of a lack of association between apolipoprotein E ϵ4 and Alzheimer's disease in Nigerians, even though the strength of this association in African Americans is similar to that in Whites (Hendrie et al. 1995b). These findings raise the possibility of genetic protection against Alzheimer's disease in Nigerians.

Little has been reported about risk factors for dementia in Asian populations. However, we should note a summary observation by Jorm (1990) that vascular dementia is more frequently diagnosed than AD in Japan, China and Russia. However, Jorm points out that this may reflect regional differences in diagnostic practice rather than differences in the true prevalence of this subtype of dementia. On the other hand, the incidence of cerebrovascular disease has been reported to be high among Japanese people (Worth et al., 1975).

CONCLUSIONS

The last few years have witnessed a small but significant number of prevalence studies that have allowed the comparison of dementia rates across diverse countries. Cross-cultural studies of dementia present formidable methodological difficulties and require a trade–off between the desirability for standardization to enable cross–site comparison and the need to adapt assessment instruments and procedures (most of which are devised in Europe or the USA) for different populations.

Yet, faced with this challenge, some valuable findings have emerged from carefully planned and executed cross-cultural studies. Perhaps the most striking of these is the apparent rarity of dementia among Nigerians (Hendrie *et al.*, 1995a). Only adequate longitudinal studies will distinguish whether this finding arises from underascertainment of cases or whether Nigerians (and, by implication, other Black African populations) are protected against dementia incidence. Demonstration of the latter possibility would provide increased focus in the search for aetiological or protective factors for dementia. To date, little is known about the risk factors for dementia in cross-cultural studies, although some emphasis has been placed on cardiovascular disease, which is in part associated with urbanization and may be an important factor in dementia aetiology in Asian populations and in African Americans. There is also some evidence from studies of apolipoprotein E to suggest that Nigerians are at lower genetic risk for dementia than African Americans. Further studies of risk factors for dementia across different populations are required to shed light on these important questions.

ACKNOWLEDGEMENT

The author gratefully acknowledges the Alzheimer's Disease Society for financial support during preparatory work for this chapter.

REFERENCES

American Heart Association (1995). *Heart and Stroke Facts: 1995 Statistical Supplement*. AHA, Dallas, TX.

American Psychiatric Association (1994). *Diagnostic and Statistical Manual of Mental Disorders, (4th edn.)*. American Psychiatric Association, Washington, DC.

Chandra, V.J. (1995). The diagnosis of dementia in trans–cultural studies. Paper presented at the World Federation of Neurology Dementia Research Group workshop, The Dementias in Africa: epidemiological, clinical and therapeutic issues. Second SONA International Conference, Marrakesh, Morocco, 18–19 April, 1995.

Chandra, V.J., Ganguli, M., Ratcliff, G. *et al.* (1994). Studies of the epidemiology of dementia: comparisons between developed and developing countries. *Aging Clin Exp Res* **6**, 307–321.

De la Monte, S.M., Hutchins, G.M. and Moore, G. (1989). Racial differences in the etiology of dementia and frequency of Alzheimer lesions in the brain. *J Natl Med Assoc* **81**, 644–652.

Hendrie, H.C., Osuntokun, B.O., Hall, K.S. *et al.* (1995a). Prevalence of Alzheimer's disease and dementia in two communities: Nigerian Africans and African Americans. *Am J Psychiatry* **152**, 1485–1492.

Hendrie, H.C., Hall, K.S., Hui, S. *et al.* (1995b). Apolipoprotein E genotype and Alzheimer's disease in a community study of elderly African Americans. *Ann Neurol* **37**, 118–120.

Heyman, A., Fillenbaum, G., Prosnitz, B., Raiford, K., Burchett, B. and Clark, C. (1991). Estimated prevalence of dementia among elderly black and white community residents. *Arch Neurol* **48**, 594–598.

Hofman, A., Rocca, W.A., Brayne, C. *et al.* (1991). The prevalence of dementia in Europe: a collaborative study of 1980–1990 findings. *Int J Epidemiol* **20**, 736–748.

Jorm, A.F. (1990). *The Epidemiology of Alzheimer's Disease and Related Disorders.* Chapman & Hall, London.

Li, G., Shen, Y.C., Chen, C.H., Zhall, Y.W., Li, S.R. and Lu, M. (1989). An epidemiological survey of age–related dementia in an urban area of Beijing. *Acta Psychiatr Scand* **79**, 557–563.

McKhann, G., Drachman, D., Folstein, M. *et al.* (1984). Clinical diagnosis of Alzheimer's disease: report of the NINCDS–ADRDA Work Group under the auspices of Department of Health and Human Services Task Force on Alzheimer's Disease. *Neurology* **34**, 939–944.

Miller, D., Hicks, S.P., D'Amato, C.J. and Landis, J.R. (1984). A descriptive study of neurotic plaques and neurofibrillary tangles in an autopsy population. *Am J Epidemiol* **120**, 331–341.

Osuntokun, B.O., Hendrie, H.C., Ogunniyi, A.O. *et al.* (1992). Cross–cultural studies in Alzheimer's disease. *Ethnic Dis* **2**, 352–357.

Osuntokun, B.O., Ogunniyi, A., Akang, E.E.U. *et al.* (1994). A4–amyloid in the brains of non–demented Nigerian Africans [Letter]. *Lancet* **343**, 56.

Osuntokun, B.O., Sahota, A., Ogunniyi, A.O. *et al.* (1995). Lack of an association between Apolipoprotein E ϵ4 and Alzheimer's disease in elderly Nigerians. *Ann Neurol* **38**, 463–465.

Schoenberg, B.S., Anderson, D.W. and Haerer, A.F. (1985). Severe dementia: prevalence and clinical features in a biracial US population. *Arch Neurol* **42**, 740–743.

Still, C.N., Jackson, K.L., Brandes, D.A., Abramson, R.K. and Macera, C.A. (1990). Distribution of major dementias by race and sex in South Carolina. *J SC Med Assoc* **86**, 453–456.

Treves, T., Korczyn, A.D., Zilber, N. *et al.* (1986). Presenile dementia in Israel. *Arch Neurol* **43**, 26–29.

van Duijn, C.M., Stijnen, T. and Hofman, A. (1991). Risk factors for Alzheimer's disease: overview of the EURODEM collaborative re–analysis of case–control studies. *Int J Epidemiol* **20** (suppl 2).

World Health Organization (1992). *The ICD–10 Classification of Mental and Behavioural Disorders.* WHO, Geneva.

Worth, R.M., Kato, H., Rhoads, G.G., Kagan, A. and Syme, S.L. (1975). Epidemiology studies of coronary heart disease and stroke in Japanese men living in Japan, Hawaii and California: mortality. *Am J Epidemiol* **102**, 481–490.

Zhang, M., Katzman, R., Salmon, D. *et al.* (1990). The prevalence of dementia and Alzheimer's disease in Shanghai, China: impact of age, gender, and education. *Ann Neurol* **27**, 428–437.

Advances in Old Age Psychiatry: Chromosomes to Community Care
Edited by C. Holmes and R. Howard
© 1997 Wrightson Biomedical Publishing Ltd

3

Apolipoprotein E: Implications and Applications

CLIVE HOLMES

Section of Old Age Psychiatry, Institute of Psychiatry, London, UK

A considerable amount of interest had already been shown in apolipoprotein E (ApoE) long before an association was found with Alzheimer's disease. This was principally because of its involvement in lipid transport and metabolism. ApoE is one of a number of protein constituents of plasma lipoproteins that mediate binding of lipoproteins to the low-density lipoprotein receptors. Lipoprotein binding to these receptors initiates the cellular uptake and degradation of the lipoproteins leading to the use of lipoprotein cholesterol in the regulation of intracellular cholesterol metabolism.

ApoE has a polymorphic nature with three major isoforms, referred to as apo-E2, apo-E3 and apo-E4, these being the product of three alleles (ε2, ε3 and ε4) at a single gene locus on chromosome 19. ApoE ε3 is considered the parent form because of its relatively increased frequency compared with the other two major alleles. The other two alleles, ApoE ε2 and ApoE ε4 differ from the parent form by a single amino acid substitution. Apo-E2 differs from the parent form because of a switch of the amino acid arginine to cysteine at residue 158, and apo-E4 differs from the parent form because of a switch from cysteine to arginine at residue 112. Three homozygous phenotypes (apo-E2/2, E3/3 and E4/4) and three heterozygous phenotypes (apo-E2/3, E3/4 and E2/4) arise from the expression of any two of these three alleles.

One large population study (Utermann *et al.*,1980) has shown that the three most common phenotypes are E3/3 (accounting for approximately 60% of all phenotypes) followed by E3/4 (approximately 23%) and E3/2 (approximately 12%), the estimated frequency of alleles in this study being ApoE ε4 allele at 15%, ApoE ε3 at 77% and ApoE ε2 at 8%. The variants apo-E2 and apo-E4 differ in their binding capacity to the low-density lipoprotein receptors, apo-E2 having relatively low binding activity compared to normal (decreased to less than 2%) and apo-E4 a high activity (increased by 100%) compared to normal. These alterations in binding activity result in hyper-cholesterolaemia in individuals homozygous for the ApoE ε4 allele and to type III hyperlipoproteinaemia in ApoE ε2 homozygotes. Thus most studies until three years ago had principally been concerned with the association of carriers of these alleles with the development of heart disease.

In March 1993 this focus of attention on cardiovascular disease switched with the publication by Strittmatter *et al.* of a paper which appeared to show an increased frequency of the ApoE ε4 allele in late-onset familial Alzheimer's disease (Strittmatter *et al.*, 1993). This paper also pointed towards a possible biological mechanism of action in that apo-E4 appeared to have higher avidity binding to beta-amyloid compared with other allelic forms. In August 1993 another paper confirmed this association with late-onset familial cases and also showed it in sporadic Alzheimer's disease (Saunders *et al.*, 1993). Since that time there have been over 1000 publications on various aspects of ApoE and its association with Alzheimer's disease, of which over 100 simply confirm this increased ApoE ε4 frequency in a number of different population groups.

Tables 1 and 2 show the frequencies of the ApoE ε4 allele in a number of early studies of familial and sporadic Alzheimer's disease (Strittmatter *et al.*,

Table 1. Frequency of the ApoE ε4 allele in familial late-onset Alzheimer's disease.

Authors, year	Country	No. AD	Criteria	Age	AD ε4 freq.	Control ε4 freq.
Strittmatter *et al.*, 1993	USA	30	NINCDS	60+	0.50	0.16
Corder *et al.*, 1994	USA	150	NINCDS	60+	0.52	0.15
Yoshizawa *et al.*, 1994	Japan	75	NINCDS	75	0.31	0.09
Liddle *et al.*, 1994	UK	73	NINCDS	73	0.40	0.12

NINCDS, National Institute for Neurological Communicable Disease and Stroke.

Table 2. Frequency of the ApoE ε4 allele in sporadic late-onset Alzheimer's disease.

Authors, years	Country	No. AD	Criteria	Age	AD ε4 freq.	Control ε4 freq.
Saunders *et al.*, 1993	USA	35	PM	66	0.36	0.16
Poirier *et al.*, 1993	Canada	91	NINCDS	75	0.38	0.12
Brousseau *et al.*, 1994	France	36	DSM-III-R	78	0.42	0.11
Yoshizawa *et al.*, 1994	Japan	47	NINCDS	75	0.34	0.09
Kuusisto *et al.*, 1994	Finland	46	NINCDS	69–78	0.36	0.17

PM, post mortem study; NINCDS, National Institute for Neurological Communicable Disease and Stroke; DSM, Diagnostic and Statistical Manual of Mental Disorders.

1993; Corder *et al.*, 1994; Yoshizawa *et al.*, 1994; Liddle *et al.*, 1994; Saunders *et al.*, 1993; Poirier *et al.*,1993; Brousseau *et al.*, 1994; Kuusisto *et al.*, 1994). These studies show an increased ApoE ε4 frequency compared with control groups in both familial and sporadic Alzheimer's disease of late onset. This increase in ApoE ε4 frequency was shown in a wide range of nationalities including those of the USA, Japan and a number of European countries, in both clinically defined Alzheimer's disease and in autopsy studies. One can also see that there is a slightly raised ApoE ε4 frequency in the familial group compared with the sporadic group. Of interest is the finding that the ApoE ε4 frequency in the control group of some nationalities appeared to be quite low; for example, a Japanese frequency of 9% compared with the Finnish frequency of 17%.

The Finnish study (Kuusisto *et al.*, 1994) was initially set up to look at ApoE ε4 as a risk factor for heart disease and is particularly important since it remains the best population study to date, all the other studies being predominantly of case–control methodology. Nine hundred and eighty individuals were followed up over a 3.5-year period, and because of the new interest in an association with Alzheimer's disease these individuals were also assessed for cognitive impairment. Nine hundred and seventy-six individuals were successfully genotyped, of whom 911 appeared to be nondemented, 46 had Alzheimer's disease, and 19 fulfilled criteria for other dementias. Table 3 shows the distribution of the nondemented and the Alzheimer's disease groups according to the number of alleles of ApoE ε4 that they possessed. As we can see, as the number of ApoE ε4 alleles increases so does the percentage of patients with Alzheimer's disease, from 2.9% in those who have no ApoE ε4 alleles to 21.4% in those individuals who are homozygous for ApoE ε4. This gives rise to an odds ratio of 2.7 times for those individuals who possess one ApoE ε4 allele and 9.1 times for those who are homozygous for the ApoE ε4 allele compared with non-carriers. However, it is of interest to note that there are 22 individuals out of 28 who are homozygous for the ApoE ε4 allele who do not have a dementing illness. Likewise there are also 19 out of the 652 subjects who do have Alzheimer's disease despite having no ApoE ε4 allele. Thus it is clear that possession of the ApoE ε4

Table 3. Associated relative risk of Alzheimer's disease according to the number of ApoE ε4 alleles (derived from Kuusisto *et al.*, 1994).

No. of ε4 alleles	No. of patients	No. nondemented	No. (%) with Alzheimer's disease
0	652	633	19 (2.9)
1	277	256	21 (7.6)
2	28	22	6 (21.4)

Odds ratios: 2.7 for ε4/* and 9.1 for ε4/ε4.

allele is neither a necessary nor sufficient condition for the development of Alzheimer's disease.

The other important issue raised by this study was the relatively high frequency of the ApoE ε4 allele in the control population compared with other populations in Japan, North America and other European countries. The prevalence of Alzheimer's disease appears similar in Finland to North America and other European countries where the ApoE ε4 frequency is much lower. Thus it did not appear, despite having a higher frequency of the ApoE ε4 allele in this population, that the prevalence of Alzheimer's disease was raised. Comparisons with Japan are more difficult because of claims of a relative increase in vascular dementia in this country (Yoshitake *et al.*, 1995). These studies point to a possible ethnic difference in the association between the ApoE ε4 allele and the development of Alzheimer's disease. Further studies on a wider range of ethnic populations have confirmed these initial findings. Thus, one small study in Nigeria (Osuntokun *et al.*, 1995) failed to show an increased frequency of the ApoE ε4 allele in native Nigerians with Alzheimer's disease compared with nondemented individuals. A more recent study based in Manhattan (Tang *et al.*, 1996) showed that, while the relative risk for Caucasians was similar to that found in the Kuusisto study, individuals homozygous for the ApoE ε4 allele having a 7.3 times increased risk and those heterozygous for the ApoE ε4 allele a 2.9 times increased risk, this was not the case for other ethnic groups. Hispanics who were homozygous had a much reduced increased relative risk, by some 2.5 times, and heterozygotes an increased risk by only 1.6 times. Even more striking was the finding that African Americans who were homozygous had an increased risk by some 3.0 times but that the individuals who were heterozygous appeared to have a significantly reduced risk by some 0.6 times. Thus it becomes apparent that there may be important ethnic considerations to take into account when one is determining relative risk. The reasons for these apparent ethnic differences may reside in differing genetic or environmental factors that reduce the risk of developing Alzheimer's disease in carriers of the ApoE ε4 allele.

A number of the early studies also showed that the ApoE ε4 allele is associated with an earlier age of onset in late-onset Alzheimer's disease. This was seen as giving additional proof that the ApoE ε4 allele acts as a risk factor for the development of Alzheimer's disease. Thus one study of sporadic Alzheimer's disease (Tsai *et al.*, 1994) showed an approximately six-year earlier age of onset for those individuals who were homozygous for the ApoE ε4 allele compared with those individuals who did not possess the allele. This finding of an earlier age of onset has been repeated in a number of studies, including both sporadic and familial cases (Houlden *et al.*, 1994; Gomez-Isla *et al.*, 1996) and it appears to be a robust finding. Some researchers would argue, in fact, that the main role of the ApoE ε4 allele as a risk factor is predominantly because of this effect (Corder *et al.*, 1995).

Given the evidence in support of the role of the ApoE ε4 allele as a risk factor for Alzheimer's disease, one might postulate that possession of this allele would lead to a greater rate of decline in carriers of the ApoE ε4 allele. A number of studies have looked at rates of cognitive decline, using tools such as the Mini-Mental State Examination (Folstein et al., 1975), to see if there is any corresponding association with rates of yearly decline with the possession of the ApoE ε4 allele. Of these studies few have supported such an association. Three studies (Basun et al., 1995; Gomez-Isla et al., 1996; Forno et al., 1996) failed to show any relationship and one study (Frisoni et al.,1995) appeared to show a negative correlation between possession of the ApoE ε4 allele and rates of cognitive decline. This latter study differed from the rest in that it used estimates of Mini-Mental State decline rather than actual yearly measurements, and so this may be an artefactual finding due to nonlinear progression. Few studies have looked at noncognitive parameters and their association with the ApoE ε4 allele, but in general it would appear that there is also a lack of clear correlation between possession of the ApoE ε4 allele and greater psychopathology. Of some interest is the finding of an association between depressive psychopathology in individuals who are carriers of the ApoE ε2 allele (Holmes et al., 1996). An association of increased depressive symptomatology in individuals with lowered cholesterol levels has been established (Morgan et al., 1993; Gallerani et al., 1995) and the possibility that this may be ApoE-mediated is intriguing.

Possession of the ApoE ε4 allele is only one of a number of other risk factors which appear to be associated with Alzheimer's disease. A number of studies have shown that these risk factors have modulating effects on the relative risk of possession of the ApoE ε4 allele and development of the disease. It appears that, with increasing age, the association between possession of the ApoE ε4 allele and the relative risk of development of the disease diminishes. Thus a study of centenarians failed to show an increased frequency of the ApoE ε4 allele in Alzheimer subjects compared with age-matched controls (Schächter et al., 1994).

The evidence that gender is a risk factor for Alzheimer's disease independent of ApoE genotype is uncertain although some incidence studies do indicate an increased risk of females developing the disease (Rorsman et al., 1986). Some studies have looked at the interaction between sex and the possession of the ApoE ε4 allele and shown that females are particularly susceptible to the risks of possession of the ApoE ε4 allele, with female heterozygotes developing the disease much earlier than male heterozygotes (Payami et al., 1994). An interaction between gender, ApoE genotype and cholesterol levels has also been cited elsewhere (Jarvik et al., 1995).

The association with family history is also of interest. Some studies, as already pointed out, appear to show an increase in the frequency of the ApoE ε4 allele in individuals who have a positive family history. However, assessment of familiality is particularly problematic in diseases of late onset. Any individuals who are genetically predisposed to Alzheimer's disease may die of other causes before the disease is expressed, and relatives may be studied before the age at which the disease is evident. Both of these problems are likely to lead to an underestimate of familiality and a corresponding overestimate of what appears to be sporadic illness. The implication of increased risk in carriers of the ApoE ε4 allele who also have a family history is that other genetic modifiers are present, but while some have been proposed such as α-1 antichymotrypsin (Kamboh *et al.*, 1995) few have been substantiated. An association with mutations in the PS-1 gene with late-onset Alzheimer's disease has also been found in some studies (Kehoe *et al.*, 1996: Wragg *et al.*, 1996). It is thus likely that other genetic factors will also have an impact on the development of late-onset Alzheimer's disease and interactions with these genes will need to be taken into account once they are established.

Other environmental risk factors such as head injury and smoking history may also influence relative risk according to ApoE genotype. Thus one study (Mayeaux *et al.*, 1995) has shown a possible synergistic effect between carriers of the ApoE ε4 allele and the risk of developing Alzheimer's disease after head injury. A 10-fold increase in the risk of Alzheimer's disease was associated with both ApoE ε4 and a history of traumatic head injury, compared with a twofold increase in risk with ApoE ε4 alone. Association with smoking is more contentious, but one study (van Duijn *et al.*, 1995) of early-onset Alzheimer's disease suggests that smokers who are ApoE ε4 allele carriers have a reduction in the risk of developing Alzheimer's disease. This reduction in risk was some 10-fold in those individuals who also had a positive family history of dementia, and did not appear to be explainable by an increased mortality in carriers of the ApoE ε4 allele who smoked.

PREDICTIVE VALUE OF ApoE GENOTYPE

It is evident from the preceding discussion that there are a number of factors which need to be taken into account when making predictions of the future risk of an individual developing Alzheimer's disease based on ApoE genotyping.

The first consideration, which is of primary importance, is that the best estimates that we have of relative risk are currently based on prevalence data. Such data cannot take into account the effects that possession of the ApoE ε4 allele has on the duration of the illness. Thus, incident studies may reveal a lower relative risk than previously reported if the ApoE ε4 allele increases survival time.

The second factor is the genotype of the individual. While it is relatively easy to assess risk in individuals who are homozygous for the ApoE ε4 allele, complications arise in individuals who possess the ApoE ε2 allele. This is because some studies indicate that the ApoE ε2 allele has a protective effect on the development of Alzheimer's disease (Corder *et al.*, 1994; Talbot *et al.*, 1994). Given the overall small numbers of ApoE-ε2-carrying individuals, assessment of relative risk in such individuals will be difficult until very large, epidemiologicaly-based studies are completed. Thus, at present, it is difficult confidently to predict the relative risk of such combinations of alleles.

Thirdly, as already discussed, the basic demographic variables of age, sex and ethnicity all appear to influence the relative risk of ApoE ε4 carrying individuals developing the disease.

Fourthly, assessment of family history is particularly difficult, and the lack of clear evidence of any other gene involvement at this stage makes interpretation of a positive family history problematic. Assessment of environmental risk factors becomes increasingly difficult if we have some risk factors which appear to increase the associated risk of the ApoE ε4 allele, such as head injury, and other risk factors, such as smoking, which appear to decrease the risk.

Fifthly, assessment of the cognitive state of the individual at interview would also add some weight as to whether or not there is increased risk of the development of Alzheimer's disease. This will, of course, occur independently of possession of ApoE ε4 allele, but it is of some interest to note that one paper (Petersen *et al.*, 1995) implies that individuals who would be considered to have a borderline dementing syndrome appear to have a particularly high risk of developing Alzheimer's disease if they also carry the ApoE ε4 allele.

Finally, the association of the ApoE ε4 allele with other diseases, such as heart disease, also means that other risk factors for heart disease, such as hypertension, would have to be taken into consideration because an individual with such risk factors would be less likely to survive to an age when late-onset Alzheimer's disease presents.

Clearly, a full assessment of the interaction of these variables and their translation into a meaningful risk value in any one individual is unlikely to be practicable. While predictive testing is a feasible option for relatives of patients with early-onset, autosomal, dominant Alzheimer's disease, multifactorial risk assessment as a tool for the prediction of late-onset disease seems unlikely to be of any clinical value.

DIAGNOSTIC VALUE OF ApoE GENOTYPING

Most of the early studies were concerned with the association of the ApoE ε4 allele with Alzheimer's disease subjects. However, questions relating to the biological mechanism of action of Apo-E4 led to interest in other dementing disorders. Table 4 shows a summary of the ApoE ε4 allele

Table 4. Apolipoprotein E ε4 allele frequency in other diseases.

Authors, year	Disease group	Disease group freq.	Control group freq.	p
Kawanashi et al., 1996	Dementia of Lewy	0.30	0.15	< 0.001
Galasko et al., 1994	body type	0.29	0.14	< 0.001
St Clair et al., 1994		0.35	0.13	< 0.001
Frisoni et al., 1994	Vascular dementia	0.45	0.18	< 0.0005
Isoe et al., 1996		0.21	0.06	< 0.01
Amouyel et al., 1994	CJD	0.33	0.11	< 0.01
Al-Chalabi et al., 1996	MND	0.42	0.21	0.015

CJD, Creutzfeldt–Jakob disease; MND, motor neurone disease.

frequency in a number of neurodegenerative conditions. The ApoE ε4 allele appears to be increased in dementia of Lewy body type (Kawanashi et al., 1996; Galasko et al., 1994; St Clair et al., 1994), Creutzfeldt–Jakob disease (Amouyel et al., 1994) and motor neurone disease (Al-Chalabi et al., 1996). The finding of an increased ApoE ε4 allele frequency in vascular dementia is more contentious, but two studies appear to support this (Frisoni et al., 1994; Isoe et al., 1996). Thus it can be seen that possession of the ApoE ε4 allele is not a good discriminating factor for the different types of dementia.

CLINICAL COURSE AND ApoE GENOTYPING

Apart from age at onset, possession of the ApoE ε4 allele also appears to have little significance in determining the clinical course of patients who have already been diagnosed as having the disease. Thus there seems to be little evidence that possession of the ApoE ε4 allele is associated with greater rates of cognitive decline or a more severe noncognitive psychopathology. Early studies seemed to indicate that the ApoE ε4 allele was associated with a longer duration of illness. On closer examination it seems that this association was artefactual, with age at onset acting as a confounding variable (Gomez-Isla et al., 1996).

Finally, on a more optimistic note, one area in which ApoE genotyping may prove to be of clinical value is in therapeutics. Clinical trials of drugs for Alzheimer's disease now include ApoE genotyping as part of their experimental protocol in the belief that treatment response may be partially genetically determined. Some evidence in support of this is available (Poirier et al., 1995) which indicates that response to the anticholinesterase tacrine may be more pronounced in individuals who do not possess the ApoE ε4 allele. Thus one double-blind, 30-week clinical trial study has shown that more than

80% of Alzheimer patients who did not carry the ApoE ε4 allele improved on measures of overall performance as measured by the Alzheimer Disease Assessment Schedule. This compares with a decline in the performance of some 60% in ApoE ε4 carriers. Clearly, a great deal of interest is being shown in these findings and future therapeutic agents will need to be assessed in the light of possible genetic influences on treatment outcome .

REFERENCES

Al-Chalabi, A., Enayat, Z.E., Bakker, M.C. *et al.* (1996). Association of apolipoprotein E ε4 allele with bulbar-onset motor neurone disease. *Lancet* **347**, 159–160.

Amouyel, P., Vidal, O., Launay, J.M. *et al.* (1994). The apolipoprotein E alleles as major susceptibility factors for Creutzfeldt–Jakob disease. *Lancet* **344**, 1315–1317.

Basun, H., Grut, M. and Lannfelt, L. (1995). Apolipoprotein e4 allele and disease progression in patients with late-onset Alzheimer's disease. *Neurosci Lett* **183**: 32–34.

Brousseau, T., Legrain, S., Berr, C. *et al.* (1994). Confirmation of the epsilon 4 allele of the apolipoprotein E gene as a risk factor for late-onset Alzheimer's disease. *Neurology* **44**, 342–344.

Corder, E.H., Saunders, A.M., Risch, N.J. *et al.* (1994). Protective effect of apolipoprotein E type 2 allele for late-onset Alzheimer disease. *Nat Genet* **7**, 180–184

Corder, E.H., Saunders, A.M., Strittmatter, W.J. *et al.* (1995). Apolipoprotein E, survival in Alzheimer's disease patients, and the competing risks of death and Alzheimer's disease. *Neurology* **45**, 1323–1328.

Folstein, M.F., Folstein, S.E. and McHugh, P.R. (1975). Mini-mental state: a practical method for grading the cognitive state of patients for the clinician. *J Psychiatr Res* **12**, 189–198.

Forno, G.D., Rasmusson, X., Brandt, J. *et al.* (1996). Apolipoprotein E genotype and rate of decline in probable Alzheimer's disease. *Arch Neurol* **53**, 345–350.

Frisoni, G.B., Calabresi, L., Geroldi C. *et al.* (1994). Apolipoprotein E epsilon-4 allele in Alzheimer's disease and vascular dementia. *Dementia* **5**, 240–242.

Frisoni, G.B., Govoni, S., Geroldi, C. *et al.* (1995). Gene dose of the e4 allele of apolipoprotein E and disease progression in sporadic late-onset Alzheimer's disease. *Ann Neurol* **37**, 596–604.

Galasko, D., Saitoh, T., Xia, L.J. *et al.* (1994). The apolipoprotein E allele ε4 is overrepresented in patients with the Lewy body variant of Alzheimer's disease. *Neurology* **44**, 1950 1951.

Gallerani, M., Manfredini, R., Caracciolo, S. *et al.* (1995). Serum cholesterol concentrations in parasuicide. *BMJ* **310**, 1632–1636.

Gomez-Isla, T., West, H.L., Rebeck, G.W. *et al.* (1996). Clinical and pathological crrelates of apolipoprotein E ε4 in Alzheimer's disease. *Ann Neurol* **39**, 62–70.

Holmes, C., Levy, R., McLoughlin, D.M. *et al.* (1996). Apolipoprotein E: non-cognitive symptoms and cognitive decline in late-onset Alzheimer's disease. *J Neurol Neurosurg Psychiatry* **61**, 580–583.

Houlden, H., Crook, R., Hardy, J. *et al.* (1994). Confirmation that familial clustering and age of onset in late-onset Alzheimer's disease are determined at the apolipoprotein E locus. *Neurosci Lett* **174**, 222–224

Isoe, K., Urakami, K., Sato, K. *et al.* (1996). Apolipoprotein E in patients with dementia of Alzheimer type and vascular dementia. *Acta Neurol Scand* **93**, 133–137.

Jarvik, G.P., Wijsman, E.M., Kukull, W.A. *et al.* (1995). Interactions of apolipoprotein E genotype, total cholesterol level, age, and sex in prediction of Alzheimer's disease. *Neurology* **45**, 1092–1096.

Kamboh, M.I., Sanghera, D.K., Ferrell, R.E. and DeKosky, S.T. (1995). APOE*4-associated Alzheimer's disease risk is modified by α1-antichymotrypsin polymorphism. *Nat Genet* **10**, 486–488.

Kawanashi, C., Suzuki, K., Odawara, T. *et al.* (1996). Neuropathological evaluation and apolipoprotein E gene polymorphism analysis in diffuse Lewy body disease. *J Neurosci* **136**, 140–142.

Kehoe, P., Williams, J., Lovestone, S., Wilcock, G., Owen, M. and the UK Alzheimer's Disease Collaborative Group (1996). Presenilin-1 polymorphism and Alzheimer's disease. *Lancet* **347**, 1185.

Kuusisto, J., Koivisto, K., Kervinen, K. *et al.* (1994). Association of apolipoprotein E phenotypes with late-onset Alzheimer's disease: population-based study. *BMJ* **309**, 636–638.

Liddle, M., Williams, J., Bayer, A. *et al.* (1994). Confirmation of association between the e4 allele of apolipoprotein E and Alzheimer's disease. *J Med Genet* **31**, 197–200.

Mayeaux, R., Ottman, R., Maestre, G. *et al.* (1995). Synergistic effects of traumatic head injury and apolipoprotein ε4 in patients with Alzheimer's disease. *Neurology* **45**, 555–557.

Morgan, R.S., Palinkas, L.A., Barrett-Connor, E.L. and Wingard, D.L. (1993). Plasma cholesterol and depressive symptoms in older men. *Lancet* **341**, 75–79.

Osuntokun, B.O., Sahota, A., Ogunniyi, A.O, *et al.* (1995). Lack of an association between apolipoprotein E ε4 and Alzheimer's disease in elderly Nigerians. *Ann Neurol* **38**, 463–465.

Payami, H., Montee, K.R., Kaye, J.A. *et al.* (1994). Alzheimer's disease, apolipoprotein E4 and gender [letter]. *JAMA* **271**, 1316–1317.

Petersen, C.R., Smith, G.E., Ivnik, R.J. *et al.* (1995). *JAMA* **273**, 1274–1278.

Poirier, J., Davignon, J., Bouthillier, D. *et al.* (1993). Apolipoprotein E polymorphism and Alzheimer's disease. *Lancet* **342**, 697–699.

Poirier, J., Delisle, M.C., Quirion, R. (1995). Apolipoprotein E4 allele as a predictor of cholinergic deficits and treatment outcome in Alzheimer's disease. *Proc Natl Acad Sci USA* **92**, 12260–12264.

Rorsman, B., Hagnell, O., Lanke, J. (1986). Prevalence and incidence of senile and multi-infarct dementia in the Lundby study: a comparison of time periods 1947–1957 and 1957–1972. *Neuropsychobiology* **15**, 122–129.

Saunders, A.M., Strittmatter, W.J., Schmechel, D. *et al.* (1993). Association of apolipoprotein E allele epsilon 4 with late-onset familial and sporadic Alzheimer's disease. *Neurology* **43**; 1467–1472.

Schächter, F., Faure-Delanef, L., Guénot, F. *et al.* (1994). Genetic associations with human longevity at the APOE and ACE loci. *Nature Genet* **6**, 29–32.

St Clair, D., Normann, J., Perry, R. *et al.* (1994). Apolipoprotein E ε4 allele frequency in patients with Lewy body dementia, Alzheimer's disease and age-matched controls. *Neurosci Lett* **176**, 45–46.

Strittmatter, W.J., Saunders, A.M., Schmechel, D. *et al.* (1993). Apolipoprotein E: high-avidity binding to beta-amyloid and increased frequency of type 4 allele in late-onset familial Alzheimer's disease. *Proc Natl Acad Sci USA* **90**, 1977–1981.

Talbot, C., Lendon, C., Craddock, N. *et al.* (1994). Protection against Alzheimer's disease with apoE ε2. *Lancet* **343**, 1432–1433.

Tang, M.X., Maestre, G., Tsai, W.Y. *et al.* (1996). Relative risk of Alzheimer's disease and age-at-onset distributions, based on APOE genotypes among elderly African Americans, Caucasians, and Hispanics in New York City. *Am J Hum Genet* **58**, 574–584.

Tsai, M.S., Tangalos, E.G., Petersen, R.C. *et al.* (1994). Apolipoprotein E: risk factor for Alzheimer disease. *Am J Hum Genet* **54**, 643–649.

Utermann, G., Lagenbeck, U., Beisiegel, U. and Weber, W. (1980). Genetics of the apolipoprotein E system in man. *Am J Hum Genet* **32**, 339–347.

van Duijn, C.M., Havekes, L.M., van Broeckhoven, C., de Knijff, P. and Hofman, A. (1995). Apolipoprotein E genotype and association between smoking and early onset Alzheimer's disease. *BMJ* **310**, 627–631.

Wragg, M., Hutton, M., Talbot, C. *et al.* (1996). Genetic association between intronic polymorphism in presenilin-1 gene and late-onset Alzheimer's disease. *Lancet* **347**, 509–512.

Yoshitake, T., Kiyohara, Y., Kato, I. *et al.* (1995). Incidence and risk factors of vascular dementia and Alzheimer's disease in a defined elderly Japanese population – the Hisayama study. *Neurology* **45**, 1161–1168.

Yoshizawa, T., Yamakawa-Kobayashi, K., Komatsuzaki, Y. *et al.* (1994). Dose-dependent association of apolipoprotein E allele epsilon 4 with late-onset, sporadic Alzheimer's disease. *Ann Neurol* **36**, 656–659.

II

Clinical and Pathological
Features of Dementia

Advances in Old Age Psychiatry: Chromosomes to Community Care
Edited by C. Holmes and R. Howard
© 1997 Wrightson Biomedical Publishing Ltd

4

Molecular Pathogenesis of Alzheimer's Disease

SIMON LOVESTONE

Section of Old Age Psychiatry, Institute of Psychiatry, London, UK

The road from chromosomes to community care is long and winding and, without wanting to push the analogy too far, is barren in places. If understanding of chromosomes represents the genetic research in Alzheimer's disease, and community care the clinical outcomes, then the road itself is molecular biology. For it is molecular biology that will translate advances in the one to outcomes in the other. Understanding the molecular pathogenesis of disease is the best, perhaps the only, hope for developing treatments for Alzheimer's disease (AD) and other disorders of interest to old age psychiatry that go beyond the palliative measures currently undergoing clinical trials. Despite exciting advances, only a few steps have been taken on this road and the goal of useful clinical outcomes remains far off.

This chapter briefly reviews current understanding of the molecular pathogenesis of AD, making reference principally to review articles, where available, for further information. Understanding of the generation of the plaques and tangles of AD has grown over the past few years although controversy still abounds in a number of areas. However, plaques and tangles are only markers of the disease process and we are not yet substantially closer to an understanding of how neurones are lost and dementia ensues in AD. Turning first to plaques, these are relatively large extracellular structures which, in their mature form, contain a central dense core of amyloid protein surrounded by a halo of degenerating neurites. The amyloid of the core is composed of peptides derived from the larger transmembranous amyloid precursor protein (APP) (Selkoe, 1994; Wisniewski *et al.*, 1994; Hyman and Tanzi, 1992). APP is an ubiquitously expressed protein of unknown function, although it may have a role in cell-to-cell communication (Yamamoto *et al.*, 1994). Much research is concentrated upon understanding the metabolism of APP and the hope that modulation of this might be one way to reduce the extent of plaque formation. Amyloid is formed from a small segment of the APP parent compound and at least two main routes of APP metabolism have been described, one of which results in the formation of amyloid-containing fragments (amyloidogenic metabolism) while the other does not (nonamyloidogenic) (Selkoe *et al.*, 1996). Thus cleavage of APP at the extracellular surface of the membrane results in cleavage within the amyloid-forming (Aβ) moiety itself. This nonamyloidogenic metabolism yields a soluble fragment called APP$_s$, and a smaller intracellular component. In contrast, cleavage of the APP compound on either side of the Aβ peptide (by β and γ secretase) yields a number of fragments, some of which contain intact Aβ. Both amyloidogenic and nonamyloidogenic metabolism occur as a normal process and, indeed, Aβ fragments are found in cerebrospinal fluid (CSF) from healthy individuals (Vigo-Pelfrey *et al.*, 1993). It does not seem as if generation of Aβ itself results in AD, but decades or a lifetime of a relative increase in Aβ production might well be harmful. The relative amount of Aβ peptides in CSF does change, however, with both age and disease (Carroll *et al.*, 1995; Lannfelt *et al.*, 1995a). This has been suggested as a diagnostic marker for AD (Lannfelt *et al.*, 1995b) although such a test would be complicated by the fact that the relationship between disease progression and Aβ concentration becomes inverse with advanced disease (Nitsch *et al.*, 1995). Although Aβ generation is not itself pathognomonic of disease, nor do Aβ peptides cause disease automatically, it appears that Aβ peptides vary in length by a few amino acids; some of these peptides aggregate more readily than others and thus may be relatively more pathogenic (Snyder *et al.*, 1994; Selkoe *et al.*, 1996).

Little is known at present about the regulation of APP processing although this remains of foremost importance as a site of potential therapeutic intervention (Gandy and Greengard, 1992). Mutations in the APP gene do cause AD in 20 or fewer families from around the world (Goate *et al.*, 1991; Schellenberg *et al.*, 1991; Mullan *et al.*, 1992). These mutations tend to aggregate on either side of the Aβ peptide, perhaps suggesting that they exert a pathogenic effect by interfering with the balance of amyloidogenic and nonamyloidogenic metabolism (Haass *et al.*, 1994; Citron *et al.*, 1992; Haass *et al.*, 1995). Another genetic influence on Aβ deposition is thought to be Down's syndrome, trisomy 21 (Holland and Oliver, 1995). All patients with Down's syndrome develop the neuropathological features of AD and frequently a dementia in mid-life (Mann, 1988). Because the APP gene is coded for on chromosome 21, all patients with Down's syndrome have three copies of this gene and it is likely that this overprovision of genetic information results in an overproduction of APP protein and consequently Aβ peptide (Armstrong *et al.*, 1996). Another cause of increased Aβ deposition in plaques is head injury and there may well be other environmental influences on plaque formation (Roberts *et al.*, 1990; Mayeux *et al.*, 1995). Some evidence suggests that APP itself might be a stress protein with an increase in expression being part of the normal cellular response to brain injury (Dewji *et al.*, 1995; Lewén *et al.*, 1995; Pappolla *et al.*, 1995). One other intriguing mechanism whereby APP metabolism is regulated is in response to signal transduction following binding of neurotransmitters to their receptors. Many neurotransmitters share similar intracellular signalling events and APP processing has been shown to be affected by a number of different neurotransmitters. However, of particular interest is the demonstration that muscarinic agonists reduce the generation of Aβ containing metabolic products (Wolf *et al.*, 1995; Felder *et al.*, 1993; Eckols *et al.*, 1995). This suggests that the muscarinic agonists currently in Phase II and III clinical trials as palliative treatments for cholinergic deficit in AD may turn out to have a more substantial long-term beneficial effect on disease progression (Fisher *et al.*, 1996).

While the effects on the causes of Aβ deposition are under examination, so too are the consequences of plaque formation. Aβ fibrils are toxic to neurones in culture although the means whereby this occurs has not been determined (Kowall, 1994; Howlett *et al.*, 1995). At least one study suggests that Aβ-induced neurotoxicity is dependent upon expression of glycogen synthase kinase-3 (GSK-3) (Takashima *et al.*, 1993), an enzyme discussed in another context below. Other studies have suggested that calcium influx is one of the neurotoxic effects consequent to Aβ deposition (Fukuyama *et al.*, 1994).

The second major pathological characteristic of AD is the accumulation within neurones of paired helical filament structures seen at the light microscopic level as neurofibrillary tangles (Goedert *et al.*, 1995; Mandelkow *et al.*, 1995; Lovestone and Anderton, 1992). These fibrillar structures are composed of massive accumulations of a microtubule-associated protein, tau, an essential component of the neuronal cytoskeleton. Microtubules are part of the cytoskeleton present in all cells but in neurones have a highly specialized role in maintaining neuronal morphology and function. In neurones microtubules are relatively long and rigid structures, a morphologic characteristic confirmed by the neuronal-specific microtubule-associated proteins, one of which is tau. The contribution of microtubules to the structure and function of the neurone depends upon the binding of tau. Tau is phosphorylated at multiple sites and the binding of tau to microtubules is regulated largely by the amount of phosphorylation (Anderton *et al.*, 1995). In developing fetal neurones when microtubules are relatively dynamic and the cytoskeleton needs to be a plastic structure, tau is heavily phosphorylated (Brion *et al.*, 1993; Hasegawa *et al.*, 1993). *In vitro* studies confirm that heavily phosphorylated tau does not bind to microtubules and thereby fails to strengthen them (Iqbal *et al.*, 1994; Bramblett *et al.*, 1993). In AD, tau is heavily phosphorylated (Lovestone and Anderton, 1992; Trojanowski and

Lee, 1994) and this leads to microtubule collapse and the loss of microtubules from degenerating neurones (Gray *et al.*, 1987; Flamen-Durand and Couck, 1979). The phosphorylation of tau is therefore of utmost importance in regulating neuronal function. During development, highly phosphorylated tau permits dynamic microtubules in growing neurones. With maturation tau is relatively lightly phosphorylated, thereby promoting microtubule stability and maintaining neuronal integrity. In AD the abnormal phosphorylation of tau results in the loss of microtubules and, presumably, the loss of neuronal function and subsequent death of the neurone. This suggests that perhaps AD is, after all, a disorder of neurodevelopment.

The finding that tau is heavily phosphorylated in AD and that microtubules are lost led to the search for regulatory mechanisms of tau phosphorylation (Pines, 1995). A number of enzymes add or remove phosphates from tau *in vitro* but only one, GSK-3, has been shown to do this in intact cells (Lovestone *et al.*, 1994; Latimer *et al.*, 1995; Sperber *et al.*, 1995). Moreover, GSK-3 phosphorylation of tau in intact cells results in more fragile microtubules, a change in microtubule morphology and a reduction in tau binding to microtubules (Lovestone *et al.*, 1996a). Studies are now concentrated on the next step in the regulatory process – that of the regulation of GSK-3 itself – in the hope that an intervention in this process will also lead to a therapy that would slow down or prevent neurofibrillary tangle accumulation.

Two other major advances in the understanding of AD have come from molecular genetics, although it is not clear how either of these affects the molecular process of pathogenesis as yet. One gene (presenilin-1; PS-1) was found on chromosome 14, mutations in this gene being associated with early-onset, autosomal dominant, familial AD (Sherrington *et al.*, 1995). The protein product of the gene predicts a structure that transverses the membrane seven times, suggesting a role as a receptor, possibly coupled to G protein (Levy-Lehad *et al.*, 1995a). The importance of this gene to AD pathogenesis was demonstrated by the finding of a near-identical gene on chromosome 1 (PS-1), mutations in which also cause early-onset familial AD (Levy-Lahad *et al.*, 1995b) and also by the association of an intronic polymorphism in PS-1 with late-onset AD (Wragg *et al.*, 1996; Kehoe *et al.*, 1996). It is not clear how the presenilins function in AD, but they might alter APP processing directly or perhaps alter the signal transduction cascades that affect APP processing and tau phosphorylation.

The second major advance was the identification of apolipoprotein E (ApoE) polymorphisms as susceptibility factors in AD (Liddell *et al.*, 1994; Poirier *et al.*, 1993; Saunders *et al.*, 1993). Some data suggested that apo-E4 protein bound more readily to $A\beta$ and might thereby promote plaque formation or reduce plaque clearance (Strittmatter *et al.*, 1993; Sanan *et al.*, 1994). However, this work was not replicated (LaDu *et al.*, 1994; LaDu *et al.*, 1995) and other laboratories suggested that apo-E3 bound more tightly to tau and to other microtubule-associated proteins (Strittmatter *et al.*, 1994a; Huang *et al.*, 1994). This led to the hypothesis that apo-E3 or apo-E2 might protect tau from hyperphosphorylation (Huang *et al.*, 1995; Strittmatter *et al.*, 1994b) and studies of cells in culture have suggested that apo-E4 is in fact toxic to microtubules (Nathan *et al.*, 1994; Holtzman *et al.*, 1995). The present author's own studies suggest that the distribution of ApoE within tau-containing cells (like neurones) is dependent upon ApoE isoform with only apo-E3 being retained within cytoplasm (Lovestone *et al.*, 1996b). Thus, work in progress from a number of different laboratories suggests that ApoE has a role in the brain in contributing to the tau-induced stabilization of microtubules, with apo-E3 or apo-E2 having a positive effect and apo-E4 a destabilizing effect. Although small, such an effect might be enough, over a lifetime, to alter an individual's risk of suffering from microtubule collapse and hence AD.

The molecular biology of AD has advanced to such an extent that the basis of a molecular model can now be outlined. A variety of genetic and environmental insults (APP mutations, trisomy 21, head injury) result in an increased deposition of Aβ in plaques, probably by altering APP metabolism. Aβ fibrils are neurotoxic to cells in culture and plaque formation in brain may be neurotoxic to surrounding cells. No link between Aβ deposition in plaques and tau phosphorylation in tangles has yet been demonstrated, although the two pathological processes must be dependent upon each other or on another common factor. Tau phosphorylation results in changes in the properties of tau and results in more fragile microtubules with a consequent loss of function and eventual death of neurones. This process may be enhanced by the pathogenic isoform of ApoE (E4) and might be reduced by the protective isoform of ApoE (apo-E2). The location of presenilins in this model is uncertain at present.

While such a molecular model is at best sketchy, and may be frankly incorrect in places, it does point the way to potential drug treatments. One very promising site for intervention is metabolism of APP and the search is intensifying for a means to regulate the APP proteases to bias metabolism in favour of the nonamyloidogenic route. Similarly, the confirmation that GSK-3 phosphorylation of tau in intact cells results in destabilized microtubules offers the way to intervene to reduce the loss of neuronal function in the accumulation of neurofibrillary tangles. Although an essential enzyme for cellular function, the development of specific neuronal GSK-3-inhibitors or compounds regulating GSK-3 in neurones is a feasible project for modern pharmaco-technology. As the pharmacologists increasingly perceive sites where their knowledge and skills might be put to good use, it does seem as though the first glimpses of the destination on that long road from chromosomes to community care are indeed in sight.

REFERENCES

Anderton, B.H., Couck, A., Davis, D.R. *et al.* (1995). Modulation of PHF-like tau phosphorylation in cultured neurones and transfected cells. *Neurobiol Aging* **16**, 389–402.

Armstrong, R.A., Cairns, N.J., Myers, D., Smith, C.U.M., Lantos, P.L. and Rossor, M.N. (1996). A comparison of β-amyloid deposition in the medial temporal lobe in sporadic Alzheimer's disease, Down's syndrome and normal elderly brains. *Neurodegeneration* **5**, 35–41.

Bramblett, G.T., Goedert, M., Jakes, R., Merrick, S.E., Trojanowski, J.Q. and Lee, V.M. (1993). Abnormal tau phosphorylation at Ser396 in Alzheimer's disease recapitulates development and contributes to reduced microtubule binding. *Neuron* **10**, 1089–1099.

Brion, J.-P., Smith, C., Couck, A.-M., Gallo, J.-M. and Anderton, B.H. (1993). Developmental changes in τ phosphorylation: fetal τ transiently phosphorylated in a manner similar to paired helical filament-τ characteristic of Alzheimer's disease. *J Neurochem* **61**, 2071–2080.

Carroll, R.T., Lust, M.R., Kim, K.S., Doyle, P.D. and Emmerling, M.R. (1995). An age-related correlation between levels of β-amyloid precursor protein and β-amyloid in human cerebrospinal fluid. *Biochem Biophys Res Commun* **210**, 345–349.

Citron, M., Oltersdorf, T., Haass, C. *et al.* (1992). Mutation of the β-amyloid precursor protein in familial Alzheimer's disease increases β-protein production. *Nature* **360**, 672–674.

Dewji, N.N., Do, C. and Bayney, R.M. (1995). Transcriptional activation of Alzheimer's β-amyloid precursor protein gene by stress. *Mol Brain Res* **33**, 245–253.

Eckols, K., Bymaster, F.P., Mitch, C.H., Shannon, H.E., Ward, J.S. and DeLapp, N.W. (1995). The muscarinic M1 agonist xanomeline increases soluble amyloid precursor protein release from Chinese hamster ovary-m1 cells. *Life Sci* **57**, 1183–1190.

Felder, C.C., Ma, A.L., Briley, E.M. and Axelrod, J. (1993). Muscarinic acetylcholine receptor subtypes associated with release of Alzheimer amyloid precursor derivatives activate multiple signal transduction pathways. *Ann NY Acad Sci* **695**, 15–18.

Fisher, A., Heldman, E., Gurwitz, D. *et al.* (1996). M1 agonists for the treatment of Alzheimer's disease – novel properties and clinical update. *Ann NY Acad Sci* **777**, 189–196.

Flament-Durand, J. and Couck, A. (1979). Spongiform alterations in brain biopsies of presenile dementia. *Acta Neuropathol (Berl)* **46**, 159–162.

Fukuyama, R., Wadhwani, K.C., Galdzicki, Z., Rapoport, S.I. and Ehrenstein, G. (1994). β-amyloid polypeptide increases calcium-uptake in PC12 cells: a possible mechanism for its cellular toxicity in Alzheimer's disease. *Brain Res* **667**, 269–272.

Gandy, S. and Greengard, P. (1992). Amyloidogenesis in Alzheimer's disease: some possible therapeutic opportunities. *Trends Pharmacol Sci* **13**, 108–113.

Goate, A., Chartier-Harlin, M.C., Mullan, M. *et al.* (1991). Segregation of a missense mutation in the amyloid precursor protein gene with familial Alzheimer's disease. *Nature* **349**, 704–706.

Goedert, M., Spillantini, M.G., Jakes, R. *et al.* (1995). Molecular dissection of the paired helical filament. *Neurobiol Aging* **16**, 325–334.

Gray, E.G., Paula Barbosa, M. and Roher, A. (1987). Alzheimer's disease: paired helical filaments and cytomembranes. *Neuropathol Appl Neurobiol* **13**, 91–110.

Haass, C., Hung, A.Y., Selkoe, D.J. and Teplow, D.B. (1994). Mutations associated with a locus for familial Alzheimer's disease result in alternative processing of amyloid β-protein precursor. *J Biol Chem* **269**, 17741–17748.

Haass, C., Lemere, C.A., Capell, A. *et al.* (1995). The Swedish mutation causes early-onset Alzheimer's disease by β-secretase cleavage within the secretory pathway. *Nature Med* **1**, 1291–1296.

Hasegawa, M., Watanabe, A., Takio, K. *et al.* (1993). Characterization of two distinct monoclonal antibodies to paired helical filaments: further evidence for fetal-type phosphorylation of the τ in paired helical filaments. *J Neurochem* **60**, 2068–2077.

Holland, A.J. and Oliver, C. (1995). Down's syndrome and the links with Alzheimer's disease. *J Neurol Neurosurg Psychiatry* **59**, 111–114.

Holtzman, D.M., Pitas, R.E., Kilbridge, J. *et al.* (1995). Low-density lipoprotein receptor-related protein mediates apolipoprotein E-dependent neurite outgrowth in a central nervous system-derived neuronal cell line. *Proc Natl Acad Sci USA* **92**, 9480–9484.

Howlett, D.R., Jennings, K.H., Lee, D.C. *et al.* (1995). Aggregation state and neurotoxic properties of Alzheimer beta-amyloid peotide. *Neurodegeneration* **4**, 23–32.

Huang, D.Y., Goedert, M., Jakes, R. *et al.* (1994). Isoform-specific interactions of apolipoprotein E with the microtubule-associated protein MAP2c: implications for Alzheimer's disease. *Neurosci Lett* **182**, 55–58.

Huang, D.Y., Weisgraber, K.H., Goedert, M., Saunders, A.M., Roses, A.D. and Strittmatter, W.J. (1995). ApoE3 binding to aut repeat I is abolished by tau serine$_{262}$ phosphorylation. *Neurosci Lett* **192**, 209–212.

Hyman, B.T. and Tanzi, R.E. (1992). Amyloid, dementia and Alzheimer's disease. *Curr Opin Neurol Neurosurg* **5**, 88–93.

Iqbal, K., Zaidi, T., Bancher, C. and Grundke-Iqbal, I. (1994). Alzheimer paired helical filaments: restoration of the biological activity by dephosphorylation. *FEBS Lett* **349**, 104–108.

Kehoe, P., Williams, J., Lovestone, S., Wilcock, G., Owen, M.J. and the UK Alzheimer's Disease Collaborative Group (1996). Confirmtion of an association between a presenilin-1 intronic polymorphism and late onset Alzheimer's disease. *Lancet* **347**, 1185.

Kowall, N.W. (1994). Beta amyloid neurotoxicity and neuronal degeneration in Alzheimer's disease. *Neurobiol Aging* **15**, 257–258.

LaDu, M.J., Falduto, M.T., Manelli, A.M., Reardon, C.A., Getz, G.S. and Frail, D.E. (1994). Isoform-specific binding of apolipoprotein E to β-amyloid. *J Biol Chem* **269**, 23403–23406.

LaDu, M.J., Pederson, T.M., Frail, D.E., Reardon, C.A., Getz, G.S. and Falduto, M.T. (1995). Purification of apolipoprotein E attenuates isoform-specific binding to β-amyloid. *J Biol Chem* **270**, 9039–9042.

Lannfelt, L., Basun, H., Vigo-Pelfrey, C. *et al.* (1995a). Amyloid β-peptide in cerebrospinal fluid in individuals with the Swedish Alzheimer amyloid precursor protein mutation. *Neurosci Lett* **199**, 203–206.

Lannfelt, L., Basun, H., Wahlund, L.-O., Rowe, B.A. and Wagner, S.L. (1995b). Decreased α-secretase-cleaved amyloid precursor protein as a diagnostic marker for Alzheimer's disease. *Nature Med* **1**, 829–832.

Latimer, D.A., Gallo, J.-M., Lovestone, S. *et al.* (1995). Stimulation of MAP kinase by *v-raf* transformation of fibroblasts fails to induce hyperphosphorylation of transfected tau. *FEBS Lett* **365**, 42–46.

Levy-Lehad, E., Wasco, W., Poorkaj, P. *et al.* (1995a). Candidate gene for the chromosome 1 familial Alzheimer's disease locus. *Science* **269**, 973–977.

Levy-Lehad, E., Wijsman, E.M., Nemens, E. *et al.* (1995b). A familial Alzheimer's disease locus on chromosome 1. *Science* **269**, 970–972.

Lewén, A., Li, G.L., Nilsson, P., Olsson, Y. and Hillered, L. (1995). Traumatic brain injury in rat produces changes of β-amyloid precursor protein immunoreactivity. *Neuroreport* **6**, 357–360.

Liddell, M., Williams, J., Bayer, A., Kaiser, F. and Owen, M. (1994). Confirmation of association between the e4 allele of apolipoprotein E and Alzheimer's disease. *J Med Genet* **31**, 197–200.

Lovestone, S. and Anderton, B.H. (1992). Cytoskeletal abnormalities in Alzheimer's disease. *Curr Opin Neurol Neurosurg* **5**, 883–888.

Lovestone, S., Reynolds, C.H., Latimer, D. *et al.* (1994). Alzheimer's disease-like phosphorylation of the microtubule-associated protein tau by glucogen synthase kinase-3 in transfected mammalian cells. *Curr Biol* **4**, 1077–1086.

Lovestone, S., Hartley, C.L., Pearce, J. and Anderton, B.H. (1996a). Phosphorylation of tau by glycogen synthase kinase-3β in intact mammalian cells: the effects on organisation and stability of microtubules. *Neuroscience* **73**, 1145–1157.

Lovestone, S., Anderton, B.H., Hartley, C., Jensen, T.G. and Jorgensen, A.L. (1996b). The intracellular fate of tau is apolipoprotein E isoform specific and tau dependent. *Neuroreport* **7**, 1005–1008.

Mandelkow, E., Song, Y.-H., Schweers, O., Marx, A. and Mandelkow, E.-M. (1995). On the structure of microtubules, tau, and paired helical filaments. *Neurobiol Aging* **16**, 347–354.

Mann, D.M. (1988). Alzheimer's disease and Down's syndrome. *Histopathology* **13**, 125–137.

Mayeux, R., Ottman, R., Maestre, G. *et al.* (1995). Synergistic effects of traumatic head injury and apolipoprotein-ε4 in patients with Alzheimer's disease. *Neurology* **45**, 555–557.

Mullan, M., Crawford, F., Axelman, K. *et al.* (1992). A pathogenic mutation for probable Alzheimer's disease in the APP gene at the N-terminus of beta-amyloid. *Nature Genet* **1**, 345–347.

Nathan, B.P., Bellosta, S., Sanan, D.A., Weisgraber, K.H., Mahley, R.W. and Pitas, R.E. (1994). Differential effects of apolipoproteins E3 and E4 on neuronal growth *in vitro. Science* **264**, 850–852.

Nitsch, R.M., Rebeck, G.W., Deng, M. *et al.* (1995). Cerebrospinal fluid levels of amyloid beta-protein in Alzheimer's disease: inverse correlation with severity of dementia and effect of apolipoprotein E genotype. *Ann Neurol* **37**, 512–518.

Pappolla, M.A., Sambamurti, K., Efthimiopoulos, S., Refolo, L., Omar, R.A. and Robakis, N.K. (1995). Heat-shock induces abnormalities in the cellular distribution of amyloid precursor protein (APP) and APP fusion proteins. *Neurosci Lett* **192**, 105–108.

Pines, J. (1995). GFP in mammalian cells. *Trends Genet* **11**, 326–327.

Poirier, J., Davignon, J., Bouthillier, D., Kogan, S., Bertrand, P. and Gauthier, S. (1993). Apolipoprotein E polymorphism and Alzheimer's disease. *Lancet* **342**, 697–699.

Roberts, G.W., Allsop, D. and Bruton, C. (1990). The occult aftermath of boxing. *J Neurol Neurosurg Psychiatry* **53**, 373–378.

Sanan, D.A., Weisgraber, K.H., Russell, S.J. *et al.* (1994). Apolipoprotein E associates with β amyloid peptide of Alzheimer's disease to form novel monofibrils. Isoform ApoE4 associates more efficiently than ApoE3. *J Clin Invest* **94**, 860–869.

Saunders, A.M., Schmader, K., Breitner, J.C.S. *et al.* (1993). Apolipoprotein E ε4 allele distributions in late-onset Alzheimer's disease and in other amyloid-forming diseases. *Lancet* **342**, 710–711.

Schellenberg, G.D., Anderson, L., O'dahl, S. *et al.* (1991). APP717, APP693, and PRIP gene mutations are rare in Alzheimer's disease. *Am J Hum Genet* **49**, 511–517.

Selkoe, D.J. (1994). Normal and abnormal biology of the β-amyloid precursor protein. *Ann Rev Neurosci* **17**, 489–517.

Selkoe, D.J., Yamazaki, T., Citron, M. *et al.* (1996). The role of APP processing and trafficking pathways in the formation of amyloid β-protein. *Ann N Y Acad Sci* **777**, 57–64.

Sherrington, R., Rogaev, E.I., Liang, Y. *et al.* (1995). Cloning of gene bearing missense mutations in early-onset familial Alzheimer's disease. *Nature* **375**, 754–760.

Snyder, S.W., Ladror, U.S., Wade, W.S. *et al.* (1994). Amyloid-β aggregation: selective inhibition of aggregation in mixtures of amyloid with different chain lengths. *Biophys J* **67**, 1216–1228.

Sperber, B.R., Leight, S., Goedert, M. and Lee, V.M.-Y. (1995). Glycogen synthase kinase-3 beta phosphorylates tau protein at multiple sites in intact cells. *Neurosci Lett* **197**, 149–153.

Strittmatter, W.J., Weisgraber, K.H., Huang, D.Y. *et al.* (1993). Binding of human apolipoprotein E to synthetic amyloid β peptide: isoform-specific effects and implications for late-onset Alzheimer disease. *Proc Natl Acad Sci USA* **90**, 8098–8102.

Strittmatter, W.J., Saunders, A.M., Goedert, M. *et al.* (1994a). Isoform-specific intercations of apolipoprotein E with microtubule-associated protein tau: implications for Alzheimer disease. *Proc Natl Acad Sci USA* **91**, 11183–11186.

Strittmatter, W.J., Weisgraber, K.H., Goedert, M. *et al.* (1994b). Microtubule instability and paired helical filament formation in the Alzheimer disease brain are related to apolipoprotein E genotype. *Exp Neurol* **125**, 163–171.

Takashima, A., Noguchi, K., Sato, K., Hoshino, T. and Imahori, K. (1993). Tau protein kinase I is essential for amyloid beta-protein-induced neurotoxicity. *Proc Natl Acad Sci USA* **90**, 7789–7793.

Trojanowski, J.Q. and Lee, V.M.-Y. (1994). Paired helical filament τ in Alzheimer's disease: the kinase connection. *Am J Pathol* **144**, 449–453.

Vigo-Pelfrey, C., Lee, D., Keim, P., Leiberburg, I. and Schenk, D.B. (1993). Characterization of β-amyloid peptide from human cerebrospinal fluid. *J Neurochem* **61**, 1965–1968.

Wisniewski, T., Ghiso, J. and Frangione, B. (1994). Alzheimer's disease and soluble Aβ. *Neurobiol Aging* **15**, 143–152.

Wolf, B.A., Wertkin, A.M., Jolly, Y.C. *et al.* (1995). Muscarinic regulation of Alzheimer's disease amyloid precursor protein secretion and amyloid β-protein production in human neuronal NT2N cells. *J Biol Chem* **270**, 4916–4922.

Wragg, M., Hutton, M., Talbot, C. *et al.* (1996). Genetic association between intronic polymorphism in presenilin-1 gene and late-onset Alzheimer's disease. *Lancet* **347**, 509–512.

Yamamoto, K., Miyoshi, T., Yae, T. *et al.* (1994). The survival of rat cerebral cortical neurons in the presence of trophic APP peptides. *J Neurobiol* **25**, 585–594.

Advances in Old Age Psychiatry: Chromosomes to Community Care
Edited by C. Holmes and R. Howard
© 1997 Wrightson Biomedical Publishing Ltd

5

Dementia with Lewy Bodies

IAN G. McKEITH

*Department of Old Age Psychiatry, Institute for the Health of the Elderly, Newcastle
General Hospital, Newcastle upon Tyne, UK*

INTRODUCTION

Lewy bodies (LB) are an important histological feature of several neurode-generative diseases which are typified by Parkinson's disease (PD). Lowe (1997) describes a family of primary LB disorders in which the LB pathology is believed to be closely related to the fundamental biology of the disease and not merely an 'incidental' bystander. The major clinical correlate of LB formation in the cerebral cortex, as seen in Table 1, is a characteristic dementia syndrome, for which the preferred term is dementia with LB (DLB).

DLB has been reported under one of its many pseudonyms (diffuse LB disease (DLBD) (Kosaka *et al.*, 1984); senile dementia of LB type (SDLT) (R.H. Perry *et al.*, 1990); LB variant of Alzheimer's disease (LBV) (Hansen *et al.*, 1990)), in 12–36% of elderly demented cases coming to autopsy in hospital-based research series, making it a common, if not the most common, dementia subtype after pure Alzheimer's disease (AD). Prevalence rates from community-based samples are, however, still lacking.

Table 1. Primary Lewy body disorders. (After Lowe, 1997.)

Region affected	Clinical sydrome	Name
Nigrostriatal system	Extrapyramidal movement disorder	Parkinson's disease
Cerebral cortex	Cognitive decline	Dementia with Lewy bodies
Sympathetic neurones in spinal cord	Autonomic failure	Primary autonomic failure
Dorsal vagal nuclei	Dysphagia	Lewy body dysphagia

THE PATHOLOGICAL SIGNIFICANCE OF LEWY BODIES IN DEMENTIA

The neurofilaments in neurones are key cytoskeletal proteins which determine the calibre of axons. LB are comprised of neurofilament proteins which have been phosphorylated by protein kinases, as a consequence of which the neurofilaments have become cross-linked, forming insoluble complexes which constitute the dense central core of the classical LB. They also contain ubiquitin, ubiquitin carboxyl-terminal hydroxylase (PGP9.5), the multicatalytic protease (MCP) and αB-crystallin, all of which are involved in the elimination of abnormal or damaged proteins within the neurone. This suggests that LB are the manifestation of a cytoprotective response and therefore a beneficial phenomenon (Pollanen et al., 1993; Lowe et al., 1997). LB are thus fundamentally different from the neurofibrillary tangle (NFT) which is the corresponding cytoskeletal lesion seen in AD. NFTs do not appear to have a cytoprotective potential and are probably 'tombstone' markers of dysregulation of another major constituent of the cytoskeleton, namely the microtubules which are required for the axonal transport of essential material travelling between the cell body and synapses of neurones. The microtubule-associated protein tau is hyperphosphorylated in AD and this is believed to contribute to the formation of paired helical filaments which are the main structural subunits of NFT.

A hypothetical scheme for LB formation suggested by Lowe involves a cell stress response in neurones which leads to a collapse of the intermediate neurofilament network under the influence of αB-crystallin, itself a cell stress protein which is known to associate with intermediate filaments. Once collapsed, neurofilaments become phosphorylated and truncated by proteolysis. Finally, ubiquitin and enzymes of the ubiquitin system become associated with the LB. This scheme is, however, speculative and much work is yet to be done to further elucidate the pathogenesis of the LB, an understanding which may be necessary to develop primary and secondary preventions. Dickson et al. (1991,1994) have additionally described ubiquitin-positive neuritic degeneration (Lewy neurites) in the hippocampal CA2–3 region of DLB cases, an LB-related phenomenon which is also seen in the substantia nigra (SN), dorsal vagus nucleus (DVN) and nucleus basalis of Meynert (nbM) (Gai et al., 1995).

WHAT CAUSES THE DEMENTIA IN DLB?

It is unlikely that any one pathological abnormality can be singled out as the unitary cause for all of the clinical manifestations of DLB. Strategic losses of subcortical and cortical neurones are likely to result in specific motor and mental impairments, the most clearly established being a correlation between

SN neurone loss and the severity of extrapyramidal symptoms. Although counts of LB density may not be a reliable surrogate for the extent of neuronal loss, some groups have found moderate correlation between the global severity of cognitive impairment and cortical LB density (Lennox et al., 1989; Samuel et al., 1996). R.H. Perry et al. (1990) did not find higher LB density to be correlated with a greater severity of dementia on the 37-item Mental Test Score (MTS) in a series of DLB cases, but did find higher cortical LB counts in the anterior cingulate gyrus of 22 cases with PD and dementia, (80.6 ± 73.2 per cm²) compared with 13 nondemented PD cases (34.5 ± 50.1), suggesting that cortical LB are associated with the development of cognitive impairment, presumably via associated neuronal dysfunction and loss. As with the DLB cases there was no significant direct correlation ($r = 0.25$) between severity of cognitive impairment on the MTS ($n = 17$, range 1–33) in the demented PD group and cingulate LB density (R.H. Perry et al., 1996).

There are at least two interpretations of these findings. First, instruments like the MTS, which were devised for the assessment of the severity of cognitive impairment in AD, may not be entirely appropriate for investigating DLB in which there is a predominance of attentional over purely mnemonic deficits. Secondly, the fluctuating pattern of the mental symptoms in DLB may be more closely related to perturbations in neurochemical parameters rather than to fixed changes in structural pathology. For example, activity of the cholinergic enzyme, choline acetyltransferase, was lower in the neocortex (particularly temporal and parietal) in DLB compared with AD patients (E.K. Perry et al., 1994), particularly in hallucinating cases. nbM neurone numbers were also significantly reduced in hallucinating compared to nonhallucinating DLB cases. However, an index of 5-HT turnover (5-hydroxytryptamine) (5HIAA : 5HT ratio) was higher in nonhallucinating cases, and 5-HT$_2$ receptor binding, which diminishes in AD, was normal in hallucinating DLB cases, suggesting that hallucinations may be related to a neocortical transmitter imbalance based on hypocholinergic and (relatively) hypermonoaminergic function. Clouding of consciousness, confusion and visual hallucinations are recognized effects of anticholinergic drug toxicity and it is likely that the summative effects of subcortical and cortical cholinergic dysfunction play a major role in the spontaneous generation of similar symptoms in DLB.

THE NEUROCHEMICAL PATHOLOGY OF DLB – IMPLICATIONS FOR TREATMENT

Cholinergic agents

Early reports that patients showing substantial symptomatic improvement with cholinesterase inhibitors (velnacrine and tacrine) were more likely to have DLB at autopsy than pure AD (Levy *et al.*, 1994) still require substantiation by appropriate randomized controlled trials.

Witjeratne and colleagues, from the Institute of Psychiatry, reported the case of an 81-year-old man 'with fleeting grandiose delusions and fluctuating cognitive performance ... in whom a provisional diagnosis of cortical Lewy body dementia was made' (Witjeratne *et al.*, 1995). Trifluoperazine (dosage not stated) quickly led to parkinsonism. During treatment with tacrine 40–80 mg over nine weeks, his cognitive state deteriorated rapidly with increased agitation and aggression. This diminished to pretreatment levels once the tacrine was discontinued. Witjeratne *et al.* conclude that, although it is difficult to draw conclusions from a single case-study, they are not planning to prescribe tacrine in further cases of DLB. One might, however, question the reliability of a diagnosis of DLB in this case (fluctuating confusion and delusions are insufficient for Newcastle SDLT criteria (McKeith *et al.*, 1992a) and would reach only the *possible* DLB category in the newly formulated consensus criteria). The possibility of a significant proportion of DLB patients being responsive to non-aminoacridine cholinesterase inhibitors justifies a cautiously conducted, double-blind, randomized controlled trial, and several such studies are in the late phases of development.

Antipsychotic agents

The potential hazards of sensitivity to severe adverse effects of standard neuroleptics in DLB (McKeith *et al.*, 1992b) have been widely publicized (CSM, 1994) and appear to be mediated via a subclinical reduction in SN neurones coupled with a failure of striatal (putamen) D_2 receptors to upregulate, either in response to substrate depletion or receptor blockade (Piggott *et al.*, 1994). Although a substantial proportion of DLB patients may be able to tolerate low doses of neuroleptics and derive considerable benefit from them, it is unfortunately not yet possible to predict which patients will fall into this category. If clinicians now consider the prescription of standard neuroleptics to DLB patients to be a hazardous practice, it may prove difficult to carry out further 'naturalistic' studies of the outcome of neuroleptic use in DLB. Not only will the number of patients available for study in future be small, but they will probably also be a highly selected group with extreme levels of behavioural disturbance, already having a worse prognosis than those patients in whom neuroleptics can be successfully avoided. A randomized, double-blind, placebo-controlled trial of low-dose neuroleptics in DLB might obtain ethical approval, but it is unclear what the outcome measures might be. Even a marginally raised mortality risk would appear to be a substantial disincentive to take part for all patients except those with the most severe psychotic symptoms or behavioural disturbance. Not only would this produce sampling biases of the type already described, but the acceptability of and compliance with a placebo regimen would prove extremely difficult.

Faced with these difficulties clinicians are currently seeking to develop safer strategies for the management of noncognitive symptoms of DLB. In the absence of data from explanatory trials only general guidelines can be offered. In patients with pre-existing PD there may be the option to reduce and, if necessary, stop antiparkinsonian medication, the preferred order of reduction/withdrawal probably being L-deprenyl, then anticholinergics, followed by direct, then indirect, dopamine agonists. The best outcome on this therapeutic see-saw is a compromise between a relatively mobile, but psychotic, patient and a nonpsychotic, but immobile, individual. The patient and his or her carer(s) may only be able to decide which is the lesser of these evils after experiencing both states.

If an antipsychotic is required a cautious approach should be taken. Pretreatment baseline measures of cognitive, noncognitive and extrapyramidal function should be recorded, preferably using standardized scales, and these should be repeated once or twice weekly during the initial period of dose titration. In this way the relative benefits and adverse consequences of treatment are monitored and the earliest signs of deterioration will be noted. Neuroleptics should be stopped if extrapyramidal symptoms appear for the first time in a DLB patient who previously displayed no evidence of parkinsonism, and should be substantially reduced or stopped in patients whose pre-existing parkinsonism worsened. A reintroduction of the drug at a lower dose probably should only be contemplated once extrapyramidal function has returned to pretreatment level. Since the majority of severe sensitivity reactions occur within the first two weeks of receiving medication, it may be wise to admit patients with a suspected diagnosis of DLB into hospital during initiation of neuroleptic therapy and to ensure that very regular clinical assessments are recorded.

Novel (atypical) antipsychotics

Early case-reports of the efficacy and safety of risperidone (Lee *et al.*, 1994; Allen *et al.*, 1995) should be treated with caution since it is a potent D_2-receptor-blocker and severe exacerbations of parkinsonism have been seen in DLB patients after only two or three days of low-dose treatment (0.5–1.0 mg daily) (McKeith *et al.*, 1995). Nevertheless, the 5-HT$_2$-antagonist properties of risperidone may confer lower risk of extrapyramidal side-effects, and it is now available in suspension, allowing for precise low dose titration.

Clozapine, which has relatively low D_2-antagonism, has been reported as a useful antipsychotic in patients with PD (Factor *et al.*, 1994) and it has very recently been made available for this purpose in the UK. Clozapine also has potent antimuscarinic activity which may exacerbate confusion and cognitive impairment, thereby limiting its use in DLB patients. The maximum tolerated dose of clozapine in such patients falls in the range 12.5–50.0 mg daily and, as with risperidone (above), antipsychotic efficacy needs to be established at such low dosage.

Psychopharmacology of DLB – the next generation

In summary, the limited evidence available suggests that future symptomatic therapies in DLB may need to be targeted on selectively increasing cholinergic and decreasing monoaminergic, particularly serotinergic, neurotransmission (Harrison and McKeith, 1995). The new generations of non-aminoacridine cholinesterase inhibitors (E2020, ENA 713, metrifonate, galanthamine) and M_1-agonists (xanomeline, SB202026) and of atypical antipsychotics with high 5-HT_2 but low D_2 and muscarinic receptor antagonism (seroquel, sertindole) should offer a series of rationally based therapeutic options for the treatment of cognitive and noncognitive symptoms of DLB.

CONSENSUS GUIDELINES FOR THE CLINICAL AND PATHOLOGICAL DIAGNOSIS OF DLB

Reference has already been made to the multiple terminology which has developed over the last decade to describe DLB. Hansen and Galasko (1992) listed 15 competing pathological labels, each of which puts a slightly different spin on what are essentially the same, or at least closely related, clinico-pathological entities. Hansen and Galasko argue that many of these terminological discrepancies stem from underlying tautologies about neuropathological and clinical criteria for the diagnoses of AD and PD. The most striking example of this is seen in relation to the interpretation of Alzheimer-type pathology in these cases. Some (predominantly North American) authorities cite the National Institute on Aging (NIA) (Khachaturian, 1985) and the Consortium to Establish a Registry for Alzheimer's Disease (CERAD) (Mirra et al., 1991) criteria as the basis for a pathological diagnosis of AD. NIA and CERAD criteria are largely based on plaque densities and, since the majority of DLB cases have increased numbers of plaques, they are considered to be AD cases with an LB 'flavouring'. Those who argue that the diagnosis of AD additionally requires the presence of frequent neocortical neurofibrillary tangles do not, however, find these changes in the majority of DLB cases and, for them, the cases cannot be regarded as variants of AD. They argue, therefore, that the LB pathology is of more significance, and the coexisting Alzheimer-type pathology is regarded as being incidental or merely age-related. New evidence from molecular genetics suggests that DLB cases may share both an increased risk for AD in the form of an increased ApoE ϵ4 allele frequency (Morris et al., 1996) whilst additionally having an increase in CYP2D6B allele frequency similar to that identified as a significant risk factor for PD (Saitoh et al., 1995).

One reason why the emerging concept of DLB has simultaneously excited so much interest but also met with considerable resistance is precisely because it has exposed these unresolved issues about the pathological and clinical classification of AD and PD.

THE CONSORTIUM ON DEMENTIA WITH LEWY BODIES

In order to address some of these challenging questions, clinical and scientific representatives of all groups actively involved in researching DLB (by whatever name!) were invited from around the globe to attend a two-day workshop in Newcastle upon Tyne in October 1995. Three major themes were identified: pathological diagnosis, clinical diagnosis, and treatment. The major output of this consortium was the formulation of consensus guidelines for the clinical and pathological diagnosis of 'dementia with Lewy bodies' (McKeith et al., 1996). DLB was universally accepted as a term which is adequately descriptive while at the same time sufficiently nonjudgemental about the precise aetiological role of LB in symptom formation. Standard procedures for post-mortem brain sampling, staining and regional semiquantitative quantification of LB were devised. These generate three broad pathological diagnostic categories: brainstem, transitional or neocortical LB disease. The move towards a common set of descriptive pathological criteria will enable direct comparisons to be made between cases from different centres, something which has previously been obstructed by pre-existing variations in nosological classification. The precise nature of the relationship between LB disease and AD was not resolved by the workshop participants and it was agreed that Alzheimer-type pathology should continue to be quantified and reported according to the practices of each individual laboratory. The pathology workshop additionally established guidelines for the handling of tissues for neurochemical analysis.

The new clinical diagnostic guidelines for DLB are shown in Table 2 and share many features with the criteria previously proposed by the Newcastle and Nottingham groups (McKeith et al., 1992a; Byrne et al., 1991).

The clinical workshop participants concentrated upon describing the constellation of neuropsychiatric manifestations thought to be associated with cortical LB – namely fluctuating cognitive impairment, attentional deficits and perceptual disturbances – and to position this correctly in

Table 2. Consensus criteria for the clinical diagnosis of probable and possible dementia with Lewy bodies (DLB). (From McKeith *et al.*, 1996.)

1. The central feature required for a diagnosis of DLB is progressive cognitive decline of sufficient magnitude to interfere with normal social or occupational function. Prominent or persistent memory impairment may not necessarily occur in the early stages but is usually evident with progression. Deficits on tests of attention and of frontal-subcortical skills and visuospatial ability may be especially prominent.

2. **Two** of the following core features are essential for a diagnosis of **probable** DLB; **one** is essential for **possible** DLB:
   a) Fluctuating cognition with pronounced variations in attention and alertness
   b) Recurrent visual hallucinations which are typically well formed and detailed
   c) Spontaneous motor features of parkinsonism

3. Features **supportive** of the diagnosis are:
   a) Repeated falls
   b) Syncope
   c) Transient loss of consciousness
   d) Neuroleptic sensitivity
   e) Systematized delusions
   f) Hallucinations in other modalities

4. A diagnosis of DLB is **less likely** in the presence of:
   a) Stroke disease, evident as focal neurological signs or on brain imaging
   b) Evidence on physical examination and investigation of any physical illness, or other brain disorder, sufficient to account for the clinical picture

relation to existing diagnostic systems, in particular those for AD and for PD. Usually in clinical practice the important diagnostic discrimination is from other causes of dementia, particularly AD, but DLB may also present as a late development in a patient already diagnosed as having PD. In these latter circumstances, the consortium recommend that the term 'PD with dementia' should be used. Many elderly patients present a complex admixture of extrapyramidal and mental symptoms of almost simultaneous onset; it was agreed that, if dementia occurs within 12 months of the onset of the motor symptoms, the patient may be considered to have a primary diagnosis of DLB rather than PD with dementia, an arbitrary distinction which may need reevaluation in the light of further knowledge.

A demonstration of impaired cognition by formal testing is essential to establishing a diagnosis of DLB. Symptoms of severe or persistent memory impairment are not essential early in the course of DLB but are likely to develop with time. Prominent deficits on tests of attention and of frontal-subcortical skills and visuospatial ability are more likely early indicators of DLB. This cognitive profile, combined with a tendency to fluctuating performance and periods of delirium, does not conform to standard definitions of the dementia syndrome which have largely been developed around AD, and a broader definition of dementia is therefore required to encompass DLB patients, certainly in the initial stages.

Although fluctuating performance was agreed by the workshop partici-pants to be an important and common defining characteristic of LB disor-ders, a proportion (perhaps 10–20%) of all cases do not show such variations. There are also considerable difficulties inherent in defining and quantifying fluctuation, particularly in the later stages of illness when it becomes submerged in the general cognitive decline. Caregiver reports via diary-keeping may be the most productive approach to identifying a fluctuating state, a strategy which has been successfully employed to measure motor fluctuations in PD. Because of these difficulties in adequately operationaliz-ing and quantifying cognitive fluctuation, it has been retained as a core feature of DLB, i.e. one with considerable diagnostic weight, but it is no longer mandatory as it was in the Newcastle criteria.

Visual hallucinations, typically recurrent, detailed and well formed, are a second core feature of DLB. McShane *et al.* (1995) found that visual hallu-cinations were present on 'more than five days a month over a period of at least four months' in pathologically confirmed DLB cases and that halluci-nators were significantly more likely to be visually impaired. The final core feature of DLB is spontaneous evidence of parkinsonism, i.e. not related to neuroleptic administration. Rigidity (47%) and bradykinesia (33%) were the most common extrapyramidal features reported by Galasko *et al.* (1996) in 26 autopsy-confirmed DLB cases and these symptoms were mild in the majority of affected individuals. Masked facies (39%) and parkinsonian gait (33%) were also relatively common. No patients exhibited classical parkin-sonian tremor. It is important to understand that the majority of DLB cases do not have extrapyramidal symptoms, particularly in the early stages, and clinicians who only suspect DLB once there is evidence of parkinsonism are likely to be missing a substantial proportion of cases.

The consensus guidelines allow for a diagnosis of *probable* DLB to be made if two core features are present in conjunction with the characteristic dementia syndrome as briefly described above. Preliminary autopsy valida-tion of the *probable* DLB category in a research sample suggests it to be in excess of 90%, a performance similar to that of the NINCDS–ADRDA crite-ria for AD, applied in a similar setting. A requirement for only one core feature enables a diagnosis of *possible* DLB to be made, and this may prove to be useful in clinical differential diagnosis when a higher index of diagnos-tic suspicion is required (increased sensitivity), although this inevitably will be at a cost of making some false-positive clinical diagnoses (reduced speci-ficity).

A list of features 'supportive of' the diagnosis of DLB have been incor-porated into the consensus criteria. These include repeated falls, syncope, transient loss of consciousness, neuroleptic sensitivity, systematized delusions, and hallucinations in other modalities. Repeated falls have been identified as a presenting symptom in one-third of DLB cases (McKeith *et al.*, 1992a; Kuzuhara and Yoshimura, 1993) but the consensus view was that there is a high background rate of falling in the cognitively impaired elderly, making it a relatively nonspecific symptom of limited diagnostic specificity. Syncopal attacks with complete loss of consciousness and muscle tone have been described by several DLB investigators and may represent the extension of LB-associated pathology to involve the autonomic nervous system. Focal neurological symptoms and signs do not generally appear in conjunction with these episodes, aiding in their discrimination from transient ischaemic attacks. The associated phenomena of transient episodes of unresponsiveness without loss of muscle tone may represent the extreme of fluctuating attentional impairment due to perturbations in central nervous system cholinergic function. The precise details of these symptom groups need further clarification and investigation before they warrant inclusion as core features of DLB.

Severe adverse reactions to standard neuroleptic medication (neuroleptic sensitivity) may be an important consequence of underlying LB disorder, but it is of limited clinical application in the diagnostic process, especially if neuroleptic prescribing is routinely and desirably avoided in patients suspected of having DLB. Systematized delusions in DLB are usually secondary to hallucinations and other perceptual disturbances and as such often have bizarre content, in contrast to the frequently mundane delusions of AD patients which are usually based upon forgetfulness and misinterpretation of events. Auditory, olfactory and tactile hallucinations, although substantially less common than visual perceptual disturbances, may be important features in some DLB cases.

REFERENCES

Allen, R.L., Walker, Z., D'Ath, P.J. and Katona, C.L.E. (1995). Risperidone for psychotic and behavioural symptoms in Lewy body dementia. *Lancet* **346**, 185.

Byrne, E.J., Lennox, G.G., Godwin-Austen, R.B. *et al.* (1991) Diagnostic criteria for dementia associated with cortical Lewy bodies. *Dementia* **2**, 283–284.

Committee on Safety of Medicines (1994). Neuroleptic sensitivity in patients with dementia. *Curr Probl Pharmacovigil* **20**, 6.

Dickson, D., Ruan, D., Crystal, H *et al.* (1991). Hippocampal degeneration differentiates diffuse Lewy body disease (DLBD) from Alzheimer's disease: light and electron microscopic immunohistochemistry of CA-3 neurites specific to DLBD. *Neurology* **41**, 1402–1409.

Dickson, D.W., Schmidt, M.L., Lee, V.M., Zhao, M.L., Yen, S.H. and Trojanowski, J. (1994). Immunoreactivity profile of hippocampal CA2/3 neurites in diffuse Lewy body disease. *Acta Neuropathol (Berl)* **87**, 269–276.

Factor, S.A., Brown, D., Molho, E.S. and Podskalny, G.D. (1994) Clozapine: a 2-year open trial in Parkinson's disease patients with psychosis. *Neurology* **44**, 544–546.

Gai, W.P., Blessing, W.S. and Blumberger, P.C. (1995). Ubiquitin-positive degenerating neurites in the brainstem in Parkinson's disease. *Brain* **118**, 1447–1460.

Galasko, D., Katzman, R., Salmon, D.P. and Thal, L.J. (1996). Clinical and neuropathological findings in Lewy body dementias. *Brain Cognition* **31**, 166–175.

Hansen L.A. and Galasko D. (1992) Lewy body disease. *Curr Opin Neurol Neurosurg* **5**, 889–894.

Hansen, L.A., Salmon, D., Galasko, D. *et al.* (1990). The Lewy body variant of Alzheimer's disease: a clinical and pathologic entity. *Neurology* **40**, 1–8.

Harrison, R.W.S. and McKeith, I.G. (1995). The diagnosis and treatment of Lewy body dementia. *Int J Geriatr Psychiatry* **10**, 919–926.

Khachaturian, Z.S. (1985). Diagnosis of Alzheimer's disease. *Arch Neurol* **42**, 1097–1105.

Kosaka, K., Yoshimura, M., Ikeda, K. and Budka, H. (1984). Diffuse type of Lewy body disease: progressive dementia with abundant cortical Lewy bodies and senile changes of varying degree – a new disease? *Clin Neuropathol* **3**, 185–192.

Kuzuhara, S. and Yoshimura, M. (1993). Clinical and neuropathological aspects of diffuse Lewy body disease in the elderly. *Adv Neurol* **65**, 464–469.

Lee, H., Cooney, J.M. and Lawlor, B.A. (1994). Case report: the use of risperidone, an atypical neuroleptic in Lewy body disease. *Int J Geriatr Psychiatry* **9**, 415–417.

Lennox, G., Lowe, J., Morrell, K., Landon, M. and Mayer, R. (1989). Antiubiquitin immunocytochemistry is more sensitive than conventional techniques in the detection of diffuse Lewy body disease. *J Neurol Neurosurg Psychiatry* **52**, 67–71.

Levy, R., Eagger, S., Griffiths, M. *et al.* (1994). Lewy bodies and response to tacrine in Alzheimer's disease. *Lancet* **343**, 176.

Lowe, J. (1997). The pathological significance of Lewy bodies in dementia. In: Perry, E.K., McKeith, I.G. and Perry, R.H. (Eds), *Dementia with Lewy Bodies*. Cambridge University Press, New York (in press).

McKeith, I.G., Perry, R.H., Fairbairn, A.F., Jabeen, S. and Perry, E.K. (1992a). Operational criteria for senile dementia of Lewy body type (SDLT). *Psychol Med* **22**, 911–922.

McKeith, I.G., Fairbairn, A.F., Perry, R.H., Thompson, P. and Perry, E.K. (1992b). Neuroleptic sensitivity in patients with senile dementia of Lewy body type. *BMJ* **305**, 673–678.

McKeith, I.G., Harrison, R.W.S. and Ballard, C.G. (1995). Neuroleptic sensitivity to risperidone in Lewy body dementia. *Lancet* **346**, 699.

McKeith, I.G., Galasko, D., Kosaka, K. *et al.* (1996). Consensus guidelines for the clinical and pathological diagnosis of dementia with Lewy bodies (DLB): report of the Consortium on DLB International Workshop. *Neurology* **47**, 1113–1124.

McShane, R., Gedling, K., Reading, M., McDonald, B., Esiri, M.M. and Hope, T. (1995). Prospective study of relations between cortical Lewy bodies, poor eyesight and hallucinations in Alzheimer's disease. *J Neurol Neurosurg Psychiatry* **59**, 185–188.

Mirra, S.S., Heyman, A., McKeel, D. *et al.* (1991). The Consortium to Establish a Registry for Alzheimer's Disease (CERAD). Part II. Standardisation of the neuropathologic assessment for Alzheimer's disease. *Neurology* **41**, 479–486.

Morris, C.M., Massey, H.M., Benjamin, R. *et al.* (1996). Molecular biology of APO E alleles in Alzheimer's and non-Alzheimer's dementias. *J Neural Transm* **47**, 205–218.

Perry, E.K., Haroutunian, V., Davis, K.L. *et al.* (1994). Neocortical cholinergic activities differentiate Lewy body dementia from classical Alzheimer's disease. *Neuroreport* **5**, 747–749.

Perry, R.H., Irving, D., Blessed, G., Fairbairn, A. and Perry, E.K. (1990). Senile dementia of Lewy body type: a clinically and neuropathologically distinct type of Lewy body dementia in the elderly. *J Neurol Sci* **95**, 119–135.

Perry, R.H., Jaros, E., Irving, D. *et al.* (1996). What is the neuropathological basis of dementia associated with Lewy bodies? In: Perry, E.K., McKeith, I.G. and Perry, R.H. (Eds), *Dementia with Lewy Bodies*. Cambridge University Press, New York.

Piggott, M.A., Perry, E.K., McKeith, I.G., Marshall, E. and Perry, R.H. (1994). Dopamine D_2 receptors in demented patients with severe neuroleptic sensitivity. *Lancet* **343**, 1044–1045.

Pollanen, M.S., Bergeron, C. and Weyer, L. (1993). Deposition of detergent-resistant neurofilaments into Lewy body fibrils. *Brain Res* **603**, 121–124.

Saitoh, T., Xia, Y., Chen, X. *et al.* (1995). The CYP2D6B mutant allele is overrepresented in the Lewy body variant of Alzheimer's disease. *Ann Neurol* **37**, 110–112.

Samuel, W., Galasko, D., Masliah, E. and Hansen, L.A. (1996). Neocortical Lewy body counts correlate with dementia in the Lewy body variant of Alzheimer's disease. *J Neuropathol Exp Neurol* **55**, 44–52.

Witjeratne, C., Bandyopadhyay, D. and Howard, R. (1995). Failure of tacrine treatment in a case of cortical Lewy body dementia. *Int J Geriatr Psychiatry* **10**, 808.

Advances in Old Age Psychiatry: Chromosomes to Community Care
Edited by C. Holmes and R. Howard
© 1997 Wrightson Biomedical Publishing Ltd

6

Frontal Lobe Dementia

DAVID M.A. MANN
Department of Pathological Sciences, Division of Molecular Pathology, University of Manchester, Manchester, UK

INTRODUCTION

In 1906, Arnold Pick described a clinical syndrome of a progressive behavioural disorder associated with bilateral atrophy of the frontal lobes of the cerebral hemispheres. Further reports concerning similar cases came to adopt the eponym 'Pick's disease' in recognition of the first description by Pick himself, thus providing a taxonomical way of distinguishing this from the other major neurodegenerative disorder – Alzheimer's disease – occurring in the presenium. Latterly, the term frontal (lobe) dementia has become widely used to depict the clinical features of a progressive disordering of character and personal and social conduct of sufficient magnitude as to render individuals incapable of managing their own affairs while retaining, for the most part, and at least in early stages of the condition, an acceptable level of general memory and intellect. However, it is also clear that functional changes within the frontal lobes can either arise directly from the presence of neurodegenerative disease within this brain region or result secondarily from a failure to engage the otherwise normal frontal lobes in appropriate neurophysiological responses because of loss, or inactivity, of neural pathways from other, possibly damaged, areas of brain which provide stimulatory inputs into the frontal lobes. Consequently, a frontal lobe syndrome can form a major or a minor part of a wide range of neurological conditions which could include atypical presentations of cortical disorders like Alzheimer's disease or the subcortical disorders of Parkinson's disease, progressive supranuclear palsy, corticobasal (ganglionic) degeneration and vascular dementia. However, the main cause is, as termed by the Manchester group, frontotemporal dementia (FTD) due to frontal lobe degeneration, a neurodegenerative disorder with a neuropathology distinct from that of

Alzheimer's disease. The author and colleagues have recently published a book on this subject (Snowden *et al.*, 1996) which describes in full, with illustrative case histories, the clinical, neuropsychological, demographic, neuropathological, neurochemical and genetic aspects of this and other closely related disorders. The present chapter represents an overview taken from a decade's experience of clinical observation of some 200 patients, with pathological follow-up of about a quarter of these.

CLINICAL OVERVIEW

The clinical syndrome of FTD has been principally elucidated by longitudinal studies of patients in Lund, Sweden (Gustafson, 1987, 1993) and Manchester, UK (Neary *et al.*, 1987, 1988, 1993a) culminating in the joint publication by these two groups of the consensus clinical diagnostic criteria for FTD (Brun *et al.*, 1994).

Clinical features

The clinical characteristics of FTD involve an insidious, though striking, change in affect and personal and social behaviour, with individuals rapidly becoming unable to manage their lives, yet failing to have any insight regarding their altered situation. With disease progression, some patients become withdrawn and apathetic while in others disinhibition, restlessness, inattention or inappropriate affect prevails. In all, speech becomes more economical, repetitive and stereotypic until a mute state is reached. Spatial and temporal orientation and executive abilities remain preserved throughout the illness. Stereotypic and ritualistic behaviours are seen, particularly so of eating, where overeating, food faddism or hyperoral activity occurs, and repetitive rituals of speech or song, dress, toileting or walking are usually present. While memory is inefficient, dense amnesia is not seen; patients show severe impairment of mental flexibility, are unable to generate or abstract information and lack organizational skills. Extrapyramidal signs of akinesia and rigidity may emerge late in the illness though patients usually remain physically well throughout most of its course; this presumably contributes to their relative longevity, with survivals of 10–15 years or more being commonplace.

Although the disorder occurs chiefly in the presenium, most commonly with onset between 45 and 60 years of age, in the Manchester series 21 years has been the youngest onset age recorded and 75 years the oldest. Men and women appear equally likely to be affected and a previous family history of similar disease, with an autosomally dominant mode of inheritance, has been noted in about half the patients.

Investigations

The electroencephalogram (EEG) usually remains normal, despite advanced dementia, with slow waveforms occurring only late in the illness. Computerized tomography (CT) and magnetic resonance imaging (MRI) reveal a nonspecific diffuse cerebral atrophy in many patients though in others there is pronounced widening of the interhemispheric and Sylvian fissures indicative of atrophy within the frontal and temporal lobes; the lateral ventricles may become dilated, especially anteriorly. Single photon emission computed tomography (SPECT) imaging (Neary et al., 1987) reveals a reduced tracer uptake in frontal (especially) and temporal lobes which is sometimes asymmetric, favouring the left side of the brain. With disease progression an involvement of the posterior hemispheres is seen.

NEUROPATHOLOGICAL CHANGES

These have been extensively reported by Mann and colleagues (Mann et al., 1993; Mann and South, 1993; Neary et al., 1993a) and Brun (Brun, 1987, 1993) and are summarized here.

Gross neuropathological findings

At autopsy, prototypical cases show a gross loss of brain tissue, the weight of the brain usually being reduced to 1000 g or less. Atrophy is most severe within the frontal gyri, frontoparietal cortex and cingulate gyrus and the temporal pole often adopts a narrow, 'knife-edge' appearance. Compared with the inferior and middle temporal gyri, the superior temporal gyrus is conspicuously spared. Posterior parietal cortex and occipital regions are less or little affected and the brainstem and cerebellum usually appear externally normal (Figure 1). On coronal sectioning, atrophy within the frontal and temporal lobes is obvious and severe, with the anterior two-thirds of the temporal lobe being more affected than the posterior third (Figure 2). The superior temporal gyrus appears (relatively) normal. Atrophy is usually symmetrical though sometimes there is a left-sided emphasis. The anterior cerebral cortical areas lose much white matter (myelin), this becoming rather brownish and softened with the usually clear distinction between it and the grey matter becoming blurred. In most instances the amygdala and entorhinal cortex are much atrophied, though the hippocampus and parahippocampal gyrus are more variably affected and are often seemingly spared. The caudate nucleus (particularly) and the putamen are frequently atrophied and other basal regions may be smaller than usual. The corpus callosum is thinned at all levels, especially anteriorly, and the lateral ventricles are much

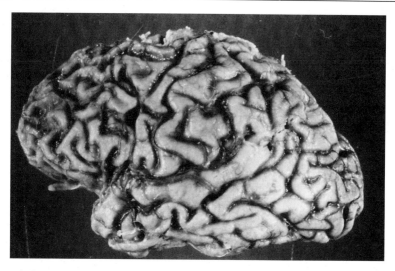

Figure 1. Lateral view of the brain of a 69-year-old female showing severe atrophy of frontal and anterior temporal lobes. The superior temporal gyrus and the posterior hemisphere regions are relatively spared. (Reproduced, with permission, from Snowden *et al.*, 1996.)

enlarged, though the extensions of these into the temporal lobes are not always similarly dilated. In most instances the substantia nigra appears normal, though on occasions some underpigmentation is apparent. The cerebellum usually appears normal.

Morphometry (Mann and South, 1993) confirms this topographic distribution of atrophy, emphasizing the loss of tissue from the frontal and temporal cortex, amygdala and striatum where decreases to about half the original size are seen; grey and white matter are mostly lost proportionately, though in some instances a greater loss of white matter may occur. In cases where apathy forms the major clinical profile, preferential loss of the dorsolateral convexity of the frontal cortex occurs, whereas when disinhibition is present the orbitofrontal cortex and the temporal pole are distinctly affected (Figure 3).

In some patients the overall degree of atrophy is less, with the brain weighing between 1000–1500 g and in these atrophy is mostly confined to frontal and frontoparietal structures.

Tissue histopathology

This has been described in detail elsewhere (Brun, 1987; Mann *et al.*, 1993). Essentially, one of two histological profiles is present, though neither can be

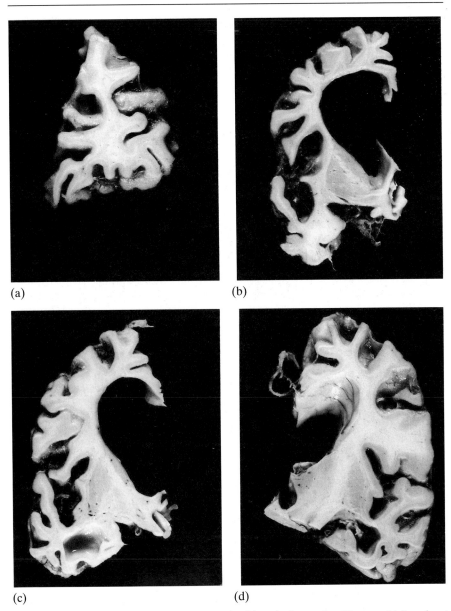

Figure 2. Coronal sections of the left cerebral hemisphere of a 69-year-old female at the level of the frontal pole (a), corpus striatum (b), amygdala (c), and mid-hippocampus (d). There is severe gyral atrophy in frontal (a), anterior parietal (b) and anterior temporal (b), (c) regions, with gross enlargement of the lateral ventricle (b)–(d) and thinning of the corpus callosum (b)–(d). The amygdala (c) is atrophic though the hippocampus (d) is relatively spared, as is the superior temporal gyrus (d). (Parts (a) and (b) reproduced, with permission, from Mann *et al.*, 1993.)

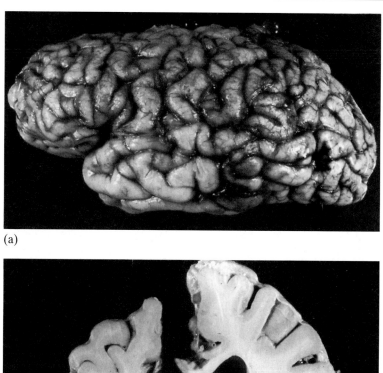

(a)

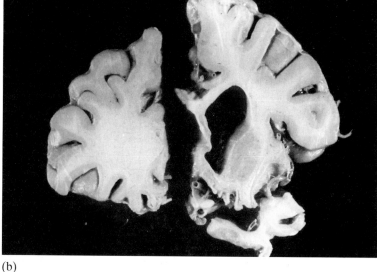

(b)

Figure 3. Lateral view (a) of the brain of a 58-year-old male showing less severe atrophy of frontal and temporal lobes and (b) coronal sections of the brain of a 68-year-old male showing severe orbitofrontal and anterior temporal atrophy with preservation of the dorsolateral convex cortex. (Reproduced, with permission, from Snowden *et al.*, 1996.)

predicted from the gross appearance of the brain (Mann *et al.*, 1993) nor from the degree and distribution of the atrophy (Mann and South, 1993). One histological type is associated with a transcortical gliosis with (or

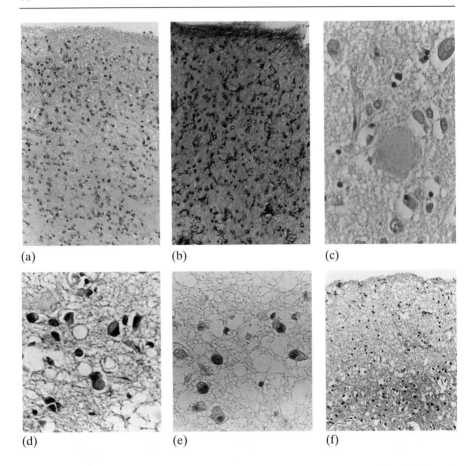

Figure 4. Histopathological changes of FTD. In Pick-type histology (a)–(e) there is severe loss of nerve cells from layers II and III (a) with intense astrocytosis (b). Some surviving cells are swollen (Pick cells) (c), and others contain inclusions (d) that are tau-positive (Pick bodies) (e). In the microvacuolar-type histology there is a 'sponginess' of layers II and III with severe loss of neurones but minimal gliosis (f). Weigerts haematoxylin (a), (c), (d), (f); phosphotungstic acid haematoxylin (b); immunoperoxidase (e). Orginal magnifications: (a), (b), (f) × 125; (c), (d), (e) × 250; (Parts (a), (b), (e), (f) reproduced, with permission, from Mann *et al.*, 1993); (parts (c), (d) reproduced, with permission, from Snowden *et al.*, 1996.)

without) inclusion bodies and swollen cells; in the other gliosis is mild and a microvacuolation of the superficial cortex is the predominant pathology (Mann *et al.*, 1993). Additionally, clinical assessment and neuropsychological profiling likewise fails to discriminate either type of histology. Familial and (apparently) nonfamilial cases are associated with both histologies, though within families, where the brain from more than one affected individual has been examined at autopsy, only a single type of histology has been seen.

In those cases where gliosis is the major histological feature there is a severe, and often virtually complete, loss of the large and small pyramidal and nonpyramidal cells of cortical layers II and III, whereas layer V pyramidal cells may be more shrunken than lost (Figure 4). Surviving nerve cells show distinctive features. First, the nerve cell, usually a larger pyramidal neurone of layer III or V (mostly) is swollen, argyrophilic and chromatolytic (loses basophilic Nissl substance); immunohistochemically such cells are weakly reactive to tau and ubiquitin antibodies (Mann et al., 1993) but are strongly so to antibodies against αB crystallin (Cooper et al., 1995). This is the so-called 'Pick cell' or 'ballooned neurone'. In the other change, a single rounded inclusion, well stained by silver impregnation methods and strongly reactive to tau and ubiquitin antibodies (Mann et al., 1993), is present in the perikaryon, mostly in layer II neurones. This change is termed the 'Pick body'. Along with these neuronal changes, a dense astrocytosis involving all cortical laminae is present (Mann et al., 1993; Cooper et al., 1996). In some instances, while a similar degree of neuronal loss and astrocytosis is seen, Pick cells and Pick bodies are absent (Mann et al., 1993) whereas on other occasions Pick cells, but not Pick bodies occur (Cooper et al., 1995), though the converse never occurs. These cytological changes are most severe in the frontal, frontoparietal, cingulate and insular cortices and in the inferior and middle temporal gyri; the superior temporal gyrus is relatively spared, as are other neocortical regions. Similar inclusion bodies are seen in the hippocampal dentate gyrus granule cells and in the pyramidal cells of areas CA1 and subiculum, and in cells of the basolateral amygdala. Although the basal ganglia may be atrophic no distinctive histological changes other than a mild astrocytosis are present. The midbrain, brainstem and cerebellum are normal, though sometimes a mild to moderate loss of cells from the substantia nigra (Mann et al., 1993) and locus caeruleus (Manaye et al., 1994) occurs.

In the microvacuolar type of histology, neither Pick cells nor Pick bodies are present (Brun, 1987, 1993; Mann et al., 1993; Cooper et al., 1995). Despite there again being a substantial loss of pyramidal and nonpyramidal nerve cells of layers II and III, with shrinkage rather than loss of nerve cells of layer V, astrocytosis is mild and usually limited to immediate subpial regions or the junction of the grey and white matter (Brun, 1987, 1993; Mann et al., 1993; Cooper et al., 1996). The microvacuolation affects layer II (chiefly) and the superficial parts of layer III and is due to an atrophy and loss of neurones from these areas, thereby contrasting with the tissue cavitation in the human spongiform encephalopathies which arise from a swelling and a vacuolation of cell processes. Immunohistochemistry using antibodies to tau, ubiquitin and αB crystallin confirms the absence of inclusion bodies and swollen cells and reveals no other distinctive changes. The same areas of cortex are affected, to the same relative degree, as in the gliotic cases. The hippocampus may also be atrophic, showing severe loss of neurones from areas CA1 and subiculum with heavy astrocytosis. Likewise, the basal ganglia, particularly the caudate nucleus, may show atrophy and gliosis, and the substantia nigra (Mann *et al.*, 1993) and locus caeruleus (Manaye *et al.*, 1994) may suffer mild to moderate cell loss.

White matter changes

While in both microvacuolar- and gliotic-type histologies the underlying cortical white matter shows extensive loss of myelin and axons, immunohistochemistry (Cooper *et al.*, 1996) reveals some distinctions. Astrocytosis within the white matter is seen only in the gliotic-type cases, though microglial cell activity is abundant in the white matter in both histologies (Cooper *et al.*, 1996). Such data suggest that in the microvacuolar-type cases the principal site of pathology may lie in the white matter, affecting the grey matter secondarily, whereas in the gliotic cases the grey matter might be primarily involved.

Atypical cases

Within the clinical spectrum of FTD there are some pathological variants, though in these the same kinds of histological changes as those seen in the prototypical cases prevail (Mann *et al.*, 1993). In such patients stereotypic behaviours form the principal clinical symptomatology. The brain is less, or little, reduced in weight and externally shows only mild overall atrophy, though focal accentuations within the temporal lobe may be seen in some instances or in the frontal lobes in others. On coronal section, however, a severe and distinctive atrophy of the caudate nucleus (particularly) and putamen occurs, the former adopting a flattened or concave profile; histology shows severe nerve cell loss and intense gliosis in these areas (Figure 5). In some patients the temporal lobe, including the middle and inferior, but not the superior, temporal gyri, the parahippocampus, hippocampus and amygdala, is severely and selectively atrophied whereas in others temporal lobe structures are spared and frontal atrophy predominates. In all such cases so far examined by the author a microvacuolar type of histology has been present in the cortex. The relationship of these striatocortical atrophies to the more prototypical cases of FTD remains uncertain, neither is it clear whether they represent a 'natural' subgroup of this.

Unresolved issues

The histopathological findings raise two issues. First, to what extent is each histological type a different tissue manifestation of the same disease process

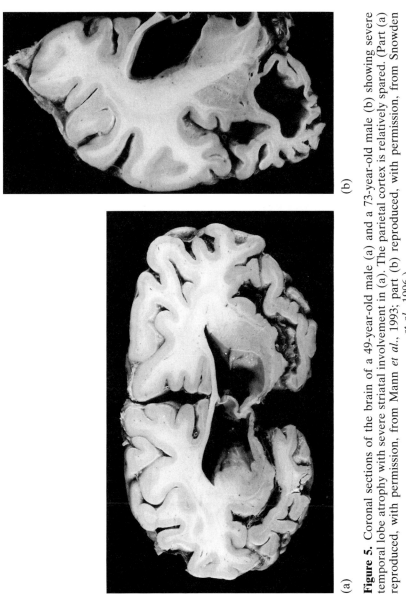

(b)

(a)

Figure 5. Coronal sections of the brain of a 49-year-old male (a) and a 73-year-old male (b) showing severe temporal lobe atrophy with severe striatal involvement in (a). The parietal cortex is relatively spared. (Part (a) reproduced, with permission, from Mann *et al.*, 1993; part (b) reproduced, with permission, from Snowden *et al.*, 1996.)

and, secondly, within this constellation of pathological change, how can the entity of 'Pick's disease' be defined?

As regards the first issue, it is clear that genetic changes probably underlie both the gliotic and microvacuolar types of pathology, though in the absence of defining genes it is not yet possible to say whether these might represent the pathological consequences of heterogeneous changes in the same gene, or analogous changes in separate, though functionally related, genes. Certainly, the first suggestion is possible since the various mutations in the prion protein gene in the human spongiform encephalopathies lead to highly variable clinical and pathological phenotypes, as do those in the amyloid precursor protein (APP) gene in Alzheimer's disease and similar disorders. Moreover, Alzheimer's disease itself is genetically heterogeneous, with four different chromosomal loci being involved; these various changes all presumably act through a common pathogenetic pathway to produce a similar pathological picture.

Secondly, what is 'Pick's disease'? Over the years this term has been used in rather cavalier fashion to ascribe a diagnostic label to cases of frontal lobe dementia where an Alzheimer-type histopathology was absent. In some instances the term was loosely applied to describe the presence of a focal atrophy of the frontal lobes despite a lack of the 'classic' histological changes of Pick bodies and Pick cells, whereas others have adopted a more stringent approach, restricting this to include only such cases where both of these cellular changes were present. The author and colleagues have noted (Cooper *et al.*, 1995) that in the gliotic cases of FTD many αB-crystallin-positive swollen cells are *always* present, even if Pick inclusion bodies are absent. By contrast, when gliosis is not seen, and a microvacuolar change prevails, such cells are rare or absent. While this suggests that within the gliotic-type cases the presence of such defining swollen cells implies the same underlying pathological cause, whether Pick bodies are present or not, this still leaves the microvacuolar-type cases outside this umbrella of change. Clearly, at present, it is not possible to reconcile these differences using conventional histopathological distinctions or to define 'Pick's disease' in a way that will satisfactorily account for all cases of FTD irrespective of histological type; this will have to wait upon clarification of the extent of genetic heterogeneity within FTD. In the meantime the author prefers the term 'Pick-type histology' to describe the gliotic forms since this avoids an implication of aetiological significance attached to an all-embracing label like Pick's disease, and also does not preclude the inclusion of cases where Pick bodies may not occur. Hence, the disorder we have termed FTD can be represented by one of two histologies, microvacuolar- and Pick-type. Within this latter category are cases which, according to strict, traditional criteria, would be known, and universally accepted, as ones of 'Pick's disease'. Defined in this way, classical Pick's disease becomes just one cause of FTD.

THE NEUROCHEMISTRY OF FTD

Initial neurochemical studies (Francis *et al.*, 1993; Qume *et al.*, 1995a, b) have indicated a neurochemical profile distinct from that of Alzheimer's disease. Cerebral cortical choline acetyl transferase activity and muscarinic M1 receptors are unaltered, in either of the histological forms, suggesting that the cholinergic system is, on the whole, preserved – a finding consistent with the normal histological appearance of the nucleus basalis of Meynert and associated structures. The decreases in receptors associated with cortical pyramidal cells (e.g. $5\text{-}HT_{1a}$ and glutamate) might be anticipated given the histological loss of such cells. However, somatostatin-like immunoreactivity is elevated in the frontal cortex indicating that the interneurone population, or at least that proportion containing this substance, is unchanged, since biochemical increases like these will reflect a maintenance of somatostatin *content* within an overall decreasing (atrophic) tissue volume. At present, FTD appears therefore to be a disease of pyramidal cells. Differential changes in 5-HT may occur in the gliotic- and microvacuolar-type cases with an increased concentration of this occurring in the gliotic cases alone; the clinical or pathological significance of this elevation of 5-HT is not known.

THE GENETICS OF FTD

As has already been mentioned, about half of the cases of FTD, irrespective of histological type, show a family history of the disease consistent with an autosomal-dominant mode of inheritance. Nonetheless, the gene, or genes, responsible for this disorder remain unknown. The author and co-workers have so far been able to exclude the possibility that FTD represents an unusual presentation of other, more common neurological disorders since changes in the APP gene (as associated with Alzheimer's disease), the prion protein gene (as in the human spongiform encephalopathies) (Owen *et al.*, 1993), the superoxide dismutase gene (as in familial motor neurone disease) or excessive CAG repeats in the IT15 gene (as in Huntington's disease) have all been ruled out. Neither do any unusual allelic variations in the apolipoprotein E gene occur (Pickering-Brown *et al.*, 1995).

Linkage analysis in a few families with FTD has indicated genetic loci on chromosome 3 (Brown *et al.*, 1995) or chromosome 17 (Lynch *et al.*, 1994). Moreover, the finding of anticipation (i.e. a gradual lowering of age at onset of disease across affected family members of different generations) in FTD pedigrees (Craufurd *et al.*, unpublished data) is suggestive, as is the case in Huntington's disease, of the presence of an expanded trinucleotide repeat sequence. However, genetic linkages to chromosome 3, 17 or elsewhere remain to be widely established in other pedigrees, and while the possession of an expanded trinucleotide repeat is a tempting possibility, this also remains to be verified. Like Alzheimer's disease, FTD may turn out to be genetically heterogeneous with the histopathological and topographical anatomical variations relating to specific, though fundamentally related, genetic changes.

ASSOCIATED DISORDERS

Clinical or pathological changes, or both, similar to FTD have been reported in several other, probably related, disorders such as frontal lobe dementia with motor neurone disease (FTD + MND) (Neary et al., 1990, 1993a; Wightman et al., 1992), semantic dementia (SD) (Snowden et al., 1994) and progressive aphasia (PA) (Snowden et al., 1992; Neary et al., 1993b). Furthermore, a Pick-type histology has been observed in the cerebral cortex of some patients with otherwise typical histological changes of subcortical disorders like progressive supranuclear palsy and corticobasal (ganglionic) degeneration. Cases such as these raise the possibility that FTD is just one clinical and pathological form of a wider spectrum of disease in which the nature, or the topography, of the tissue damage, and hence the defining clinical features, are dictated by specific, and perhaps multigenic, aetiologies.

CONCLUSION

FTD, and similar disorders like FTD + MND, PA and SD, represent prototypical syndromes of frontotemporal lobar atrophy and each is associated with a distinctive topographical distribution of a particular histopathology within the brain. The link between these various syndromes is supported by findings of overlaps between symptomatology and a blurring of diagnostic distinctions as the disorders progress. FTD may commence in the orbitofrontal cortex, then spread into the dorsolateral cortex and the temporal lobes; in the progressive language disorders of SD and PA, spread may be reversed from temporal to frontal lobes. The histologies underlying these various frontotemporal atrophies can be classed as gliotic (Pick-type) or microvacuolar, though neither can be predicted from the clinical symptomatology nor from the macroscopic appearance of the brain. Whether the histologies are aetiologically separate or represent a range of possible pathological phenotypes is not known. Similar histopathological changes associated with disorders like motor neurone disease, progressive supranuclear palsy and corticobasal degeneration widen the spectrum of disease. The nosology and aetiology of these (overlapping) disorders remain uncertain, and much will depend upon molecular genetics for their future characterization.

REFERENCES

Brown, J., Ashworth, A., Gydesen, S. *et al.* (1995). Familial non-specific dementia maps to chromosome 3. *Hum Mol Genet* **4**, 1625–1628.

Brun, A. (1987). Frontal lobe degeneration of non-Alzheimer type. I Neuropathology. *Arch Gerontol Geriatrica* **6**, 193–207.

Brun, A. (1993). Frontal lobe degeneration of non-Alzheimer type revisited. *Dementia* **4**, 126–131.

Brun, A., Englund, E., Gustafson, L. *et al.* (1994). Clinical and neuropathological criteria for fronto-temporal dementia. *J Neurol Neurosurg Psychiatry* **57**, 416–418.

Cooper, P.N., Jackson, M., Lennox, G., Lowe, J. and Mann, D.M.A. (1995). Tau, ubiquitin and alpha B crystallin immunohistochemistry define the principal causes of degenerative fronto-temporal dementia. *Arch Neurol* **52**, 1011–1015.

Cooper, P.N., Siddons, C.A. and Mann, D.M.A. (1996). Patterns of glial cell activity in fronto-temporal dementia (lobar atrophy). *Neuropathol Appl Neurobiol* **22**, 17–22.

Francis, P.T., Holmes, C., Webster, M.-T., Stratmann, G.C., Procter, A.W. and Bowen, D.M. (1993). Preliminary neurochemical findings in non-Alzheimer dementia due to lobar atrophy. *Dementia* **4**, 172–177.

Gustafson, L. (1987). Frontal lobe degeneration of non-Alzheimer type. II Clinical picture and differential diagnosis. *Arch Gerontol Geriatrica* **6**, 209–223.

Gustafson, L. (1993). Clinical picture of frontal lobe degeneration of non-Alzheimer type. *Dementia* **4**, 143–148.

Lynch, T., Sano, M., Marder, K.S. *et al.* (1994). Clinical characteristics of a family with chromosome 17-linked disinhibition-dementia-parkinsonism-amyotrophy complex. *Neurology* **44** 1878–1884.

Manaye, K.F., Woodward, K., McIntyre, D.D., White, C.L., Mann, D.M.A. and German, D.C. (1994). Locus caeruleus cell loss in lobar atrophy. *Neurodegeneration* **3**, 205–210.

Mann, D.M.A. and South, P.W. (1993). The topographic distribution of brain atrophy in frontal lobe dementia. *Acta Neuropathol* **85**, 335–340.

Mann, D.M.A., South, P.W., Snowden, J.S. and Neary, D. (1993). Dementia of frontal lobe type: neuropathology and immunohistochemistry. *J Neurol Neurosurg Psychiatry* **56**, 605–614.

Neary, D., Snowden, J.S., Shields, R.A. *et al.* (1987). Single photon emission tomography using 99m TcHMPAO in the investigation of dementia. *J Neurol Neurosurg Psychiatry* **50**, 1101–1109.

Neary, D., Snowden, J.S., Northen, B. and Goulding, P. (1988). Dementia of frontal type. *J Neurol Neurosurg Psychiatry* **51**, 353–361.

Neary, D., Snowden, J.S., Mann, D.M.A., Northen, B., Goulding, P.J. and McDermott, N. (1990). Frontal lobe dementia and motor neurone disease. *J Neurol Neurosurg Psychiatry* **53**, 23–32.

Neary, D., Snowden, J.S. and Mann, D.M.A. (1993a). The clinical pathological correlates of lobar atrophy. A review. *Dementia* **4**, 154–159.

Neary, D., Snowden, J.S. and Mann, D.M.A. (1993b). Familial progressive aphasia: its relationship to other forms of lobar atrophy. *J Neurol Neurosurg Psychiatry* **56**, 1122–1125.

Owen, F., Cooper, P.N., Pickering-Brown, S., McAndrew, C., Mann, D.M.A. and Neary, D. (1993). The lobar atrophies are not prion encephalopathies. *Neurodegeneration* **2**, 195–199.

Pickering-Brown, S.M., Siddons, M., Mann, D.M.A. *et al.* (1995). Apolipoprotein E allelic frequencies in patients with lobar atrophy. *Neurosci Lett* **188**, 205–207.

Qume, M., Misra, A., Zeman, S. *et al.* (1995a). Serotonergic profiles of lobar atrophies. *Biochem Soc Trans* **23**, 600S.

Qume, M., Misra, A., Zeman, S. *et al.* (1995b). Non-serotonergic profiles of lobar atrophies. *Biochem Soc Trans* **23**, 601S.

Snowden, J.S., Neary, D., Mann, D.M.A., Goulding, P.J. and Testa, H.J. (1992). Progressive language disorder due to lobar atrophy. *Ann Neurol* **31**, 174–183.

Snowden, J.S., Griffiths, H. and Neary, D. (1994). Semantic dementia: autobiographical contribution to preservation of meaning. *Cogn Neuropsychol* **11**, 265–288.

Snowden, J.S., Neary, D. and Mann, D.M.A. (1996). *Fronto-Temporal Lobar Degeneration: Fronto-Temporal Dementia, Progressive Aphasia, Semantic Dementia*. Churchill Livingstone, Edinburgh.

Wightman, G., Anderson, V.E.R., Martin, J. *et al.* (1992). Hippocampal and neocortical ubiquitin-immunoreactive inclusions in amyotrophic lateral sclerosis with dementia. *Neurosci Lett* **139**, 269–274.

Advances in Old Age Psychiatry: Chromosomes to Community Care
Edited by C. Holmes and R. Howard
© 1997 Wrightson Biomedical Publishing Ltd

7

Vascular Cognitive Impairment: A New Approach

ASHOK DEVASENAPATHY AND VLADIMIR HACHINSKI

Department of Clinical Neurological Sciences, University of Western Ontario, London, Ontario, Canada

INTRODUCTION

The dementias pose a significant health problem in developed nations, afflicting 10% of people over 65 years of age and 25–50% of people over 85 (Heyman *et al.*, 1984). The prevalence of the dementias doubles every five years in the age group 65–85, an important fact since this age group is the fastest-growing segment of our population in the Western world. Although senile dementia of the Alzheimer's type (SDAT) constitutes up to two-thirds of all dementias, vascular causes represent from 15 to 20% (Forette *et al.*, 1991). The prevalence of vascular dementia increases linearly with age and varies greatly from country to country, ranging from 1.2 to 4.2% in people over 65 years of age (Brayne, 1995).

Strokes are a common occurrence in the elderly segment of our population. In the Rochester, Minnesota, study, the incidence of stroke increased ninefold between ages 55–64 and 85 years and over (Broderick *et al.*, 1989). A substantial proportion of nondegenerative dementia in old age may very well be the early presentation of cerebrovascular disease, which may eventually manifest itself as ischaemic and haemorrhagic stroke, thus increasing the economic significance of the vascular dementias (Ferrucci *et al.*, 1996).

Vascular disease in general and the vascular causes of dementia in particular are potentially treatable and preventable. The basis for treatment is dependent on the early identification of risk factors, yet epidemiological studies suffer from many shortcomings related to the definition, diagnostic criteria, and assessment of the subject. This hinders recognition of the risk factors which may make it possible to identify patients at the 'brain-at-risk' stage, where preventive measures are most effective (Hachinski and Bowler, 1993).

PROBLEMS WITH THE CURRENT CONCEPT OF VASCULAR DEMENTIA

'Vascular dementia', as a concept, is obsolete. 'Vascular' is too generic and fails to identify specific aetiology which may be subject to current and future preventive measures. 'Dementia' identifies patients too late to do much about the problem.

An alternative approach is to identify patients across the entire spectrum of vascular cognitive impairment, from the high-risk, with no definite clinical symptoms (brain-at-risk stage), to full-blown dementia (Hachinski, 1994).

RISK FACTORS

It is widely believed that the risk factors for vascular-mediated dementia are the same as those for cerebrovascular disease (Butler et al., 1993). Clearly age and race are of prime importance, since cognitive loss is an age-associated phenomenon, although the aetiology for the decline is neither the same in all age groups nor in all races. The significance of other risk factors, such as gender, and those acquired, such as hypertension, diabetes, cholesterol, smoking, heart disease and atrial fibrillation, are less well established (Skoog, 1994); therefore, the impact of modification of these acquired risks is still unclear.

Additionally, it is widely accepted that up to a quarter of stroke patients may go on to develop vascular dementia (Tatemichi et al., 1992). The risk appears greater in patients with lacunar infarcts; indeed the incidence can be five times as high as that of the general population (Loeb, 1995). This may be an indication of the relative importance of certain vascular risk factors, i.e. hypertension, diabetes, etc., over others. Genetic susceptibility may also be an important contributing factor.

Epidemiological studies on the effectiveness of primary and secondary prevention in the vascular dementias are scant, and those isolated studies which have looked at individual risk factors lack adequate numbers of participants. Large-scale studies, such as the Sys–Eur Vascular Dementia Project, whose aim is to identify the importance of isolated systolic hypertension in the prevention of vascular dementia, are rarities (Forette et al., 1991). The results of this study are still pending.

PATHOLOGY AND PATHOPHYSIOLOGY

The syndromic nature of vascular cognitive impairment is reflected by a diversity of underlying vascular pathologies and pathophysiology. The widely accepted pathologic entities accounting for the vast majority of vascular causes of cognitive dysfunction include multi-infarct dementia and strategic infarct dementia caused by injury to one or more vital structures involved in cognition, i.e. left thalamus, dominant angular gyrus, etc. Strategic cerebral infarcts may contradict the widely accepted notion of a stepwise deterioration in intellectual functions as a hallmark of the vascular dementias. Indeed, an abrupt onset of cognitive symptoms is encountered in up to 20% of patients with vascular cognitive impairment (Erkinjuntii and Sulkava, 1991).

The most controversial of all is 'Binswanger's disease'. This ill-defined entity has no characteristic pathology and may lie in the spectrum of the so called 'état lacunare', or lacunar state. Both the lacunar state and Binswanger's disease have similar clinical manifestations, typically characterized by the slowing of information-processing, impaired memory and poor sustained attention. Executive dysfunction includes poor wordlist generation, verbal fluency, impaired motor programming, with perseveration and impersistence, and difficulty with set-shifting. Memory loss in the subcortical vascular dementias is characterized by poor retrieval and intact recognition (Cummings, 1994).

It is felt that the pathological lesions of the subcortical vascular dementias affect the circuitry interconnecting the caudate nucleus, globus pallidus, thalamus and the frontal lobes, thus producing similar clinical symptomatology to that seen with other subcortical diseases. Gait problems are also a common accompaniment and may be the result of the involvement of the frontal subcortical periventricular white matter and disruption of the thalamo-cortico-mediocapsular pathways (Hennerici et al., 1994). There is controversy as to whether the gait problem may be the early hallmark of cognitive decline (Hennerici et al., 1994). Rarefaction of the fibres of the corpus callosum may yet be another contributing factor (Yamanouchi et al., 1990).

THE VEXING AREA OF WHITE MATTER

The subcortical white matter is a watershed region situated between the territories of perfusion of the cortical perforators and the deep terminal subcortical penetrating branches of the anterior and posterior circulation. Perfusion damage secondary to multiple pathological causes and pathophysiological mechanisms has been identified, and has the radiological hallmark of decreased density on computerized tomography (CT) and increased signal on the long TR and long TE spin sequences on magnetic resonance imaging (MRI) scans.

Rarefaction of the white matter has been referred to as leukoaraiosis (Hachinski et al., 1986), but says little about the underlying pathology. Although white matter loss and gliosis have been identified in some cases, the vast majority of individuals with leukoaraiosis have ventricular 'caps' and 'rims', frequently seen in normal young individuals, and which become more pronounced with ageing (Verny *et al.*, 1991). In some cases no clear-cut pathological lesions can be identified. Alzheimer's disease and other degenerative dementias have also been described in the brains of patients with leukoaraiosis, and the mechanism of its formation may be multifactorial (cerebral atrophy, amyloid angiopathy, associated hypertensive arteriopathy, etc.) (Verny *et al.*, 1991).

Studies on the significance of leukoaraiosis show conflicting data. There are references in the literature showing these individuals to be at risk for recurrent strokes (Inzitari *et al.*, 1987), possibly even at risk for coronary artery disease (Raiha *et al.*, 1993) and carotid stenosis. These studies contradict some retrospective studies that have shown leukoaraiosis to be more common in the Alzheimer's disease groups than in the vascular dementia cohorts, but the Alzheimer's group of patients lacked vascular risk factors (Mirsen *et al.*, 1991). Leukoaraiosis, rather than being a risk factor itself, may act in synergy with cortical atrophy and ischaemia to the basal ganglia/thalamic regions, which may present themselves as increased signal (bright spots) on heavily proton weighted (so called T-2) MRI scans (Schmidt, 1992).

The possibility that the underlying pathological and neurochemical processes may be one of the provocative factors for cognitive loss should be addressed. MR-spectroscopy may help in our quest to understand this vexing problem. This imaging modality has demonstrated that there are regional metabolic variations in the white matter in the brains of patients with probable Alzheimer's disease, ischaemic vascular dementia and in asymptomatic individuals with leukoaraiosis, thus validating the diversity of aetiologies and pathologies that account for leukoaraiosis with its variable clinical significance (Constans *et al.*, 1995).

It is possible that the explanation for cognitive decline may not only be as the result of decreased cortical metabolic function due to subcortical white matter ischaemia. The likelihood that subcortical grey nuclei such as the thalamus and basal ganglia may in part contribute to the loss of intellect cannot be excluded. Cerebral radionuclide single photon emission computerized tomography (SPECT) studies have shown that in patients with Binswanger's disease the most hypoperfused regions are the thalami and the basal ganglia (Kawabata *et al.*, 1993). These findings have good correlation with data obtained from cerebral positron emission tomography (PET), suggesting a subcortical influence for the loss of cognitive abilities. Cerebral PET has the added potential of evaluating the physiological 'circuits' which may be responsible for the subcortical dementias; thus it may serve as fertile ground for application in clinical studies.

The density and the distribution of leukoaraiosis in the region of important white matter tracts may make some forms more clinically significant than others. One of the important neuroanatomical sites where white matter damage may produce profound cognitive deficits is at the level of the third ventricle in the region of the genu of the internal capsule. Lesions at this site can disrupt the important fibre tracts interconnecting the dorsomedial nuclei of the thalamus, cingulate gyrus, the frontal lobes and the medial temporal lobe regions. Clinically, these patients have profound deficits in their verbal memory (Tatemichi *et al.*, 1995). Cerebral MRI scans in such patients may show white matter atrophy in the third ventricular region (Charletta *et al.*, 1995).

Data from cerebral PET show that mean global cortical metabolic activity is lower in patients with anterior subcortical and periventricular hyperintensities, and metabolic rates in the frontal cortical regions are lower in patients with lacunar infarcts in the basal ganglia and the thalamus (Sultzer *et al.*, 1995). Cerebral perfusion studies in such patients with leukoaraiosis, but without dementia, have revealed that in the nondemented there is increased oxygen extraction with less of a decrease in cortical perfusion as compared with the demented.

This suggests that some forms of leukoaraiosis may, in fact, be the preclinical stages of vascular dementia (Yao *et al.*, 1992). Magnetic resonance perfusion and diffusion techniques may help to differentiate leukoaraiosis and basal ganglia hyperintensities which are associated with significant ischaemic neuronal damage from sublethal lesions that may still be responsive to treatment (Hossmann *et al.*,1995). Functional MRI holds similar potential in the judicious identification of patients with subclinical cognitive loss. Many published clinical studies utilizing the functional neuroimaging modalities lack detailed neuropsychological testing of their subjects. Were such tests to be incorporated it might be possible to correlate subtle but significant psychometric test findings with focal cerebral metabolic and perfusion abnormalities; data such as these might be useful in identifying patients when their cognitive deficits are still subclinical.

Although Binswanger's original description may not have been sufficient for the purpose of defining a new neurological disease, leukoaraiosis requires further research to determine its significance in the syndrome of vascular cognitive impairment (Pantoni and Garcia, 1995).

THE MIXED DEMENTIAS

The combined incidence of Alzheimer's disease and vascular dementias of various aetiologies (i.e. the mixed dementias) ranges from 5 to 20%, based on different autopsy series (Brun and Englund, 1986). It is often problematic to differentiate the mixed dementias from severe vascular dementias and the lacunar state, unless there are definite neuroimaging correlates. Cerebral MRI may be an invaluable aid in this task, for vascular causes of cognitive impairment have some characteristic radiological correlates, which include:

total white matter lesion area; left cortical infarction area; left parietal infarction area; and the total infarction area. There is a strong association between dominant hemisphere infarcts and dementia. Subcortical infarctions in the basal ganglia, thalamus and the frontotemporal lobes, especially in the left hemisphere, have also been implicated (Liuck *et al.*, 1992).

The committee that formulated the NINDS–AIREN (National Institute for Neurological Diseases and Stroke/Association Internationale pour la Recherche et l'Enseignement en Neuroscience) criteria for the diagnosis of vascular dementia has recommended that the term 'mixed dementia' not be used. It was felt that vascular contribution to dementia is ill-defined while the role of neuronal depopulation is clear. Furthermore, they recommend that stroke patients who have a concomitant dementia (such as Alzheimer's disease) which meets the NINCDS–ADRDA criteria for the concomitant dementia, should be considered to have nonvascular dementia rather than a mixed dementia (Roman *et al.*, 1993). These recommendations, however, fail to identify a very important issue which the clinician often encounters and may be seen in up to 20% of autopsy series. The clinician often encounters patients with undiagnosed early dementia whose cognition acutely worsens, which could potentially be the result of a small stroke, such as a lacunar infarct. If the vascular component is neither identified nor treated the resultant effect could be preventable premature 'senility'.

Even the issue of age associated memory impairment has made researchers question when Alzheimer's disease should be diagnosed (Storandt and Hill, 1989), for it seems clear that all of us will develop the pathological changes of Alzheimer's disease if we live long enough. At a time when there is so much uncertainty as to whether age associated memory loss is physiological or pathological, neglecting the vascular component of cognitive impairment seems unscientific.

In some autopsy series the nonvascular/non–Alzheimer's dementias constitute as much as 10–15% of the dementias. Although they are not as common as Alzheimer's disease they often mimic clinical symptomatology encountered with the subcortical vascular dementias (Heyman *et al.*, 1992).

AN ALTERNATIVE APPROACH

Although cerebrovascular disease has been implicated as a cause for cognitive impairment for well over a century, it is only within the past three decades that we have come to realize its exact importance. There has been a revival of interest in this area, in part due to our understanding that vascular disease can be prevented, its progression slowed, and sometimes it may be effectively treated.

The present authors propose that an alternative approach should be used in the evaluation, diagnosis and treatment of such patients. The first step in achieving this task should be the redefinition of the syndrome of vascular dementia as 'vascular cognitive impairment' (Hachinski and Bowler,1993).

Cognition is a generic term embracing the qualities of knowing, which includes perceiving, recognizing, conceiving, judging, sensing, reasoning and intuition (Concise Oxford Medical Dictionary). Dementia, however refers to multiple cognitive deficits including memory. The term dementia is adequate only for Alzheimer's disease, with its early involvement of the mesial temporal lobe structures and resultant early loss of memory. Furthermore, dementias are typically thought to be progressive and untreatable. Though cerebrovascular disease may, in its terminal manifestation, produce a dementia, the ravages of a dementia can be prevented if it is identified early . It is most desirable to identify patients at the brain-at-risk stage, where cognitive loss is minimal or subclinical and therapy most effective (Hachinski, 1992).

CLINICAL CRITERIA FOR THE DIAGNOSIS OF VASCULAR DEMENTIA – HISTORICAL ASPECTS

In the early 1970s the widespread understanding that cerebrovascular disease was treatable prompted the development of an ischaemic score (Hachinski *et al.*, 1975). This scoring system was aimed at clarifying the concept of multi-infarct dementia as not being a syndrome of global and progressive mental decline. This scale has been widely used in the diagnosis of multi-infarct dementia, either in its original or modified forms. The Hachinski ischaemic scoring scale has often been applied in different clinical criteria to operationalize for vascular risk factors. Prospective clinicopathological correlations show ischaemic scores to be fairly sensitive for the differentiation of pure Alzheimer's disease and multi-infarct dementia (approximately 70–80%), but relatively insensitive to the presence of mixed dementias (17–50%) (Chui, 1989). This scoring system was not developed to operationalize vascular risk factors in these other groups and its use in these other populations risks overdiagnosing vascular dementia, as patients with cerebrovascular disease or stroke score highly on the ischaemic scale regardless of whether or not the cerebrovascular disease has anything to do with their dementia (Brust, 1988; Fischer *et al.*, 1991).

CLINICAL CRITERIA: THE 'DEMENTIA' CONCEPT OF VASCULAR COGNITIVE IMPAIRMENT

The continued pursuit of a definition of the vascular dementias has resulted in the development of several clinical criteria, none of which is complete, nor do they agree on any one simple classification. The DSM-IV (American Psychiatry Association, 1994) and the ICD-10 (International Classification of Disease) (WHO, 1991) criteria for multi-infarct dementia and Alzheimer's disease are very similar, and place a great deal of emphasis on the presence of 'long tract signs' and focal neurological deficits as key elements in diagnosis. These two clinical criteria are difficult to operationalize and, as emphasized, the desire to make a diagnosis of vascular cognitive impairment in its early stages should preclude the use of clinical criteria that identify patients after the development of any overt neurological deficits. The second group of clinical criteria are from the California Alzheimer's Disease Diagnosis and Treatment Centers (CADDTC) (Chui et al., 1992), the National Institute of Neurological Diseases and Stroke (NINDS), and the Association Internationale pour la Recherche et l'Enseignement en Neuroscience (AIREN).

The NINDS and AIREN criteria are developments of the DSM-IV and ICD-10 in an attempt to facilitate the operability of the clinical criteria. Both NINDS and AIREN are based on clinical and neuroimaging features of cerebral infarcts and fail to address the issues of anoxic and haemorrhagic cerebral injury. All four sets of clinical criteria (NINDS, AIREN, DSM-IV and the ICD-10) fall short of identifying patients before the onset of frank cognitive impairments (Bowler and Hachinski, 1995).

THE NEED FOR THE STANDARDIZATION OF CORE NEUROPSYCHOLOGICAL TESTS

Since there is neither agreement in the clinical classification of the vascular dementias, nor has there been success in identifying individuals at the brain-at-risk stage, where clinical symptomatology may not be overtly apparent or evident on neurological examination, an attempt should be made to standardize core neuropsychological examinations that may serve as effective screening tools in high-vascular-risk groups. The successful development of such tests requires an understanding of the complex task at hand. No neuropsychological battery exists at present which successfully demonstrates the cortical and subcortical cognitive impairments encountered in the vascular dementias (Roman et al., 1993). The aim here is not to discuss the specific merits and shortcomings of the numerous neuropsychological batteries which may be clinically useful, but to provide a brief overview of some features that should be incorporated in the development of the 'ideal' test battery.

Although strategic cerebral infarcts in the basal ganglia, thalamus or caudate may cause profound impairment in global psychomotor tests such as the Mini-Mental State Examination (MMSE), typically there is progressive impairment of cognition over time rather than an acute worsening, unless there is bilateral involvement of these structures. Therefore tests such as the

MMSE are clinically not very useful. The MMSE places an emphasis on language and memory and lacks the recognition portion of the clinical test (Roman *et al.*, 1993). Studies typically show that patients with vascular dementia do poorly on tests that are influenced by frontal and subcortical mechanisms that are involved in executive functioning, verbal fluency, attention, and motor performance (Kertesz and Clydesdale, 1994). Not unexpectedly, patients with vascular dementia do poorly on tests such as the Mattis Dementia Rating Scale (MDRS), motor performance subsets; the Wechsler Adult Intelligence Scale (revised) (WAIS–R), picture arrangement subsets; the Wechsler Aphasia Battery (WAB), writing subsets; the WAIS–R object assembly subsets; and the WAB block design subsets. On the other hand, patients with early Alzheimer's disease do poorly on tests such as the WAB repetition subsets, and patients with severe Alzheimer's disease do poorly on story recall tests (Kertesz and Clydesdale, 1994). The above-mentioned psychometric tests are best for those patients with clinically apparent cognitive impairment, and for those with early or 'borderline disease'. Subjective questionnaires, such as the Functional Activities Questionnaire, may increase the sensitivity of screening (Hershey *et al.*, 1987).

More insight into the neuropsychology of the vascular dementias may be gained if the deficits found on different psychometric test batteries are correlated with functional neuroimaging studies such as cerebral PET scans to evaluate for metabolic abnormalities of the cerebral cortical regions which are in question. Cerebral PET has its greatest value in the differentiation of early Alzheimer's disease from vascular cognitive impairment (Mielke *et al.*, 1994). PET features which are typically seen in multi–infarct dementia include an asymmetric pattern of hypometabolism that is variable in distribution from patient to patient.

DEGREES OF CERTAINTY IN A DIAGNOSIS OF VASCULAR COGNITIVE IMPAIRMENT

The current clinical diagnostic criteria for the vascular dementias embodied in the NINDS–AIREN and CADDTC clinical criteria include the subheadings 'probable', 'possible', and 'definite'. The criteria for 'definite' include the tissue diagnosis of vascular disease, either by brain biopsy or autopsy. The present authors agree that at this time this is the only means of making a conclusive diagnosis, and feel that the 'mixed' dementias cannot be neglected, for it becomes necessary to recognize the vascular component, since at the moment this is the only major component which is treatable and therefore preventable. Furthermore, many patients with early stages of Alzheimer's disease may not come to clinical attention prior to worsening of their cognition, either as the result of a stroke or another brain insult. Not recognizing vascular disease in these patients may prevent the early institution of effective therapy.

Clinical criteria such as those in the NINDS–AIREN have 'probable' and 'possible' categories of clinical certainty in the diagnosis of vascular dementia. Although there is widespread acceptance that recognition for the need to causally link evidence for cerebrovascular disease and 'dementia', the current clinical criteria fail to endorse the spectrum of clinical manifestations encountered with vascular cognitive impairment. Furthermore, both categories have requirements for the involvement of multiple cognitive domains, focal neurological signs and neuroradiological evidence of stroke(s), which need not be features of all vascular dementias. In addition, the emphasis on memory in both these categories fails to acknowledge the subtle cognitive impairment that individuals may have due to vascular causes, thus excluding patients from consideration at a stage when further damage could be prevented.

Evidence of one or more strokes on cranial MRI or CT may exclude patients with no overt clinical signs until their brains are devastated enough to produce a dementia. It is the authors' feeling that the first step in the evolution of such clinical criteria for less than definite vascular 'dementia', should be to adopt a set of hierarchical, qualitative, standardized instruments to determine cognitive impairment. The simplest would be clinical, moving in a modular fashion to the most complex of neuropsychological batteries, with an emphasis on accepted definitions for the stages and clinical symptoms encountered in the spectrum of vascular cognitive impairment. This aim, to more expeditiously implicate a vascular aetiology, may be facilitated by incorporating newer technological advances such as the biological markers for Alzheimer's disease. Such tests may become the standard components of the core diagnostic work-up battery for the cognitively impaired.

BIOLOGIC MARKERS FOR ALZHEIMER'S'S DISEASE AND THEIR CLINICAL APPLICATIONS IN THE DIAGNOSIS OF VASCULAR DEMENTIA

Even at best, only 80% of autopsy-proven Alzheimer's patients who will eventually meet the NINCDS–ADRDA (National Institute for Neurological, Communicable Diseases and Stroke, Alzheimer's Disease and Related Disorders Association) criteria will meet clinical criteria for probable Alzheimer's disease (Risse et al., 1990). Over the last several years the important role of apolipoprotein E (ApoE) in the pathogenesis of Alzheimer's disease has unexpectedly emerged.

Genetic and biochemical studies have shown that ApoE is crucial in the pathogenesis of this disease. ApoE is a 299 amino acid compound found in

serum and cerebrospinal fluid which plays a crucial role in normal cholesterol metabolism. This protein has two functional domains; one end binds to
cholesterol and the other to cellular low-density lipoproteins (LDL) and
other receptors for lipids, thus facilitating endocytosis. The brain has an
abundant source of ApoE messenger RNA (Mahley, 1988).

As shown by an experiment on regenerating nerves by Shooter and
colleagues (Gebicke-Haerter and Shooter, 1989; Ignatius et al., 1986), ApoE
is involved in the transport and delivery of cholesterol in regenerating nerve
cells, and is felt to be crucial in the repair process in the brain after injury.
ApoE has three primary isoforms Apo-E2, Apo-E3, Apo-E4, each form
differing from the others by a single amino acid and having different avidity
for LDL receptors (Mahley, 1988). Apo-E2 is unable to bind to LDL receptors and is felt to be a major risk factor for coronary artery disease and
strokes. Apo-E4 is felt to be the major determinant in the development of
late-onset Alzheimer's disease (Mahley, 1988).

Large demographic studies have shown that the Apo-E3 allele is the most
common, with a frequency of 0.73, and Apo-E4 is much less common, with
a frequency of 0.14. In families of late-onset Alzheimer's disease the
frequency of the Apo-E4 phenotype is markedly increased to 0.40 (Menzel
et al., 1983). Patients without the Apo-E4 allele have an average age of onset
of dementia of 84 years. In patients with one Apo-E4 allele the age of onset
is 79 years and in those with two it is 68 years (Strittmatter et al., 1993). Over
90% of patients with two Apo-E4 phenotypes develop dementia by 90 years
of age. Although the inheritance of this phenotype appears to be a major
risk factor in the development of dementia, patients without this allele may
also develop the disease. Young patients with early-onset Alzheimer's
disease associated with the mutation of the gene for amyloid precursor
protein (APP) on chromosome 21 do not have the same risks. Therefore, it
is felt that the Apo-E4 phenotype is specific for late-onset Alzheimer's
disease, and it is seen in approximately 66% of patients with sporadic and
late-onset disease (Corder et al., 1993).

A SEROLOGICAL AND SPINAL FLUID DIAGNOSTIC TEST FOR ALZHEIMER'S DISEASE

Since the incorrect clinical diagnosis of Alzheimer's disease ranges from 15
to 40% (Berg and Morris, 1994), our understanding of the molecular
chemistry of Alzheimer's disease has been applied to the development of a
diagnostic test for the ApoE phenotype, spinal fluid tau protein and beta-
amyloid 42. These three biological markers have high correlation with
Alzheimer's disease. Spinal fluid concentration of tau has high correlation
with the brain's burden of neurofibrillary tangles, whose concentration in

turn is directly proportional to the severity of dementia (Delacourte and Defossez, 1986).

Cerebrospinal fluid beta-amyloid 42 (Aβ 42) is the by-product of metabolism of APP (amyloid precursor protein), and it is currently felt that this protein is widely deposited in amyloid plaque. The spinal fluid level of Aβ 42 is reduced in patients with Alzheimer's disease, probably from deposition in plaques rather than spinal fluid. A high spinal fluid Aβ 42 suggests Alzheimer's disease is unlikely (Yonkin, 1995).

As described, Apo-E4 is strongly associated with Alzheimer's disease. Since Alzheimer's disease is felt to be the cause of dementia in up to 66% of individuals, if there are more than two Apo-E4 alleles, then the possibility of the diagnosis being Alzheimer's disease is in excess of 90%. The correlation of tau and Aβ 42 results may help make a diagnosis of Alzheimer's disease with a specificity of 95% and a sensitivity in excess of 60% (Yonkin, 1995; Vigo–Pelfrey et al., 1995; Munroe et al., 1995; Motter et al.,1995).

The presence of markers for Alzheimer's disease may help identify the nature of the dementia, particularly in cases of mixed aetiology.

ADVANCES IN OUR UNDERSTANDING OF THE VASCULAR DEMENTIA SYNDROMES

Recent advances in molecular biology and chemistry have not only been applied to the understanding of Alzheimer's disease, but also to several syndromes associated with the vascular dementias. Some specific areas which may serve as fruitful ground for future research are highlighted in the following paragraphs.

One of the best-known causes of preventable vascular morbidity, especially in younger individuals, is associated with the lupus anticoagulant/antiphospolipid antibody syndrome. This syndrome may occur, either as a primary disorder not associated with any other autoimmune disease, or with 'lupus-like' rheumatological disorders and as a paraneoplastic phenomenon.

Several distinct stroke-associated immunological disorders such as Sneddon's syndrome and Kohlmeier–Degos disease also have associated antiphospholipid antibodies. Anticoagulation with warfarin and the maintenance of a high International Normalized Ratio (INR) have been clearly shown to be effective. Refractory cases with recurrent thromboembolic events may be treated with concomitant immunosuppression. Although the significance of this syndrome as a cause for vascular dementia and coronary morbidity in younger individuals has been clearly established, the significance of the same antibodies in the elderly is less clear. There are references in the literature that show these antibodies to be associated with vascular headaches, recurrent strokes, and temporal arteritis/polymyalgia rheumatica (Chakravarthy *et al.*, 1995). There is widespread belief that the incidence of all autoantibodies increases with age (Xavier *et al.*, 1995). Further epidemiological studies may add to the significance of these antibodies as a vascular risk factor in the elderly population.

Although the significance of subcortical arteriosclerotic encephalopathy is still in question, a well-established syndrome associated with recurrent subcortical ischaemia and leucoencephalopathy is the cerebral autosomal dominant arteriopathy with subcortical infarcts and leucoencephalopathy syndrome (CADASIL). This disorder was formerly referred to as hereditary multi–infarct dementia.

Recently the locus of the gene responsible for this disorder has been mapped to chromosome 19 (Tournier–Lasserve *et al*; 1993). The frequency of the above disorder is not known, but is felt to be underestimated for 25 Caucasian families have thus far been identified in Europe since its description (Bousser and Tournier–Lasserve, 1994). CADASIL affects middle-aged adults without any vascular risk factors. These patients have recurrent transient ischaemic attacks and strokes and eventually develop vascular dementia with pseudobulbar palsy. Death usually occurs within 10 years of the onset of symptoms. About 40% of these patients have vascular headaches and the noncoincidental nature of this syndrome is related to the gene for familial hemiplegic migraine which has its locus on the same chromosome (no. 19) (Joutel *et al.*, 1993). Patients with CADASIL often have psychosis and mood disorders characterized by either mania and/or depression, which often precede the cerebrovascular symptoms by years (Bousser and Tournier–Lasserve, 1994).

RESEARCH IN THE 'COMMON' RISK FACTORS FOR VASCULAR DEMENTIA

The above-mentioned vascular dementia syndromes may be fascinating but are less common than other risk factors for cerebral embolism, the significance of which is less clear. Some of these will be discussed briefly. About 25% of ischaemic strokes in older individuals are the result of embolic events from the heart. A large proportion of cardioembolic events are secondary to atrial fibrillation. In recent years, the application of transoesophageal echocardiography has contributed much, not only to an expeditious diagnosis of left atrial thrombi, but also to a clearer understanding of the dynamics of the left atrium which may predispose susceptible individuals to cerebral emboli. Such phenomenan as spontaneous echo contrast (i.e. a sign of a slow flow state in a cardiac chamber) (Fatkin *et al.*, 1994) deserve more attention regarding their influence on 'silent' cerebral embolism (European Atrial

Fibrillation Trial, 1996), as a cause for cognitive decline. This diagnostic modality may help us to find answers to questions relating to the significance of cardiac arrhythmias in 'haemodynamic' dementias (and other poorly understood phenomena including embolic events from patent foramen ovale and aortic arch atheroma) (Sulkava and Erkinjuntti, 1987).

In the same manner, large-scale studies such as the North American Symptomatic Carotid Endarterectomy Trial (NASCET) may provide answers to questions concerning the risks of cognitive impairment associated with 'asymptomatic' or high-grade carotid stenosis and the influence of treatments, either medical or surgical, in halting its progression. This study has shown that carotid stenosis is not an independent risk factor for leukoaraiosis (Streifler *et al.*, 1995).

Many of these elaborate studies should complement and not supplant basic epidemiological studies, which are currently scarce or not available, and may aid in the identification of risk factors for vascular cognitive impairment before the onset of frank dementia.

CONCLUSIONS

'Vascular dementia' may be the leading cause of cognitive impairment in the world, but we lack agreement as to what it encompasses or how it should be defined. The term falsely implies a single mechanism and consistent manifestations. An alternative approach consists of identifying patients across the whole spectrum of vascular cognitive impairment, from high-risk subjects with no deficit (brain-at-risk stage) to patients with full-blown dementia, and then describing the cognitive impairment in terms of standard neuropsychological measures, and relating the dementia to specific vascular aetiologies, so that prevention and therapy can be instituted. The decade of the brain is witnessing spectacular advances in genetics, functional imaging and the neurosciences that will help the understanding of vascular cognitive impairment. The challenges are immense but the opportunities are even greater.

REFERENCES

American Psychiatric Association (1994). *Diagnostic and Statistical Manual of Mental Disorders (4th edn)*. American Psychiatric Association, Washington DC.

Berg, L. and Morris, J.C. In: Terry, R.D., Katzman, R. and Bick, K.L. (Eds) (1994). *Alzheimer's Disease*. Raven Press, New York, pp. 9–22.

Bousser, M.G. and Tournier–Lasserve, E. (1994). Summary of the proceedings of the first international workshop on CADASIL, Paris, May 19–21. *Stroke* **25**, 704–707.

Bowler, J.V. and Hachinski, V.C. (1995). Vascular cognitive impairment: a new approach to vascular dementia. *Bailliere's Clin Neurol* **42**, 357–376.

Brayne, H.R. (1995). Epidemiology of vascular dementia. *Neuroepidemiology* **14**, 240–257.

Broderick, J.P., Phillips, S.J., Whisnant, J.P., O'Fallon, W.M. and Bergstrahl, E.J. (1989). Incidence rate of stroke in the eighties: the end of the decline in stroke? *Stroke* **23**, 1701–1704.

Brun, A. and Englund, E. (1986). A white matter disorder in dementia of the Alzheimer type: a patho–anatomical study. *Ann Neurol* **19**, 253–262.

Brust, J.C. (1988). Vascular dementia is overdiagnosed. *Arch Neurol* **45**, 799– 801.

Butler, R.N., Ahronheim, J., Fillit, N., Rapoport, S.I. and Tatemichi, J.K. (1993). Vascular dementia: stroke prevention takes on a new urgency. *Geriatrics* **48**, 32–34, 40–42.

Chakravarthy, K., Fountain, G., Marry, P., Byron, M., Hazleman, S. and Scott, D.G. (1995). A longitudinal study of anticardiolipin antibodies in polymyalgia rheumatica and giant cell arteritis. *J Rheumatol* **22**, 1694–1697.

Charletta, A. *et al.* (1995). CT and MRI findings among African-Americans with Alzheimer's disease, vascular dementia and stroke without dementia. *Neurology* **45**, 1456–1461.

Chui, H.C. (1989). Dementia: a review emphasizing clinico–pathological correlations and brain–behavior relationships. *Arch Neurol* **46**, 806–814.

Chui, H.C., Victoroff, J.I., Margolin, D. *et al.* (1992). Criteria for the diagnosis of ischemic vascular dementia proposed by the State of California Alzheimer's Disease Diagnostic and Treatment Centers. *Neurology* **42**, 473–480.

Constans, J.M., Meyerhoff, D.J., Gerson, J. *et al.* (1995). H–1 Mr spectroscopic imaging of white matter signal hyperintensities: Alzheimer's disease and ischemic vascular dementia. *Radiology* **197**, 517–523.

Corder, E.H., Saunders, A.M., Strittmatter, W.J. *et al.* (1993). Association of apolipoprotein E allele with late onset familial and sporadic Alzheimer's disease. *Science* **261**, 921–923.

Cummings, J.L. (1994). Vascular subcortical dementias: clinical aspects. *Dementia* **5**, 177–180.

Delacourte, A. and Defossez, A. (1986). Alzheimer's disease: tau protein promoting factors of microtubule assembly are major components of paired helical filaments. *J Neurol Sci* **76**, 173–186.

Erkinjuntii, T. and Sulkava, R. (1991). Diagnosis of multi-infarct dementia. *Alzheimer Dis Assoc Disord* **5**, 112–121.

European Atrial Fibrillation Trial (1996). Silent brain infarction in nonrheumatic atrial fibrillation. The EAFT Study Group. *Neurology* **46**, 159–165.

Fatkin, D., Herbert, E. and Feneley, M.P. (1994). Hematological correlates of spontaneous echo contrast in patients with atrial fibrillation and implications for thromboembolic risks. *Am J Cardiol* **73**, 672–676.

Ferrucci, L., Guralnik, J.M., Salive, M.E. *et al.* (1996). Cognitive impairment and the risk of stroke in the older population. *J Am Geriatr Soc* **44**, 237–241.

Fischer, P, Jellinger, K, Gatterer, G *et al.* (1991). Prospective neuropathological validation of Hachinski's ischemic scores in dementia. *J Neurol Neurosurg Psychiatry* **54**, 580–583.

Forette, F., Amery, A., Staessen, J. *et al.* (1991). Is prevention of vascular dementia possible? The Sys–Eur Vascular Dementia Project. *Aging* **3**, 373–382.

Gebicke-Haerter, P.J. and Shooter, E.M. (1989). Sulfation of rat apolipoprotein E. *J Neurochem* **53**, 912–916.

Hachinski, V.C. (1992). Preventable senility: a call for action against the vascular dementias. *Lancet* **340**, 645–648.

Hachinski, V.C. (1994). Vascular dementia: a radical redefinition. *Dementia* **5**, 130–132.

Hachinski, V.C. and Bowler, J.V. (1993). Vascular dementia. *Neurology* **43**, 2159–2160.

Hachinski, V.C., Ilif, L.D., Zikha, E. *et al.* (1975). Cerebral blood flow in dementia. *Arch Neurol* **32**, 632–637.

Hachinski, V.C., Potter, P. and Merskey, H. (1986). Leuko-araiosis: an ancient term for a new problem. *Can J Neurol Sci* **13**(suppl 4), 533–534.

Hennerici, M.G., Oster, M., Cohen, S. *et al.* (1994). Are gait disturbances and white matter degeneration early indicators of vascular dementia? *Dementia* **5**, 197–202.

Hershey, L.A., Jaffe, D.F., Greenough, P.G. and Yang, S.L. (1987). Validation of cognitive and functional assessment instruments in vascular dementia. *Int J Psychiatry Med* **17**, 183–192.

Heyman, A., Wilkinson, W.E., Stafford, J.A. *et al.* (1984). Alzheimer's disease: a study of epidemiological aspects. *Ann Neurol* **15**, 335–341.

Heyman, A., Filenbaum, G., Mirra, S. *et al.* (1992). Clinical misdiagnosis of Alzheimer's disease – a review of the CERAD autopsy findings. *Ann Neurol* **32**, 270–277.

Hossman, R.A. and Hoehn–Berlage, M. (1995). Diffusion and perfusion MR imaging of cerebral ischemia. *Cerebrovasc Brain Metab Rev* **7**, 187–217.

Ignatius, M.J., Gebicke–Haerter, P.J., Skene, J.H.P. *et al.* (1986). Expression of apolipoprotein E during nerve degeneration and regeneration. *Proc Natl Acad Sci* **83**, 1125–1129.

Inzitari, D., Diaz, F., Fox, A. *et al.* (1987). Vascular risk factors in leukoaraiosis. *Arch Neurol* **44**, 42–47.

Joutel, A., Bousser, M.G., Biousse, V. *et al.* (1993). A gene for familial hemiplegic migraine maps on chromosome 19. *Nat Genet* **5**, 40–45.

Kawabata, K., Tachibana, H., Sugita, M. *et al.* (1993). A comparative I–123 IMP SPECT study in Binswanger's and Alzheimer's disease. *Clin Nucl Med* **18**, 329–336.

Kertesz, A. and Clydesdale, S. (1994). Neuropsychological deficits in vascular dementia vs Alzheimer's disease. Frontal lobe deficits prominent in vascular dementia. *Arch Neurol* **51**, 1226–1231.

Liuck, A., Miller, B.L., Howng, S.L. *et al.* (1992). A quantitative MRI study of vascular dementia. *Neurology* **42**, 138–143.

Loeb, C. (1995). Dementia due to lacunar infarctions: a misnomer or a clinical entity? *Eur Neurol* **35**, 187–192.

Mahley, R.W. (1988). Apolipoprotein E, cholesterol transport protein with an expanding role in cell biology. *Science* **240**, 622–630.

Menzel, J., Kladetzky, K.G,. Assmann, G. *et al.* (1983). Apolipoprotein E polymorphism and coronary artery disease. *Arteriosclerosis* **3**, 310–315.

Mielke, R., Pietrzyk, U., Jacobs, A. *et al.* (1994). HMPAO SPECT and FDG PET in Alzheimer's disease and vascular dementia: comparison of perfusion and metabolic patterns. *Eur J Nucl Med* **21**, 1052–1060.

Mirsen, T.R., Lee, D.H., Wong, C.J. *et al.* (1991). Clinical correlations of white matter changes on magnetic resonance imaging scans of the brain. *Arch Neurol* **48**, 1015–1021.

Motter, R., Vigo-Pelfrey, C., Kholodenko, D. *et al.* (1995). Reduction of β-amyloid peptide-42 in cerebrospinal fluid of patients with Alzheimer's disease. *Ann Neurol* **38**, 643–647.

Munroe, W.A., Southwick, P.C., Chang, L. *et al.* (1995). Tau protein in CSF as an aid in the diagnosis of Alzheimer's disease. *Ann Clin Lab Sci* **25**, 207–217.

Pantoni, L. and Garcia, J.H. (1995). The significance of cerebral white matter abnormalities 100 years after Binswanger's report. A review. *Stroke* **26**, 1293–1301.

Raiha, I. *et al.* (1993). Relationship between vascular factors and white matter low attenuation of the brain. *Acta Neurol Scand* **87**, 286–289.

Risse, S.C., Raskind, M.A., Nochlin, D. *et al.* (1990). Neuropathological findings in patients with a clinical diagnosis of probable Alzheimer's disease. *Am J Psychiatry* **144**, 168–172.

Roman, G.C., Tatemichi, T.K., Erkinjuntii, T. *et al.* (1993) Vascular dementia diagnostic criteria for research studies. Report of the NINDS–AIREN international workshop. *Neurology* **43**, 250–260.

Schmidt, R. (1992). Comparison of magnetic resonance imaging in Alzheimer's disease, vascular dementia and normal aging. *Eur Neurol* **32**, 164–169.

Skoog, I. (1994). Risk factors for vascular dementia: a review. *Dementia* **5**, 137–144.

Storandt, M. and Hill, R.D. (1989). Very mild senile dementia of the Alzheimer s type. *Arch Neurol* **46**, 383–386.

Streifler, J.Y., Eliasziw, M., Benevente, O.R. *et al.* (1995). Lack of relationship between leukoaraiosis and carotid artery disease. The North American Symptomatic Carotid Endarterectomy Trial. *Arch Neurol* **52**, 21–24.

Strittmatter, W.J., Saunders, A.M., Salvesen, G.S. and Roses, A.D. (1993). Apolipoprotein E: high avidity in binding to amyloid and increased frequency of type 4 allele in late onset Alzheimer's disease. *Proc Natl Acad Sci* **90**, 1977–1981.

Sulkava, R. and Erkinjuntti, T. (1987). Vascular dementia due to cardiac arrhythmias and systemic hypotension. *Acta Neurol Scand* **76**, 123–128.

Sultzer, D.L., Mahler, M.E., Cunnings, J.L. *et al.* (1995). Cortical abnormalities associated with subcortical lesions in vascular dementia. Clinical and positron emission tomographic findings. *Arch Neurol* **52**, 773–780.

Tatemichi, T.K., Desmond, D.W., Mayeux, R. *et al.* (1992). Dementia after stroke: baseline frequency, risks and clinical features in a hospitalized cohort. *Neurology* **42**, 1185–1193.

Tatemichi, T.K., Desmond, D.W. and Prohovnik, I. (1995). Strategic infarcts in vascular dementia. A clinical and brain imaging experience. *Arzneimittelforschung* **45**, 371–385.

Tournier–Lasserve, E., Joutel, A., Melki, J. *et al.* (1993). Cerebral autosomal dominant arteriopathy with subcortical infarcts and leukoencephalopathy maps to chromosome 19q12. *Nature Genet* **3**, 256–259.

Verny, M., Duyckaerts, C., Pierot, L. *et al.* (1991). Leuko–araiosis. *Dev Neurosci* **13**, 245–250.

Vigo-Pelfrey, C., Seubert, P., Barbour, R. *et al.* (1995). Elevation of microtubule-associated protein tau in cerebrospinal fluid of Alzheimer's patients. *Neurology* **45**, 788–793.

World Health Organization (WHO) (1991). *The Neurological Adaptation of the International Classification of Diseases (ICD–10NA)*. World Health Organization, Geneva (draft).

Xavier, R.M., Yamauchi, Y., Nakamura, M. *et al.* (1995). Antinuclear antibody in healthy aging people: a prospective study. *Mech Aging Dev* **78**, 145–154.

Yamanouchi, H., Sugiura, S. and Shimada, H. (1990). Loss of nerve fibers in the corpus callosum of progressive subcortical vascular encephalopathy. *J Neurol* **237**, 39–41.

Yao, H., Sadoshima, S., Ibayashi, S. *et al.* (1992). Leukoaraiosis and dementia in hypertensive patients. *Stroke* **23**, 1673–1677.

Yonkin, S.G. (1995). Evidence that Aβ 42 is the culprit in Alzheimer's disease. *Ann Neurol* **37**, 287–288.

III

Dementia Management

Advances in Old Age Psychiatry: Chromosomes to Community Care
Edited by C. Holmes and R. Howard
© 1997 Wrightson Biomedical Publishing Ltd

8

Principles of Drug Treatment in Alzheimer's Disease

ANDREW W. PROCTER

Department of Psychiatry, Manchester Royal Infirmary, Manchester, UK

INTRODUCTION

The major motivation for the neurobiological study of neurodegenerative diseases has been the hope that effective treatments might thereby be developed. The description of the neurochemical pathology of Parkinson's disease led to the introduction of a rational neurotransmitter-based therapy for this condition and set the scene for the systematic study of other disorders, including Alzheimer's disease (AD), which was one of the first conditions subject to intensive neurochemical study.

Rational drug treatments may aim to act at different points in the pathological process of AD. The ultimate aim is to prevent or reverse pathology; however, less ambitious aims include prevention of death of subpopulations of neurones, correction of the resulting neurotransmitter imbalances, or enhancement of the function of the remaining neurones. To date, the majority of proposed treatments are based on the restoration of selective neurotransmitter dysfunction, an approach dependent upon reliable and valid studies of the neurochemical pathology to identify the important early neurotransmitter losses.

NEUROCHEMICAL PATHOLOGY OF ALZHEIMER'S DISEASE

It is assumed that, if any particular neurochemical finding is to be considered of primary importance in AD, then it should meet two key criteria: first, that it be present in the early stages of the disease and, secondly, that the magnitude of that change be correlated with the severity of some clinical or pathological hallmark of the disorder. The study of tissue obtained by

neurosurgery early in the course of the disease demonstrates neurotransmitter changes which meet these criteria (Procter, 1996).

The neocortical cholinergic system

The early demonstrations of substantial losses of the enzyme for the synthesis of acetyl choline, choline acetyltransferase (ChAT) from the brains of
patients with AD in both post-mortem and ante-mortem tissue has stimulated much subsequent research of this neurotransmitter (Procter, 1996).
Other evidence also establishes a cholinergic deficit as one of the most
prominent features of AD. Neuropathological studies have shown that there
is usually considerable loss of the neurones which give rise to the cortical
cholinergic innervation, the neurones of the nucleus basalis of Meynert
(nbM) which is associated with loss of nucleolar volume of the cells. The
observations of neurofibrillary tangle formation in the nbM and cholinergic
neurites in senile plaques suggested a link between the cholinergic system
and the pathological features of AD.

Biochemical measures of cholinergic function have shown consistent and
extensive losses of those biochemical activities which are associated with
cholinergic terminals. In particular, ChAT activity seems to be reduced post-
mortem in all areas of the cerebral cortex of patients with AD. Neurosurgical
specimens taken early in the course of the disease confirm this loss of activity and a reduced ability of the tissue to synthesize acetyl choline (ACh).

The magnitude of this cholinergic dysfunction is correlated with the severity of both the cognitive impairment (Neary et al., 1986), and the neuropathological changes, including senile plaque formation and loss of pyramidal
neurones (Neary et al., 1986). Considerable emphasis has been placed on the
significance of this cholinergic deficit and it has been suggested that the
dementia of AD is due primarily to this (Coyle et al., 1983).

However, doubts have been raised as to the validity of the view of AD as
primarily a disorder of the cholinergic system. Subsets of patients with
dementia have been reported with the typical neuropathological features, yet
cortical ChAT activity was not selectively reduced (Palmer et al., 1986).
Other patients with AD, particularly the elderly, had at most only minimal
loss of cholinergic neurones from the nbM. Reduction in numbers of these
basal forebrain neurones, which innervate the neocortex, and in cortical
ChAT activity of similar magnitude occurs in another neurodegenerative
condition, olivopontocerebellar atrophy, yet cognitive impairment in this
condition is not prominent (Kish et al., 1988).

Thus the neocortical cholinergic deficit probably only explains a part of
the cognitive decline, as has been suggested by neuropsychological studies
of the effects of cholinergic antagonists (Kopelman and Corn, 1988). Drugs
which aim to correct this deficiency are likely to affect only those aspects

of cognitive function mediated through this cholinergic system. Probably the most extensively studied drug for the treatment of AD is the cholinesterase inhibitor, tetrahydroaminoacridine (THA). This appears to have beneficial effects on attentional function rather than on memory directly. This is indicated by an improvement in choice reaction time with no effect on a classic test of short-term memory, delayed matching to sample (Sahakian and Coull, 1993).

Other corticopetal neurotransmitters

The cortex receives inputs from at least three other populations of subcortical neurones, each using a different transmitter. The catecholamines noradrenaline and dopamine are relatively unaffected whereas the situation regarding serotonin (5-hydroxytryptamine, 5-HT) is complex.

Biochemical determinations of 5-HT-containing neurones in AD have mostly relied on determinations of concentrations of 5-HT and its major metabolite, 5-hydroxyindoleacetic acid (5-HIAA), in post-mortem samples. In many areas of the neocortex of AD subjects the content of these may be reduced, and neurofibrillary degeneration and neuronal loss in the raphe nucleus has been reported. However, this is by no means a consistent finding, and even in AD brains at autopsy half of the cortical areas may have no selective reduction of presynaptic 5-HT activity.

This discrepancy between studies may in part be explained by the inadvertent selection of cases for which institutional care had been necessary because of behavioural symptoms. Many of these studies have been based on predominantly hospitalized patients. In an attempt to examine this in an epidemiologically representative sample of AD patients, subjects from a community-based study of AD have been examined for structural and functional markers of serotonergic innervation in two cortical areas (Chen et al., 1996). Loss of 40% of immunoreactive cells occurred from the dorsal raphe nucleus (DRN), yet loss of presynaptic uptake sites ([3H] paroxetine binding) of comparable magnitude was confined to the temporal cortex. Individual DRN neurones project diffusely to several areas of brain and no significant loss of [3H] paroxetine binding was found in frontal cortex. This may provide evidence for some plasticity in the system by sprouting of remaining serotonergic innervation in a region less affected by the pathological process of AD. Concentrations of 5-HT were unchanged in either area and, as has been found in other series, the ratio of 5-HIAA to 5-HT was significantly increased in both areas. This has been interpreted as evidence for increased turnover of 5-HT in surviving serotonergic terminals. Furthermore, 5-HIAA concentration in lumbar cerebrospinal fluid (CSF) positively correlated with the dementia rating in a series of histologically verified AD patients.

The study of patients assessed retrospectively indicates that patients judged to be aggressive during life had more severe loss of both 5-HT concentration and postsynaptic receptors (Palmer *et al.*, 1988; Procter *et al.*, 1992). The assessment of behavioural symptoms retrospectively is potentially unreliable, but compatible results were obtained when patients were assessed prospectively (Chen *et al.*, 1996). The loss of the structural markers of cortical serotonergic pathology, [³H] paroxetine binding, from the neocortex was most prominent in those subjects with behavioural symptoms in life. On the basis of these results it is difficult to assign particular symptoms to pathology in the serotonergic system, as patients with aggression, depression and overactivity all showed loss of [³H] paroxetine binding of comparable magnitude. In other studies aggressive behaviour has been linked to more advanced disease (Procter *et al.*, 1992), compatible with the view that loss of 5-HT$_2$ receptors is a feature of more extensive pathology found towards the end-stage of the disorder.

Nonetheless, drugs acting on the serotonergic system appear to be of some benefit in the treatment of the behavioural symptoms. The selective 5-HT reuptake blocker, citalopram, and other compounds such as trazodone and buspirone, are of little benefit on the cognitive symptoms of AD, yet emotional and mood disturbance may be improved (Nyth and Gottfries, 1990; Lawlor *et al.*, 1994). Theoretically it is possible that enhancement of serotonin function may be detrimental to cognitive function (see below).

Cortical interneurones

Within the cortex there are large numbers of interneurones containing the inhibitory transmitter gamma-aminobutyric acid (GABA), often co-localized with one or more of a variety of neuropeptides. The balance of evidence indicates that loss of these substances is not a fundamental characteristic of AD. Post-mortem assessment of GABA-releasing neurones has been complicated by artefacts and epiphenomena (Lowe *et al.*, 1988). Thus, no change in the activity of the enzyme responsible for GABA synthesis, glutamic acid decarboxylase (GAD), was found in a careful study where AD and control subjects were matched for the nature of the terminal illness (Reinikainen *et al.*, 1988). Normal GAD activity and GABA content have been confirmed with cortical biopsy tissue, and an attempt at treating AD with a GABA agonist was unsuccessful (Mohr *et al.*, 1986).

Many studies have demonstrated that the concentration of the neuropeptide somatostatin is reduced but this was not confirmed in biopsy samples. Larger reductions in somatostatin and GABA content have been reported in post-mortem studies that included only subjects displaying severe histopathology rather than in those where no such selection criteria were employed (Lowe *et al.*, 1988). Taken together, these data support the view that loss of somatostatin is not a hallmark of the disease process. A clinical trial with the synthetic somatostatin analogue octreotide failed to improve cognition of AD patients (Mouradian *et al.*, 1991).

Cortical pyramidal neurones

There is now accumulating evidence that glutamic acid (GLU) is the principal transmitter of the corticocortical association fibres and the major hippocampal pathways. Histological and some neurochemical studies indicate that these pathways degenerate quite early in AD.

Several independent studies indicate that severity of dementia correlates with degeneration of corticocortical pyramidal neurones in association areas. Positron emission tomography (PET) shows temporal and parietal lobes of AD patients are major and early sites of pathological changes. Neuropsychological test scores correlate with both PET data and the pyramidal cell and synapse counts in layer III (Neary *et al.*, 1986). Thus, cognitive symptoms seem to be due to shrinkage or loss of pyramidal neurones from parietotemporal areas.

Results obtained using a variety of techniques are consistent with GLU being the major neurotransmitter of these neurones. The major input and output pathways of the hippocampus (except the septohippocampal cholinergic pathway) use GLU as transmitter. There was cell loss and tangle formation in the entorhinal cortex and in the CA1 area in AD patients at post-mortem. Evidence from *in vivo* imaging suggests that atrophy of the hippocampus occurs by the mid-point of the disease process. Hyman and colleagues (1987) measured the concentration of GLU in the terminal zone of the perforant pathway where there was an 80% decrease in AD specimens. Consistent with this, decreased GLU staining was observed in the molecular layer of the dentate gyrus (Kowall and Beal, 1991). Although this latter study did not examine the entorhinal cortex, GLU and glutaminase immunoreactive pyramidal neurones in the CA fields were decreased in number, and the remaining neurones showed irregular shortening and disorganized dendritic fields. Many also showed tangle formation. These data imply that if the glutamatergic pathways are considered to be involved in memory (Hyman *et al.*, 1990) it follows that the loss of glutamatergic function may contribute to the memory dysfunction in AD, and enhancement of the activity of glutamatergic neurones may be beneficial.

RECEPTOR REGULATION OF CORTICAL PYRAMIDAL NEURONES

The excitability of pyramidal neurones of the neocortex is affected by many transmitters, according to *in vitro* electrophysiological studies (McCormick and Williamson, 1989). However, such studies have consistently shown that only a proportion of cells respond to a particular drug, which suggests that there is a substantial degree of heterogeneity with respect to the transmitter receptors on pyramidal neurones. The receptors present on cortical pyramidal cells can be identified by selective lesioning studies (Chessell *et al.*, 1994). These studies show consistent reductions in binding of [^{3}H] pirenzipine to M_1 receptors in areas of neocortex that showed pyramidal neurone loss and emphasize the potential importance of M_1 receptors for regulating the activity of both corticofugal and corticocortical pyramidal neurones. The most selective marker of the subpopulation of corticofugal neurones is the 5-HT_{1A} receptor. Hence, positive modulation of impulse flow by the M_1 receptor, perhaps in combination with an antagonist of the 5-HT_{1A}-receptor-induced hyperpolarization, may represent a promising therapeutic strategy.

The action of drugs on pyramidal cell activity may be determined by measuring the release of glutamate from pyramidal neurones forming the corticostriatal pathway by intracerebral microdialysis in anaesthetized rats (Dijk *et al.*, 1995). Such studies may be used to test these hypotheses and show that selective 5-HT_{1A} antagonists can potentiate the effect of a depolarizing agent (*N*-methyl-D-aspartate) on the activity of glutamatergic pyramidal neurones, as well as facilitate endogenous neurotransmission in the rat, and may therefore be useful for the symptomatic treatment of patients with AD.

One theoretical side-effect of such cognition-enhancing drugs could be excitotoxicity, although this is usually considered in the context of ischaemia, where a massive release of excitatory amino acids may be followed by neuronal degeneration. Moreover, while an increase in glutamate might be viewed as potentially excitotoxic in normal individuals, cholinomimetics would be acting to ameliorate *decreased* glutamate release in AD. In addition, the role of glucose in glutamate excitotoxicity has to be considered. Studies using the PET technique indicate that, in AD, glucose utilization is relatively more impaired than oxygen metabolism (Fukuyama *et al.*, 1994) and the quantity of the glucose transporter in Alzheimer brains is reported to be reduced compared with normal controls (Simpson *et al.*, 1994). Experimental studies in the rat indicate that glutamate loses most of its excitotoxic capability when glucose concentrations in the brain are reduced to low physiological concentrations (Dijk *et al.*, 1995).

PUTATIVE LINKS BETWEEN NEURONAL PATHOLOGY AND ABERRANT PROTEIN METABOLISM

No direct link between the two cardinal features of AD, amyloid deposition, exemplified by senile plaque formation, and tangle formation within, or loss of, subpopulations of cortical pyramidal neurones has been established

(Neary *et al.*, 1986; Braak and Braak, 1991). Recent studies suggest that the effects of reduced activity of glutamatergic neurones might include the promotion of the formation of senile plaques.

Tau

Hyperphosphorylation of tau protein probably accounts for its abnormal transformation into paired helical filament (PHF) tau, a key constituent of tangles, but the mechanism(s) is not well described. Activation of a protein kinase which can generate PHF tau may thereby promote tangle formation. Hypoactivity of glutamatergic neurones is also implicated in aberrant mechanisms of tau hyperphosphorylation since glutamate stimulation of rat cortical neurones in culture depresses production of PHF-like tau.

Amyloid precursor protein

The major component of the extracellular amyloid is the 4 KDa β-amyloid protein, (βA4). This is encoded within a much larger protein, the amyloid precursor protein (APP). APP comprises a family of glycoproteins, including APP_{695} and other isoforms such as APP_{751} and APP_{770} which are characterized by a serine protease inhibitory domain or KPI. They are all derived by alternative splicing. At least two pathways have been described for the processing of APPs, a secretory pathway dependent on protein kinase C, and a lysosomal/endosomal pathway. The secretory pathway involves phosphorylation and insertion of APP into the cell membrane followed by cleavage of a large N-terminal fragment. This pathway does not appear to yield intact βA4 as the cleavage site is within that sequence. The lysosomal/endosomal pathway yields small C-terminal fragments, some of which contain the βA4 sequence. Lysosomal/endosomal processing of APPs is thought to be responsible for the secreted βA4 found in cerebrospinal fluid; it is not yet clear whether the secreted βA4 forms the characteristic β-pleated sheet amyloid found in senile plaques following changes in the extracellular environment or if aberrant intracellular handling or catabolism of APP is responsible. Although various groups have proposed that the mismetabolism of APP and deposition of βA4 is the seminal pathogenic event in AD (Hardy and Higgins, 1992) no association has been found between senile plaque formation and dementia score (Neary *et al.*, 1986).

Glial cells in culture have been shown to express APP but do not appear to secrete large amounts of the soluble form; however, pyramidal neurones appear to be a major source of APP.

The secretion of APP from pyramidal cells appears to be regulated by neuronal activity, in particular, transmitter transduction mechanisms. This includes M_1 and other receptors which use products of phosphatidylinositol bisphosphate (PIP_2) hydrolysis as second messengers and, following activation, increase APP secretion.

While the precise nature of the neurotoxic process in AD remains to be identified, further work is required to establish whether the intracellular accumulation of soluble APP is toxic or whether the lack of one or both of the secreted forms so disrupts normal neuronal integrity as to be the pathogenic agent.

CONCLUSIONS

Studies of the neurochemical pathology of AD have indicated that early in the course of the disease abnormalities of relatively few neurotransmitters are obvious. This is in contrast to the situation late in the disease, which is usually examined in post-mortem tissue. Thus the most reliable and consistent changes are those seen in the cholinergic innervation of the cortex and the cortical pyramidal neurones. The likely consequence of this is that there is a functional underactivity of the remaining cortical pyramidal neurones and excitatory inputs due to loss of excitatory inputs such as terminals of cholinergic neurones acting via the M1 receptor, as well as functional preservation of inhibitory inputs such as serotonergic neurones acting via 5-HT_{1A} receptors.

Well-designed trials with adequate numbers of subjects showed that the anticholinesterase THA benefits some patients, expressed either as improvement in the core deficits of AD, or as a reduced rate of deterioration (Wilcock, 1995). However, only a few patients benefit greatly, and only certain symptoms and cognitive deficits are improved. While it is clear that THA is not an ideal cholinesterase inhibitor, another approach to supplementing the deficit in acetylcholine in the AD brain could be to use M_1 agonists, which may be at least as useful as any improved cholinesterase inhibitor. However, the functional status of the M_1 receptor in AD needs to be clarified (Bowen *et al.*, 1995). In view of this it may transpire that the most effective treatment requires polypharmacy, such as an M_1 agonist in combination with a 5-HT_{1A} antagonist.

While this strategy is essentially aimed at providing a symptomatic treatment, a serendipitous consequence of enhancing the activity of pyramidal neurones might be to affect the disease process itself by altering the deranged protein metabolism which appears to be at the core of the disease.

ACKNOWLEDGEMENTS

I am grateful to colleagues formerly of the Department of Neurochemistry, Institute of Neurology, London, for helpful discussions during the preparation of this chapter, in particular, Professor D.M. Bowen and Drs P.T. Francis, M. Qume and C. Chen. I also wish to thank Professor D. Neary, and Drs B. Doshi, M. Esiri, T. Hope, B. McDonald, D. Mann and J. Snowden for the collection and classification of samples.

REFERENCES

Bowen, D.M., Francis, P.T., Chessell, I.P. *et al.* (1995). Alzheimer's disease: is the improvement of cholinergic transmission the correct strategy ? In: Cutler, N.R., Gottfries, C.G. and Siegfried, K.R. (Eds), *Alzheimer's disease: clinical and treatment aspects*. John Wiley & Sons, Chichester, pp. 89–116.

Braak, H. and Braak, E. (1991). Neuropathological staging of Alzheimer's disease. *Acta Neuropathol* **82**, 239–259.

Chen, C.P.L.-H., Alder, J.T., Bowen, D.M. *et al.* (1996). Presynaptic serotonergic markers in community-acquired cases of Alzheimer's disease: correlations with depression and neuroleptic medication. *J Neurochem* **66**, 1592–1598.

Chessell, I.P., Francis, P.T., Webster, M.-T. *et al.* (1994). An aspect of Alzheimer neuropathology after suicide transport damage. *J Neural Transm Suppl* **44**, 231–243.

Coyle, J.T., Price, D.L., and DeLong, M.R. (1983). Alzheimer's disease: a disorder of cortical cholinergic innervation. *Science* **219**, 1184–1190.

Dijk, S.N., Francis, P.T., Stratmann, G.C. and Bowen, D.M. (1995). Cholinomimetics increase glutamate outflow by action of the corticostriate pathway: implications for Alzheimer's disease. *J Neurochem* **115**, 1169–1174.

Fukuyama, H., Ogawa, M., Yamauchi, H. *et al.* (1994). Altered cerebral energy metabolism in Alzheimer's disease: a PET study. *J Nucl Med* **35**, 1–6.

Hardy, J. and Higgins, G.A. (1992). Alzheimer's disease: the amyloid cascade hypothesis. *Science* **256**, 184–185.

Hyman, B.T., van Hoesen, G.W. and Damasio, A.R. (1987). Alzheimer's disease: glutamate depletion in the hippocampal perforant pathway zone. *Ann Neurol* **22**, 37-40.

Hyman, B.T., van Hoesen, G.W. and Damasio, A.R. (1990). Memory-related neural systems in Alzheimer's disease: an anatomic study. *Neurology* **40**, 1721–1730.

Kish, S.J., Munir, E.-A., Schut, L., Leach, L., Oscar-Berman, M. and Freedman, M. (1988). Cognitive deficits in olivopontocerebellar atrophy: implications for the cholinergic hypothesis of Alzheimer's dementia. *Ann Neurol* **24**, 200–206.

Kopelman, M.D. and Corn, T.H. (1988). Cholinergic 'blockade' as a model for cholinergic depletion. *Brain* **111**, 1079–1110.

Kowall, N.W. and Beal, M.F. (1991). Glutamate-, glutaminase- and taurine-immunoreactive neurons develop neurofibrillary tangles in Alzheimer's disease. *Ann Neurol* **29**, 162–167.

Lawlor, B.A., Radcliffe, J., Molchan, S.E., Martinez, R.A., Hill, J.L. and Sunderland, T. (1994). A pilot placebo-controlled study of trazodone and buspirone in Alzheimer's disease. *Int J Geriatr Psychiatry* **9**, 55–59.

Lowe, S.L., Francis, P.T., Procter, A.W., Palmer, A.M., Davison, A.N. and Bowen, D.M. (1988). Gamma-aminobutyric acid concentration in brain tissue at two stages of Alzheimer's disease. *Brain* **111**, 785–799.

McCormick, D.A. and Williamson, A. (1989). Convergence and divergence of neurotransmitter action in human cerebral cortex. *Proc Natl Acad Sci USA* **86**, 8098–8102.

Mohr, E., Bruno, G., Foster, N. *et al.* (1986). GABA-agonist therapy for Alzheimer's disease. *Clin Neuropharmacol* **9**, 257–263.

Mouradian, M.M., Biln, J., Giuffra, M. *et al.* (1991). Somatostatin replacement therapy of Alzheimer disease. *Ann Neurol* **30**, 610–630.

Neary, D., Snowden, J.S., Mann, D.M.A. *et al.* (1986). Alzheimer's disease: a correlative study. *J Neurol Neurosurg Psychiatry* **49**, 229–237.

Nyth, A.L. and Gottfries, C.G. (1990). The clinical efficacy of citalopram in treatment of emotional disturbance in dementia disorders. A Nordic multi-centre study. *Br J Psychiatry* **157**, 894–901.

Palmer, A.M., Procter, A.W., Stratmann, G.C. and Bowen, D.M. (1986). Excitatory amino acid-releasing and cholinergic neurones in Alzheimer's disease. *Neurosci Lett* **66**, 199–204.

Palmer, A.M., Stratmann, G.C., Procter, A.W. and Bowen, D.M. (1988). Possible neurotransmitter basis of behavioral changes in Alzheimer's disease. *Ann Neurol* **23**, 616–620.

Procter, A.W. (1996). Neurochemical pathology of neurodegenerative conditions in old age. In: Jacoby, R and Oppenheimer, C (Eds), *Textbook of Psychiatry in the Elderly*, Oxford University Press, Oxford.

Procter, A.W., Francis, P.T., Stratmann, G.C. and Bowen, D.M. (1992). Serotonergic pathology is not widespread in Alzheimer patients without prominent aggressive symptoms. *Neurochem Res* **17**, 917–922.

Reinikainen, K.J., Paljarvi, L., Huuskonen, M., Soininen, H., Laasko, M. and Reikkinen, P.J. (1988). A post mortem study of noradrenergic serotonergic and GABAergic neurons in Alzheimer's disease. *J Neurol Sci* **84**, 101–116.

Sahakian, B.J. and Coull, J.T. (1993). Tetrahydroaminoacridine (THA) in Alzheimer's disease: an assessment of attentional and mnemonic function using CANTAB. *Acta Neurol Scand Suppl* **149**, 29–35.

Simpson, I.A., Koteswara, R., Chundu, M.D., Davis-Hill, T., Honer, W.G. and Davies, P. (1994). Decreased concentrations of GLUT1 and GLUT3 glucose transporters in the brains of patients with Alzheimer's disease. *Ann Neurol* **35**, 546–551.

Wilcock, G.K. (1995). Pharmacological approaches to treating Alzheimer's disease. In: Dawbarn, D and Allen, S.J. (Eds), *Neurobiology of Alzheimer's Disease*. BIOS Scientific Publishers, Oxford, pp. 289–304.

Advances in Old Age Psychiatry: Chromosomes to Community Care
Edited by C. Holmes and R. Howard
© 1997 Wrightson Biomedical Publishing Ltd

9

Behavioural and Environmental Treatment in Dementia

STEVEN H. ZARIT

The Gerontology Center, The Pennsylvania State University, Pennsylvania, USA

Behavioural and environmental interventions have a long history in the treatment of dementia. These treatments can reduce or control a variety of disturbing behaviours and allow patients to function at an optimal level, despite their underlying illness. Although there is considerable evidence of their effectiveness (Hinchliffe, *et al.*, 1995; Teri and Logsdon, 1990; Teri *et al.*, 1992; Stokes, 1996), behavioural and environmental treatments remain relatively underutilized. Clinicians who understand the basic principles behind these interventions can make an immediate impact on dementia patients and the lives of their caregivers, including both family members or staff in an institutional setting.

It is clear that many different approaches are needed in dementia. A recent editorial in the *American Journal of Geriatric Psychiatry* reviewed the limited effects of tacrine in Alzheimer's disease and recommended that the standard treatment should focus instead on caregivers, helping them to obtain more help with managing the patient as well as learning better skills for doing so themselves (GAP Committee on Aging, 1994). Similarly, reviews of the effectiveness of neuroleptics with behavioural problems in dementia suggest that, despite their widespread usage, they often have little or no benefit (Schneider *et al.*, 1990). Adverse side-effects or even paradoxical effects are also common in dementia. In this context behavioural and environmental interventions make sense as additional tools in the treatment of dementia, having few or no adverse side-effects and a reasonable degree of efficacy in controlling difficult behaviours.

Because the dementing illnesses have such dramatic and unrelenting progressive effects, it is easy to adopt a reductionist viewpoint when confronted with problem behaviours. By automatically assuming that a problem is caused by the illness, we may miss events which trigger the

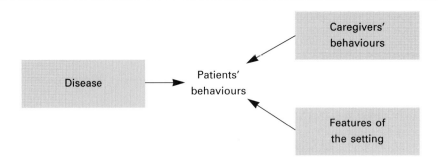

Figure 1. A model of behavioural problems in dementia.

behaviour or which reinforce it. In contrast to a reductionist perspective, behaviour in dementia can best be understood as the interaction of disease and environment, as shown in Figure 1. From this interactive perspective, the effect of dementing illness is to increase the probability that a variety of problematic behaviours will occur. The illness reduces thresholds for disturbed or agitated behaviour at several levels. One immediate impact is the loss of neurones in key regions of the brain and the corresponding deficits of critical neurotransmitters involved in regulation of mood and behaviour. The cognitive changes in the disease also make problem behaviour more likely. Because of their cognitive deficits patients are more likely to misunderstand or miscommunicate with other people or become frightened by their inability to relate present to past. They also have more difficulty initiating activities and keeping themselves occupied. Nonetheless, behaviours do not occur in a vacuum. Patients remain responsive to the surrounding environment, with behaviour occurring in response to specific events or as the consequence of previous patterns of reinforcement. Even in advanced dementia, events trigger problem behaviour, and responses to problems have the inadvertent effect of reinforcing them. The dementing illness, then, makes a variety of problems more likely to occur, but when and how often they occur are related to patterns of interaction and stimulation within a particular setting.

This can be illustrated with a common example involving dementia that clinicians learn about early in their careers. If someone walks up behind a dementia patient (with moderate or moderately severe impairment) and begins talking without first making eye contact, a frequent response is that the patient is startled and hits out. A reductionist approach is to view this situation as illustrating that dementia *causes* aggressive behaviour. But the real cause is an interaction of disease and an inexpert way of approaching the patient. The behavioural episode might further be altered by characteristics of the setting, such as the noise level or amount of other activities.

Sleep problems provide another example of the complex relationship of disease and environment. It is well known that sleep disturbances are very common in dementing illnesses and that centres in the brain that regulate sleep and waking are damaged. Yet it is also clear that sleep problems are more common among patients who nap during the daytime. Interventions which increase activity during the daytime can be an efficient and effective way of improving sleep at night. As an example, in an ongoing study of adult day care for dementia patients (Zarit *et al.*, 1996), a majority of family members using adult day care for relatives suffering from dementing illnesses report that patients sleep better on days when they attend the programme. A combination of structured activity and decreased opportunities for unscheduled naps may improve sleep during the night for dementia patients (as they do for the rest of us). Characteristics of settings which are conducive to sleep and activity can also contribute to the establishment of appropriate patterns.

A BASIC BEHAVIOURAL APPROACH TO DEMENTIA

First, this chapter will explore a basic approach to behavioural treatment in dementia, which the author and colleagues have used over the years in management of a variety of problems (Zarit *et al.*, 1985; Zarit, 1996; see also Stokes, 1996; Teri and Logsdon, 1990). This approach represents a process of how to think about and identify behavioural treatments, rather than a set of stock responses for specific problems. The author believes that this strategy is necessary because the specific events that trigger or reinforce a problem can vary widely depending on the patient and setting. This method involves working with caregivers, whether the family of the patient or staff, to gather key information and implement interventions.

There are two components of this approach: (1) viewing behaviour in the context of a memory-impairing disease and (2) problem-solving. The starting-point is to help caregivers to look at specific behaviour problems as due to a memory-impairing disease. Caregivers often misunderstand or misinterpret common problems. They may, for example, believe that a patient asks the same question over and over again to annoy the caregiver or to get attention, or because of laziness. The author's team encourage caregivers to think about why someone with a memory-impairing disease would behave in this way; that is, that the patient actually cannot remember.

An important step is helping caregivers to avoid reasoning or arguing with patients over factual issues. Families, particularly, become caught in logical traps. They believe they can reason with patients and thereby change incorrect beliefs or memories, but patients stubbornly insist they are right. Patients may insist, for example, that they want to see their long-deceased mothers, or to go home when they are already at home. Reorienting them to reality (or to our notion of reality) does not work. It is simply not possible to persuade patients with massive cognitive deficits that they are mistaken. In fact, reminding patients that their mothers are dead is often upsetting, since they experience it as a new loss, and the result is more agitation. This type of argument often causes a lot of distress among caregivers and unnecessary agitation among patients.

As an alternative way of approaching these situations, the author encourages caregivers to think about why someone with memory loss would behave in this way, and what they must be feeling at this time. Although caregivers cannot respond effectively to the content of these types of communications, it is possible to respond to the underlying emotions, for example by providing comfort or reassurance, or by reminiscing about the patient's mother. In this way, the patient's feelings are validated, and the emotion which may be driving the agitated behaviour is diminished.

Increasing the caregiver's understanding of problem behaviours flows naturally into the second step, problem-solving. Problem-solving is used to address persistent troubling behaviours. Drawn from contemporary behaviour therapy, problem-solving involves a series of steps to identify causes and reinforcers of current problems and to generate and implement possible solutions (see Table 1). The starting-point is to pinpoint a specific behaviour or problem (e.g. agitation, depressed behaviours) and to have the caregiver observe it over a period of several days. Caregivers should note when the problem occurs, what went before it (antecedents) and what followed the behaviour (reinforcers). In dementia, for example, inactivity is a frequent antecedent of agitated behaviour and the consequence, or reinforcer, is attention. This initial step also provides a baseline of how often the problem occurs, against which interventions can be measured.

Once a pattern of antecedents and consequences is identified, one can work with caregivers to identify strategies to change or head off the problem. Strategies need to be specific and practical and within the ability of the caregiver to manage. Family members who are feeling overwhelmed may need encouragement to identify possible solutions. They can be encouraged to brainstorm ideas, saying anything that comes to mind without censoring their responses. This approach sometimes helps them to overcome their feelings of hopelessness and to use their own coping resources to identify solutions.

The next step is to select a solution. Sometimes the best choice is obvious. Again, however, caregivers experiencing a lot of stress may have difficulty in selecting a solution. In that case they can compare different strategies using the method of pros and cons, which was developed by Beck and his associates in the treatment of depression (Beck et al., 1979). In this approach, caregivers write down advantages and drawbacks of each approach (includ-

Table 1. The problem-solving approach
to management of behaviour problems.

1. Assessment
2. Identify antecedents and consequences
3. Generate solutions
4. Select a solution
5. Rehearse the solution
6. Implement and evaluate

ing doing nothing). By putting down on paper their assessment of different approaches, they can more easily make a decision to try out one strategy.

Rehearsing the steps involved in the behavioural intervention before it is actually tried out can head off problems. Caregivers can identify parts of the plan that are not realistic or if there are obstacles that they need to take into account.

Finally, the solution is implemented. At that point caregivers should continue monitoring how often the problem occurs in order to evaluate how successful this strategy has been.

Typical interventions to prevent problems from occurring include changing a routine or, particularly, introducing activities. Having patients become more active in structured programmes that build on well-learned motor skills which are not affected until late in the disease can reduce agitated behaviour and other common problems (Zarit *et al.*, 1996). Other solutions include showing patients more affection, changing which staff interact with a patient or how they interact, or making a change in the patient's daily routine (because, after all, patients cannot remember other people's schedules for them). Scheduling is a particularly effective way of managing incontinence, which frequently occurs from not remembering to go to the toilet. A related behavioural approach has been effective for the treatment of depression among dementia patients, resulting in improved mood both for them and for their caregivers (Teri, 1994).

Problem-solving is compatible with the use of medications. In fact, medications to control behaviour or mood should be considered as one of the possible strategies for intervention. If the caregiver obtains a baseline of the frequency of the targeted problem before a medication is introduced, then it will be possible to make an accurate evaluation of the effectiveness of treatment. By viewing medications as one possible strategy and carefully monitoring their effectiveness, clinicians can develop more rational treatment approaches.

Problem-solving can also be used to identify antecedents and consequences of caregiver stress. Rather than pinpointing a specific behaviour problem, caregivers can note when they feel the most stress, and what has led up to that. Sometimes, it will be revealed that no one problem or behaviour is overwhelming. Instead, the accumulation of small stressors without a break leads to difficulties. Solutions can then focus on how the caregiver can prevent the build-up of stress, such as arranging for respite care.

Like any other treatment, behavioural approaches are complex and require training to use them effectively. Because they often appear simple and direct, clinicians often take too casual an approach, applying them incorrectly or inadequately. To be effective, behavioural treatment must be systematic and follow certain general principles

ENVIRONMENTAL INTERVENTIONS IN DEMENTIA

An extensive literature has developed in environmental features that promote adaptive behaviour in dementia patients. Much of this literature emphasizes the institutional setting, and careful, empirical research on which specific aspects of settings make a difference remains to be done. Some general recommendations can be made, however, based on case-studies of special settings designed for dementia patients (Cohen and Day, 1994; Malmberg and Zarit, 1993; Parmalee and Lawton, 1990; Regnier, 1994).

First, settings need to be secure to prevent continuing struggles over entrances and, especially, exits from the facility. Disguising the main entrance and providing residents with areas where they can walk freely can be very helpful. Many newer institutional settings include garden areas where patients can walk freely. Although the specific value of these open areas has not been assessed, they are used frequently by a subset of patients and may serve to provide reassurance to others that they could go out if they wanted to.

Secondly, a variety of environmental reminders can be used so that patients can identify their own rooms and stay out of the rooms of other residents. Besides names, photographs can be useful cues. Varying the decor and colours can also be helpful. These reminders should not take on the heavy-handed approach often seen in orientation training. Instead, staff can use simple and practical procedures to identify what kinds of reminders help with important concerns, such as helping patients to find their own rooms.

Thirdly, settings need to have relatively low levels of background noise. Noise can be agitating as well as contributing to problems in communication for hearing-impaired individuals. A major characteristic of successful settings for the treatment of dementia may be low levels of noise (Malmberg and Zarit, 1993).

Fourthly, settings need to have programmes of activities that engage patients. A general strategy is to build on established skills, rather than teaching new activities. Patients may have a variety of intact motor skills and functional behaviours that can serve as the basis for a programme of activities (Baum et al., 1993). Simple repetitive activities such as weight-bearing exercise may engage some patients and improve their overall fitness. Staff may find that they must provide a lot of individual attention, especially as the disease advances (Malmberg and Zarit, 1993), but involvement remains possible.

Fifthly, regular exposure to daylight has been found by some facilities to reduce sundowning (periods of disorientation during the later afternoon and early evening) among residents. If there is an area of the facility with windows where patients can sit, this can serve as the focus of a lot of informal social activity, as well as reducing problems due to inadequate exposure to light.

More than any single environmental characteristic, an overriding principle in the development of a setting for dementia patients is allowing for autonomy (Hofland, 1995). That can be accomplished through design of the setting; for example, avoiding conflict over the entrance to the facility, or providing residents with single rooms. Autonomy is conveyed, however, through the attitudes and behaviours of staff. Staff can convey respect to patients, redirecting their behaviour only when necessary and always in kind ways. A skilled staff who understand the effects of dementia on behaviour and who can tolerate the disordered communications and behaviour of dementia patients can create an effective programme, even in facilities that are not modern.

CONCLUSIONS

Behavioural and environmental treatments can result in substantial improvements in behaviours, with few or no adverse consequences. Staff in dementia care facilities and families can be trained in basic approaches that maximize the remaining abilities of patients and minimize disruptive behaviours. These interventions contribute to an overall programme of treatment for dementia.

REFERENCES

Baum, C., Edwards, D.F. and Morrow-Howell, N. (1993). Identification and measurement of productive behaviors in senile dementia of the Alzheimer type. *Gerontologist* **33**, 403–408.

Beck, A.T., Rush, D., Shaw, D. and Emery, G. (1979). *Cognitive Therapy of Depression*. Guilford, New York.

Cohen, U. and Day, K. (1994). Emerging trends in environments for people with dementia. *Am J Alzheimer's Care Relat Disord Res* **9**, 3–11.

GAP Committee on Aging (1994). Impact of tacrine in the care of patients with Alzheimer's disease. *Am J Geriatr Psychiatry* **2**, 285–288.

Hinchliffe, A.C., Hyman, I.L., Blizard, B. and Livingston, G. (1995). Behavioural complications of dementia – can they be treated? *Int J Geriatr Psychiatry* **10**, 839–847.

Hofland, B.F. (1995). Resident autonomy in long–term care: paradoxes and challenges. In: Gamroth, L.M., Semradek, J. and Tornquist, E.M. (Eds), *Enhancing Autonomy in Long–Term Care: Concepts and Strategies.* Springer, New York, pp. 15–33.

Malmberg, B. and Zarit, S.H. (1993). Group homes for dementia patients: an innovative model in Sweden. *Gerontologist* **31**, 682–686.

Parmelee, P.A. and Lawton, M.P. (1990). The design of special environments for the aged. In: Birren, J.E. and Schaie, K.W. (Eds), *Handbook of the Psychology of Aging (3rd edn).* Academic Press, San Diego, CA, pp. 464–488.

Regnier, V. (1994).*Assisted Living Housing for the Elderly: Design Innovations from the United States and Europe.* Van Nostrand Reinhold, New York.

Schneider, L.S., Pollock, V.E. and Lyness, S.A. (1990). A metaanalysis of controlled trials of neuroleptic treatment in dementia. *J Am Geriatr Soc* **38**, 553–563.

Stokes, G. (1996). Challenging behaviour in dementia: a psychological approach. In: Woods, R.T. (Ed.), *Handbook of the Clinical Psychology of Aging.* John Wiley & Sons, London, pp. 601–828.

Teri, L. (1994). Behavioral treatment of depression in patients with dementia. *Alzheimer's Dis Assoc Discord* **8** (suppl 3), 66–74.

Teri, L. and Logsdon, R. (1990). Assessment and management of behavioral disturbances in Alzheimer's disease. *Compr Ther* **16**, 36–42.

Teri, L., Rabins, P., Whitehouse, P. *et al.* (1992). Management of behavior disturbance in Alzheimer disease: current knowledge and future directions. *Alzheimer Dis Assoc Disord* **6**, 77–88.

Zarit, S.H. (1996). Interventions with family caregivers. In: Zarit, S.H. and Knight, B. (Eds), *A Guide to Psychotherapy and Aging: Effective Interventions in a Life Span Context.* American Psychological Association, Washington, DC, pp. 139–162.

Zarit, S.H., Orr, N.K. and Zarit, J.M. (1985). *The Hidden Victims of Alzheimer's Disease: Families Under Stress.* New York University Press, New York.

Zarit S.H., Stephens, M.A.P., Townsend, A. and Greene, R. (1996). Stress reduction for family caregivers: effects of day care use. Paper presented at the Meeting of the American Psychological Association, Toronto, Canada.

Advances in Old Age Psychiatry: Chromosomes to Community Care
Edited by C. Holmes and R. Howard
© 1997 Wrightson Biomedical Publishing Ltd

10

Ethical and Legal Issues in the Care of Demented Old People

ROB JONES

Department of Health Care of the Elderly, University of Nottingham Medical School, Nottingham, UK

INTRODUCTION

Glimpsing the approaching dawn of a new millennium, it seems right to look forward to see what will be the issues of the future – though the future in so many ways grows from the past. The possible new ethical and legal themes are legion and necessarily only a few can be briefly highlighted. However, the horizon of the next century seems worth scanning.

One broad background perspective from the past remains a firm feature of the present and seems set to figure large in the future: the very negative, unattractive stereotypes and prejudices so many have about dementia and services for dementia, a perceptual problem against which we struggle to provide good ethical care.

Further background arises from Francis Fukuyama's declaration in America in 1991 of the end of history (Fukuyama, 1992) – since when history seems to have moved on apace – but Jonsen followed in 1992 by his declaration of the end of medical ethics (Jonsen, 1992). The latter assertion also seems not to have been quite right. But Jonsen's great concern was that overweening bureaucratic regulation and cost-containment were destroying the freedom of doctors to exercise professional clinical judgement with good ethical decisions. Again, this is important background for us, also looking forward into the future.

Although for many health professionals dealing with dementia the deliberations of lawyers about their work may seem like a perception of hell, this would, of course, be quite wrong. But certain legal deliberations will be most important for dementia services (Law Commission, 1995). The Law Commission's proposed Bill for a legal framework to deal with mental incapacity seems certain to become law by the year 2000 and its thinking seems set to dominate our practice at least until 2010.

Interestingly, Grimley Evans (1987) around a decade ago lambasted, or at least categorized, the law and lawyers as anethical – without ethics – and in the Law Commission report it is hard to find any mention of the words ethics or ethical. But this will be a key document impacting on clinical practice and some themes from it merit exploration here.

CONCERNS WITH RESEARCH IN DEMENTIA

This major area can only briefly be mentioned but there must be some concern in relation to the proposed Bill's regulation of research in people with dementia. A new Mental Incapacity Research Committee will be set up, in addition to present mechanisms, a national body whose agreement would be necessary for any research of a nontherapeutic nature with incapable demented people. It seems certain that, during the parliamentary passage of any Bill, attempts would be made to strengthen what some might see as 'anti-research provisions' in it. In the interests of furthering dementia research vigilance will be necessary, as some take the extreme attitude that, by definition, no research whatsoever should be undertaken on demented people incapable of consent. Certainly, Fulford and Hope rightly argue against a too black and white approach, an unwarranted desire for ethical certainty here and in other areas (Fulford and Hope, 1994). Clearly, it is in the interests of the whole community to ensure that appropriate and effective research with dementia is able to continue.

PRACTICAL CONCERNS IN THE MEDIA

Research is a special area but, of course, day by day a host of familiar and unfamiliar practical problems with demented people arise. Some concerns which have crept into the media in recent years include:

- prolonging life through 'flu vaccinations;
- high-cost potential new treatments, such as tacrine – limiting the budget and deciding who should get them;
- genetic screening: the right to know for patient and family, and the patient's choice to know, which may limit the knowledge of other family members;
- the value (for whom?) and ethics of presymptomatic diagnosis.

Such issues will require increasing and wide ethical debate.

Long-standing common themes are decision-making without consent and the possible need for compulsion. But confidentiality and telling the truth (Jackson, 1991) are also difficult areas. Clear-cut, hard-and-fast answers are not yet, perhaps, available here, but it is the mark of a good service to consider properly dignity, privacy, confidentiality, and truth-telling with demented patients.

Public opinion on telling the truth to patients may be surprising. A Canadian survey showed that one-third of the public wanted doctors to conceal facts from patients at the request of family members. And this was not particularly with dementia. Only 58% wanted spouses to make decisions for them if they became impaired, revealing a perhaps surprisingly lower level of trust of spouses than might have been anticipated.

ETHICAL PRINCIPLES

In dealing with the multiplicity of practical problems, it seems wisest to approach them by applying the well accepted medical ethical principles (Bloch and Chodoff, 1991): autonomy; beneficence; non-maleficence; equity or justice. But even these have been criticized as an uneasy compromise when ethical issues need to be addressed in our so-called post-modernist society. Some hold at an extreme level that we are now a society of moral strangers to each other – we no longer agree on what is the right thing to do. This may be going a little far, but certainly there are tensions between the seemingly clear principles, any consensus on their application, and the realities of day-to-day care and provisions (Hope, 1994). The practicality may be a little battered and not quite reflect the pure principles.

MENTAL INCAPACITY

Also perhaps a little vague and battered are approaches to assessing mental incapacity. These need sharpening up, and a spur will come with the proposed new Bill as it will develop a Code of Practice on the topic. Experienced clinicians need to be ready to advise sensibly on this. People should not need PhDs to be competent but some greater clarity and consistency in competency assessment is needed. In Toronto useful work has been underway with special Competency Clinics developing the area (Silberfeld and Fish, 1994). One feature the team has found there is the phenomenon of people who are capable of recognizing the consequences of their actions but who refuse to face them. Such seemingly sufficient cognitive capacity with insufficient concern for consequences is a difficult feature of the increasingly recognized frontal dementia syndromes.

Also relevant here is the concept of akrasia: being competent but being very weak-willed. This comes in particularly with some demented patients, as does also Gillon's idea of adequate autonomy (Gillon, 1994).

The present common-law test of capacity is 'does the person understand what is proposed to be done and why?' The Law Commission (1995) developed the area by proposing that mental incapacity should be 'by reason of mental disability', and that the person would be so classified because of being incapable of at least one of the following:

1. Of understanding the information relevant to a decision about, for example, treatment or care, including information about the consequences of the decision
2. Of retaining the information
3. Of making a decision independently in the light of this information
4. Of communicating a decision.

AUTONOMY

The four principles are the best ethical principles so far to achieve wide support and merit some examination of their practicality. The scope of their application, as Gillon has suggested, is most important, especially with dementia (Gillon, 1994). Autonomy, that is, personal choice, is clearly difficult with demented people, but there are a number of possible ways of promoting autonomy and the proposed new Bill will promote them.

Advance Statements about Health is the terminology which it uses to cover what previously has variously been called an Advance Directive or a Living Will – a witnessed and signed statement made while the individual is still capable, describing how health care decisions should be approached if mental incapacity should occur. Advance Directives, probably, already have legal weight, but with this new Bill they certainly will. A Code of Practice will be drawn up to cover them, and Continuing Powers of Attorney, which will be like the present Enduring Powers of Attorney: drawn up ahead of time while the individual is still mentally capable, and naming a specific individual to take over decision-making if mental incapacity supervenes, but they will be able essentially to cover all decisions including health and social care.

Again, it will be most important for clinicians to give sensible, practical advice guiding the construction of any Codes of Practice for these areas, with their awareness of the realities of therapeutic and health care decisions.

These mechanisms will rightly seek to further autonomy, seeking at least partly the substitute judgement, the choice the demented person would have made if not impaired.

However, this could go too far. Doctors know well the old lady who happily settles into residential care, having forgotten her previous vehement rejection of such 'terrible homes', clearly now enjoying a secure and high quality of life compared with her perhaps previously rather bleak, vulnerable, or even greatly suffering existence. Rejecting such help, without real knowledge of it, would not be an informed judgement and should have limited use in forming an appropriate substitute judgement. But too narrowly interpreting 'autonomy', too rigidly reaching substitute judgements, would outlaw such a happy outcome. The skinny and superficial young man might well view the fat, middle-aged man whom he is likely to become as better off dead, but think differently when actually living this reality himself. It would be wrong if real therapeutic benefit were ruled out by ill-judged, supposed expressions of informed autonomy, made much earlier in life.

And, we have evidence that intimate surrogate decision-makers frequently decide in ways conflicting with the expressed wishes of the patient, taking account of how decisions will affect their own lives or other family members, or affect family unity. Nelson (and others) have rightly noted that our model for family substitute judgements rather presupposes ideal family relationships, often not present with the author's patients, or perhaps at least rather strained by the effects of the dementia (Sonnenblick *et al.*, 1993; Emanuel and Emanuel, 1993). Perhaps for this reason, the Law Commission (1995) rejected granting any *automatic* proxy decision-making powers to the next of kin.

However, family-carer substitute decision-makers seem to me to be much more likely to be in tune with the patient's best interests, but we do need more work (as Elliott has said) to define how the interests of such family intimates could impact upon substitute judgements (Elliott and Weiger, 1994). Certainly we must avoid rigid bureaucratic processes and the delays which excessive legal mechanisms could introduce, preventing timely relief of distress. Decisions should be kept as close as possible to the patient.

BENEFICENCE

Turning to beneficence, clearly we will be in some difficulty here about doing good if we really are all moral strangers to each other and cannot decide what is good. But leaving that aside, here we surely come to the difficult area of judging quality of life. The Elliotts have argued with some justice (Elliott and Elliott, 1991) that it is no more possible logically to imagine a demented person's life than to imagine the life of a dog. But it is important that we do try to empathize and to understand as far as we can. Actually, the typical loss of insight protects against much distress for the demented patient, and though friends and family may experience keen distress, perceiving deterioration and 'indignity', the 'sufferer' involved commonly seems to suffer little, if at all. In fact, a bad quality of life is usually fairly obvious, and suffering easy to see. But whether people get the right skilled care which they need can be highly influential in constructing the picture we see. If, due to lack of necessary staff and resources, dependency needs are not met and relievable suffering is not properly dealt with, then the quality of life may 'artificially' be made to appear much worse. We cannot collaborate with judgements that the patient would be better off dead, when really what is needed is better and more appropriate care (Jones, 1987).

With quality of life, surprising judgements may be made. Grimley Evans (1987) describes a patient left after a stroke in a highly disabled, dependent and, seemingly, most undignified state but whose enjoyment of life was actually probably greater than he had ever previously known. He had always led a lonely, downtrodden, impoverished and unhappy life, and now found himself waited on hand and foot by charming, caring, attractive female nurses, attentive to his every need. What could be a private hell for one person may be experienced as quiet contentment by another. And how much should be the family's feelings be decisive in this area? True substitute judgement may be very hard to exercise.

ACTING REASONABLY IN THE BEST INTERESTS

The proposed new Bill will give a General Authority to carers, family, professionals – or whoever may be reasonably involved with mentally incapable persons – to act reasonably within limits in their best interests without any necessary legal procedure, and this should also have associated with it a Code of Practice.

In order to be seen to be acting reasonably in the best interests of the individual, the Law Commission (1995) would have you consider:

1. the ascertainable past and present wishes of the person concerned, and the factors that person would consider if able to do so;
2. the need to permit and encourage the person to participate, or improve his or her ability to participate, as fully as possible in anything done for, and any decisions affecting him or her;
3. the views of other people whom it is appropriate and practicable to consult about the person's wishes and feelings, and what would be in his or her best interests;
4. whether the purpose for which any action or decision is required can be as effectively achieved in a manner less restrictive of the person's freedom of action.

Various points arise for further discussion, but only a few can be briefly considered here. 'The ascertainable past and present wishes of the person concerned, and feelings and factors they would consider' sounds straightforward. But, in reality, these may often be in conflict. Does the doctor resolve that conflict, and how? Other family members will probably have to help in this process. How will their wishes and feelings affect matters? At any rate, if the doctor's behaviour is objected to, these will be legal standards against which it is judged.

Who are the other appropriate people? What happens when they disagree, which is usually the case with difficult cases?

Most of these 'best interests' criteria are noticeably less concerned with the more traditional, narrower view of what constitutes best interests, but rather with involving and balancing various wishes and views. The Law Commission's view is that consideration of 'best interests' must necessarily include attention to autonomy and require involving others to help determine decisions. But, to the experienced clinician, it is clear that competing and contradictory themes could well arise, leading to great difficulty and delay before they are resolved. If people are to receive necessary treatment in a timely fashion to relieve disease, and distress, the need for another Code of Practice seems to loom into view again.

NON-MALEFICENCE

Non-maleficence means 'above all to do no harm'. But sometimes a difficult balance has to be achieved between, say, the risk of unwanted side-effects, with neuroleptics, for example, and the severe distress or dangerous agitation otherwise being untreated. Recent concern has been expressed following a study of the use of neuroleptics in residential care homes in Glasgow (McGrath and Jackson, 1996) and their possible inappropriate use. In 1996 a study got underway to obtain valuable evidence on this matter in Nottingham, and has already shown significant long-term repeat prescribing with such patients with little evidence of necessary reviews and monitoring.

Using medication only as kind of chemical restraint seems clearly unethical. The goal must be therapeutic benefit, though in the real world the team may need to balance possible over-sedation of one seriously violent patient against even greater possible harm to other frail patients. Again, though, we cannot collude with a real need for more care staff being improperly covered up by medication used for restraint.

Similar workers apply to means of physical restraint of demented patients (Pitt, 1988). In an emergency special measures may be necessary, but the routine use of physical mechanisms of restraint appears unethical. Rather, this is likely to be merely for the convenience of staff or to save resources (Royal College of Nursing, 1986).

In this area, to make good judgement an effective and skilled multidisciplinary team is essential. Proper training and supervised experience are needed for team members, as are proper resources. Although judging quality of life is difficult, it is central to proper ethical care. And the effectively collaborating, experienced multidisciplinary team, working carefully with all those involved, especially with family carers, seems better placed than any other body or group sensitively and accurately to make appropriate judgements.

Working in this way, aiming for beneficence, the team should be aiding, seeking, and promoting the best interests, including the autonomy, of the incapable individual (Jones, 1993).

EQUITY

Equity, or justice, means allowing everyone the same consideration and chance to benefit and, from our perspective, this especially includes the demented. Stereotyping, prejudice and ageism may mean the community accords a very low priority to resource provision (Dickson and Welsh, 1991). Some of the deficits and impairments which we find clinically in dementia have been seen by some as diminishing the individual's serious 'right to life' (Tooley, 1972). It has been argued that demented individuals lack 'valid claims on grounds of justice to health care treatment' because of a lack of 'personhood' – because they are not persons (Brock, 1988).

Too easy and too rigid categorization in this area seems unhelpful and dangerous. A temporary delirium state can mean that a demented person – or even a relatively normal person – can appear, albeit temporarily, to have 'diminished personhood' in this frame of reference.

In some senses the demented patient can become a 'new person' as the ravages of dementia proceed. Insight, recent memory, and more subtle functions are lost. But personal and individual responses to a less well understood world are nevertheless still evident until the final stages – whilst a capacity for joy remains. Such persons should not be simply dismissed.

As demented people are so vulnerable perhaps more rather than less attention should be given to their ethical claims. But we cannot ethically ignore the cost of treatment, and must also consider health care provision for the wider community.

The Quality Adjusted Life Years (QALYs) approach has been one attempt to standardize consideration of the usefulness of treatment of various illnesses: how many Quality Adjusted Life Years are added by the treatment (Rosser and Watts, 1972)? With some approaches it is possible to categorize certain states as 'worse than death' – and many might view dementia in this way. But the approach can be as discriminating against the elderly as they are inevitably less able to look forward to large numbers of 'quality' years (Black, 1991) and it may be insufficiently sensitive to the complexities of the 'quality' calculations which are appropriate in the context of elderly people (Williams, 1987, 1992). Harris worries also that with such techniques some (including, presumably, the demented elderly) may be seen as 'the enemy': unfortunate enough to be sick and dependent and threatening the culture of contentment of the young, fit 'good guys' by making competing claims on resources, concern and taxation (Harris, 1991).

PROBLEMS AT THE END OF LIFE

Certain areas should be mentioned as major practical problems, though only brief consideration can be given here: suicide; assisted death; euthanasia; letting die.

Suicide as yet does not often arise as a problem with dementia and the elderly, but this may change with refinement of techniques for the early detection of mild dementia and more accurate presymptomatic testing or genetic screening. When is suicide a reasonable or at least allowable choice for such an elderly person? Clearly there is great scope for debate here, with people with bleak, empty, isolated and, perhaps, foreseeably, disability-ridden and decline-ridden lives.

Assisted death (the deliberate killing of a patient through humane medical means) has been seen as ethically acceptable in some circumstances (Institute of Medical Ethics, 1990, 1991) such as persistent vegetative state, and the Tony Bland case (Appeal Case 789, 1993) and indeed the more recent case considered by the Scottish courts (Dyer, 1996) arguably have legalized passive euthanasia in the UK.

What about demented patients and assisted death? Governments and others want to cut costs. Could 'assisted death' gradually become accepted as reasonable and in the best interests of the elderly demented?

The British Medical Association (1993) has rejected significant change in the law to legalize euthanasia or assisted death, viewing this as too major a change in clinical practice. Once permissible, standards would tend to drift downwards, with gradual creeping acceptance of the previously unaccept-able. Interestingly, British work with relatives of patients who had recently died showed non-spouse relatives significantly more likely than spouse relatives to have felt that a significantly earlier death should have occurred. This suggests considerable scope for intergenerational conflict about the patient's best interests.

In the UK there appears to be a consensus (Stanley, 1989; Jones, 1993) that psychiatrists, working closely with their multidisciplinary teams and with family carers, with good professional practice, with relief of patients' suffer-ing as the prime aim, can withhold or withdraw life-sustaining treatment in the hopeless, final stages of life for some physically ill severely demented patients. Assisted death seems neither clinically necessary nor ethically appropriate with demented old people.

There is also a wider view. The inevitable coarsening effect on professional morale and practice – and on society – if it became routine for perplexed, nonconsenting, helpless, elderly demented people to be 'assisted' into death seems alarming. To the trust given to doctors and nurses incalculable harm could be done. The potential for misuse seems enormous and always likely to be far ahead of attempts at its prevention.

CONCLUSIONS

A useful illustration is provided by giving the six basic principles of medical ethics established by Stanford University Medical Center Committee on Ethics (quoted in Williams, 1992): preserve life; alleviate suffering; do no harm; tell the truth; respect patient autonomy; deal justly with patients. From the perspective of health care of the elderly in the UK, we might suggest that 'preserve life' should not be the first principle and that it be modified to 'respect life', at least when considering older people with dementia. But this, perhaps, also shows how our perspective changes, as such a shift in emphasis seems much more obviously appropriate and acceptable now than it did, say, a decade ago. Also with a UK perspective and a broader public health perspective, perhaps, we would add: respect all possible patients; respect carers.

And the professional duty for the doctor here amidst this conflict is to find the appropriate ethical balance. It is important that doctors retain flexibility for their practice, though bound by a clear ethical duty and obligation. We must all seek to avoid excessive legalistic, bureaucratic, and overweening control over good professional and ethical practice. We must demonstrably have the highest regard for patients' best interests, which must centrally include autonomy. But we must also promote wide and continuing debate, as there are no final answers here. The best care is likely where most decisions are taken flexibly and properly at grass-roots level. We need to assert this message and to win the support and trust of our communities through our demonstrable good ethical practice.

REFERENCES

Appeal Cases 789 (1993). *Airedale NHS Trust* v. *Bland*.
Black, D. (1991). Paying for Health. *J Med Ethics* **17**, 117–123.
Bloch, S. and Chodoff, P. (1991). *Psychiatric Ethics (2nd edn.)* Oxford University Press, Oxford.
British Medical Association (1993). *Report to the House of Lords Select Committee on Medical Ethics from the British Medical Association*. Medical Ethics Committee, BMA.

Brock, D.W. (1988). Justice and the severely demented elderly. *J Med Phil* **13**, 73–99.

Dickson, J. and Welsh, H.G. (1991). Priority setting: lessons from Oregon. *Lancet* **337**, 891–894.

Dyer, C. (1996). Judge rules doctors can let coma woman die. *The Guardian* 25 Apr, 7.

Elliott, C. and Weiger, C. (1994). Mental capacity, responsibility and mental health legislation. *Curr Opin Psychiatry* **7**, 423–425.

Elliott, C. and Eliott, B. (1991). From the patient's point of view: medical ethics and the moral imagination. *J Med Ethics* **17**, 173–178.

Emanuel, L.L. and Emanuel, E.J. (1993). Decisions at the end of life: guided by communities of patients. *Hastings Cent Rep* **5**, 6–14.

Fukuyama, F. (1992). *The End of History and the Last Man*. Hamish Hamilton, London.

Fulford, K.W. and Hope, T. (1994). Psychiatric ethics: a bioethical ugly duckling? In: Gillon, R. (Ed.), *Principles of Health Care Ethics*. John Wiley & Sons, Chichester, pp. 681–695.

Gillon, R. (1994). Medical ethics: four principles plus scope. *BMJ* **309**, 184–188.

Grimley Evans, J. (1987). The sanctity of life. In: Elford, R.J. (Ed.), *Medical Ethics and Elderly People*. Churchill Livingstone, Edinburgh, pp. 78–92.

Harris, J. (1991). Unprincipled QUALYs: a response to Cubbon. *J Med Ethics* **17**, 185–188.

Hope, T. (1994). Ethics of treatment and research in psychiatry. *Curr Opin Psychiatry* **7**, 430–433.

Institute of Medical Ethics Working Party (1990). Assisted death. *Lancet* **336**, 610–613.

Institute of Medical Ethics Working Party (1991). Withdrawal of life-support from patients in a persistent vegetative state. *Lancet* **337**, 96–98.

Jackson, J. (1991). Telling the truth. *J Med Ethics* **17**, 5–9.

Jones, R.G. (1987). Problems in senile dementia. In: Elford, R.J. (Ed.), *Medical Ethics and Elderly People*. Churchill Livingstone, Edinburgh, pp. 49–68.

Jones, R.G. (1993). Ethical and legal issues in the care of demented people. *Rev Clin Gerontol* **3**, 55–68.

Jonsen, A.R. (1992). The end of medical ethics. *J Am Geriatr Soc* **40**, 393–397.

Law Commission (1995). *Mental Incapacity. Report No. 231*. London: HMSO.

McGrath, A.M. and Jackson, G.A. (1996). Survey of neuroleptic prescribing in residents of nursing homes in Glasgow. *BMJ* **312**, 611–612.

Pitt, B. (1988). Exercising restraint [Editorial]. *Int J Geriatr Psychiatry* **2**, 207–210.

Rosser, R.M. and Watts, V.C. (1972). The measurement of hospital output. *Int J Epidemiol* **1**, 361–366.

Royal College of Nursing (1986). *Improving Care of Elderly People in Hospital.* Joint publication of the Royal College of Nursing, British Geriatrics Society and the Royal College of Psychiatrists, London.

Silberfeld, M. and Fish, A. (1994). *When the Mind Fails: A Guide to Dealing with Incompetency*. University of Toronto Press, Toronto.

Sonnenblick, M., Friedlander, Y. and Steinberg, A. (1993). Dissociation between the wishes of terminally ill patients and decisions of their offspring. *J Am Geriatr Soc* **41**, 599–604.

Stanley, J.M. (1989). The Appleton Consensus: suggested international guidelines for decisions to forego medical treatment. *J Med Ethics* **15**, 129–136.

Tooley, N. (1972). Abortion and infanticide. *Phil Public Affairs* **2**, 37–65.

Williams, A. (1987). Quality-adjusted life-years. *Lancet* **i**, 1372.

Williams, A. (1992). Cost-effectiveness analysis: is it ethical? *J Med Ethics* **18**, 7–11.

Advances in Old Age Psychiatry: Chromosomes to Community Care
Edited by C. Holmes and R. Howard
© 1997 Wrightson Biomedical Publishing Ltd

11

Dementia Care in the UK: Looking Towards the Millenium

ELAINE MURPHY

Professor of Psychiatric Services Research and Development, United Medical and Dental Schools, London, UK

INTRODUCTION

Fifteen years ago the UK was the undisputed world leader in the field of psychiatry of old age and at present it remains the only country where there is a specialist consultant and separate identified service in nine out of ten districts. It is probable that within a year or two there will be a separate specialty of psychiatry of old age in every health district.

Developments in the UK were stimulated by the rapidly rising proportion of retired people, now one of the highest in the world at 17% of the population, but crucially also by the organizational structure of the National Health Service (NHS). There were large numbers of beds in old psychiatric institutions which during the 1950s and 1960s were rapidly being vacated by younger mentally ill people. Psychiatrists had not hitherto been very keen to provide a service for old people with dementia, but the old mental hospitals had traditionally accepted severely disabled dementia sufferers in the absence of any other institutional or community provision.

Until the early l980s, when the Government provided direct financial incentives for the independent sector to establish nursing homes, there were very few nursing home places in Britain. Elderly people with dementia who were too physically frail or behaviourally disturbed to be cared for adequately in residential care homes provided by the local authority were admitted by default to the psychiatric hospitals.

This difficult situation, in which general psychiatric services found themselves increasingly responsible for an unwanted but needy client group, undoubtedly encouraged the development of the new psychiatric subspecialty. If ordinary general psychiatrists did not want to take on the task of caring for these people, then someone needed to be specially appointed to do the job.

This unique combination of demographic and organizational pressures provided the structural context in which a handful of enthusiastic psychiatrists in the late 1960s and early 1970s took up the challenge, not only of improving the care of those who were admitted to psychiatric hospitals, but also of providing a service to those older people with dementia and their families living in the community who were often receiving very little help at all from the statutory services (Arie, 1981).

Psychiatric services for older people in the UK are remarkably homogeneous in their organization. This is not only because of the structural organization of the NHS but also because of the influence of the Royal College of Psychiatrists in vetting job descriptions of consultant appointments. The regional college adviser refuses to sanction the creation of jobs by health authorities or trusts which fail to provide certain physical facilities in hospital, including assessment and continuing care beds and a certain number of nursing and therapy staff. This has had the very beneficial effect of ensuring that inexperienced new consultants embarking on their first job at least have the bare minimum of essential tools in order to provide a basic assessment service. It has, however, also had the negative effect of producing a uniform model of care which has been detrimental to planning creative solutions to providing care in closer collaboration with local authority social care services, the independent sector and voluntary organizations. It has also fixed the lion's share of health service resources devoted to the care of people with dementia firmly in the hospital, with health care staff. There has been relative neglect of the essential social care support services which enable a confused old person to be cared for satisfactorily in the community. This is partly the fault of psychiatrists but also a result of the division between the health and social care systems. In the UK we now have the best-developed psychiatric assessment and treatment service for old people in the world, but it is much hampered in its effectiveness by the gaping hole in the community social care services. Social care developments, that is domestic and personal care, respite care, day care, overnight care, residential and nursing home care, and support systems for relatives, are remarkably varied both in content and volume from one geographical area to another (Murphy and Banerjee, 1993).

Paradoxically, the very people the system was set up to provide care for – those with dementia – are the least likely to be the focus of continuing input from the NHS service. The burgeoning numbers of Community Teams tend to focus on people with functional disorders and on those on whom they feel their professional skills are best deployed.

If the current situation is to be rectified – and it ought to be remembered that it is far too late to make dramatic changes by the year 2000 – then a shared vision must be established of where services should be nationally in five or ten years' time and a clear strategy for getting there developed. As

Goethe said, 'when you want to reach infinity, advance on all sides right until the end'.

PRINCIPLES OF CARE FOR PEOPLE WITH DEMENTIA

Any strategy aimed at improving the health of people with dementia must be driven by a vision of what can be achieved in terms of what public health experts now call 'health gain' for individuals and for populations of older people as a whole. Services for people with dementia are not only geared to the relief of burden of carers, as is sometimes assumed by health care planners, but should also be directed at relieving the distress and disability of the individuals themselves (Murphy and Banerjee, 1993). Service evaluations must be couched in terms of clinical and functional outcome for patients as well as outcomes as perceived by the satisfaction of caring families. This is self–evident for most medical disorders; it should be more widely recognized by public health planners and managers. How to measure outcomes is, however, exceedingly difficult. Establishing criteria and measures for judging the quality of life of people with dementia has been attempted in a variety of ways, but still needs much further development. Neverthless, we can start with some basic principles.

The principles proposed here will serve, in fact, as principles for any community health service for people who are seriously dependent on others for their well-being as a result of enduring physical and/or mental disorders. They are derived, but modified, from principles established by the USA National Institute of Mental Health in 1980 (Murphy, 1991). The criteria for an effective dementia care system are as follows:

- There must be a mechanism for identifying persons with dementia who are in need; it may also at times be necessary to reach out to those who do not wish to have help but are at risk of harm to themselves or others.
- The system must offer assistance in obtaining financial entitlements in the form of income support and disability allowances, to improve patients' and their carers' choices.
- It must offer 24–hour crisis assistance so that individuals are not left uncared for or unsupported during an acute episode of illness, no matter what time of the day or night a crisis arises.
- It must provide for social care needs of patients on a 24-hour basis.
- Services must be provided indefinitely and be available for an individual's lifetime if necessary.
- Services must provide adequate medical and psychiatric treatment on a continuing basis.
- Services must provide back–up support for family, friends and members

of the local community in order to minimize the burden of care which falls on other people's shoulders.

- The system must engage voluntary groups, community organizations and other members of the local community to maximize involvement in normal community activities.
- The system must operate so as to protect patients' rights and ensure that their civil liberties are not denied.
- Finally, the system must provide for the co–ordination, integration and binding together of services so that they function as one 'seamless service'.

HEALTH CARE AND SOCIAL CARE

Having established these basic service principles, it is also helpful to consider our services' ability to deliver two distinct types of care: first, those that provide for the 'ordinary needs' of daily life which every citizen needs and, second, those that provide for 'special needs' generated by mental disorder. This distinction is vitally important because dementia has a profound impact on the ability to carry out the tasks of daily life and to orchestrate the business of living in the community. 'Ordinary needs' include adequate income, housing, food and clothing, plus protection from physical harm, a means of daily occupation and the opportunity for emotional, spiritual and social fulfilment. The 'special needs' of a mentally disordered person are for specific medical and psychological treatments and rehabilitation.

In wealthier developed parts of the world, where health care provision has been dominated by a professional model of care emphasizing the importance of doctors, nurses and therapists, service provision has developed in a curiously lopsided way. We now have a system in the UK where the health care parts of our system are developing quickly, but where the basic social care support systems to enable people to live satisfactory lives in the community are rudimentary. As a consequence of this imbalance, families caring for people with mental disorders in old age still experience serious burden and stress. They lack assistance with the basic, practical, 'hands–on', domestic and personal care for the necessary numbers of hours per day, lack information about financial benefits available from the State – which are in any case insufficient to meet the real expenses of caring for a disabled old person – and have little choice of services. The Alzheimer's Disease Society in the UK stresses the need for, first, financial grants to caring relatives to enable them to choose the practical care services they judge most appropriate for their circumstances, and, secondly for an army of 'hands–on', practical carers who will provide a flexible number of hours of care to people in their own homes at times best suited to the client and their family carers. Research surveys have confirmed that these are key priorities for carers (Levin *et al.*, 1989).

BLOCKS TO IMPLEMENTING THE PRINCIPLES

Our current disparate system of services in which primary care health teams are remote, both from Social Services, from hospital-based teams, from voluntary organizations and from the independent sector is a clear recipe for fragmentation of services and poor overall planning. Furthermore, staffing structures and professional training remain a serious block to developing a more accessible and responsive service and one which can deliver effective social care.

Traditionally, the strongest influence on service development has come from the specialist NHS services, and it is unsurprising that we have created a world in our own image. We have to embrace the real need for change in our own style of service if the overall system is to more nearly meet our vision.

Table 1 outlines the current major blocks to implementing the service principles and also highlights the major action which needs to be taken at both Government and local level to achieve these goals.

A STRATEGY FOR THE MILLENIUM

We know that services do not change without first there being a shift in the hearts and minds of those who deliver them and also the provision of the right financial incentives to foster desired developments. In Table 1, the actions required fall into the following main categories:

1. *Financial resource transfer*: Allocation of care funds needs to shift from health care to social care and from secondary care to primary care. Benefits and tax incentives to foster the influence of older people themselves on making choices for their own care need to be devised.
2. *Human resources*: A major change in the staffing of services requires a rethink about the role of the senior health care professional. He or she needs to become an educator, 'consultant' and intermittent supporter rather than a pure clinician. We need also to review the skill-mix of those who provide care. Management training for community staff in the NHS is currently poor and hence there is little understanding of how to manage services in an operationally effective way in domiciliary and community settings. There are also huge multiprofessional training implications for general practitioners (GPs) and primary care staff.
3. *Recognize and strengthen the mixed economy of care*: Dementia care has always largely been provided by individuals themselves and their families. The statutory sector services, who traditionally have resourced, planned and delivered any services which were added on to this basic

Table 1. Dementia care action plan.

Principles of an effective service	Blocks in the system	Action required to achieve an effective service
Access mechanisms for identifying people in need	No active outreach by primary care team or social services; lack of GP awareness and involvement	Improve professional training for primary and social care staff Involve community groups Improve access through education of public
Maximize income to improve choices	Welfare rights workers remote from service system Cultural attitudes of 'property owners' – the cascade of wealth	Target benefits and tax mechanisms on sustaining people at home Welfare rights workers in service teams
24-hour crisis service	Currently a 9–5 work day only system in both NHS and LA	24-hour responsive primary care team with access to specialist advice quickly
24-hour social care service	No effective case-management system in place; insufficient resources invested in hands–on care; staff in teams are often trained professionals only	Transfer resources from specialist teams to primary health and social care teams Review and dramatically change skill mix and number of staff in primary care Train professionals to do more education, supervision and support in primary care
Continuing medical and psychiatric treatment if required	Poor co–ordination of specialist medical and psychiatric services for older people Poor GP training, especially in nursing homes Residents of institutions often denied appropriate care from all disciplines	Integrate specialist services in one consulting team; plan all services for elderly people as a whole Concentrate training for GPs in nursing home medicine Deploy specialist professionals in institutions
Focus on carers; services to reduce carer burden	Services are inflexible, do not engage carers in plans or offer real choices	Offer real choice by giving resources to carer to spend Statutory involvement of carers in planning system
Involvement of nonstatutory organizations in services	Private sector not involved in service development Voluntary organizations are insufficiently resourced and supported by statutory sector	Obligatory involvement of independent sector in planning, service development, training and quality assurance programmes Abolish competition Develop closer long-term relationships with providers
Protect patients' rights to liberty and rights to receive care	Advocacy services and service users' groups poorly developed for this group Institutionalization still too frequent Abuse common	Promote advocacy services Involve users with early dementia and 'proxy' users of same age Train for awareness of abuse
One integrated, co–ordinated 'seamless service' – a 'one-stop shop'	Health and social services operate separately; primary and secondary care are not integrated	Integrate health and social care primary care teams at GP practice level

family care, now need to realize that there are many other significant providers of care – notably the private 'for profit' residential and domiciliary care providers and a huge and growing independent sector of voluntary organizations and housing associations. Mechanisms for involving *all* the key players, as well as family carers, in the development of service policies and planning are largely in the gift of central Government through funding mechanisms.

To paraphrase the watchword of the American War of Independence, – 'No taxation without representation' – the author would say to the independent sector, 'No registration without representation'. The independent sector must get involved in planning, service development and training if public money is to be invested in such care homes.

No one organization or professional alone has the wisdom or skills to achieve the ideal service, but having seen the heartening major improvements that have been achieved over the past 20 years, the author cannot but help be optimistic that this vision can be achieved.

REFERENCES

Arie, T. (1981). Healthcare of the very elderly. Too frail a basket for so many eggs. In: Arie, T.(Ed.), *Health Care of the Elderly*. Croom Helm, London, pp. 11–19

Levin, E., Sinclair, I. and Gorback, P. (1989). *Families, services and confusion in old age*. Avebury, Aldershot.

Murphy, E. (1991). *After the Asylums*. Faber and Faber, London.

Murphy, E. and Banerjee, S. (1993). The organization of old age psychiatry services. *Rev Clin Gerontol* **3**, 367–378.

IV

Treatment and Prognosis
of Affective Disorders

12

Defeating Depression in Old Age

BRICE PITT
Department of Mental Health of the Elderly, St Charles' Hospital, London, UK

*The days of our years are threescore years & ten; and though men be so
strong that they come to fourscore years: yet is their strength then but
labour & sorrow*
Psalm 90, 10

*Crabbed age and youth cannot live together
Youth like summer morn, age like winter weather*
Shakespeare, *The Passionate Pilgrim*

In old age natural melancholy is almost an inseparable accident
Burton, *The Anatomy of Melancholy*

There are ageist assumptions that old age is necessarily fraught and gloomy
both in our classical literature and in our contemporary mythology and
attitudes. A popular television character, Victor Meldrew, in the series 'One
Foot in the Grave' epitomises 'crabbed age', and many young people, including doctors and nurses, assume that late life is dreary, empty, full of woes
and that to be miserable as well as old is normal (Cohen *et al.*, 1994). The
notion that late life depression is justified by bereavement, ill health, loneliness and having no further role is a pernicious obstacle to the recognition
and treatment of depressive illness (Pitt, 1995). In 1964 Williamson *et al.*
found that dementia and depression in elderly people were largely unknown
to their general practitioners, and matters were no better in Iliffe *et al.*'s
(1991) survey of general practice in north London. Macdonald (1986) found
that GPs could diagnose depression if put on their mettle by having a
researcher using the Brief Assessment Schedule to make an assessment
before or after the consultation, but making the diagnosis had no effect on
stimulating treatment.

The charter of the Royal College of Psychiatrists states that one of the
three aims of which it was founded is 'to further public education in the

science and practice of psychiatry and related subjects'. To this end a Public Education Committee was formed (hardly too soon!) in 1986. Its national objectives were:

- to achieve greater awareness and understanding of mental illness in order to overcome fear and prejudice
- to achieve greater awareness and understanding of psychiatry and its successes
- to raise awareness of the College and its functions
- to become the authoritative source of information on mental illness and on psychiatry

This entails approaches to the public, the professions (notably general practice), the National Health Service (purchasers, providers, advisers), the education system (catch 'em young!) and the media. Techniques include media training for the members of the College and its officers, press briefings and conferences, publishing commissioned articles (with 'a member of the Royal College of Psychiatrists' added to the by-line), fact sheets and leaflets distributed through GPs surgeries, the setting up of a Patients' Liaison Group (Lamont and Pitt, 1993) and special campaigns.

In the 150th anniversary year of the College the President's target was the stigma which attached to mental illness and the mentally ill; then in 1992, following an initiative by Dr Peter White and Mrs Vanessa Cameron developed by the PEC, the College launched a Defeat Depression campaign. This was partly inspired by the DART Campaign (Depression: awareness, recognition & treatment) in the USA, supported by the American Psychiatric Association.

Robert Burton wrote in his *Anatomy of Melancholy* in 1621: 'I say of our melancholy man, he is the cream of human adversity, the quintessence and upshot; all other diseases whatsoever are but flea-bitings to melancholy in extent: 'tis the pith of them all.' Three hundred and seventy years later it would be good to put that message across, especially as the disorder is now often treatable.

The objectives are, for the public:

- to raise awareness of the nature, course and treatment of depressive disorders
- to encourage people to seek help more readily from primary health care and mental illness services
- to make those at particular risk more aware of the existence of depressive illness and its responsiveness to treatment
- to measure the effectiveness of the campaign

And for doctors and other health care professionals:

- to publish consensus statements on the recognition and treatment of depressive disorders in general practice
- to increase the knowledge of GPs and other health care professionals in the recognition and effective treatment of depressive illness
- to explore the potential for the prevention of depressive illness through early recognition of its symptoms (i.e. secondary prevention)
- to measure the effectiveness of the professional education campaign

A MORI poll of 2000 members of the public at the outset of the campaign found that 73% regarded depression as a medical condition like any other, 89% did not regard depressed people as mad or unstable, 97% thought that anyone could be afflicted, 22% had personally suffered depression, and 55% knew someone who had. Personal distress and tragedy, economic and financial stress, other stresses and physical illness were considered to be the causes of depressive illness, in that order.

As regards treatment, 91% favoured counselling and support through social networks, but only 16% antidepressants, which were believed by 78% to be addictive. Sixty per cent expected help from the GP, 34% from family, 14% from friends, 3% from counselling (i.e. it was favoured but not regarded as readily available) and 2% from psychiatry. To summarize, in many respects the public were already well informed, except for the value of antidepressants.

The 'Help is at Hand' leaflets, aimed directly at the public, were launched with *Depression*, and *Depression in the Elderly* (by Dr Robert Baldwin) appeared a couple of years later. The present author wrote for the campaign a popular book, *Down with Gloom*, with witty and apt cartoons by the late Mel Calman (Pitt, 1995). Humour was used to illustrate the symptoms of depression, its causes, those at risk, the effects of depression on the family, bereavement and other causes and self-, psychological, social and drug treatments.

A survey to assess the effectiveness of the College's communications used press coverage from September 1992 to September 1993. There were 736 press cuttings mentioning the College. Twenty-six per cent dealt with depression, 8% with the psychiatry of old age. Twenty-seven per cent of 226 positive 'patient-focused' references were to depression, and 4% to 'old age'; 42% of the few negative patient-focused references were to depression, none to old age. Thirty-four per cent of 382 positive service-focused references were to depression, 12% to old age; 10% of 159 negative service-focused references were to depression and 3% to old age.

Twenty-eight per cent of references were to material published by the College, of which the majority were to depression and sleep disorders, and 8% to depression in the elderly.

A MORI poll after three years of the campaign showed some small improvement in those who regarded antidepressant treatment as appropriate and reduction in those who thought antidepressants addictive.

On the professional front, meetings between the Royal Colleges of Psychiatrists and General Practitioners resulted in a consensus statement on the recognition and treatment of depression summarized for the *British Medical Journal* (Paykel and Priest, 1992) and distributed to every general practice by the Department of Health. A subsequent series of meetings between the two Colleges, chaired by Professors Cornelius Katona and Paul Freeling, addressed depression in later life. The resulting paper was eventually published in *Primary Care Psychiatry* (Royal Colleges of General Practitioners and Psychiatrists, 1995) but otherwise the contents were not widely distributed. Some of the chief points, therefore, are summarized below.

Depression in late life:

- is common
- the prevalence is 15% in those over 65, 30% in GP attenders
- is common in dementia
- is hard to detect
- 'endogenous' and 'reactive' concepts are not helpful
- minor depression may have a Hamilton Depression Scale rating approaching major
- risk factors include
  a previous and family history of depression
  poor health (stroke, myocardial infarction, arthritis, bronchitis)
  widowhood
  personality
  lack of confidant
- precipitating factors include
  losses
  medication
- important indicators include
  recent changes in health
  recent changes in circumstances
  recent changes in consulting behaviour

Missing depression
- old people tend not to report their mood
- they are ashamed of being depressed
- they stress, instead, bodily symptoms
- the doctor may consider the depression justified
- the doctor may be wary of prescribing antidepressants

Screening
- is a useful step to diagnosis
- may be used opportunistically or at the over-75 health check
- the 15-item Geriatric Depression Scale (Yesavage *et al.*, 1983) is favoured

Suicide
- increases with
  age
  bereavement
  isolation
  deteriorating health
  pain
- actual and attempted suicide are closely linked
- the psychiatrist should be involved where there is suicidal risk

Antidepressants
- work in major depression
- probably don't in minor
- comparing new drugs with old:
  are equally effective
  all have side-effects, but the new are different
  the cost-benefit of new drugs is as yet unclear
- every GP should know one old and one new drug
- GPs should be prepared to refer to a psychiatrist

Psychosocial management
- understanding, support and regular review by the GP
- cognitive behavioural therapy and brief dynamic therapy are both effective
- group therapy has reduced readmission rates (Ong et al., 1987)
- counselling, family therapy and long-term psychotherapy are of more doubtful benefit
- focused (e.g. bereavement) counselling may be protective
- so may social interventions

How long to treat?
- at least six months
- there is evidence from hospital practice that continuing antidepressants for at least two years reduces relapse (Jacoby et al., 1993)
- long-term medication needs review if physical health worsens
- the whole primary health care team needs to be mobilized and co-ordinated by, say, a practice nurse

Specialist help
- for difficult diagnostic and management problems
- as support for GP
- where resources are needed which are under specialist control
- in failure to respond to primary treatment
- in physical illness, self-neglect, agitation, stupor, suicidal risk

Outcomes
- 30% of patients are still depressed after 3 years
- those who remain depressed have shortened lives of diminished quality
- continuing treatment may improve prognosis
- more data are needed from primary care

Conclusions
- depression in late life is treatable
- health services should identify and manage depression
- the role of the primary health care team is crucial in:
  detection
  providing a range of physical and psychological treatments
  indefinite monitoring after recovery
- advice and support are needed from the specialist old age psychiatry service
- there needs to be an infrastructure of well organized social care
- further education of primary HCTs and the public is paramount

REFERENCES

Cohen, R., Kennard, D. and Pitt, B. (1994). Attitudes towards mental illness and the elderly. *Psychiatr Bull* **18**, 721–725.

Iliffe, S., Haines, A., Gallivan, S. *et al.* (1991). Assessment of elderly people in general practice. 1. Social circumstances and mental state. *Br J Gen Pract* **41**, 9–12.

Jacoby, R., Lunn, A. and OADIG (1993). How long should the elderly take antidepressants? A double-blind placebo-controlled study of continuation/prophylaxis therapy with dothiepin. *Br J Psychiatry* **162**, 175–182.

Lamont, L. and Pitt, B. (1993). The Patients' Liaison Group. *Psychiatr Bull* **317**, 377.

Macdonald, A. (1986). Do general practitioners 'miss' depression in elderly patients? *BMJ* **292**, 1365–1367.

Ong, Y.-L., Martineau, F., Lloyd, C. and Robbins, I. (1987). Support group for the depressed elderly. *Int J Geriatr Psychiatry* **2**, 119–123.

Paykel, G. and Priest, R. (1992). Recognition and management of depression in general practice: a consensus statement. *BMJ* **305**, 1198–2102.

Pitt, B. (1995). Depressed and physically ill: how to diagnose and what to do? *Curr Opin Psychiatry* **8**, 235–236.

Pitt, B. and Calman, M. (1995). *Down with Gloom, or How to Defeat Depression.* Gaskell, London

Royal Colleges of General Practitioners and Psychiatrists (1995). Recognition and management of depression in late life in general practice. *Prim Care Psychiatry* **1**, 107–113.

Williamson, J., Stokoe, I., Gray, M. *et al.* (1964). Old people at home: their unreported needs. *Lancet* **i**, 1117–1120.

Yesavage, J., Brink, T., Rose, T. *et al.* (1983). Development and validation of a geriatric depression screening scale: a preliminary report. *J Psychiatr Res* **17**, 37–49.

13

New Antidepressants in the Elderly

CORNELIUS L.E. KATONA

Department of Psychiatry, University College London Medical School, London, UK

INTRODUCTION

This chapter updates an earlier review of the role of newer antidepressants in older people (Katona, 1993). Since that review was written, four new antidepressants have become available in the UK: citalopram (a serotonin-specific reuptake inhibitor (SSRI)); venlafaxine (which selectively blocks reuptake of both serotonin and noradrenaline); nefazodone (an SSRI which also blocks 5-HT$_2$ receptors); and a novel monoamine-oxidase inhibitor (MAOI), moclobemide. In this chapter the problems of antidepressant treatment in the elderly and the parameters relevant to assessing newer drugs are outlined. In the light of this background information, the evidence regarding the efficacy and tolerability of the relatively newly introduced tricyclic (TCA) lofepramine, the SSRIs, and of venlafaxine and moclobemide will be discussed in turn. In particular, the question of whether their advantages in elderly patients might be sufficient to outweigh their higher cost will be addressed.

PROBLEMATIC AREAS IN THE DRUG TREATMENT OF DEPRESSION IN OLD AGE

There have been surprisingly few placebo-controlled trials of TCAs and other older antidepressants in the elderly (Gerson *et al.*, 1988; Rockwell *et al.*, 1988; Anstey and Brodaty, 1995). Considerably more trials have compared antidepressants with each other. With few exceptions the placebo-controlled trials have found the active antidepressant to be superior and the head-to-head comparisons have shown therapeutic equivalence (with or without differences in side-effect rate or profile). The head-to-head comparisons have, however, almost always been underpowered to allow confidence that no real differences exist.

The extent to which these conclusions can be extrapolated to routine clinical practice is also questionable. Most trials specify major depression as an entry criterion, whereas the majority of elderly patients with significant depression fulfil criteria for dysthymia rather than major depression (Kivela et al., 1988). Equally important, virtually no antidepressant trials have examined patients aged 80 and over, since such patients almost invariably fulfil one or more trial exclusion criteria (Salzman, 1993). These considerations serve, perhaps, to temper the current enthusiasm for 'evidence-based' treatment evaluations relying solely on randomized controlled trial data – at least until more representative trials have been completed.

A further difficulty in evaluation arises from the fact that the outcome measures used do not take into account the clinical differences between older depressed patients and their younger counterparts. The Hamilton Depression Rating Scale (HDRS; Hamilton, 1960), for example, contains many somatic items whose presence may in older people reflect coexistent physical disease. More representative results in older patients would be seen if more appropriate scales were used. These include less somatically weighted scales such as the Montgomery–Asberg Depression Rating Scale (MADRS; Montgomery and Asberg, 1979); measures of global response, and scales specifically designed for older subjects such as the Geriatric Depression Scale (GDS) or the recently devised depression change scale derived from the Geriatric Mental Status interview (Ravindran et al., 1994). Related to this is the excessive reliance in trials to date on measures of severity of and change in depressive symptoms as opposed to measures of resource utilization or quality of life. The potential benefits of newer antidepressants need to be assessed in the context of the problems associated with the use of older antidepressants such as the TCAs. These problems are summarized briefly below.

THE SIDE-EFFECTS OF OLDER ANTIDEPRESSANTS IN THE ELDERLY

Elderly patients are more likely to suffer side-effects when taking older antidepressants and are also vulnerable to serious adverse consequences. The most important such adverse consequences are accidents (Ray, 1992) and falls (Campbell, 1991).

Using epidemiological data from the USA, Ray (1992) demonstrated a clear relationship between antidepressant use and car-accident-related injuries in people aged 65–84. In particular, the use of TCAs was associated with a doubling in the risk of crash involvement. The major mechanism implicated in vulnerability to falls is alpha-adrenoceptor blockade (a property of most TCAs and MAOIs) which aggravates the postural hypotension present in many older people because of age-associated blunting of baroreceptor reflexes (Woodhouse, 1992). Falls in older people are themselves more hazardous because of the increased risk of long-bone fractures due to age-related osteoporosis (Melton, 1993). It has been reported that hip-fracture risk increases approximately threefold in elderly subjects treated with TCAs (Glassman and Roose, 1994). The antihistaminic sedative effect of many TCAs is probably a further contributor to antidepressant-associated accidents and falls.

Most older antidepressants also have adverse effects on cognitive function (Knegtering et al., 1994). This is largely a function of cholinergic receptor blockade (Moskowitz and Burns, 1986), which also causes the well-known side-effects of constipation, blurred vision and impaired urinary flow which are all potentially more problematic in older subjects.

Age-related changes in drug handling may exacerbate the whole range of drug side-effects in the elderly. Age-related decreases in protein synthesis can increase free plasma drug levels. Antidepressant elimination may be slowed by the reduction with increasing age in creatinine clearance and hepatic blood flow.

The evidence summarized above relies mainly on epidemiological data, in vitro studies and studies in healthy volunteers. The problems identified correspond well to those identified in routine clinical practice in the psychiatry of old age. Clinical trial data (e.g. the studies summarized by Anstey and Brodaty (1995)), confirm the high rate of side-effects associated with the use of older antidepressants in an aged population. It is noteworthy, and perhaps surprising, however, that most studies show little if any increase in adverse-event-related trial withdrawal from older compared with newer antidepressants. Nortriptyline has a particularly good tolerability record in clinical trials in older subjects. Kanba et al. (1992) found no difference in adverse effect rates between older and younger subjects and no age-associated increase in blood levels achieved. Similarly, Miller et al. (1991), in an open-label study, found that only 5/45 elderly depressed subjects were unable to tolerate nortriptyline, which also did not cause measurable exacerbation in orthostatic hypotension. These findings probably reflect the relative physical health of older subjects who are able to participate in antidepressant clinical trials.

In the 'real-life' context, as opposed to that of clinical trials, antidepressant treatment is often given inadequately or not at all. The problem may be partly one of compliance which is hampered both because of troublesome side-effects (even if these are insufficiently severe as to warrant withdrawal from a clinical trial) and because many older antidepressants require several tablets to be taken two or even three times a day. The great majority of older depressed patients, however, are not given antidepressants at all. This is evident from studies both in community (Livingston et al., 1990; Manela et al., 1996) and primary care (Macdonald, 1986; Mullan et al., 1994) settings. Reluctance on the part of general practitioners to use antidepressants in their older patients may be due to the high likelihood (Mullan *et al.*, 1994) that such patients have contraindications to the use of TCAs or are taking other drugs liable to interact adversely with them. A recent study of antidepressant prescribing in primary care found that older patients were significantly less likely to receive newer antidepressants than their younger counterparts and that nearly half the sample on older tricyclics were receiving therapeutically inadequate doses (Katona *et al.*, 1996a).

CRITERIA FOR ASSESSING NEW ANTIDEPRESSANTS IN AN OLDER POPULATION

The above considerations are very relevant to the evaluation of whether a particular new antidepressant has a useful contribution to make to the management of older depressed patients. The specific questions to be asked about each new drug can be summarized as follows:

- Are there any age-related differences in its pharmacokinetics?
- What data are available on safety and tolerability?
- As regards efficacy:
  is there evidence against placebo?
  how representative are the subjects studied?
  how relevant are the measures used?
  is the drop-out rate sufficiently low to make 'completer'
  analysis meaningful and/or are 'intention-to-treat' data available?
  are there data on global outcome, resource utilization and/or
  quality of life?
  is there evidence in 'difficult-to-treat' groups such as the
  physically frail or those with dementia?
  is there evidence of long-term efficacy in preventing
  relapse or recurrence?

In the remainder of this chapter, evidence (or the lack of it) regarding these questions will be reviewed for each of the newer antidepressants.

THE SAFETY, TOLERABILITY AND EFFICACY OF NEWER ANTIDEPRESSANTS IN OLD AGE

Lofepramine

Lofepramine is a TCA in structure. It appears, however, from *in vitro* studies to be only weakly anticholinergic; trials in younger adults support its relative lack of anticholinergic side-effects (Sjögren, 1980). Lofepramine (70–140 mg) has been compared in single-dose studies with 50 mg amitriptyline and placebo in healthy elderly volunteers. Lofepramine did not differ significantly in side-effects from placebo, whereas even at the relatively low dose used, amitriptyline was associated with more frequent subjective side-effects as well as significantly reducing standing diastolic blood pressure. Salivary volume (an objective measure of dry mouth) was reduced by amitriptyline compared with either placebo or lofepramine. Lofepramine actually improved choice reaction time, in contrast with amitriptyline which impaired it (Ghose and Sedman, 1987). In the pharmacokinetic arm of the same studies, Ghose and Spragg (1989) found lofepramine to have an elimination half-life of 2.5 hours, suggesting that its pharmacokinetics in old age are similar to those in younger subjects, despite its very extensive (99%) protein binding (Sjogren, 1980).

The efficacy of lofepramine in elderly depressed patients has been compared with that of amitriptyline (Jessel et al., 1981), and dothiepin (Fairbairn et al., 1989). Both studies were underpowered (20/19 and 30/32 respectively) but had high completer rates. In completer analyses of global outcome, lofepramine was found to be significantly more effective than amitriptyline (72% versus 47% responding) and as effective as dothiepin. As far as side-effects were concerned, lofepramine did not differ significantly from amitriptyline but was associated with less dry mouth and drowsiness than dothiepin.

Tan et al. (1994) have reported a double-blind randomized 28-day trial of low-dose lofepramine (70 mg once daily) compared with placebo in 63 depressed elderly inpatients on medical wards. Forty-six patients completed the trial. Overall, lofepramine and placebo groups showed similar improvement, but lofepramine tended to be more effective than placebo in those patients who were more severely depressed.

These results suggest that lofepramine appears to be a reasonably effective and well tolerated antidepressant for elderly people. The small sample sizes render these conclusions somewhat guarded, however, especially in the absence of any long-term efficacy data.

SSRIs

Studies in younger subjects suggest that SSRIs have similar efficacy to TCAs. They are generally better tolerated with a distinct side-effect profile characterized by freedom from cardiotoxicity, anticholinergic effects and postural hypotension but with a greater tendency to provoke headache and nausea. All SSRIs have some effects on the cytochrome P450 system and may thus increase plasma levels of co-administered drugs such as TCAs and warfarin (Taylor and Lader, 1996). SSRIs may also (on the basis of clinical trial evidence in younger patients) be more rapidly effective than TCAs in reducing suicidal thoughts (Muijen et al., 1988). If true in older subjects, this may be of particular importance in view of the relatively high suicide rate in such patients and the closer link between suicide and depression than earlier in life (Cattell and Jolley,

1995). A recent primary care case-note study (Mullan *et al.*, 1994) suggests that elderly patients (particularly those with depressive symptoms) are more likely to be fit to take SSRIs than TCAs. The evidence regarding safety and tolerability of each of the currently available SSRIs is reviewed below.

Fluvoxamine

Fluvoxamine is chemically unrelated to the TCAs and is a potent and selective inhibitor of serotonin reuptake which does not block cholinergic receptors and has only negligible effects on noradrenaline reuptake (Classen *et al.*, 1977). It is rapidly absorbed, has no active metabolites and is excreted renally. Its plasma half-life of 15 hours is unaffected by age (Benfield and Ward, 1986). Nausea may be particularly troublesome at the higher end of the recommended dose range (Wagner *et al.*, 1992).

Four double-blind controlled comparisons between fluvoxamine against older antidepressants in elderly patients have been published. Only one (Wakelin, 1986) incorporated a small ($n = 12$) placebo group. This study was also of relatively young (age range 60–71) subjects, only lasted four weeks and had relatively high drop-out rates. Both fluvoxamine and imipramine were superior to placebo in completer analyses, but on an intention-to-treat basis this superiority was only marginal. Rahman *et al.* (1991) and Phanjoo *et al.* (1991) carried out relatively small (26 and 25 entrants to each study arm) trials of fluvoxamine against dothiepin and mianserin respectively. The subjects had a wide age range (up to 87 years) and were exposed to the trial drug for six weeks. As in the Wakelin (1986) study, drop-out rates were high. Rahman *et al.* (1991) and Phanjoo *et al.* (1991) both reported fluvoxamine to be as effective as the comparator drugs, the response rate in the former study being 64% for fluvoxamine and 60% for dothiepin. Surprisingly, side-effect profiles were similar for fluvoxamine and comparators in all the studies, although Wakelin (1986) found fluvoxamine to give rise to significantly less dry mouth than imipramine. A further study (Bocksberger *et al.*, 1993) compared fluvoxamine (up to 200 mg) with moclobemide (up to 450 mg) in a total of 40 patients, and showed the latter to be superior (in terms of global rating) at both 14 and 28 days, with response rates at 28 days of 84% and 55% respectively. Both drugs were well tolerated, though fluvoxamine was associated with nausea and anxiety, and moclobemide with headache and dizziness.

Fluvoxamine thus appears reasonably well tolerated, though the moclobemide comparison sheds some doubt as to efficacy. There is no evidence regarding long-term treatment.

Fluoxetine

Like the other SSRIs currently available, fluoxetine is structurally unrelated to the TCAs, is highly selective in blocking serotonin reuptake and is relatively free of cardiovascular, anticholinergic, antihistaminic and hypotensive effects (Feighner, 1983). It has a relatively long half-life (two to three days) and is metabolized in the liver; its major (and probably active) metabolite, norfluoxetine, has a half-life still longer (seven to nine days) than the parent compound. Lucas and Osborne (1986) found no age-related alteration in the time-course of elimination of fluoxetine and norfluoxetine. Fluoxetine may precipitate atrial fibrillation or sinus bradycardia in elderly patients (Buff *et al.*, 1991). A serious fluoxetine/MAOI interaction, involving hypothermia and confusion and resulting in a number of deaths, has also been noted (Feighner *et al.*, 1990). With these provisos, however, fluoxetine appears safe and well tolerated by older depressed patients. Kerr *et al.* (1992) noted improvement in critical flicker fusion threshold in elderly depressed patients on fluoxetine, compared with some deterioration in an amitriptyline control group. Orengo *et al.* (1996) reported from an open trial in inpatients that fluoxetine was associated with improvements in cognitive functioning as well as depressive symptoms. In this study, side-effect ratings while on fluoxetine were actually reduced from baseline; this presumably reflected increased tolerance of side-effects as depressive symptoms receded.

There has been one published study of fluoxetine against placebo (Tollefson and Holman, 1993). It was, however, very large, with over 250 subjects in each study arm. Drop-out rates were low, and similar to fluoxetine and placebo. Significantly more fluoxetine patients were classified as responders, but overall response rates were low (36% versus 27%).

In addition to this, four controlled comparisons between fluoxetine and older antidepressants have been published (Feighner and Cohn, 1985; Altamura *et al.*, 1989; Falk *et al.*, 1989; La Pia *et al.*, 1992). In the largest (*n* = 78/79) of these (Feighner and Cohn, 1985), the comparator was doxepin. Dose and treatment duration were adequate and global response assessed. The drop-out rate approached 50% in the fluoxetine group and exceeded it in the doxepin group. Drop-out was adverse-event-related in 32% of the fluoxetine patients and 43% of the doxepin patients. Reasonable and similar intention-to-treat response rates (approaching 50%) were found. Altamura *et al.* (1989) compared fluoxetine with amitriptyline (75 mg only); drop-out rates were low. Completer analysis showed equivalent efficacy. Amitriptyline appeared to have a faster onset of action, probably reflecting its early sedative, anxiolytic and appetite-stimulating effects. The only significant difference in side-effects reported was less frequent dry mouth on fluoxetine.

The study by Falk *et al.* (1989) comparing fluoxetine and trazodone is marred by the fact that only 10/14 patients on fluoxetine and 3/13 on trazodone completed the study. Significantly more responders and fewer drop-outs were found in the fluoxetine group; constipation was commoner on trazodone and insomnia on fluoxetine. La Pia *et al.* (1992) found fluoxe

tine and mianserin to have similar efficacy over six weeks in a study involving 75 subjects; mianserin was associated with more anticholinergic side-
effects.

There have also been two studies comparing fluoxetine with other 'new'
antidepressants. Altamura and Aguglia (1994) have published preliminary
results of a study comparing fluoxetine with moclobemide in 68 elderly
depressed patients; they report equivalent efficacy. Geretsegger et al. (1994)
compared fluoxetine with paroxetine in 106 older depressed subjects.
Paroxetine was associated with earlier onset of action and greater cognitive
improvements as well as a higher responder rate (figures not given) and
modest superiority in some end-point measures. No difference in tolerability between the drugs was found.

There is some, though limited, evidence attesting to the long-term efficacy
and tolerability of fluoxetine. Feighner and Cohn (1985) continued their
study against doxepin for 48 weeks and showed very low relapse rates over
48 weeks in both groups, with no difference emerging between the two drugs.

Fluoxetine has also received very preliminary evaluation in elderly
depressed patients with concurrent physical illness. In a prospective study of
consecutive admissions to an acute geriatric medical unit (Evans, 1993),
depression 'cases' were treated with open-label fluoxetine. Outcome was
significantly better in those continued on treatment than in those who discontinued it early. A subsequent and recently completed randomized placebo-
controlled trial also favours fluoxetine (M. Evans, personal communication).

On the basis of these studies, fluoxetine appears to have a different side-
effect profile to tricyclic antidepressants and to be comparable with them in
efficacy. Fluoxetine has also been fully evaluated against placebo, though
with only modest evidence for its superiority, and has some track record in
maintenance treatment and in the physically ill.

Paroxetine

Paroxetine is a highly selective serotonin reuptake inhibitor which is rapidly
absorbed and extensively (95%) protein-bound, with a complex metabolic
pathway of oxidation, methylation and conjugation prior to excretion in the
urine. There is some evidence (Kaye et al., 1989) that the plasma half-life of
approximately 24 hours is prolonged in the elderly.

There have been no placebo-controlled trials of paroxetine in older
depressed patients, but five controlled comparisons against older antidepressants have been published. Dunner et al. (1992) compared paroxetine
with doxepin in 271 patients whose mean age was relatively young at 68
years. There were no overall differences in efficacy. Hutchinson et al. (1991)
found no differences in efficacy between paroxetine and amitriptyline in a
total of 90 subjects identified in primary care; drop-out rates were low in

both groups. In a similar comparison with amitriptyline in elderly hospital inpatients, Geretsegger *et al.* (1995) also achieved a high completer rate and found no differences either in efficacy or overall side-effects. Paroxetine was associated with more anxiety and agitation, whereas more anticholinergic effects were seen with amitriptyline. Guillibert *et al.* (1989) found paroxetine (20–30 mg) to have similar efficacy and withdrawal rate to clomipramine (at the relatively low dose of up to 75 mg) in 79 patients aged 60 and over. Dorman (1992) found paroxetine to be superior to mianserin in 60 elderly patients, though it should be noted that the dose of mianserin used was small and associated with a remarkably low (18%) response rate. All the above studies reported more anticholinergic side-effects with comparator drugs than paroxetine. In addition, Guillibert *et al.* (1989) found more tremor and somnolence with clomipramine, and Dunner *et al.* (1992) reported more diarrhoea and nausea with paroxetine.

There has also (as cited earlier) been a comparison (Geretsegger *et al.*, 1994) between paroxetine and another SSRI, with some evidence of superior efficacy for paroxetine.

Paroxetine thus appears to be of at least equal efficacy to comparator drugs. Its side-effect profile in elderly patients is in keeping with that predicted from *in vitro* studies and found in younger subjects. Paroxetine remains to be evaluated against placebo and in long-term maintenance.

Sertraline

Sertraline is unrelated chemically to other SSRIs and desensitizes 5-HT_2 receptors directly as well as inhibiting 5-HT reuptake. It is relatively free of anticholinergic, antihistaminic and adverse cardiovascular side-effects (Doogan and Caillard, 1988). Pharmacokinetic studies (Invicta Pharmaceuticals, Sandwich, UK, data on file) suggest that although the pharmacokinetics of the parent compound are similar in elderly and younger volunteers, levels of its major metabolite, desmethylsertraline, are higher in the older group. In these older subjects, the plasma half-life of sertraline was about 22 hours and that of desmethylsertraline about 48 hours. Hindmarch *et al.* (1990) compared the cognitive effects of sertraline against mianserin in a nine-day study in elderly volunteers and found sertraline to have a neutral psychomotor profile whereas mianserin was sedating. The same group reported sertraline (in comparison with placebo) to improve vigilance (Hindmarch and Bhatti, 1988).

The only controlled study of sertraline in elderly patients published in full form (Cohn *et al.*, 1990) compared it with amitriptyline in a total of 241 patients, two-thirds of whom were on sertraline. The completer rate in both sertraline and amitriptyline groups was less than 50%, in the light of which it is noteworthy that although efficacy of the two drugs was similar in the completers, the intention-to-treat analysis showed somewhat greater improvement in depression rating in the amitriptyline group. This may of course reflect amitriptyline's sedative and anxiolytic effects. Side-effect-related withdrawal occurred in 28% of subjects on sertraline and 35% of those on amitriptyline; anticholinergic side-effects were commoner on amitriptyline and gastrointestinal ones on sertraline. Low relapse rates were seen in both groups of completers during the 16-week continuation phase (Invicta Pharmaceuticals, Sandwich, UK, data on file).

More recently, an abstract reporting a 12-week controlled comparison between sertraline and nortriptyline in a total of 204 depressed subjects with a mean age of 68 has been published (McEntee, 1995). Sertraline appeared superior at the end of the study, with differences most evident in patient-completed scales and measures of quality of life. Patients on sertraline also improved more in some cognitive tests.

Sertraline appears reasonably well tolerated by elderly patients with modest evidence of longer-term efficacy. The high withdrawal rate and lack of a placebo arm in the only detailed published trial to date limit the confidence that can be placed in these results.

Citalopram

Citalopram is the most highly specific inhibitor of 5-HT reuptake currently available. It is metabolized rapidly by oxidation and demethylation (some of the metabolites probably being active) and is an effective antidepressant in younger adults with significantly fewer anticholinergic side-effects than TCAs (Luo and Richardson, 1993). Studies in elderly volunteers suggest that breakdown of citalopram is slowed, with higher resultant plasma levels (Fredrickson Overo et al., 1985). In the only controlled trial to date in elderly depressed subjects, Nyth et al. (1992) compared citalopram with placebo in 149 subjects aged 65 and over, two-thirds of whom received citalopram. All were clinically depressed though only 74% fulfilled criteria for major depression. Twenty per cent had a concomitant diagnosis of dementia and 63% had at least one somatic illness. Global improvement was greater in the citalopram-treated subjects but this superiority was less evident in depression ratings, particularly when the analysis was restricted to subjects with major depression. Patients with dementia treated with citalopram displayed modest improvements in some aspects of cognitive functioning. Citalopram was well tolerated but was associated with significantly more side-effects early in treatment than placebo.

While limited, these results provide some support for the use of citalopram in the elderly. Though data from only one controlled trial are available, the findings are strengthened by the use of placebo and the relatively representative sample used. There are no available data on continuation treatment with citalopram. A recent pilot study provides very preliminary evidence for citalopram's role in refractory depression. Uehlinger *et al.* (1995) assessed the safety and efficacy of adding lithium to citalopram in 5/14 elderly patients not responding after four weeks' treatment with citalopram alone. Four responded, three of them within a week. The lithium/citalopram combination was generally well tolerated.

Nefazodone

Nefazodone is an SSRI which also blocks 5-HT$_2$ receptors. It is only a weak blocker of noradrenaline reuptake and has very little effect on alpha$_2$-adrenergic, histaminic and cholinergic receptors (Eison *et al.*, 1990). Its major metabolites (hydroxynefazodone and meta-chloprophenylpiperazine (mCPP)) are active, predominantly on the 5-HT system, though mCPP may also affect alpha$_2$-adrenoceptors (Hamik and Peroutka, 1988). Nefazodone is an effective antidepressant in younger adults (Feighner *et al.*, 1989).

The half-life of nefazodone is increased in elderly volunteers (Shea *et al.*, 1988), in whom it has also been shown to be free of significant cardiovascular effects except for causing a modest reduction in supine blood pressure (Breuel *et al.*, 1993). Van Laar *et al.* (1995) compared the acute and subchronic (seven-day) effects of nefazodone and imipramine on cognitive functioning, daytime sleepiness and on-the-road driving skill in 12 elderly and 12 younger volunteers. High-dose (200 mg b.d.) nefazodone was associated with significant but slight cognitive and driving impairment at seven days; the lower dose (100 mg b.d.) had no significant effects. No age-related differences in the effects of nefazodone were found. These results suggest that nefazodone may well be a well tolerated antidepressant in older depressed subjects; no published efficacy or tolerability data in such subjects are currently available, however.

Venlafaxine

Venlafaxine inhibits the reuptake of both serotonin and (more weakly) noradrenaline. It is essentially devoid of effects on alpha-adrenergic, histaminic and cholinergic receptors (Muth *et al.*, 1991) and is an effective antidepressant in younger adults (Schweitzer *et al.*, 1991). Saletu *et al.* (1992) reported that, at least in healthy young volunteers, venlafaxine did not appear to have deleterious cognitive or psychomotor effects. Following multiple dosing, the clearance of venlafaxine and its major metabolite (o-desmethylvenlafaxine) is reduced by 18% in older subjects, with the half-life of both compounds consequently increased by one to two hours (Wyeth Laboratories, Maidenhead, UK, data on file).

There are no published data available concerning the safety and efficacy of venlafaxine in older depressed patients. Wyeth Laboratories (data on file) have, however, analysed the data from a six-week randomized controlled study against dothiepin in 92 patients aged between 64 and 87, and from an open study in 77 subjects (age range 63–89) lasting up to 12 months. The main side-effects occurring on venlafaxine were nausea, headache, dry mouth, constipation, somnolence and dizziness. Adverse-event-related withdrawal occurred in fewer than 10% of subjects in both studies. In the dothiepin comparison, efficacy was equal in the two groups, with 60% response rate in each. Although only 49/77 patients in the open continuation study completed 12 months' treatment, the results suggest some prophylactic efficacy, with 75% of patients classified as remitted at nine months.

Moclobemide

Moclobemide is a benzamide derivative which is short-acting and selectively and reversibly inhibits MAO-A (Da Prada *et al.*, 1989). In contrast with conventional MAOIs, no formal dietary restrictions are required. The pharmacokinetics of moclobemide are very similar in younger and elderly volunteers (Stoeckel *et al.*, 1990) and depressed subjects (Maguire *et al.*, 1991).

Two studies have examined the cognitive effects of moclobemide in older volunteers under controlled conditions. Wesnes *et al.* (1989) compared the cognitive effects of moclobemide, trazodone and placebo with and without alcohol. The effects of moclobemide were neutral or slightly enhancing (with the exception of slight reduction in vigilance) whereas trazodone was associated with widespread and marked cognitive impairment. Similarly, Kerr *et al.* (1992) compared the cognitive effects of moclobemide, amitriptyline and placebo in elderly volunteers and found no significant differences between moclobemide and placebo, whereas amitriptyline significantly impaired short-term memory.

Two placebo-controlled trials of moclobemide in older subjects have been published. Both used relatively low (400 mg/day) dosage. The first (Nair *et al.*, 1995) was a three-arm design with nortriptyline as active comparator. A total of 109 subjects aged between 60 and 90 were randomized to receive moclobemide (400 mg/day), nortriptyline (with blood levels maintained within the therapeutic window) or placebo. Remission rates (intention-to-treat analysis) were 23%, 33% and 11% respectively, the only significant difference being between nortriptyline and placebo. Tolerability of moclobemide was, however, significantly superior to that of nortriptyline. In the second, very large, trial (Roth *et al.*, 1996) all subjects were cognitively impaired. Of these, 511 had a primary diagnosis with significant depressive features; the remainder ($n = 183$) had major depression. Moclobemide was significantly superior to placebo in terms of depression ratings; this was less apparent in terms of global rating with the superiority of moclobemide only being significant in the primary dementia subgroup. Moclobemide was generally well tolerated.

In addition to these placebo-controlled studies, pooled clinical trial data show moclobemide to be similar both in efficacy and (unlike its tricyclic comparators) in tolerability in elderly and younger depressed subjects (Angst and Stabl, 1992). There have also been several smaller published comparison studies against other antidepressants. De Vanna et al. (1990) found moclobemide to be as effective as both mianserin ($n = 40/40$) and maprotiline ($n = 20/19$). Similarly, Tiller et al. (1990) found no significant difference in efficacy between moclobemide ($n = 20$) and mianserin ($n = 19$). Pancheri et al. (1994) compared moclobemide with imipramine (maximum dose 100 mg) in a total of 30 patients and found moclobemide to have a faster onset of action and to be associated with some degree of cognitive improvements as well as alleviation of depressive symptoms. There were five dropouts in the moclobemide group, however, and one in those taking imipramine. Comparisons between moclobemide and other newer antidepressants have been described earlier in this chapter (Bocksberger et al., 1993; Altamura and Aguglia, 1994). These found moclobemide to be somewhat superior to fluvoxamine and as effective as fluoxetine.

Though long-term efficacy data on moclobemide in the elderly have yet to be published, the drug has received more extensive clinical trial evaluation in older subjects than most other antidepressants. The interpretation of these studies is hampered by the relatively low doses used and some doubts as to efficacy exist in the light of the Nair et al. (1995) study. Moclobemide nonetheless appears to be a well tolerated drug with some promise in this patient group, particularly in subjects with co-morbid dementia.

CONCLUSIONS

The number of available 'newer' antidepressants and the nature and extent of clinical trial data on them has increased considerably since the previous edition of this chapter. It remains the case that newer antidepressants appear as effective as, and somewhat better tolerated than, their older tricyclic comparators, with clearer advantages in terms of cognitive functioning. Placebo-controlled data remain scanty but provide some measure of reassurance as far as fluoxetine and citalopram (and, to a lesser extent, lofepramine, fluvoxamine and moclobemide) are concerned. Head-to-head comparisons between 'newer' antidepressants remain few and far between and none emerges as clearly superior to the others, although paroxetine and moclobemide may claim a slight edge in terms of numbers of patients studied and the results of head-to-head comparisons.

The new generation of antidepressant drugs probably do represent a step forward in the treatment of depression in elderly patients, their main advantage lying in the fact that they have fewer contraindications and a less disabling side-effect profile, which may enable a higher proportion of the many depressed elderly patients in the real world who would not be eligible for entry into controlled clinical trials to be treated effectively (Mullan *et al.*, 1994). It is noteworthy that both citalopram (Nyth *et al.*, 1992) and moclobemide (Roth *et al.*, 1996) were most clearly superior to placebo in the context of co-morbid depression and dementia.

Data on long-term efficacy remain lacking, with none of the newer drugs able to claim the superiority over placebo in relapse prevention demonstrated for dothiepin (Old Age Depression Interest Group, 1993) and phenelzine (Georgotas *et al.*, 1989). There is also a lack of evidence on the efficacy of newer antidepressants in physically ill older people, which is perhaps unsurprising in view of the formidable difficulties in carrying out such studies (Koenig *et al.*, 1989). Critical cost–benefit appraisal (Maynard, 1993) of newer antidepressants is also necessary to determine whether reductions in health and social care utilization offset their greater costs. In the light of recent evidence on the high costs of care associated with depression in older people (Katona *et al.*, 1966b) this question needs urgent attention.

REFERENCES

Altamura, A.C. and Aguglia, E. (1994). Moclobemide vs fluoxetine in elderly out-patients with major depression or dysthymia: a double blind trial. *Eur J Psychiatry* **9**(suppl 1), 163S.

Altamura, A.C., Percudani, M., Guercetti, G. and Invernizzi, G. (1989). Efficacy and tolerability of fluoxetine in the elderly: a double-blind study versus amitriptyline. *Int Clin Psychopharmacol* **4**, 103–106.

Angst, J. and Stabl, M. (1992). Efficacy of moclobemide in different patient groups: a meta-analysis of studies. *Psychopharmacology* **106**, S109–S113.

Anstey, K. and Brodaty, H. (1995). Antidepressants and the elderly: double-blind trials 1987–1992. *Int J Geriatr Psychiatry* **10**, 265–279.

Benfield, P. and Ward, A. (1986). Fluvoxamine: a review of its pharmacodynamic and pharmacokinetic properties, and therapeutic efficacy in depressive illness. *Drugs* **32**, 313–334.

Bocksberger, J.P., Gachoud, J.P., Richard, J. and Dick, P. (1993). Comparison of the effects of moclobemide and fluvoxamine in elderly patients with a severe depressive episode. *Eur Psychiatry* **8**, 319–324.

Breuel, H.-P., de Lenheer, I., Coninx, L. and Gammans, R. (1993). Comparison of the cardiovascular effects of nefazodone, imipramine and placebo in healthy elderly volunteers. *Eur Neuropsychopharmacol* (special issue) **3**, 423.

Buff, D.D., Brenner, R., Kirtane, S.S. and Gilboa, R. (1991). Dysrhythmia associated with fluoxetine treatment in an elderly patient with cardiac disease. *J Clin Psychiatry* **52**, 174–176.

Campbell, A.J. (1991). Drug treatment as a cause of falls in old age: a review of offending agents. *Drugs Aging* **1**, 289–302.

Cattell, H. and Jolley, D.J. (1995). One hundred cases of suicide in elderly people. *Br J Psychiatry* **166**, 451–457.

Classen, V., Davies, J.E., Hertting, G. et al. (1977). Fluvoxamine: a specific 5-hydroxy-
tryptamine uptake inhibitor. Br J Pharmacol 60, 505–516.

Cohn, C.K., Shrivastava, R., Mendels, J. et al. (1990). Double-blind, multicenter
comparison of sertraline and amitriptyline in elderly depressed patients. J Clin
Psychiatry 51, 28–33.

da Prada, M., Kettler, R., Keller, H.H. et al. (1989). Neurochemical profile of
moclobemide, a short-acting and reversible inhibitor of monoamine oxidase type
A. J Pharmacol Exp Ther 248, 400–413.

de Vanna, M., Kummer, J., Agnoli, A. et al. (1990). Moclobemide compared with
second-generation antidepressants in elderly people. Acta Psychiatr Scand Suppl
360, 64–66.

Doogan, D.P. and Caillard, V. (1988). Sertraline: a new antidepressant. J Clin
Psychiatry 49, 46–51.

Dorman, T. (1992). Sleep and paroxetine: a comparison with mianserin in elderly
depressed patients. J Clin Psychiatry 53(suppl), 53–58.

Dunner, D.L., Cohn, J.B., Walshe, T. et al. (1992). Two combined, multicenter
double-blind studies of paroxetine and doxepin in geriatric patients with major
depression. J Clin Psychiatry 52(suppl 2), 57–60.

Eison, A.S., Eison, M.S., Torrente, J. et al. (1990). Nefazodone: preclinical pharmacology of new antidepressant. Psychopharmacol Bull 26, 311–315.

Evans, M. (1993). Depression in elderly physically ill inpatients: a 12-month prospective study. Int J Geriatr Psychiatry 8, 587–592.

Fairbairn, A.F., George, K. and Dorman, T. (1989). Lofepramine versus dothiepin in
the treatment of depression in elderly patients. Br J Clin Pract 43, 55–60.

Falk, W.E., Rosenbaum, J.E., Otto, M.W. et al. (1989). Fluoxetine versus trazodone
in depressed geriatric patients. J Geriatr Psychiatry Neurol 2, 208–214.

Feighner, J.P. (1983). The new generation of antidepressants. J Clin Psychiatry 44,
49–55.

Feighner, J.P. and Cohn, J.B. (1985). Double-blind comparative trials of fluoxetine and
doxepin in geriatric patients with major depressive disorder. J Clin Psychiatry 46, 20–25.

Feighner, J.P., Pambakinan, R., Fowler, R.C. et al. (1989). A comparison of
nefazodone, imipramine and placebo in patients with moderate to severe depression. Psychopharmacol Bull 25, 219–221.

Feighner, J.P., Boyer, W.F., Tyler, D.L. and Heborsky, R.J. (1990). Fluoxetine and
MAIOs: adverse interactions. J Clin Psychiatry 51, 222–225.

Fredrickson Overo, K., Toft, B., Christophersen, L. and Gylding-Sabroe, J.P. (1985).
Kinetics of citalopram in elderly patients. Psychopharmacology 86, 253–257.

Georgotas, A., McCue, R.E. and Cooper, T.B. (1989). A placebo-controlled comparison of nortriptyline and phenelzine in maintenance therapy of elderly depressed
patients. Arch Gen Psychiatry 46, 783–785.

Geretsegger, C., Bohmer, F. and Ludwig, M. (1994). Paroxetine in the elderly
depressed patient: randomised comparison with fluoxetine of efficacy, cognitive
and behavioural effects. Int Clin Psychopharmacol 9, 25–29.

Geretsegger, C., Stuppaeck, C.H., Mair, M., Platz, T., Fartacek, R. and Hein, M.
(1995). Multicenter double-blind study of paroxetine and amitriptyline in elderly
depressed inpatients. Psychopharmacology 119, 277–281.

Gerson, S.C., Plotkin, D.A. and Jarvik, L.F. (1988). Antidepressant drug studies 1946
to 1986: empirical evidence of aging patients. J Clin Psychopharmacol 8, 311–322.

Ghose, K. and Sedman, E. (1987). A double-blind comparison of the pharmacodynamic effects of single doses of lofepramine, amitriptyline and placebo in elderly
subjects. Eur J Clin Pharmacol 33, 505–509.

Ghose, K. and Spragg, B.P. (1989). Pharmacokinetics of lofepramine and amitriptyline in elderly healthy subjects. *Int Clin Psychopharmacol* **4**, 201–215.

Glassman, A.H. and Roose, S.P. (1994). Risk of antidepressants in the elderly. Tricyclic
antidepressants and arrhythmias – revising risks. *Gerontology* **40**(suppl 1), 15–20.

Guillibert, E., Pelicier, Y., Archembault, J.C. *et al.* (1989). A double-blind, multicentre study of paroxetine versus clomipramine in depressed elderly patients. *Acta
Psychiatr Scand* **80**(suppl 350), 132–134.

Hamik, A. and Peroutka, S.J. (1988). 1-(m-Chlorophenyl)piperazine interactions with
neurotransmitter receptors in the human brain. *Biol Psychiatry* **25**, 569–575.

Hamilton, M. (1960). A rating scale for depression. *J Neurol Neurosurg Psychiatry*
23, 56–62.

Hindmarch, I. and Bhatti, J.Z. (1988). Psychopharmacological effects of sertraline in
normal, healthy volunteers. *Eur J Clin Pharmacol* **35**, 221–223.

Hindmarch, I., Shillingford, J. and Shillingford, C. (1990). The effects of sertraline on
psychomotor performance in elderly volunteers. *J Clin Psychiatry* **51**, 34–36.

Hutchinson, D.R., Tong, S., Moon, C.A.L. *et al.* (1991). A double-blind study in
general practice to compare the efficacy and tolerability of paroxetine and
amitriptyline in depressed elderly patients. *Br J Clin Res* **2**, 43–47.

Jessel, H.-J., Jessel, I. and Wegener, G. (1981). Therapy for depressive elderly
patients: lofepramine and amitriptyline tested under double-blind consitions. *Z
Allgemeinmed* **57**, 784–787.

Kanba, S., Matsumoto, K., Nibuya, M. *et al.* (1992). Nortriptyline response in elderly
depressed patients. *Prog Neuropsychopharmacol Biol Psychiatry* **16**, 301–309.

Katona, C.L.E. (1993). New antidepressants in elderly patients. In: Levy, R., Howard,
R. and Burns, A. (Eds), *Treatment and Care in Old Age Psychiatry*. Wrightson
Biomedical Publishing Ltd, Petersfield, pp. 157–167.

Katona, C., Donoghue, J., Wildgust, H. and Tylee, A. (1996a). Antidepressant
prescribing patterns in older people. (submitted).

Katona, C., Manela, M. and Livingston, G. (1996b). The costs of community care for
older people. *Br J Psychiatry* (in press).

Kaye, C.M., Haddock, R.E., Langley, P.F. *et al.* (1989). A review of the metabolism
and pharmacokinetics of paroxetine in man. *Acta Psychiatr Scand* **80**, 60–75.

Kerr, J.S., Fairweather, D.B. and Hindmarch, I. (1992). The effects of acute and
repeated doses of moclobemide on psychomotor performance and cognitive
function in healthy elderly volunteers. *Hum Psychopharmacol* **7**, 273–279.

Kivela, S.-L., Pahkala, K. and Laippala, P. (1988). Prevalence of depression in an
elderly population in Finland. *Acta Psychiatr Scand* **78**, 401–413.

Knegtering, H., Eijck, M. and Huijsman, A. (1994). Effects of antidepressants on
cognitive functioning of elderly patients: a review. *Drugs Aging* **3**, 192–199.

Koenig, H.G., Goli, V., Shelp, F. *et al.* (1989). Antidepressant use in elderly medical
inpatients: lessons from an attempted clinical trial. *J Gen Intern Med* **4**, 498–505.

La Pia, S., Giorgio, R., Ciriello, A. *et al.* (1992). Evaluation of the efficacy, tolerability and therapeutic profile of fluoxetine versus mianserin in the treatment of
depressive disorders in the elderly. *Curr Ther Res* **52**, 847–858.

Livingston, G., Thomas, A., Graham, N. *et al.* (1990). The Gospel Oak Project: the
use of health and social services by dependent elderly people in the community.
Health Trends **2**, 70–73.

Lucas, R.A. and Osborne, D.J. (1986). The disposition of fluoxetine and norfluoxetine in elderly patients with depressive illness compared to younger subjects.
Proceedings of the 16th CINP Congress, Puerto Rico.

Luo, H. and Richardson, J.S. (1993). A pharmacological comparison of citalopram, a bicyclic serotonin selective uptake inhibitor, with traditional tricyclic antidepressants. *Int Clin Psychopharmacol* **8**, 3–12.

Macdonald, A.J.D. (1986). Do general practitioners 'miss' depression in elderly patients? *BMJ* **292**, 1365–1367.

McEntee, W.J. (1995). A double-blind comparison of sertraline and nortriptyline in the treatment of depressed geriatric outpatients. Abstracts of the American Psychiatric Association Meeting, Miami, FL 20–25 May, 1995. NR264 (p. 126).

Maguire, K., Pereira, A. and Tiller, J. (1991). Moclobemide pharmacokinetics in depressed patients: lack of age effect. *Hum Psychopharmacol* **6**, 249–252.

Manela, M., Katona, C.L.E. and Livingston, G. (1996). How common are the anxiety disorders in old age? *Int J Geriatr Psychiatry* **11**, 65–70.

Maynard, A. (1993). Cost management: the economist's viewpoint. *Br J Psychiatry* **163**(suppl 20), 7–13.

Melton, L.J. (1993). Hip fractures: a worldwide problem today and tomorrow. *Bone*(suppl 1), S1–S8.

Miller, M.D., Pollock, B.G., Rifai, A.H. *et al.* (1991). Longitudinal analysis of nortriptyline side-effects in elderly depressed patients. *J Geriatr Psychiatry Neurol* **4**, 226–230.

Montgomery, S.A. and Asberg, M. (1979). A new depression scale designed to be sensitive to change. *Br J Psychiatry* **134**, 382–389.

Moskowitz, H. and Burns, M.M. (1986). Cognitive performance in geriatric subjects after acute treatment with antidepressants. *Neuropsychobiology* **15**, 38–43.

Muijen, M., Roy, D., Silverstone, T. *et al.* (1988). A comparative clinical trial of fluoxetine, mianserin and placebo with depressed out-patients. *Acta Psychiatr Scand* **78**, 384–390.

Mullan, E., Katona, P., D'Ath, P. and Katona, C. (1994). Screening, detection and management of depression in elderly primary care attenders. 2. Detection and fitness for treatment: a case record study. *Fam Pract* **11**, 267–270.

Muth, E.A., Moyer, J.A., Haskins, J.T., Andree, T.H. and Husbands, G.E.M. (1991). Biochemical, neurophysiological, and behavioural effects of Wy-45.233 and other identified metabolites of the antidepressant venlafaxine. *Drug Dev Res* **23**, 191–199.

Nair, N.P.V., Amin, M., Holm, P. *et al.* (1995). Moclobemide and nortriptyline in elderly depressed patients. A randomised, multicentre trial against placebo. *J Affect Disord* **33**, 1–9.

Nyth, A.L., Gottfries, C.G., Lyby, K. *et al.* (1992). A controlled multicentre clinical study of citalopram and placebo in elderly depressed patients with and without concomitant dementia. *Acta Psychiatr Scand* **86**, 138–145.

Old Age Depression Interest Group (1993). How long should the elderly take antidepressants? A double-blind placebo-controlled study of continuation/prophylaxis therapy with dothiepin. *Br J Psychiatry* **162**, 175–182.

Orengo, C.A., Kunik, M.E., Molinari, V. and Workman, R.H. (1996). The use and tolerability of fluoxetine in geropsychiatric inpatients. *J Clin Psychiatry* **57**, 12–16.

Pancheri, P, Delle Chiaie, R., Donnini, M. *et al.* (1994). Effects of moclobemide on depressive symptoms and cognitive performance in a geriatric population: a controlled comparative study versus imipramine. *Clin Neuropharmacol* **17** (suppl 1), S58–S73.

Phanjoo, A.L., Wonnacott, S. and Hodgson, A. (1991). Double-blind comparative multicentre study of fluvoxamine and mianserin in the treatment of major depressive episode in elderly people. *Acta Psychiatr Scand* **83**, 476–479.

Rahman, M.K., Akhtar, M.J., Savla, N.C. *et al.* (1991). A double-blind, randomised comparison of fluvoxamine with dothiepin in the treatment of depression in elderly patients. *Br J Clin Pract* **45**, 255–258.

Ravindran, A.V., Welburn, K. and Copeland, J.R.M. (1994). Semi-structured depression scale sensitive to change with treatment for use in the elderly. *Br J Psychiatry* **164**, 522–527.

Ray, W.A. (1992). Psychotropic drugs and injuries among the elderly: a review. *J Clin Psychopharmacol* **12**, 386–396.

Rockwell, E., Lam, R.W. and Zisook, S. (1988). Antidepressant drug studies in the elderly. *Psychiatr Clin North Am* **11**, 215–233.

Roth, M., Mountjoy, C.Q., Amrein, R. *et al.* (1996). Moclobemide in elderly patients with cognitive decline and depression. *Br J Psychiatry* **168**, 149–157.

Saletu, B., Grunberger, J., Anderer, P., Linzmayer, L., Semtlisch, H.V. and Magni, G. (1992). *Br J Clin Pharmacol* **33**, 589–601.

Salzman, C. (1993). Pharmacologic treatment of depression in the elderly. *J Clin Psychiatry* **54**(suppl 2), 23–28.

Schweitzer, E., Weise, C., Clary, C., Fox, I. and Rickels, K. (1991). Placebo-controlled trial of venlafaxine for the treatment of major depression. *J Clin Psychopharmacol* **11**, 233–236.

Shea, J.P., Shukla, U.A. and Pittman, K.A. (1988). Single dose pharmacokinetics of nefadozone in elderly subjects, renally impaired patients and patients with hepatic cirrhosis in comparison to healthy volunteers. *Clin Pharmacol Therap* **43**, 146.

Sjögren, C. (1980). The pharmacological profile of lofepramine: a new antidepressant drug. *Neuropharmacology* **19**, 1213–1214.

Stoeckel, K., Pfefen, J.P., Mayersohn, M. *et al.* (1990). Absorption and disposition of moclobemide in patients with advanced age or reduced liver or kidney function. *Acta Psychiatr Scand* **360**, 94–97.

Tan, R.S.H., Barlow, R.J., Abel, C. *et al.* (1994). The effect of low dose lofepramine in depressed elderly patients in general medical wards. *Br J Clin Pharmacol* **37**, 321–324.

Taylor, D. and Lader, M. (1996). Cytochromes and psychotropic drug interactions. *Br J Psychiatry* **168**, 529–532.

Tiller, J., Maguire, K. and Davies, B. (1990). A sequential double-blind controlled study of moclobemide and mianserin in elderly depressed patients. *Int J Geriatr Psychiatry* **5**, 199–204.

Tollefson, G.D. and Holman, S.L. (1993). Analysis of the Hamilton Depression Rating Scale factors from a double-blind, placebo-controlled trial of fluoxetine in geriatric major depression. *Int Clin Pharmacol* **8**, 253–259.

Uehlinger, C., Nil, R., Amey, M., Baumann, P. and Dufour, H. (1995). Citalopram–lithium combination treatment of elderly depressed patients: a pilot study. *Int J Geriatr Psychiatry* **10**, 281–287.

van Laar, M.W., van Willigenburg, A.P.P. and Volkerts, E.R. (1995). Acute and subchronic effects of nefazodone and imipramine on highway driving, cognitive functions, and daytime sleepiness in healthy adult and elderly subjects. *J Clin Psychopharmacol* **15**, 30–40.

Wagner, W., Plekkenpol, B., Gray, T.E., Vlaskamp, H. and Essers, H. (1992). Review of fluvoxamine safety database. *Drugs* **43** (suppl 2), 48–54.

Wakelin, J.S. (1986). Fluvoxamine in the treatment of the older depressed patient: double-blind placebo-controlled data. *Int Clin Psychopharmacol* **1**, 221–230.

Wesnes, K.A., Simpson, P.M., Christmas, L., Anand, R. and McClelland, G.R. (1989). The effects of moclobemide on cognition. *J Neural Transm Suppl* **28**, 91–102.

Woodhouse, K. (1992). The pharmacology of major tranquillisers in the elderly, In: Katona, C. and Levy, R. (eds), *Delusions and Hallucinations in Old Age*. Gaskell, London, pp. 84–93.

Advances in Old Age Psychiatry: Chromosomes to Community Care
Edited by C. Holmes and R. Howard
© 1997 Wrightson Biomedical Publishing Ltd

14

ECT in the Elderly

DAVID WILKINSON

Old Age Psychiatry, Elderly Mental Health Services, Western Community Hospital, and University of Southampton, Southampton, UK

INTRODUCTION

Electroconvulsive therapy (ECT) has been used to treat depression for over 50 years and, despite all the developments in antidepressant treatments, it still remains a principal treatment for the severely mentally ill. However, it remains controversial and is a subject about which even the most uninformed and taciturn feel able to provide expert comment. There is no reason for anyone to be ill-informed, as there is a wealth of data on the subject confirming its superior efficacy over sham ECT (Wilkinson, 1993). There seems to be less controversy in the elderly where it has been shown to be an effective treatment for affective disorders (Table 1), with a recent meta-analysis (Mulsant *et al.*, 1991) showing that ECT produced a significant improvement in 83% of cases and cure in 62%.

Table 1. ECT outcome studies in the elderly.

Authors	n	Electrode placement (%)		Length of course (No. of treatments)	Outcome (%)	
		Unilateral	Bilateral		Excellent/ good	Poor
Fraser and Glass (1980)	29	45	55	6.5	100	0
Gaspar and Singhe (1982)	33	0	100	8.7	79	12
Mielke *et al.* (1984)	24	57	13	13.8	75	0
Karlinsky and Shulman (1984)	33	70	9	9.3	78	21
Kramer (1987)	50	0	100	7.4	92	8
Benbow (1987)	122	3	95	8.3	80	20
Godber *et al.* (1987)	163	95	3	11.2	74	26
Magni *et al.* (1988)	30	0	100	11	63	37
Coffey *et al.* (1988)	67	51	29	9	98	2
Figiel *et al.* (1989)	51	74	6	9	82	18

It is safe, despite the likelihood of multiple system disorders and medications (Gasper and Singhe, 1982). It is well tolerated but, as will be discussed, not well liked. It will sometimes cause or exacerbate confusion but produces no evidence of brain damage (Coffey *et al.*, 1991; Lippmanns *et al.*, 1985) or lasting cognitive deficits (Devanand *et al.*, 1991). However, when bilateral ECT is used there is some evidence that it can cause some lasting effects on memory (Squire, 1986) but it seems that patients receiving brief-pulse unilateral ECT can expect to recover fully from their depressive illness without experiencing any short- or long-term memory impairment (Weiner *et al.*, 1986). The therapeutic dilemma then is that, while the evidence strongly supports the view that ECT should be considered in every patient who has either failed to respond to other treatments or is so depressed as to be at risk of suicide, or death from inanition, many patients and the general public still regard the treatment as archaic and barbaric.

This dilemma has to be our responsibility to resolve; our silent confidence in the treatment will not be enough. While we cannot ignore our patients' complaints we also have to be more positive about its prescription. The allegation of barbarism has to be dealt with in the context of other medical treatments. Many surgical procedures are profoundly disfiguring, for example, mastectomy, and yet, because they offer treatment for cancer, or physical pain rather than the intolerable distress of depression, they are accepted without comment. Certain procedures such as episiotomy are in fact often undertaken without adequate anaesthesia with the patient entirely conscious and without any hint of consent being given. ECT seems to be judged by different rules, often irrationally, so it is important that psychiatrists should not be apologetic about ECT and should offer it positively when the established criteria for its use are satisfied. However, a positive view of its use does not automatically encourage patient acceptance; therefore anxiety about its use and side-effects must be addressed.

TREATMENT-RELATED ANXIETY

Of course, anxiety is not unique to ECT; in general surgery Sheffer and Greigenstein (1960) report that 92% of their sample preoperatively demonstrated tension and fear about the use of anaesthesia and Graham and Conley (1960) found that 34 of 70 patients on the evening before surgery acknowledged being very frightened and anxious; indeed, Hughes *et al.* (1981) concluded that many patients found ECT less anxiety-provoking than a trip to the dentist. That patients will be anxious is therefore not in doubt and we need to examine ways of lessening it.

The author and colleagues looked at anxiety levels associated with ECT in their unit before each treatment, between treatment and after discharge

Table 2. Concerns expressed about ECT before and after treatment.

Concern	Patient responses		
	Pre-ECT (n = 11)	Post-ECT (n = 11)	Follow-up (n = 7)
Being made unconscious	–	4	–
Losing control of bladder	1	4	–
Memory loss	1	9	–
Possible brain damage	3	2	–
Being in pain	1	–	–
Use of electricity in treatment	1	4	–
Having a convulsion or fit	1	2	–
Use of anaesthetic	1	8	6
Not knowing what would happen	2	5	–
What others will think	1	1	–
Side-effects	4	4	–
Waiting the night before	–	1	3

Source: From Heggs (1990).

(Heggs, 1990). The results showed a general fall in anxiety levels with treatment, but in six of nine patients showing an overall fall there was a measurable rise in anxiety after the third or fourth treatment. One obvious point that we need to address, therefore, is that ECT is not a one-off operation but a repetitive procedure and this may have a bearing on anxiety. Our reassurance and persuasion is at its height before treatment starts, but we must continue to affirm the need for treatment during the course, particularly perhaps after three or four treatments, when the patient is less withdrawn and uninterested and wants to find out more about what is happening.

This study highlighted something also noted by Abrams (1988), that there are some elderly patients who improve for the first three or four treatments and then get worse with further treatment and eventually fail to regain the initial improvements. ECT should not therefore be prescribed and forgotten; we should review progress after each two or three treatments to decide whether to continue, to increase the dose, to change from unilateral to bilateral or vice versa, and to address any side-effects that might develop such as confusion, emergence delirium or headaches. Heggs (1990) also used a visual analogue scale for anxiety to rank the various treatment steps (Table 2). Clearly, many of the anxieties relate purely to the anaesthetic, with patients fearing loss of consciousness, memory and bladder control, as well as concerns over saying embarrassing things while drowsy. This is at variance with the Freeman and Kendell (1980) study showing that only 29% of patients were afraid of waiting for or having the anaesthetic. Their study was on younger patients 12 months after treatment and yet Heggs showed at

Table 3. ECT group – recurring themes.

1. How does ECT work?
2. Memory loss – reason, recovery
3. How do you decide how many?
4. 'The old days' before anaesthesia
5. Safety – has anyone died?
6. The needle
7. Would you have ECT?
8. Side-effects – headache, muzziness
9. Other patients' 'horror stories'
10. The name 'convulsive therapy'

three-month follow-up that concern about the anaesthetic was still paramount. Three of the eleven patients whom Heggs interviewed said that they would not be prepared to have ECT again if it were necessary. This is an important factor in managing depression in the elderly who, despite a good response to ECT, may relapse and benefit from a further course.

Following the study a number of changes were made to practice in the author's unit including the provision of an information sheet and the patients being offered the chance to see the treatment room and electrodes prior to treatment, but chiefly the establishment of an ECT users' group. This group has had a significant impact in the sense of 'glasnost', giving ECT patients a positive identity and a forum for open discussion. It has allowed the other ward groups to concentrate on other issues, as ECT is seldom brought up in these. The main themes are shown in Table 3 and are, in general, negative. Patients often need encouragement to share their positive feelings about their improvement with ECT, in view of the general antipathy towards it amongst them. The support group often allows these feelings to be expressed and consequently reinforces the need to continue treatment. Fear of ECT is lessened by allowing patients' misconceptions to be aired; one patient thought that ECT was administered through a large spiked helmet and was greatly reassured when encouraged to see the electrodes. Another felt the bruises on the back of her hand were due to excessive violence on the part of the anaes-thetist, rather than simply extravasation of blood following the injection.

A video made for teaching purposes is also used which shows a patient before, during and after treatment together with some explanation of the procedure. This is shown to relatives and patients who are uncertain about the treatment before they give consent. No patient shown the video has subsequently refused the treatment. As it has been made by staff in the unit it adds to the sense of openness and reassurance, demystifying the proce-dure. Baxter *et al.* (1986) felt that videos were unhelpful but the present author feels that they are useful if used as part of a range of anxiety-reduc-ing measures.

PRESCRIBING ECT

When deciding about the prescription of ECT and its continuation one must remember the initial assessment of the patient's illness; one's first interview is crucial to the understanding of the illness and the patient. It is the time when the patient is at their lowest ebb, and yet often at their most accessible, so if at that time there is enough information to suggest that the patient would respond well to ECT, this should be recorded because during trials of antidepressants and admission to hospital some of the symptoms may ameliorate and lessen one's resolve to try ECT, despite lack of adequate improvement.

WHO WILL RESPOND?

To some extent it is possible to predict who will respond to ECT; it is rare for the retarded patient with delusions of guilt and suicidal intent not to respond. Unfavourable features are long-standing anxiety, hypochondriasis, somatization symptoms and personality traits of hysterical or dependent nature. Fraser and Glass (1980) identified five items from the Hamilton Depression Rating Scale which best predicted response to ECT; these were guilt, subjectively depressed mood, psychic anxiety, loss of interests, and agitation. Others have found similar predictors and assessed their value (Table 4). However, despite having a clear picture of favourable and unfavourable features there are enough patients with atypical depression who fail to respond to other measures and who respond to ECT to justify a

Table 4. Predictive factors for response to ECT.

Favourable	Unfavourable
Sudden onset	Hypochondriasis
Insight	Neurotic traits
Less than one years' duration	Intelligence
Obsessionality	
Self-reproach	

(Hobson, 1953: 79% accuracy)

Weight loss	Anxiety
Pyknic physique	Hypocondriasis
Early morning wakening	Hysterical traits
Somatic delusions	Worse in evenings
Paranoid delusions	Self-pity

(Carney et al., 1965: 76% accuracy)

therapeutic trial of ECT as good clinical practice. In fact, in one ECT outcome study (Godber *et al.*, 1987), 27% of the sample showed predominantly neurotic features and still had a good outcome. If anxiety, panic disorder or obsessional symptoms present for the first time in late life it can well be an indication of a depressive illness; if these symptoms partially resolve with antidepressants one should be encouraged to try ECT. One should also not be too distracted by a lack of vegetative signs and symptoms of depressive illness. While diurnal variation, weight loss, constipation, and all the other signs are useful corroborative evidence, they do not tell us what the patient is thinking and feeling which the author feels is always the key to whether or not they are depressed.

PARKINSON'S DISEASE AND ECT

There is now considerable evidence (Douyon *et al.*, 1989; Lebensohn and Jenkins, 1975) that ECT *per se* improves the motor symptoms of Parkinson's disease (PD) whether or not depression is present. A study by Ward *et al.* (1980) again showed dramatic improvements in motor function but no improvement in on–off phenomena. The present author certainly feels that ECT can have a remarkable effect on Parkinsonian motor symptoms; however, like Abrams (1988) he feels that the effect on motor performance is less long-standing than the effect on mood. The author has admitted a patient with Parkinson's disease for repeat ECT who was treated previously with ECT for depression and whose mood had remained stable but whose mobility had declined. His Parkinson's disease improved rapidly after four session of unilateral ECT but the treatment was stopped due to incipient hypomania. Like others (Abrams, 1988) the author feels that maintenance ECT may be an appropriate treatment for Parkinson's disease, particularly if delusions and hallucinations are present and producing a dilemma as to whether one should use neuroleptics, with the risk of worsening the Parkinson's disease.

MAINTENANCE AND CONTINUATION ECT

In 1990 the American Psychiatric Association task force on ECT defined continued administration of ECT over a six-month period to prevent relapse after induction of remission as continuation ECT (C-ECT); treatment beyond six months was termed maintenance ECT (M-ECT). This was felt to be a viable form of management for selected patients.

Maintenance ECT has been used for many years; one recent survey of British psychogeriatricians found that 20% were using it (Benbow, 1991) but there is little more than anecdote to support its use in the literature. Such studies as there are consist mainly of case-studies and small series of hospi-talized patients, all of a 'naturalistic' nature.

One study (Mirchandani *et al.*, 1994), a one-year follow-up of nine elderly patients, is no different but did seem to indicate that continuation treatment, even if discontinued fairly quickly, may confer some lasting advantage in prevention of relapse, as did Petrides in looking at 33 courses of C-ECT (Petrides *et al.*, 1994). The conclusion seemed to be that where patients have responded to acute ECT but previously failed on continuation pharma-cotherapy there was compelling evidence for C-ECT and little therapeutic alternative. The four patients in Petrides *et al.*'s (1994) study who continued with M-ECT remained well and the five who had previously stopped did not. Naturally this result is open to other interpretations but it does suggest that C-ECT should be considered for those with recurrent depression who respond well to ECT acutely but receive no prophylaxis from pharma-cotherapy. The practicalities of using outpatient M-ECT have prevented my using it more. Bringing elderly patients to hospital for outpatient ECT early in the day, from a rural catchment area some distance from the hospital, can be problematic, they soon lose enthusiasm for the treatment and conse-quently often withdraw consent. This is an issue recently addressed by Kim *et al.* (1996). However, Schwarz's findings, that rehospitalization rates were reduced by 67% after instituting M-ECT, suggest that we should try and overcome the practical difficulties (Schwarz *et al.*, 1995).

DOES ECT CAUSE STRUCTURAL BRAIN DAMAGE?

Many psychogeriatricians (Benbow, 1991) are willing to treat depression in patients suffering from dementia with ECT. However, the response can be varied, with fewer than expected regaining complete remission of the depres-sion, and optimistic reports should be tempered by the knowledge that many patients with dementia will become more confused and disoriented with ECT, especially if bilateral treatment is given. There is now considerable evidence from prospective studies using magnetic resonance imaging (MRI) and computerized tomography (CT) (Coffey *et al.*, 1988; Pande *et al.*, 1990) to show that there is no relationship between ECT and brain damage. Interestingly, all the studies note that many of these depressed patients show significant structural brain abnormalities (often patchy white matter changes on MRI) before treatment (Table 5). This in effect means that we already give ECT to a population with some degree of brain damage and that exten-sion to overt dementia need not be feared if depression and agitation are significant features. In fact, like Parkinson's disease, it may be a more ratio-nal treatment than the usual response of escalating doses of major tranquil-lizers with all the possible problems of extrapyramidal side-effects, and

Table 5. Brain imaging findings in depressed patients for ECT.

	Coffey et al., 1988 (n = 67)	Pande et al., 1990 (n = 7)
Normal scans	14 (21%)	2 (28%)
Patchy white matter lesions	44 (66%)	5 (71%)
Cortical atrophy	46 (68%)	2 (28%)
Lateral ventricle enlargement	45 (67%)	–

increasing confusion that these can bring. ECT has been advocated (Fogel, 1988) as an alternative to tranquillizers for the profoundly demented patient who screams or shouts and shows nonverbal signs of depression such as negativism or poor appetite. It may have advantages over medication but there may be difficulty in obtaining consent from patient and family.

ELECTRODE PLACEMENT

As previously mentioned, unilateral ECT should be used in demented patients as it can produce less confusion. Fraser and Glass (1980) felt unequivocally that for the elderly unilateral treatment was as effective and carried considerably less morbidity than bilateral. Since then opinions have varied. The Royal College of Psychiatrists (1989) recommends bilateral treatment unless minimizing side-effects is a major consideration and speed of action is not of paramount importance. The present author feels that Abrams (1988) puts the vacillation over electrode placement beyond debate when he points out that unilateral ECT has a pronounced cognitive advantage over bilateral ECT and it would therefore seem foolish not use 'substantially supra threshold, brief, square wave, unilateral ECT as an initial trial in every patient', except those who are severely agitated, deluded or suicidal, have acute mania, catatonic stupor or are at risk physically from a longer course of treatment. He completely endorses that approach; however, if there is no substantial improvement after four to six unilateral treatments it could be switched to bilateral, and equally bilateral treatments can be switched to unilateral after the initial improvement has been achieved, particularly if any signs of memory disturbance are emerging. Interestingly, the first antipodean survey of ECT practice (O'Dea et al., 1991) found that 63% of patients received unilateral ECT although there were some marked regional variations.

ELECTRICAL STIMULUS

Part of the variance in views about unilateral/bilateral electrode placement is dependent on dosing. Ictal electroencephalograms (EEGs) show that grand mal seizures with full therapeutic effect are readily elicited by high-intensity bilateral ECT. Low-intensity stimulation, particularly if unilateral, produces a qualitatively different response with less generalization, less synchronicity, and less intensity, particularly over the unstimulated hemisphere, with less complete suppression of the seizure at the end. We need to ensure substantially supra-threshold stimuli if we are not to blame electrode placement for reduced efficacy rather than lack of electrical intensity.

PHYSICAL ILLNESS

The high-risk patient has been addressed elsewhere (Abrams, 1988; Benbow et al., 1991). The present author's view is that there are no absolute contraindications to ECT, only relative risks – relative, that is, to the morbidity or mortality of untreated depression itself. Many people are denied treatment due to irrational caution, related primarily to the perceived anaesthetic risk. Pacemakers are not barriers to treatment, neither is myocardial infarction; in the latter the greatest risk is in the first 10 days postinfarct and is probably negligible at three months. Equally, stroke, anaemia or anticoagulants are not contraindications. Arterial hypertension can be controlled during treatment. Insulin-dependent diabetics need careful monitoring to ensure hydration and appropriate insulin dosage, as requirements tend to reduce during treatment. In fact, dehydration is probably the major problem in severely depressed, retarded patients which can lead to deep vein thrombosis and pulmonary embolism if not managed carefully, but this is not related to the ECT use. The mortality associated with ECT according to Fink (1979) is 0.002% compared with anaesthetic induction alone of 0.003–0.04%. The main barrier to treatment is often the anaesthetist who is unsure of the procedure; the Royal College of Psychiatrists' ECT committee regards liaison with anaesthetists as part of its brief and hope that this will encourage greater understanding.

To return to the original theme, the concern of anaesthetists is that shared by many, and the way to address it is by openness and discussion. ECT is not a universal panacea without side-effects and to pretend that it is in order to persuade patients to consent is foolish. We now have clear guidelines as to when to give ECT, how and to whom. We should use it with confidence as part of an eclectic approach to treatment and it will continue to relieve intolerable distress and save lives.

REFERENCES

Abrams, R. (1988). *Electroconvulsive Therapy*. Oxford University Press, Oxford.

American Psychiatric Association Task Force (1990). The practice of electroconvulsive therapy: recommendations for treatment, training, and privileging. American Psychiatric Press, Washington, DC.

Baxter, L., Roy-Byrne, P., Liston, E. *et al.* (1986). Informing patients about electro-convulsive therapy: effects of a video-tape presentation. *Convuls Ther* **2**, 25–29.

Benbow, S.M. (1987). The use of electroconvulsive therapy in old age psychiatry. *Int J Geriatr Psychiatry* **2**, 25–30.

Benbow, S.M. (1991). Old age psychiatrists' views on the use of ECT. *Int J Geriatr Psychiatry* **6**, 317–322.

Carney, M.W.P., Roth, M. and Garside, R.F. (1965). The diagnosis of depressive syndromes and the prediction of ECT response. *Br J Psychiatry* **125**, 91–94.

Coffey, C.E., Figiel, G.S., Djang, W.T. *et al.* (1988). Leukoencephalopathy in elderly depressed patients referred for ECT. *Biol Psychiatry* **24**, 143–161.

Coffey, C.E., Weiner, R.D., Djang, W. *et al.* (1991) Brain anatomic effects of ECT. *Arch Gen Psychiatry* **48**, 1013–1021.

Devanand, D.P., Verma, A.K., Tirumalesetti, F. *et al.* (1991). Absence of cognitive impairment after more than 100 lifetime ECT treatments. *Am J Psychiatry* **148**, 929–932.

Douyon, R., Sorby, M., Kutchko, B. *et al.* (1989). ECT and Parkinson's disease revisited: a naturalistic study. *Am J Psychiatry* **146**, 1451–1455.

Figiel, G.S., Coffey, C.E. and Weiner, R.D. (1989). Brain magnetic resonance imaging in elderly depressed patients receiving electroconvulsive therapy. *Convuls Ther* **5**, 26–34.

Fink, M.F. (1979). *Convulsive Therapy: Theory and Practice*. Raven Press, New York.

Fogel, B. (1988). Electroconvulsive therapy in the elderly: a clinical research agenda. *Int J Geriatr Psychiatry* **3**, 181–190.

Fraser, R.M. and Glass, I.B. (1980). Unilateral and bilateral ECT in elderly patients: a comparative study. *Acta Psychiatr Scand* **62**, 13–31.

Freeman, C.P.L. and Kendell, R.E. (1980). ECT: one patient's experiences and attitudes. *Br J Psychiatry* **137**, 8–16.

Gaspar, D. and Samara Singhe, L.A. (1982). ECT in psychogeriatric practice – a study of risk factors, indications and outcome. *Compr Psychiatry* **23**, 170–175.

Godber, C., Rosenvinge, H., Wilkinson, D.G. *et al.* (1987). Depression in old age: prognosis after ECT. *Int J Geriatr Psychiatry* **2**, 19–24.

Graham, L.E. and Conley, E.M. (1960). Evaluation of anxiety and fear in adult surgical patients. *Nurs Res* **20**, 113–122.

Heggs, A. (1990). Does electroconvulsive therapy make people anxious? [Thesis, University of Southampton, UK].

Hobson, R.F. (1953). Prognostic factors in electric convulsive therapy. *J Neurol Neurosurg Psychiatry* **16**, 275–281.

Hughes, J., Barraclough, B. and Reeve, W. (1981). Are patients shocked by ECT? *J R Soc Med* **74**, 283–285.

Karlinsky, H. and Shulman, K. (1984). The clinical use of electroconvulsive therapy in old age. *J Am Geriatr Soc* **32**, 183–186.

Kim, E., Zisselman, M. and Pelchat, R. (1996). Factors affecting compliance with maintenance electroconvulsive therapy: a preliminary study. *Int J Geriatr Psychiatry* **11**, 473–476.

Kramer, B.A. (1987). Electroconvulsive therapy use in geriatric depression. *J Nerv Ment Dis* **175**, 233–235.

Lebensohn, J. and Jenkins, R. (1975). Improvements of Parkinsonism in depressed patients treated with ECT. *Am J Psychiatry* **132**, 283–285.

Lippmanns, R., Manshadi, M., Wehry, M. *et al.* (1985). 1250 ECT treatments without evidence of brain injury. *Br J Psychiatry* **147**, 203–204.

Magni, G., Fisman, M. and Helmes, E. (1988). Clinical correlates of ECT-resistant depression in the elderly. *J Clin Psychiatry* **49**, 405–407.

Mielke, D.H., Winstead, D.K., Goether, J.W. *et al.* (1984). Multiple monitored electroconvulsive therapy: safety and efficacy in elderly depressed patients. *J Am Geriatr Soc* **32**, 180–182.

Mirchandani, I., Abrams, R., Young, R. and Alexopoulos, G. (1994). One-year follow-up of continuation convulsive therapy prescribed for depressed elderly patients. *Int J Geriatr Psychiatry* **9**, 31–36.

Mulsant, B.H., Rosen, J., Thornton, J. and Zubenko, G. (1991). A prospective naturalistic study of electroconvulsive therapy in late life depression. *J Geriatr Psychiatry Neurol* **4**, 3–13.

O'Dea, J.F.J., Mitchell, P.B. and Hickie, I.B. (1991). Unilateral and bilateral electroconvulsive therapy for depression? *Med J Aust* **155**, 9–11.

Pande, A.C., Grunhans, L.D., Aisen, A.M. *et al.* (1990). A preliminary magnetic resonance imaging study of ECT-treated depressed patients. *Biol Psychiatry* **27**, 102–104.

Petrides, G., Dhossche, D., Fink, M. and Francis, A. (1994). Continuation ECT: relapse prevention in affective disorders. *Convuls Ther* **10**, 189–194.

Royal College of Psychiatrists (1989). *The practical administration of electroconvulsive therapy (ECT)*. Gaskell, London.

Schwarz, T., Loewenstein, J. and Isenberg, K. (1995). Maintenance ECT: indications and outcome. *Convuls Ther* **11**, 14–23.

Sheffer, M.B. and Greigenstein, F.E. (1960). Emotional responses of patients to surgery and anaesthesia. *Anesthesiology* **21**, 502–507.

Squire, L.R. (1986). Memory functions as affected by electroconvulsive therapy. *Ann NY Acad Sci* **466**, 307–314.

Ward, C., Stern, G., Pratt, R.T.C. *et al.* (1980). Electroconvulsive therapy in Parkinsonisn patients with on–off syndrome. *J Neural Transm Gen Sect* **49**, 133–135.

Weiner, R., Rogers, H. and Davidson, J. (1986). Effects of stimulus parameters on cognitive side-effects. *Ann NY Acad Sci* **462**, 315–325.

Wilkinson, D.G. (1993). Electroconvulsive therapy (ECT). In: Copeland, R., Abou-Saleh, M. and Blazer, D. (Eds), *The Psychiatry of Old Age*. J. Wiley & Sons, Chichester, pp. 77.1–77.6.

Advances in Old Age Psychiatry: Chromosomes to Community Care
Edited by C. Holmes and R. Howard
© 1997 Wrightson Biomedical Publishing Ltd

15

Non-Drug Treatment of Depression in Older People

MARTIN BLANCHARD

Department of Old Age Psychiatry, Royal Free Hospital, London, UK

INTRODUCTION

Besides the use of medications and formal therapies (such as cognitive behavioural therapy (CBT), focused analytic therapy, group therapy and family therapy) in the management in older people, there are a whole series of other activities which can benefit depression and which could occur within the aegis of the primary care health team. Many of these activities may be in addition to antidepressant medication but they may also be beneficial in less severe depression where antidepressants are not indicated or, less frequently, where antidepressants may be contraindicated due to patient frailty, intolerance or hazardous drug interactions. These non-drug treatments also do not require the training nor theoretical rigour of the psychological therapies.

This chapter will initially examine the nature of depression within the older community, its association and current management as determined by a study from Gospel Oak in Inner London, and then discuss assessment and possible management of this depression within a primary care context.

THE NATURE OF DEPRESSION IN OLDER PEOPLE IN THE COMMUNITY

The frequency of depressive symptoms appears to increase with age (Gaitz and Scott, 1972) and its concomitant disability. It was therefore surprising when results from the National Institute of Mental Health/Epidemiologic Catchment Area (NIMH/ECA) studies indicated that depression, as they identified and defined it, was less prevalent among adults aged 65 years or more than among younger age groups (Weismann *et al.*, 1985).

The findings of the NIMH/ECA studies for older people have been criticized on several points. The Diagnostic Interview Schedule (DIS) which was used excluded minor episodes of depression and also depression associated with physical disorders – increasingly common with age. The DIS is highly structured and devised to be performed by lay interviewers; denial of depressive mood and somatization are not uncommon in depression among older people.

However, a recent study by Henderson *et al.* (1993) discovered a rate of 1.0% for DSM-IIIR major depression in a community survey of people aged 70 years or older in Australia, thus apparently confirming the earlier studies. But there was also evidence of a high level of depressive symptoms among older people. These 'below case level' depressive symptoms correlated with neuroticism, poor physical health, disability and a history of previous depression. This study served to reinforce the arbitrariness of 'caseness' for depression among older people and the fact that, because someone does not reach such caseness, it does not necessarily mean that they do not possess clinically relevant depressive symptoms.

The concern that prevalent physical illnesses in older people may cause an increase in the reporting of somatic symptoms and therefore a distortion in the prevalence rate of depression was addressed by Berkman *et al.* (1986). Physical disability among their study population was associated with virtually every item on their depression scale (CES-D, Center for Epidemiologic Studies Depression Scale), not just the somatically orientated ones. A factor analysis of response on this scale from older people produced results almost identical to younger and middle-aged adults. They concluded that disability had a pervasive influence across all domains of depressive symptomatology, and that clinicians and more diagnostically-oriented research instruments tended to underestimate rates of depression among older people by attributing their somatic complaints and/or dysphoric states simply to their declining physical state.

Even if the majority of older adults do not fit DSM-IIIR criteria for major depression but rather have depressive symptoms associated with physical illness and/or adjustment to life stress, it is important to realize that health policy based on the prevalence of major depressive disorders will be ineffective if the loss of social, emotional, physiological, and cognitive function is associated with depressive symptoms that are substantial and widespread but not congruent with a diagnosis of a major disorder (Kennedy *et al.*, 1989).

There has therefore been a need to devise assessment schedules specifically for older people. The Comprehensive Assessment and Referral Evaluation (CARE) instruments (Gurland *et al.*, 1983) have been designed to identify cases of depression among older people severe enough to warrant some form of intervention (probably pervasive depression). They were used to discover very similar levels of depression in New York (13%) and London (12.9%).

Copeland *et al.* (1987) utilized a 'psychiatric' definition of caseness and developed the Geriatric Mental Scale (GMS) along with a computer program (AGECAT) in order to analyse in a repeatable fashion the responses to their semi-structured questionnaire. They discovered 3.0% 'psychotic' or more severe depression and 8.3% 'neurotic' or milder depression among their older Liverpool community. From the results of their three-year follow-up (Copeland *et al.*, 1992) they were able to estimate the incidence of GMS depression caseness as 23.7 per thousand per year.

Livingston *et al.* (1990) screened the Gospel Oak electoral ward in north London using the short-CARE (Gurland *et al.*, 1984) and discovered 15.9% 'probable pervasive depression' increasing to 18.5% when the residents of a local authority home were included. Depression was highly associated with not being currently married (but not with age), living alone, more recent contact with their general practitioner and hospital outpatient departments, and with increased prescription of benzodiazepines and antidepressants – and yet only 12% of their identified depressed cases were receiving antidepressants.

FACTORS ASSOCIATED WITH DEPRESSION IN OLD AGE

There are several significant associations with depression which may also be important in the management of the condition.

Physical illness

A strong association between depression and physical ill-health among older people has been consistently reported. Certain illnesses may have a direct aetiological role in depression either through physiological or cognitive means whilst others may act as maintaining factors. Gurland *et al.* (1983), using the CARE measure, reported a correlation of 0.4 between depression caseness and physical ill-health among New York and London older communities. Kennedy *et al.* (1989) used the CES-D, with a cut-point of 16, to study 2137 older community residents. They obtained a 72% response rate and found caseness in 11% of men and 20% of women. A hierarchy of characteristics was associated with the substantial levels of depressive symptoms: illness, disability, isolation, bereavement and poverty. The prevalence and relative risk of depressive symptoms were related to the number of medical conditions, the number of problems in activities of daily living (ADL), disability, perceived health and the number of visits to a physician. The fact that people felt that they had little or no control over their health also appeared to be important.

Bereavement

Old age is a time of bereavement and, like other losses, this may be expected to precipitate depressive states – although it has been argued that this type of life-event is expected at this time of the life cycle and may therefore cause less psychological damage than when experienced earlier. Certainly the vast majority of bereaved people do pass through the natural process of grief without recourse to doctors. Bruce *et al.* (1990) used NIMH/ECA data and compared depressive episodes and dysphoria between newly bereaved (*n* = 39) and married (*n* = 1047) people aged 45 years and older. They found that bereavement greatly increased the risk of depression and dysphoria, but that the bereaved subjects with depression reported significantly fewer symptoms of guilt compared with the nonbereaved with depression. None of the bereaved and depressed had experienced an earlier depressive episode.

To determine the relationship between recent bereavement and suicide, Bunch (1972) studied 75 consecutive cases of suicide and compared them with 150 matched controls living in the same area. She found that having lost a spouse within the previous three years was significantly more common among people who committed suicide than controls (up to five times), and that more widows than widowers killed themselves. Of the suicides, 81% compared with only 26% of controls had responded to bereavement with evidence of psychiatric disturbance.

Social factors

There have been several studies which have used measures developed by Brown and Harris (1978) but these have only examined hospital-based populations. Representative community studies tend to use briefer measures of social factors, and to compare these with the severity of depressive symptoms rather than presence of clinical case-level depression. Nevertheless, there is evidence that social factors can influence onset and course of depression among older people.

Murphy (1982), building upon Brown and Harris's (1978) assertion that working-class women were five times more likely to develop depression in the year following a severe event or major difficulty, investigated the importance of social factors in the explanation of depression as the commonest mental illness in old age. She compared 100 depressed people referred to local psychiatric services with a group of age- and sex-matched nondepressed control subjects from the general population. Only the index episode of depression had to be presenting for the first time in old age, i.e. some of the patients had experienced previous depressions in younger life. The Present State Examination (PSE) and Feighner criteria (Feighner *et al.* 1972) were used as measures of caseness, and the Life Events and Difficulties Schedule

(LEDS) (Brown and Harris, 1978) was used to examine social factors. A reliability study for the LEDS among older people demonstrated an 81% agreement between subjects' and relatives' responses, with 100% agreement about severe events – the events that are believed to be important aetiologically for depression. Taking one year before interview or one year before onset of depression as the time periods of interest, 48% of patients compared with 23% of normal subjects had a severe event in the year before onset; 42% of patients and 19% of normals had a major non-health difficulty; 39% of patients and 26% of normals had major health difficulties. Of the 200 community interviews performed, 46% of respondents were rated *a* (highest level) on the intimacy rating and 18% *d* (no confidant). Among patients, 39% were *d* on the intimacy rating. Thus 'intimacy' appears to be an important factor in old age depression.

Palinkas *et al.* (1990) studied 1615 men and women aged 65 years or over with the Beck Depression Inventory (BDI) and obtained measures of (1) social activity (the number of social clubs and voluntary associations attended); (2) social network index (size, proximity and contact); (3) frequency of face-to-face contact with close family and friends; (4) 'social distance' of a person identified as being the primary source of support; and (5) physical status from self-report. They discovered that women were less likely than men to point to their spouse as their primary source of support. The scores achieved on the BDI were inversely related to: (1) social network index and (2) participation in voluntary associations and religious institutions. Those who had no primary source of support or who depended upon a relative had significantly higher depressive symptoms. Social network index and social distance to primary source of support were independently associated with depression after controlling for age, sex and number of chronic physical conditions. The number of close friends was inversely associated with depression score whereas the number of close relatives was not. The importance of friends was perceived to indicate that the intimacy of a close friendship was psychologically valuable.

It should be realized that, when examining social factors, depressive symptoms may themselves affect social support by (a) discouraging support, (b) rendering the individual unable to perform expected 'social behaviours' to maintain a network, and (c) by influencing an individual's perception as to the availability and adequacy of support. It is therefore necessary to perform longitudinal studies to examine the outcome effect of social variables on the onset of depression and its subsequent course.

Kivela and Pahkala (1989) performed a prospective follow-up with a mean duration of 14.9 months on 264 depressed older people living in the community. Outcome was good in 41% of cases. Poor outcome was associated with low social participation, low frequency of visiting contacts and low perceived health.

Oxman *et al.* (1992) attempted to examine the effect of the characteristics of social networks and support on depressive symptoms. They utilized results on surveys carried out on 1962 community residents aged 65 years and older first seen in 1982 and followed up in 1985. Baseline depression, functional disability in 1982 and change in disability by 1985 contributed mainly to variance and required adjustment along with sociodemographic variables for their multiple regression analyses. In the psychological sphere, loss of a spouse, adequacy of emotional support and its change between 1982 and 1985 made the largest social contributions to depression and its outcome. Other significant factors were: 'tangible' support adequacy and its change, loss of a confidant, number of children making weekly visits and any change in this, and the absence of a confidant in 1982.

NON-DRUG/NON-THERAPY INTERVENTION STUDIES

There have been few nonpharmacological intervention studies examining outcome in depression in older people. Mulrow *et al.* (1990) treated hearing impairment in 95 older people compared with a waiting-list control. At a four-month follow-up, significant positive changes were seen in treated patients in communication function, social and emotional function and depression scores.

The beneficial effect of reestablishing social interaction has been demonstrated by Schonfield *et al.* (1985) who examined two groups ($n = 42, n = 47$) aged 55–91 years. They followed one group through a mental health treatment programme which emphasized the strengthening of social networks, and the other through a nutrition programme. Initially the mental health programme group scored significantly higher on the BDI and its members had fewer friends as measured on the Social Support Network Inventory. 'Graduates' of the mental health programme improved significantly in their Beck scores with a concomitant increase in friends. Their conclusion was that continued socialization in later years may serve to allay depression.

FINDINGS FROM THE GOSPEL OAK COMMUNITY STUDY

The Gospel Oak community study involved the enumeration and assessment of people of pensionable age from 3000 households in an electoral ward of Inner London. The instrument used to assess depression was the short-CARE (Gurland *et al.*, 1984). Of the cases of probable pervasive depression, 83% were female with an average age of 76.3 years; in contrast, 68.7% of the total pensionable population were female (chi square = 14.2, $p < 0.001$).

Table 1. Current treatment according to DSM-IIIR diagnosis.

	Antidepressant	Hypnotic	Counselling/supportive therapy
Major depression	4/22 (18%)	7/22 (32%)	2/22 (9%)
Dysthymia	6/32 (19%)	9/32 (32%)	1/32 (3%)
DNOS	2/23 (9%)	5/23 (22%)	0/23 (0%)
Others	1/19 (5%)	2/19 (11%)	2/19 (11%)

Further demographic and health-related features of the pervasive depression cases were that 63% were widowed and 22% married; 60% lived in council-rented accommodation and 26% lived in more supportive social services facilities; 62% lived alone, 22% lived with their spouse and 15% lived with a child; 43% had no close relative living in the borough; only 14% did not report a physical illness; only 21% were not receiving regular prescriptions from their general practitioner.

DSM-IIIR diagnoses in the community

DSM-IIIR diagnoses were made by a psychiatrist for all the cases of probable pervasive depression. Physical illness was so common that it could not be used as an exclusion criterion for diagnosis. Estimated population prevalence rates for DSM-IIIR caseness were calculated as 4% major depression, 6% dysthymia and 4% depression not otherwise specified (DNOS).

The relationship between DSM-IIIR diagnosis and current treatment can be seen in Table 1. There was a trend for more prescription of antidepressants and benzodiazepines with greater severity of depression.

Specific treatment and primary care contact

Only 12/77 (16%) DSM-IIIR depression cases were receiving antidepressant medication and 3/77 (4%) were receiving psychotherapy or counselling. Hypnotics were being taken by 21/77 (27%). These low levels of specific management for depression associated with a high level of use of primary care services were similar to findings from other studies (Waxman *et al.*, 1983; Livingston *et al.*, 1990). The lack of antidepressant prescribing could have been due to lack of recognition on the part of general practitioners but might also have been due to worries about potential side-effects of the medications concerned, not only by them but also by the patients. There was almost a complete lack of counselling and psychotherapy interventions within primary care for older depressed people, perhaps reflecting a lack of resources (people and time) but also reflecting negative therapeutic attitudes towards depressed older people.

Table 2. Summary of all interventions suggested by
the multidisciplinary team ($n = 96$).

Medication review	26/96	(27%)
Start antidepressant	41/96	(43%)
Check thyroid function	8/96	(8%)
General physical review	27/96	(28%)
Review pain control	6/96	(6%)
Review mobility	7/96	(7%)
Review eyesight	2/96	(2%)
Review hearing	9/96	(10%)
Review ADL	7/96	(7%)
Psychological symptom control	20/96	(21%)
Relationship counselling	20/96	(21%)
Bereavement counselling	17/96	(18%)
Increase socialization	44/96	(46%)
Housing/financial assistance	17/96	(18%)

PRIMARY CARE MANAGEMENT

The depression intervention part of the Gospel Oak study included the generation of management plans by an experienced secondary care multi-disciplinary team. Table 2 demonstrates the interventions suggested by the multidisciplinary team for all 96 cases.

The multifaceted nature of the interventions suggested can be inferred by the sheer number of them and is demonstrated in that over 50% of subjects required interventions in three or more areas. These interventions were to be carried through by a qualified study nurse working in close liaison with the local general practitioners and, with their agreement, making specialist referrals where necessary.

Compliance with management

Forty-three cases in the intervention study were seen by the study nurse. An average of 10 visits, each of approximately 45 minutes, were made to each of the 43 patients over the three-month period. A mean of seven hours of study-nurse time was spent face to face with each patient over a three-month period.

The interventions carried out involved, on average, six hours of 'psychological' intervention per patient in three months; this intervention process encountered the fewest difficulties with 100% success. Requests for an increase in social network and a trial of antidepressants were discovered to be the most difficult to implement: in 26/43 (60%) of cases the multidisciplinary team requested that the patient should start at a club or day centre, but 18/26 (69%) were not implemented due to patient refusal; there were

19/43 (44%) requests for a trial of antidepressants, but 12/19 (63%) were not implemented due mainly to patient refusal but also to some general practitioner resistance. Overall, 50% of activities were not implemented because of patient refusal.

Outcome of primary-care-based intervention

When examining all the cases in the study, the intervention group fell a mean of 2.7 points on the Depression Diagnostic Scale (DPDS) scale at three months while the control group fell 1.26. The difference between the two groups was statistically significant at the 5% limit. Considering, secondly, the DSM-IIIR cases, the intervention group fell a mean of 2.7 points on the DPDS scale at three months while the control group demonstrated least change, falling only 0.73 points. The difference here was significant at 0.3%.

Again, examining DSM-IIIR cases, in terms of change from case to non-case using DPDS criteria, 27% (8/30) of the cases in the control group and 46% (17/37) of cases in the intervention group became non-cases over the three months (chi square NS, $p = 0.1$).

CONCLUSIONS

Studies have demonstrated a substantial untreated psychiatric morbidity among older people in the community and it is appropriate that the management of these older people should be by the primary health care team. From a recent study it appears though that some patients do not wish to begin antidepressant medication nor to increase their social contact outside the home. It is possible that these interventions are not relevant for the type of depressed subjects living at home, who would not see themselves as psychiatrically ill, and who perhaps have never socialized in such a way. Certainly, more research is needed to study this apparent negativism towards the use of antidepressants; a greater take-up of prescriptions may have resulted in an even better improvement. Nevertheless, despite the lack of success in these two areas, the Gospel Oak intervention study did indicate that the mental state of older people who were depressed could be improved over a three-month period with limited intervention by a nurse.

This finding, if replicated, must have important implications for primary care. But then the question arises as to who could carry out such work with older depressed patients? The role could, in theory, be taken up by the specialist community psychiatric nursing service, but the small number of such nurses devoted to work with older people and the large number of potential patients precludes this. It is possible perhaps, that a practice nurse or health visitor could be trained to carry out such work. Their skills in depression recognition and management could be developed; indeed, the idea of practice nurse specialists in the mental health of older people is not inconceivable.

REFERENCES

Berkman, L.F., Berkman, C.S., Kasl, S. *et al.* (1986). Depressive symptoms in relation to physical health and functioning in the elderly. *Am J Epidemiol* **124**, 372–388.

Brown, G.W. and Harris, T.O. (1978). *Social Origins of Depression.* Tavistock, London.

Bruce, M.L., Kim, K., Leaf, P.J. and Jacobs, S. (1990). Depressive episodes and dysphoria resulting from conjugal bereavement in a prospective community sample. *Am J Psychiatry* **147**, 608–611.

Bunch, J. (1972). Recent bereavement in relation to suicide. *J Psychosom Res* **16**, 361–366.

Copeland, J., Dewey, M., Wood, N., Searle, R., Davidson, I. and McWilliam, C. (1987). Range of mental illness amongst the elderly in the community. Prevalence in Liverpool using the GMS-AGECAT package. *Br J Psychiatry* **150**, 815–823.

Copeland, J., Davidson, I., Dewey, M. *et al.* (1992). Alzheimer's disease, other dementias, depression and pseudodementia: prevalence, incidence and three-year outcome in Liverpool. *Br J Psychiatry* **161**, 230–239.

Feighner, J., Robins, E., Guzes, S. *et al.* (1972). Diagnostic criteria for use in psychiatric research. *Arch Gen Psychiatry* **26**, 57–63.

Gaitz, C. and Scott, J. (1972). Age and the measurement of mental health. *J Health Soc Behav* **13**, 55–67.

Gurland, B., Copeland, J., Kuriansky, J. *et al.* (1983). *The Mind and Mood of Aging.* Croom Helm, London.

Gurland, B., Golden, R., Teresi, J. and Challop, J. (1984). The SHORT-CARE: an efficient instrument for the assessment of depression, dementia and disability. *J Gerontol* **39**, 166–169.

Henderson, A.S., Jorm, A.F., Mackinnon, A. *et al.* (1993). The prevalence of depressive disorders and the distribution of depressive symptoms in later life: a survey using draft ICD-10 and DSM-IIIR. *Psychol Med* **23**, 719–729.

Kennedy, G., Kelman, H., Thomas, C. *et al.* (1989). Hierarchy of characteristics associated with depressive symptoms in an urban elderly sample. *Am J Psychiatry* **146**, 220–225.

Kivela, S.-L. and Pahkala, K. (1989). The prognosis of depression in old age. *Int Psychogeriatr* **1**, 119–133.

Livingston, G., Hawkins, A., Graham, N., Blizard, B. and Mann, A. (1990). The Gospel Oak Study: prevalence rates of dementia, depression and activity limitation among elderly residents in Inner London. *Psychol Med* **20**, 137–146.

Mulrow, C., Aguilar, C., Endicott, J. *et al.* (1990). Quality of life changes and hearing impairment. A randomised trial. *Ann Intern Med* **113**, 188–194.

Murphy, E. (1982). Social origins of depression in old age. *Br J Psychiatry* **141**, 135–142.

Oxman, T.E., Berkman, L.F., Kasl, S., Freeman, D.H. Jr and Barrett, J. (1992). Social support and depressive symptoms in the elderly. *Am J Epidemiol* **135**, 356–368.

Palinkas, L.A., Wingard, D.L. and Barrett-Connor, E. (1990). The biocultural context of social networks and depression among the elderly. *Soc Sci Med* **30**, 441–447.

Schonfield, L., Garcia, J. and Streuber, P. (1985). Factors contributing to mental health treatment of the elderly. *J Appl Gerontol* **4**(2), 30–39.

Waxman, H., Carner, E. and Blum, A. (1983). Depressive symptoms and health service utilization among the community elderly. *J Am Geriatr Soc* **31**, 417–420.

Weismann, M.M., Myers, J.K., Tischler, G.L. *et al.* (1985). Psychiatric disorders (DSM-III) and cognitive impairment among the elderly in a US urban community. *Acta Psychiatr Scand* **71**, 366–379.

Advances in Old Age Psychiatry: Chromosomes to Community Care
Edited by C. Holmes and R. Howard
© 1997 Wrightson Biomedical Publishing Ltd

16

Dysthymic Disorders and Chronic Minor Depression in Late Life: Description and Treatment

DAN G. BLAZER

Department of Psychiatry and Behavioral Sciences, Duke University School of Medicine, Durham, North Carolina, USA

INTRODUCTION

Subsyndromal depression, that is a depressive syndrome which does not meet criteria for major depression yet is considered clinically significant in terms of disabling older adults, is one of the more common problems encountered by primary care physicians in ambulatory practice. Subsyndromal depressions may be variously diagnosed as: prodromal or partially recovered major depressive disorders (DSM-IV and ICD-9); mood disorder due to general medical condition (DSM-IV); minor depression (DSM-IV Appendix); brief recurrent mood disorder; depressive personality (ICD-9); and dysthymic disorder (DSM-IV) or neurotic depression (ICD-9) (American Psychiatric Association, 1994; World Health Organization, 1977; Angst *et al.*, 1990). The boundaries between these diagnostic categories are not clear except that each is distinguished from the more severe mood disorders, such as bipolar disorder and unipolar disorder. This chapter will focus on the two variants above which have been most widely studied, i.e. dysthymic disorder and minor depression.

Dysthymic disorder is described in DSM-IV as 'a chronically depressed mood that occurs for most of the day more days than not for at least two years' (American Psychiatric Association, 1994). In addition, two symptoms must be present among the following: poor appetite or overeating, insomnia or hypersomnia; low energy or fatigue; low self-esteem; poor concentration or difficulty making decisions; feelings of hopelessness; the permanent presence of low interest; and self-criticism. To make the diagnosis of dysthymic disorder, these symptoms should have become 'a part of the individual's day-to-day experience'. In contrast, there are no agreed diagnostic criteria for minor depression. In the Appendix of DSM-IV, a proposed definition for minor depression is a syndrome which lasts for two or more weeks and which has three of the eight criteria for major depression, symptoms which cause clinically significant distress.

A number of questions arise, however, regarding dysthymia and minor depression. These questions derive in part from certain counterintuitive empirical observations of depressive syndromes across the life cycle. First, recovery from major depression does not occur as quickly nor as completely as many clinicians assume. One reason that clinicians tend to be misled in documenting improvement from severe mood disorders is that the typical rating scales do not identify less severe mood disturbances, or personality and interpersonal dysfunction. Frequently, it takes an individual six months to one year to recover from a severe mood disorder. These individuals may be labelled as suffering from a dysthymic disorder or minor depression. Secondly, by definition a dysthymic disorder is a relatively continuous depressive mood which is less severe than a major depressive disorder and tends not to fluctuate over time. Rarely, however, does a chronic, less severe depression not fluctuate in severity. Thirdly, our current diagnostic categories are hypotheses which should be tested empirically. In other words, major depression with melancholia, dysthymic disorder, adjustment disorder with depressed mood, etc., are hypotheses which have been stated in our nomenclature. Empirical studies, such as genetic studies, outcome studies, studies of biological markers and response to therapy, as well as statistical studies of clusters of symptoms across time in individuals themselves, should be applied to these categories to test their 'validity'. For example, many cases which meet current criteria for dysthymia or minor depression may actually be variants of a unipolar recurrent mood disorder. Therefore, a study treatment must be underpinned by an understanding of the epidemiology, risk factors and course of dysthymic disorder and minor depression if treatment is to be evaluated objectively.

EPIDEMIOLOGY

Few argue that the frequency of clinically significant depressive symptoms in community populations is relatively high compared with a diagnosis of major depression. A comparison of the estimates of various community studies of clinically significant depressive symptoms in community populations is presented in Table 1 (Blazer and Williams, 1980; Murrell et al., 1983; O'Hara et al., 1985; Berkman et al., 1986; Blazer et al., 1991; Beekman et al., 1997).

These estimates suggest that most clinically significant depressive symptoms are not captured by the diagnosis of major depression.

Table 1. Prevalence of clinically significant depressive symptoms in late life (symptom scales).

Blazer and Williams, 1980	14.7%
Murrell *et al.*, 1983	13.7% (M); 18.2% (F)
O'Hara *et al.*, 1985	9.0%
Berkman *et al.*, 1986	11.3% (M); 19.2% (F)
Blazer *et al.*, 1991	9.0%
Beekman, 1997	12.9%

In contrast, the estimates of major depression between compilations is quite low, rarely ranging above 3%, (Gurland *et al.*, 1983; Copeland *et al.*, 1987; Broadhead *et al.*, 1990; Devenand *et al.*, 1994) (see Table 2). In North Carolina, though the overall prevalence of major depression is less than 1% among the elderly, the prevalence of dysthymic disorder among the 60+ age group is 1.6%, of minor depression with mood disorder 4.5%, and of minor depression without a mood disturbance 25.6% (Stewart *et al.*, 1992).

These estimates are low and do not account for all persons with clinically significant depressive symptoms in late life.

This wide variation in the prevalence of depressive symptoms compared with major depression and dysthymic disorder suggests that many persons across the life cycle experience depressive syndromes which are probably clinically significant yet are not captured by these two diagnoses. Broadhead and colleagues (1990) found that the likelihood of impairment in persons experiencing minor depression in terms of absence from work was significantly greater than for persons without minor depression, yet was lower for persons with major depression. Impairment for minor depression approximated the impairment found among persons diagnosed with dysthymic disorder in a prospective study. In addition, these persons utilized more medical services and were more likely to be treated for depression than persons without diagnosis of depression.

Devenand *et al.* (1994) found, in a clinical study of persons between 60 and 92 years of age treated in an ambulatory mental health clinic, that 18% were diagnosed with dysthymic disorder. The average age of onset for these

Table 2. Prevalence of current major depression in late life (ICD, RDC[a] and DSM).

Blazer and Williams, 1980 (DSM-III)	1.8%
Gurland *et al.*, 1983 (ICD)	1.9%
O'Hara *et al.*, 1985 (RDC[a])	1.2%
Copeland *et al.*, 1987 (GMS-AGECAT)	2.9%

[a] Research Diagnostic Criteria.

persons experiencing dysthmic disorder in later life was 55 and the average duration of illness was 12.5 years. Most did not have a previous diagnosis of major depression. Though stressful events were frequently associatcd with the onset and continuance of dysthymic disorder, other risk factors for major depression were not found in this clinical study. For this reason, Devenand suggested that dysthymic disorder was a unique syndrome in older persons and should be investigated as such.

RISK FACTORS

A comparison of the risk factors for major depression, minor depression and dysthymic disorder in late life is presented in Table 3. As can be seen, the risk factors for major depression are virtually identical to those for minor depression. In the study by Devenand (1994), the risk factors for dysthymic disorder vary from those of major depression. According to most studies, however, the risk factors for dysthymic disorder are similar to those for major depression (American Psychiatric Association, 1994). Biological factors associated with major depression with melancholia, such as reduced rapid eye movement (REM) sleep latency have been associated with dysthymic disorder. Dexamethasone nonsuppression, however, is uncommon in dysthymic disorder. Dysthymic disorder is more common among first-degree biological relatives of persons with major depressive disorder than in the general population. Except for the relatively consistent finding of an equal distribution by gender of dysthymic disorder, the risk factor profiles for major depression, minor depression and dysthymic disorder do not appear to be significantly different.

Table 3. Risk factors for major depression, minor depression and dysthymia in late life.

Major depression	Minor depression	Dysthymia
Not married	Perceived poor health	No gender difference
Female gender	Functional limitations	Stressful life events
Younger age	Loneliness	Co-morbid disorders less
Low socioeconomic status	Internal locus of control	common (Devenand et
Cognitive impairment	Not/no longer married	al., 1994)
Co-morbid anxiety	History of major depression	
Internal locus of control	Cognitive impairment	
Loneliness	Functional impairment	
Functional impairment	Stressful life events	
(Beekman et al., 1997)	(Beekman et al., 1997;	
	Blazer et al., 1991	

OUTCOME

By definition, dysthymic disorder is a chronic condition. Yet the difficulty in diagnosing, especially in differentiating dysthymic disorder from other mood disorders is graphically presented in Figure 1. As can be seen, dysthymic disorder/major depression may be manifested by brief recurrent episodes, the

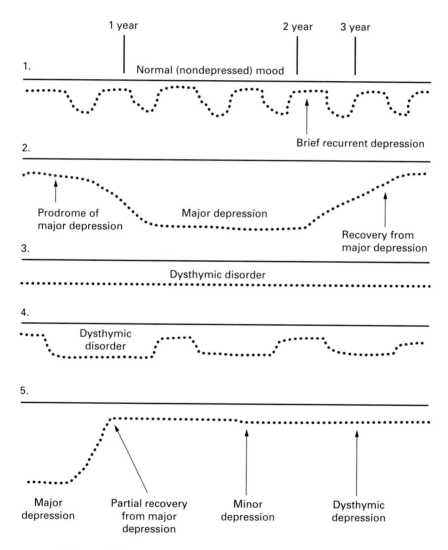

Figure 1. The course of minor depression/dysthymic disorder.

prodrome or recovery from an episode of major depression, a typical dysthymic disorder, a dysthymic disorder with periodic but short episodes of complete or almost complete recovery, and a prolonged or partial recovery from a major depressive disorder. As obtaining historical data regarding the course of a mood disorder from an older adult is notoriously difficult, it is often impossible accurately to chart the course of a dysthymic disorder except prospectively. Prospective charting often reveals that the initial diagnosis is not the final diagnosis. For example, what appears to be a dysthymic disorder/minor depression over a course of months is later found to be the prodrome of a major depressive episode. Or, recovery from a major depression may only be partial and symptoms of dysthymia are evident two year after partial recovery from the major depressive episode. In addition, a chronic minor depression/dysthymia may be superimposed with episodes of major depression which respond to treatment and return the individual to her or his previous clinical presentation of minor depression or dysthymia. Against this background, the clinician must determine what therapy to select and how to evaluate the effectiveness of that therapy. As dysthymic disorder/minor depression is protean in its manifestations over time, it is extremely difficult to study the condition in controlled treatment settings. For these reasons, the treatment of dysthymic disorder is usually individualized to the patient and the physician treating that patient must take care that the prescribed therapy is of benefit to the patient individually. Once the dysthymic patient has become engaged in therapy, either pharmacological and/or psychotherapeutic, the effectiveness of therapy must be distentangled from a dependency upon therapy during the course of therapy.

TREATMENT OF MINOR DEPRESSION/DYSTHYMIC DISORDER

The treatment of minor depression/dysthymic depression can be divided for convenience into three modes – pharmacotherapy, psychotherapy and social/environment intervention. The literature is conflicting regarding the effectiveness of medications in the treatment of dysthymic disorder/minor depression. There has been little study specifically of the treatment of dysthymic disorder with medications. For example, Stewart *et al.* (1992), in a study of over 400 outpatients with Hamilton Depression Rating Scale scores of 10 or less, found that these minor depressive syndromes responded to imipramine and phenelzine compared with placebo. In contrast, Paykel *et al.* (1988) evaluated the use of amitriptyline in treating more severe versus less severe depressive syndromes in primary care settings. They found that amitriptyline was effective in treating the more severe but not less severe syndromes.

Given the lack of empirical data regarding the effectiveness of antidepressant medications in the treatment of minor depression/dysthymia, the clinician may wish to prescribe an antidepressant medication on a trial basis to determine if that medication is effective. The guidelines for determining effectiveness are described below. Four categories of antidepressant medication should be considered. First, the clinician should consider the use of the selective serotonin reuptake inhibitors (SSRIs) such as fluoxetine, paroxetine, sertraline and nefazodone. The selection of a specific SSRI may depend upon the particular symptoms targeted. For example, an individual experiencing dysthymia/minor depression with significant sleep disturbance may be prescribed nefazodone or trazodone in low doses. Nefazodone may be started at 50 mg orally at night with an increase to 150 mg per day if tolerated by the patient. Trazodone may be started at 25–50 mg orally at night and increased to 100 or perhaps 150 mg. In subsydrome depressions, lower doses of these medications are often found to be beneficial in individual cases. If the patient is experiencing obsessive thoughts, such as excessive worry, then fluoxetine 10 mg daily may be the drug of choice. If agitation is a major concern in treatment, then the use of paroxetine 20 mg daily or nefazodone 200 mg daily or sertraline 50 mg daily would be preferred over fluoxetine.

As noted in the Stewart et al. study (1992), monoamine oxidase inhibitors (MAOIs), specifically phenelzine, were found to be effective in treating less severe depressive disorders. Nevertheless, MAOIs can lead to significant agitation in older adults and therefore SSRIs are generally preferred. The concern regarding diet and the use of MAOIs is real but perhaps overrated as a reason for not using the medication. If the clinician is seriously considering the possibility of following pharmacotherapy with electroconvulsive therapy (ECT) (which would be rare in the treatment of a minor depression/dysthymic disorder), then the MAOIs should not be used because they must be discontinued one to two weeks prior to the use of ECT because of the interaction with medications used during ECT.

Stimulants have been suggested for minor depressions in older adults for many years and evidence can be found scattered throughout the literature that such drugs are of some benefit (Gurain and Rosowsky, 1993). In the USA stimulants are frequently used to treat less severe depressions or atypical depressions, especially in long-term care facilities. These drugs frequently increase activity in persons experiencing a more retarded form of depression early in the course of treatment. Their effect frequently wanes over time and patients often become uncomfortable taking the medication. When used in low doses (such as methylphenidate, less than 20 mg/day) the medication is rarely addictive in older persons and rarely leads to significant problems with cardiovascular events.

Tricyclic antidepressants should not be neglected as a treatment for less severe depressions. The two tricyclic drugs most frequently used in older persons are nortriptyline and desipramine. Each can be used in doses ranging from 25 to 75 mg. In persons who can tolerate the side-effects, these drugs provide a viable alternative to the SSRIs, especially if cost is a major factor in assuring compliance of the patient in taking the medication.

The empirical data verifying the effectiveness of the use of medications for the treatment of dysthymia/minor depression are sparse and contradictory. Such drugs are frequently used in treating subsyndromal depression in late life because many clinicians believe them to be effective. The author suggests guidelines to ensure that the medications are used as cautiously as possible. First, the clinician should identify specific target symptoms for which it is believed that the medication will be effective. In minor depression, only rarely will a medication lead to a dramatic improvement in many symptoms as experienced in a typical treatment response of melancholic depression. Target symptoms which may respond include sleep disturbance, obsessive worrying, crying spells and anhedonia. Once the clinician talks with the patient about the specific hoped-for benefit of the medication to correct these particular symptoms (not promising that the medication will improve every symptom) then the medication can be more adequately monitored in terms of its effectiveness. Secondly, the clinician should only expect a partial remission of even the target symptoms with the use of medications alone. This partial remission may be sufficient to enable the older person to return to normal functioning, though that normal functioning may not be the desired-for functioning of a successfully ageing person. Finally, over time the clinician must consider the cost–benefit ratio of continued use of a psychotropic medication. None of these medications is without side-effects. For this reason the clinician must weigh the therapeutic advantages versus both the cost of continuing therapy and the side-effects produced. If at all possible the physician should avoid prescribing multiple medications to an individual with minor depression/dysthymia as it becomes virtually impossible to disentangle the individual therapeutic benefit of each medication under such circumstances.

The evidence for the effectiveness of psychotherapy in the treatment of minor depression/dysthymia in late life is generally positive, but also mixed (Scogin and McErath, 1994). A variety of therapies have been proposed, including group therapy, group therapy with a behavioural orientation, individual cognitive therapy, group therapy with an emphasis on reminiscence, and self-administered cognitive and behavioural therapy. Psychodynamic, insight-orientated therapy may be especially appropriate for an individual experiencing a dysthymic disorder/minor depression who is sophisticated regarding psychological factors and wishes to explore his or her feelings within the framework of psychodynamic theory.

Despite the mixed results with psychotherapy, clinicians should recognize that empirical studies of psychotherapy may not capture the nuances of its use in the treatment of chronic depression. Rarely does a 'chronic' depression become apparent to a clinician unless the situation has worsened. By definition, both the symptoms and lifestyle of a person with chronic depression tend to become adaptive (even if maladaptive on the surface) and therefore these persons typically do not seek therapy. Therefore, when therapy is sought, either from a psychiatrist, other mental health workers, or a primary care physician, the older adult experiencing the chronic, subsyndromal depression is usually in the midst of some type of minor, or major, crisis. After initial evaluation, especially if the family is brought into the evaluation, it will probably be apparent that a chronic depression has worsened as a result of some specific stressful experience. Approaching therapy from a 'crisis intervention perspective' may be especially beneficial in assisting the older person to return to their normal state of equilibrium.

The symptoms of chronic subsyndromal depression are myriad and may have evolved over months, even years. Therefore psychotherapy should not be directed towards either the entire spectrum of symptoms experienced by the older adult or the multiple problems which may have contributed to the depression over many years. Rather, therapy should be focused upon specific components of the depressive syndrome. For example, the therapist may consider some specific aspects of social functioning which have worsened over a period of months as the approach to therapy. Usually, a limited number of sessions on a relatively frequent basis (for example, weekly) should be supplanted by continued sessions at increasingly greater intervals. Given the chronicity of this disorder, however, 'discharge' from therapy may not be warranted. Therefore the patient can benefit significantly from visits every six months of approximately 30 minutes. These visits can focus upon the particular issues which were the central elements of the intense period of therapy. The patient often benefits from these infrequent contacts; they are relatively inexpensive and may save a trip (or trips) to a primary care physician. In other words, these patients need someone to talk to over time.

If the therapy is directed towards helping an individual who has suffered from a more severe depressive episode (but who is now in the midst of a dysthymic disorder/minor depression) reintegration into their former life becomes a primary goal of therapy. A recognition of the long lag necessary for integration is critical at the outset of therapy, as expectations for therapy are set.

Finally, a clinician must consider social/environmental interactions. Empirical data are virtually absent regarding social types of interventions except the impact of such interventions in nursing homes or other congregate living situations. Nevertheless, family counselling may enable the family to better manage the older adult with minor depression/dysthymic disorder. In addition, family therapy may uncover interpersonal factors which contribute to the subsyndromal depression. An alliance between patient, family and psychiatrist is one of the most positive factors in assuring that minor depression can be effectively treated. Rarely do older persons experiencing depression protest when the psychiatrist wishes to speak with a family member. In fact, most older persons come to the psychiatrist with a family member and that family member may even accompany the older person into the initial session uninvited. This should not automatically be discouraged but family dynamics should be assessed from the outset of therapy and then an approach which includes the family can be instituted when indicated.

CONCLUSION

As stated at the outset of this paper, dysthymic disorder/minor depression is protean in its manifestations and therefore difficult to define, much less treat with specific therapies. Nevertheless, lessons which have been learned in the treatment of more severe depressions and the experience of many psychiatrists with persons suffering less severe depressions over many years do provide some guidelines for the management of these disorders. By their very nature these disorders are difficult to study empirically and therefore empirically based guidelines for therapy may not emerge for many years. This does not mean, however, that treating these patients should be neglected. Rather, clinical judgement, targeting specific symptoms and monitoring overall outcome and use of health services on an individual basis are of significant benefit to the dysthymic older adult.

ACKNOWLEDGEMENTS

This study was supported in part by the Established Population for Epidemiologic Studies of the Elderly contract from the National Institutes on Aging (NIA Contract No. NO1 AG 1 2102) and the Clinical Research Center for the Study of Depression in Late Life (Grant no. MH 40159).

REFERENCES

American Psychiatric Association (1994). *Diagnostic and Statistical Manual of Mood Disorders, 4th edn.* American Psychiatric Association, Washington, DC.

Angst, K., Marikagis, K., Scheidegger, P. and Wicki, W. (1990). Recurrent brief depression: a new subtype of affective disorders. *J Affect Disord* **19**, 87–98.

Beekman, A.T.F., Deeg, D.J.H., Vantilburg, T., Schmidt, J.H., Horijar, C. and Vantilburgh, W. (1997). Major and minor depression in later life: a study of prevalence and risk factors (in press).

Berkman, L.F., Berkman, C.S., Kasl, S. *et al.* (1986). Depressive symptoms in relation to physical health and functioning in the elderly. *Am J Epidemiol* **124**, 372–388.

Blazer, D.G. and Williams, C.D. (1980). The epidemiology of dysphoria and depression in an elderly population. *Am J Psychiatry* **137**, 439–444.

Blazer, D.G., Burchet, B., Service, C. and George, L.K. (1991). The assocation of age and depression among the elderly: an epidemiologic exploration. *J Gerontol* **46**, 210–215.

Broadhead, W.E., Blazer, D.G., George, L.K. and Tse, C.K. (1990). Depression, disability days and days lost from work in a prospective epidemiologic survey. *JAMA* **264**, 2524–2528.

Copeland, J.M.R., Dewey, M.E., Wood, N., Searle, R., Davidson, I.A. and McWilliam, C. (1987). Range of mental illness among the elderly in the community: prevalence in Liverpool using the GMS-AGECAT package. *Br J Psychiatry* **150**, 85–123.

Devenand, D.P., Nobler, M.S., Singer, T. *et al.* (1994). Is dysthymia a different disorder in the elderly? *Am J Psychiatry* **151**, 1592–1599.

Gurain, B. and Rosowsky, E. (1993). Methylphenidate treatment of minor depression in very old patients. *Am J Geriatr Psychiatry* **1**, 171–173.

Gurland, B., Copeland, J., Kuriansky, J., Kelleher, M., Sharp, L. and Dean, L.L. (1983). *The Mind and Mood of Aging: The Mental Health Problems of the Community Elderly in New York and London.* Haworth Press, New York.

Murrell, S.A., Himmelfarb, S. and Wright, K. (1983). Prevalence of depression and its correlates in older adults. *Am J Epidemiol* **117**, 175–185.

O'Hara, M.W., Kohout, F.J. and Wallace, R.B. (1985). Depression among the rural elderly: a study of prevalence and correlates. *J Nerv Ment Dis* **173**, 582–589.

Paykel, E.S., Holliman, J.A., Freeling, P. and Sedgwick, P. (1988). Predictors of therapeutic benefits from amitriptyline in mild depression: a general practice placebo-control trial. *J Affect Disord* **14**, 83–95.

Scogin, F. and McErath, L. (1994). Efficacy of psychosocial treatments for geriatric depression: a quantitative review. *J Consult Clin Psychol* **62**, 69–74.

Stewart, J.W., McGrath, P.J. and Quitken, F.M. (1992). Can mildly depressed outpatients with atypical depression benefit from antidepressants? *Am J Psychiatry* **149**, 615–619.

World Health Organization (1977). *Manual of the International Statistical Classification of Diseases, Injuries and Causes of Death, (9th revision).* World Health Organization, Geneva.

Advances in Old Age Psychiatry: Chromosomes to Community Care
Edited by C. Holmes and R. Howard
© 1997 Wrightson Biomedical Publishing Ltd

17

The Prognosis of Depression in Later Life

ROBERT BALDWIN

Central Manchester Healthcare Trust, Psychiatry Directorate, Manchester, UK

This chapter reviews current knowledge concerning the outcome of depression in older people, factors which predict outcome and avenues which might improve it. Research into neurobiological factors which may be of relevance to outcome are also touched upon.

NATURALISTIC OUTCOME

In referred patients

Most studies are of patients referred to psychiatric services. The task of reviewing the literature in prognosis has been made easier thanks to a study by Cole (1990), who has conducted the only meta-analysis of depression outcome studies in the elderly. He included only studies in which there were more than 25 patients since the 1950s. This involved 990 patients. Table 1 summarizes the findings.

Table 1. Meta-analysis of prognosis studies (%) (after Cole, 1990).

Prognosis category	Studies <23 months		Studies >24 months	
	Results	*Combined results (n = 575)*	*Results*	*Combined results (n = 515)*
Well	31–64	43.7	18–33	27.4
Relapse with recovery	15–25	15.8	28–52	34.2
Continuously ill	18–69	27.3	7–30	9.9
Other	8–21	13.2	23–39	28.5

The studies included by Cole were: Kay *et al.*, 1955; Post, 1962, 1972; Gordon, 1981; Cole, 1983; Cole, 1985; Baldwin and Jolley, 1986; Godber *et al.*, 1987; Magni *et al.*, 1988.

Only a quarter of patients can be expected to remain completely well. The average follow-up in these studies was 32 months. Whether in the short term (23 months or less) or longer term (more than 24 months), about 60% either remained well or were well but had further relapses.

However, Cole also assessed these studies in the light of McMaster University Health Sciences Center criteria for prognostic research. These included: formation of an inception cohort; description of referral pattern; completion of follow-up; development and use of objective outcome criteria; blinded assessment of outcome and adjustment for extraneous prognostic factors. All of the studies, judged in this way, had serious and multiple flaws. Further criticisms include the lack of operational diagnostic criteria and a structured interview to assess subjects in some studies, and the use of retrospective designs.

Since Cole's review, there have been only a few further published studies of relevance. Burvill et al. (1991) studied subjects ($n = 103$, mainly inpatients) over 12 months, assessed using the Geriatric Mental Status Schedule (Copeland et al., 1976). Again the results were similar to Cole's meta-analysis: 47% well at one year, 18% relapsed and recovered, 24% were depressive invalids or had been continuously ill, while 11% died; though when using a more stringent dichotomized outcome only 32% were found to have unequivocally good outcomes.

Murphy (1983) found that those with delusional depressive illness had a dire prognosis. In the study of Burvill et al. (1991), 35% of the cohort had psychotic depression. Their outcome did not differ compared with the remainder. The author's own research (Baldwin, 1988) also did not find a worse prognosis for deluded compared with nondeluded elderly depressed patients.

Stoudemire and colleagues (1993) followed up 55 patients aged over 55 (mean age 72 years) who met DSM-IIIR criteria for major depression (American Psychiatric Association, 1987) at 6, 15 and approximately 48 months in a naturalistic study. At 15-month follow-up, 77% of patients given tricyclic antidepressants and 70% treated with electroconvulsive therapy (ECT) had improved (combined result 72%). Approximately four years after initial treatment, 93% of patients treated with tricyclics and 79% of those treated with ECT were in remission (combined result 84%), although numbers available for assessment were reduced to 43 by then. Although these findings are encouraging, there was a very high rehospitalization rate during the course of follow-up, 50% overall.

In a short-term study, Flint and Rifat (1996) evaluated the responses of 101 patients with major depression (DSM-IIIR) to sequential regimens of antidepressants and, if no response to drugs, ECT. The protocol allowed for up to 28 weeks' treatment. In the intention-to-treat analysis, 83% of patients recovered with one of the regimens. This will be discussed further later (see section on resistant depression).

Freyne and Wrigley (1995), in a retrospective study of 86 depressed patients covering 12 months minimum, reported outcomes similar to Baldwin and Jolley (1986) for patients seen on domiciliary consultation and similar to that reported by Murphy (1983) when those who were seen on hospital liaison were also included. Poor physical health was a predictor of poor outcome and increased mortality (three times that expected) and was accentuated in the subgroup seen in the hospital.

Lastly, Alexopoulos et al. (1996) compared the time to recovery and of remission in 63 elderly depressed patients (mean age 75) with 23 'younger' depressed patients (mean age 55). Using survival analysis there was no difference in the time course to recovery, and no evidence of a worse prognosis for the older group. Sixty per cent of each group were recovered at six months.

Although these later studies are more sound methodologically than some earlier reports, they still suffer from the same weaknesses which Cole (1990) highlighted. However, it is reasonable to assert that the prognosis of depression in elderly people presenting to psychiatrists is not as bad as has been suggested by some commentators; for example, '. . . no matter what is done, a third get better, a third stay the same, and a third get worse' (Millard, 1983); but neither is it all that rosy. Approximately 60% of patients either remain symptom-free or have relapses from which they recover over periods typically of around four years. At least half, though, will experience a recurrence of their depression and about one-third of patients will remain with unresolved symptoms.

In the community

There is less information regarding nonpsychiatric patients. The Liverpool Continuing Health in the Community Study followed up 1070 people in the community over six years (Green et al., 1994). Their original model (Green et al., 1992) proposed four vulnerability factors (female gender, smoking, loneliness and life dissatisfaction) and one trigger (bereavement) in the preceding six months in the genesis of depression. Three years on, on cross-sectional follow-up, 40% of the original group of 123 subjects were recovered. Among a large range of potential prognostic factors, the only ones associated with recurrence of depression (or persistent depression) at the year 3 interview were bereavement of a close figure in the six months prior to reassessment, loneliness, and poor life satisfaction at the time of follow-up. Factors found in studies of referred patients, for example physical ill-health, did not predict outcome. There was a trend for higher rates of admission to more supported accommodation among those who had been depressed originally and very little use of antidepressant medication.

Another series of community studies has been conducted by a Finnish group. In one of these (Kivela et al., 1991), 199 people aged over 60 years suffering from dysthymic disorder were compared with 42 similarly-aged persons with major depression episode (DSM-III). The assessment of outcome was the same as that used by Murphy (1983). Thirty-nine per cent of the men and 48% of the women had a 'good' outcome. These findings were rather better than for dysthymic disorder. No predictive variables could be identified for the depressed men. For the women, poor outcome was associated with diabetes, suicidality and psychomotor disturbance. As one would anticipate, the mean Hamilton scores of those in the study suggested that they were less severely ill than the referred patients in the meta-analysis of Cole (1990).

In the frail and ill

Koenig et al. (1992) followed up 53 hospitalized elderly men with severe medical illnesses and major depression. After 2.3 months (range ±1.6 months) 64% had persistent depression, 18% had improved and 18% were in remission. No predictors of outcome, including use of treatment, were identified in this study.

Ames (1990) identified 93 residents of residential care homes with significant depressive symptoms. A range of interventions, many of a social nature, were suggested by the local psychogeriatric team, but the outcome at three months was poor. There was no evidence of efficacy, probably because many of the suggestions had not been acted upon. At 12 months, of those who had survived, a quarter remained depressed. These findings are clearly alarming.

Depression in carers

Ballard et al. (1996) screened 109 carers of dementia patients for depression. Six had major depression (American Psychiatric Association, 1987) and 20 'minor depression'. At one year, three of six major depressives were still 'cases' and five of the 20 'minor' depressives remained so. Thus 30% of all cases persisted for the whole year. Also, 28 of the 59 (48%) nondepressed patients went on to develop depression (9 major and 19 minor). Factors associated with length of depression in carers were depression and problem behaviours in the patient. This is clearly a neglected area.

MORTALITY

Though rates for relapse and chronicity vary quite considerably, there is rather more uniformity regarding mortality. Table 2 shows results from three short-term and two longer-term studies. All the figures in Table 2 are above that expected, assuming, roughly, a 5% year-on-year mortality in this group.

Table 2. Studies of mortality in depression in old age.

Author	Number	Follow-up (months)	Mortality rate (%)
Murphy, 1983	124	12	14
Baldwin and Jolley, 1986	100	12	8
Rabins et al., 1985	62	12	13
Murphy et al., 1988	120	48	34
Baldwin and Jolley, 1986	100	48	26

In some cases, for example the study of Rabins et al. (1985), it exceeds that expected by a factor of 2.5, chiefly due to cardiovascular causes, an excess also reported by Murphy et al. (1988). It might be assumed that the excess death rate is merely due to more physical disease in those who died prematurely. In the study of Murphy et al. (1988), two groups were compared, one with depression, and an age- and sex-matched control group from the community. The groups were then matched for levels of physical morbidity, with the finding that the depressed group still had statistically higher mortality.

Burvill and Hall (1994) have, more recently, confirmed a high mortality which could not be explained by physical ill health, in a five-year follow-up of a cohort of 103 depressed patients. They also found an excess of cardiovascular causes. Self-reports by patients were as good a predictor of mortality as physician-related measures, but poor mobility was the best independent predictor of death.

Most deaths occur early in the course of illness (Baldwin and Jolley, 1986; Jorm et al., 1991). Hence, in a long-term study of elderly depressed patients referred to a psychiatric service (Robinson, 1989), it was found that the two-year mortality was high, 35%, but the 10- and 15-year mortality was hardly higher than that from the catchment population. Almost all survivors at five years and beyond remained psychiatrically well.

O'Brien and Ames (1994) postulate several possible mechanisms for the increased mortality in depression: co-morbid physical illness; occult illness; illness effects (e.g. related to psychomotor retardation); treatment effects; biological effects such as abnormality of the hypothalamic-pituitary-adrenal axis or endocrine abnormalities. Undertreatment is another explanation. Cardiovascular mortality is reportedly higher in elderly depressed men whose depression was judged to be inadequately treated (Avery and Winokur, 1976) and among elderly depressed women not given ECT (Babigian and Guttmacher, 1984).

The contribution of suicide to mortality in depression in elderly people varies between studies. In those of Baldwin and Jolley (1986) and Murphy (1983), suicides comprised a very small percentage of deaths. The same is true of a study spanning 15 years (Robinson, 1989). An exception is the study of Ciompi (1969) where, during a very long follow-up, a significant reduction in life expectancy was accounted for almost entirely by a suicide rate seven to eight times that of the general population. The reason for this discrepancy is unclear, but may because Ciompi's study included only patients whose depression had begun in earlier life.

COMPARATIVE OUTCOME

Depressive illness is prone to relapse, recurrence and chronicity, and this, contrary to popular teaching, is true irrespective of age. Lee and Murray (1988) have drawn attention to the poor outcome among younger depressed patients, and there have been several comparative studies of the outcome of older compared to younger depressed patients. The 'old age' arms of some of these are discussed elsewhere in this chapter.

Meats *et al.* (1991) recruited 56 inpatients with major depression and compared their outcome over a one-year period with 24 inpatients under the age of 65. The outcomes allowed comparison with the data of Murphy (1983) and of Baldwin and Jolley (1986). Sixty-eight per cent of elderly patients were well at one year compared with 50% of the younger patients. This was a significant difference. Many more of the latter had a poor outcome (41%) compared with the elderly group (16%).

Brodaty *et al.* (1993) also were unable to detect a difference in outcome in three groups of in- and outpatients with DSM-IIIR major depression: a group aged 18–39 (*n* = 104), another aged 40–59 (*n* = 77), and an elderly group aged 60 plus (*n* = 61). Outcome was assessed at about one year and nearly four years.

Hinrichsen (1993) examined the psychiatric status of 127 elderly patients (aged 60 and over) and found at one year that 72% had recovered. He highlighted that this did not differ significantly from the USA National Institute of Mental Health study of mixed-aged patients.

Hughes *et al.* (1993) compared depression scores at baseline (using the CES-D, a standard depression scale devised by the same group) which met DSM-IIIR criteria for a major depressive episode of 67 patients who were less than 60 years old and 46 patients who were older. At six-month follow-up the mean CES-D scores of the younger group were above the threshold for depression while those of the older age group were below it. The authors concluded that older depressed patients had a more favourable prognosis.

Reynolds *et al.* (1994) studied consecutive episodes of depression in 32 'young' elderly patients (mean age 66.8 years) with recurrent unipolar depression. These episodes were successfully treated in over 80% of cases and were comparable with a study by the same group of mixed-aged patients.

Lastly, the comparative study of Alexopoulos *et al.* (1996) already referred to challenged the view that older patients have a worse outcome.

FACTORS PREDICTING OUTCOME

Based on his meta-analysis, Cole (1990) suggested that chronic physical illness, severity and duration of the index depression, number of previous episodes, severe adverse intervening life events and cerebral organicity were all of prognostic importance. Social factors, in so far as these were examined, other than adverse intervening life-events, were not of prognostic importance. This accords with other suggestions that depression in later life may take on a more autonomous pattern which is less influenced by psychosocial factors (Hughes *et al.*, 1993; Blazer *et al.*, 1992), and with the study of Alexopoulos *et al.* (1996) in which psychosocial factors were mediators of recovery only in the younger group. Cole found conflicting evidence with regard to age of depression onset and actual age and their relationship to prognosis. In the study of Alexopoulos and colleagues (1996), late age of depression onset predicted chronicity, whereas in the study of Brodaty *et al.* (1993), the opposite was found. Slower recovery is a risk for chronicity at all ages (Alexopoulos *et al.*, 1996). Lastly, dysthymia is associated with a poorer prognosis than depressive illness (Kivela *et al.*, 1991, 1993) and its presence before the index episode can be expected to predict a poorer recovery. Unlike depressive illness, outcome from dysthymia does seem associated with social factors, for example, isolation and few hobbies (Kivela *et al.*, 1993).

In the studies from Western Australia (Emmerson *et al.*, 1989; Burvill *et al.*, 1991), physical ill health and severity of illness were not found to predict outcome, although the authors point out that the patients studied were from a relatively affluent population with few nursing homes, thus biasing the sample.

Table 3 lists these poor prognostic factors, subdivided by whether they are illness-related or general. However, with the exception of the rate of recovery and supervening ill health, these will be known at the outset of a depression. They thus permit a modest degree of prediction.

DEPRESSION OUTCOME AND BRAIN DISEASE

Although listed in Table 3, the prognostic significance of organic brain pathology is not entirely settled. It can be considered from two points of view: coarse brain disease, including dementia, and subtle brain damage.

Table 3. Factors associated with a poor prognosis.

General
Presence of cerebral organic pathology
Preceding severe physical health problems
Supervening health events

Illness-related
Slower recovery
More severe initial depression
Duration of symptoms greater than 2 years
Three or more previous episodes (for recurrence rather than chronicity)
Age of depression onset (conflicting)
Previous history of dysthymia

Naturalistic outcome

The studies described so far have almost all excluded patients with dementia. Forsell *et al.* (1994) followed 62 patients with 'depressive disorder' of whom 28 were also demented by DSM-IIIR criteria. At three-year follow-up 20 of the 34 patients initially with depression alone were reassessed. Twelve had changed little and only two were recovered. Only one had developed dementia. Of the original 28 with a dual diagnosis, 11 were re-examined and 10 were no longer depressed. Underdetection of depression in both groups was common. The authors postulate that this may have been due to co-morbid physical illness masking the depression.

Snowden and Lane (1994) also reported a poor overall prognosis, again with small numbers, but without such a difference in demented versus nondemented patients.

Depression and dementia

Depressive illness *per se* does not seem to be associated with an increased risk of dementia (Murphy, 1983; Baldwin and Jolley, 1986; Stoudemire *et al.*, 1993). However, recently Alexopoulos *et al.* (1993) studied 57 depressed inpatients subdivided by the presence or not of 'reversible dementia', defined as a dual diagnosis of DSM-IIIR major depressive disorder (MDD) plus DSM-IIIR dementia with, in addition, remission of dementia after improvement of the depression. Using survival analysis, there was an almost fivefold increase in the risk of developing dementia for those presenting originally with depression. However, one cannot rule out the possibility that some of those studied were already demented at presentation, even though their cognitive function improved temporarily with depression treatment, or that referral bias resulted in an overrepresentation of such cases.

Nevertheless, this study suggests that in a minority of elderly patients depression will be a prodrome of a dementing illness. Alexopoulos *et al.*

(1993) were unable to identify clinical predictors of those going on to develop irreversible dementia, but neuropsychological and imaging data were not systematically recorded at baseline. Reding *et al.* (1985) found that the presence of cerebrovascular, extrapyramidal or spinocerebellar disorder and confusion developing on low doses of tricyclic drugs were the best baseline predictors of future dementia in their series, based in a dementia clinic.

The tendency to exclude patients with dementia and/or structural brain damage in prognostic studies of depression is understandable. But the clinical reality is that depression and brain disease often co-exist and the depressive component may require pharmacological treatment. In a study designed to re-examine the hypothesis that cerebral disease confers a worse outcome Baldwin *et al.* (1993) compared 32 depressed patients who also had coarse cerebral disease, for example stroke or dementia, with 66 depressed patients without such co-morbidity. A check-list of DSM-IIIR criteria for major depression (MD) was applied (American Psychiatric Association, 1987). Not all patients had MD but all met criterion A1: pervasively depressed mood for a minimum of two weeks. Apart from higher scores on the Hamilton Depression Rating Scale among the latter group and more cognitive impairment in the former, there were no significant differences in demographic details, psychiatric variables, health or life-events between groups.

Cross-sectional outcome, based on a score of 11 or more for 'caseness' (Yesavage *et al.*, 1983) at one year on the Geriatric Depression Scale (GDS) showed that 54% of the nonorganic depressed group compared with 40% of those with brain disease and co-morbid depression were non-cases at one year (excluding seven missing cases). These differences were not significant. If deaths are included as missing data the corresponding figures are 62% and 54% respectively; this is not a statistical difference.

The longitudinal course of symptoms is expressed in Table 4. The method of computing outcome is described elsewhere (Baldwin *et al.*, 1993). Although two-thirds of those in the nonorganic group were improved or recovered compared with half of those with co-morbid depression and brain disease, this is largely accounted for by the (predictable) increase in mortality in the latter

Table 4. Longitudinal outcome based on questionnaire (missing cases, *n* = 15).

	Functional group	Organic group
Full recovery	26 (43%)	9 (39%)
Substantial improvement	15 (25%)	2 (9%)
No change or worse	11 (19%)	4 (17%)
Dead	8 (13%)	8 (35%)

Note: Chi square = 6.20, d.f. 3; $p = 0.10$

group. Statistical comparison of the groups revealed no differences. So reasonable short-term outcome in depression is possible even in the face of co-morbid cerebral disease.

Which factors predict recovery or chronicity? This was determined by the use of discriminant function analysis. The factor most associated with a poor outcome was the total GDS score: the higher the score, the worse the outcome.

Although initial group membership (organic or not) was entered into a stepwise logistic regression analysis, it was not selected in the final model as a variable likely to affect outcome, and, in fact, the proportions of patients with a 'good' outcome (a dichotomized classification created for the purpose of the statistical analysis) was similar in the two groups – 30 of 66 for the group without cerebral disease and 10 of 32 for those with co-morbid brain disease (for all cells: chi square = 3.51, NS; for two outcomes alone; chi square = 0.001, NS).

However, it was thought possible that different factors might influence outcome for the two groups of depressed patients. When the logistic analysis was repeated for each group separately, the initial GDS predicted 73.9% correctly of the nonorganic group but only 50% of patients with co-morbid organic cerebral disease, increasing to 78.3% and 55.6% respectively when a second variable, whether or not the patient was alone at the time of entry to the study, was included. No further variables added significantly to these predictions. Clearly the small numbers in the organic group permit only tentative conclusions, but it does seem that outcome in this latter group is unaffected by the initial GDS score, whereas for those without organic co-morbidity it is even more important than for the sample as a whole.

Logistic regression was repeated with the subgroup who were both free from organic brain disease *and* who met criteria for MD, as in DSM-IIIR (*n* = 48). This subgroup is comparable with studies such as have been reviewed by Cole (1990). This analysis selected 'initial GDS score', 'whether or not living alone' and 'age' (of the patient at entry), and correctly predicted 88.6% of the patients in this group, compared with only 58.6% of the remaining heterogeneous sample. The effect of age was not in the expected direction; that is, younger patients fared worse. However, this variable was entered at significance levels rather lower (p = 0.01) than the GDS initial score ($p < 0.01$). Its relevance is uncertain given the small sample.

In summary, the major depression group was somewhat more predictable than the minor depression group, although small numbers do not permit a satisfactory analysis of the minor depression group. An important inference is that the syndrome of major depression is amenable to treatment in a variety of co-morbid conditions, including those of the brain, a finding somewhat at odds with the earlier reports, such as that of Post (1962), when ECT was the main method of treatment. The advent of a range of antidepressant drugs has, it is hoped, resulted in more patients with depression and cerebral disease receiving treatment, with better than expected results.

Subtle brain changes and the outcome of depression

With regard to subtle cognitive impairment, a quarter of a century ago Post (1968) wrote: '. . . subtle cerebral changes may make ageing persons increasingly liable to affective disturbance.' In the classic study of Jacoby et al. (1981), a subgroup of patients (7 of 41) was identified with depression onset after the age of 60 years, enlarged ventricles and a high mortality rate, thus lending weight to this view. Furthermore, Pearlson et al. (1989) found CT scan abnormalities to be significantly commoner in patients with cognitive impairment (as defined on the Mini-Mental Status Examination (MMSE), Folstein et al., 1975).

A detailed discussion of the role of putative brain abnormalities, as visualized and increasingly reported in studies using magnetic resonance imaging (MRI), is beyond the scope of this chapter. Elsewhere, literature on MRI in depression has been summarized to draw attention to the relatively high rate of unexpected and unexplained brain abnormalities (Baldwin, 1993). These consist primarily of periventricular hyperintense (PVH) areas visualized on T_2-weighted MRI images, especially those extending into the adjacent white matter, and deep subcortical white matter hyperintensity (DSCWMH), although changes in basal ganglia grey matter (Beats et al., 1991) and an unexpectedly high rate of cortical infarcts in older depressed patients have also been reported (Fujikawa et al., 1993).

The aetiology of such lesions is not known. Although DSCWMH are common in old people, there is increasing evidence that they should be not regarded as part of 'normal ageing' (Manolio et al., 1994). Some, although not all, studies report that such lesions are related to hypertension. Moreover, recent research has identified a surprisingly high prevalence of potential thromboembolic sources in association with white matter change in otherwise apparently healthy older individuals (Lindgren et al., 1994). Recently, an excess of vascular disease and risk factors in late- compared with early-onset depression has been demonstrated, although scans were not performed (Baldwin and Tomenson, 1995).

O'Brien et al. (1996) compared 60 subjects with major depression with 39 control subjects and a comparison group with Alzheimer's disease. Significantly more of the depressed group with an onset after the age of 65 years ($n = 16$) had DSCWMH, 50% compared with 20% (and 9.5% of similarly aged controls). In this study the difference was not accounted for by an excess of vascular risk factors in the late-onset group.

Abas et al. (1980) reported subtle cognitive impairment on tests of latency using an automated test battery in 70% of patients with depressive illness.

Furthermore, residual slowing associated with a higher ventricular-to-brain ratio was observed in a substantial minority on re-testing. More recently, the same group (Beats *et al.*, 1996) studied frontal lobe function in 24 elderly depressed patients and compared them with 15 matched controls. On recovery, higher residual depression scores on the Hamilton Rating Scale were associated with slowed thinking times and increased ventricular size. Using single photon emission tomography, Curran *et al.* (1993) reported a weak positive correlation between recovery from depression and increased uptake of tracer in a number of brain areas.

Lastly, Hickie *et al.* (1995) reported that in 39 patients with a mean age of 64.4 years (range 28–86) with resistant depression (operationally defined), poor response to further individualized mood treatment regimens was predicted by the extent of DSCWMH, even allowing for the factor of age. Furthermore, changes were more extensive in patients with late-onset depression (>50 years), who also had most psychomotor change.

Hickie *et al.* (1995) studied patients referred to a tertiary referral centre for affective disorder. Might therapeutic resistance be associated with brain pathology in less refractory patients, more typical of those referred to geriatric psychiatry services? In Manchester the present author and colleagues have been exploring this. The hypothesis was that the amount of DSCWMH and degree of brain atrophy are more pronounced in a treatment-resistant group compared with responders. A subsidiary hypothesis was that frontal lobe function, as measured by an appropriate battery of neuropsychological tests, is also more impaired in resistant cases.

Consecutive patients with new episodes of major depression, as defined by DSM-IIIR, were recruited from two old-age psychiatric services in Manchester involving five consultants. Patients with dementia, again as defined in DSM-IIIR, were excluded. This was a naturalistic study, so that the clinician was free to prescribe whichever antidepressants he or she wanted to. A 'good response' was defined as a fall in the Montgomery–Asberg Depression Rating Scale (MADRS; Montgomery and Asberg, 1979) to 10 or less, fewer than five DSM-IIIR criteria met for major depression and a clinical global impression score (CBI) of at least four ('slightly improved'). Levels of resistance were defined *post hoc* as follows: *responsive to monotherapy*, i.e. good outcome with the use of a single antidepressant alone (ignoring short courses of neuroleptics); *response to second-line treatment ('relative resistance')*, i.e. good response but lithium augmentation and/or ECT required in addition to antidepressant, despite compliance and a recorded trial of an antidepressant for at least six weeks; *poor response to second-line treatment ('absolute resistance')*, i.e. if assessment at 24 weeks showed MADRS score of 11 despite the above therapies.

MRI was performed as soon as feasible after recruitment using a 0.5 Tesla scanner, using 17 slices in three planes with matched T_1- and T_2-weighted images. In addition, a neuropsychological test battery was administered comprising the Mini-Mental State Examination, a digit symbol substitution test, the Rey auditory verbal learning test (Rey, 1964), the modified Wisconson Card Sorting Test (Nelson, 1976), a word fluency test ('FAS'), the trial-making tests A and B (Army Test Battery, 1944), animal-naming test and the Rey Osterrieth complex figure test. The test battery emphasized frontal lobe function and was administered at the point at which the MADRS score was at its lowest (the patients were seen at 6, 12 and 24 weeks). For this part of the study 24 normal elderly control subjects were also examined. Neuroimaging was only conducted on the patient group. Lastly, compliance was monitored via tablet counts at each visit and during random visits.

The main comparisons were: (1) between the three treatment response groups regarding comparisons of MRI measures and neurophyschological profiles; (2) between the same three outcome groups and also the normal control group regarding neuropsychological measures.

One hundred and five patients, comprising consecutive episodes of depression, were recruited. Thirty were excluded for the following reasons: onset of dementia during the trial period (6); sudden death during trial of monotherapy (3); elective ECT before six-week period of monotherapy (2); non-response to monotherapy but no progression to second-line treatment (4); noncompliance with medication (15). This left 75 patients, all of whom consented to neuropsychological testing. Forty-four (59%) of these had an MRI scan. Of the 75, 32 were responsive to antidepressant monotherapy (43%), 28 required a second-line treatment such as ECT or lithium augmentation (37%) and 15 were poorly responsive to all treatment (20%). The corresponding figures for the 44 who had an MRI scan were: 16 (36%), 18 (41%) and 10 (23%).

The mean age of the sample was 75 years with no differences between groups. Significantly more of the controls were married as they were, in the main, spouses of patients. Physical health was rated poorer in the study patients compared with controls, and unsurprisingly there was a more frequent history of prior depression. Beyond these there were no differences in demographic variables, educational attainment or estimate of premorbid intelligence.

The data are still being analysed, but results from the neuropsychological tests and linear measures used to assess brain atrophy can be summarized. The latter was assessed using the method devised by Gomori et al. (1984), using a tracker ball on the original Vectra MRI scanner console. In brief, using analysis of co-variance (to co-vary for age), measures of temporal atrophy and the prepontine ratio (PPR), a measure of infratentorial atrophy, were significantly greater in those who were either resistant to all treatment or required a second-line treatment. The PPR measure was particularly striking in those showing complete resistance (Table 5).

Table 5. Linear measures of brain atrophy in resistant and nonresistant depression.

Brain region	Group 1 Good response (n = 16)	Group 2 Partial resistance (n = 18)	Group 3 Absolute resistance (n = 10)	MANOVA/ ANCOVA	Post hoc group differences
Bifrontal	286.6	293.0	286.5	$F = 0.57; p = 0.11$	NS
Cortico-temporal	42.9	54.9	55.1	$F = 4.3; p = 0.02$	1 < 2,3*
Lateral-ventricular	76.9 (75.0)	97.8 (90.4)	83.9 (89.0)	$F = 3.19; p = 0.052$	NS
Third ventricle	100.1 (99.1)	110.5 (109.0)	105.5 (114.1)	$F = 0.25; p = 0.72$	NS
Bicaudate ratio	123.2 (121.5)	133.3 (131.2)	124.7 (128.5)	$F = 0.34; p = 0.71$	NS
Prepontine ratio	240.5	255.4	334.6	$F = 3.72; p = 0.33$	1,2*
Combined brain ratios	345.8 (344.0)	419.7 (417.0)	424.4 (432.4)	$F = 3.69; p = 0.038$	1 < 2,3*

Note: Mean group scores with (brackets) adjusted means after ANCOVA for age.
NS, Not a significant difference.
* $p = 0.05$.

Each individual neuropsychological test was entered into an analysis of variance. Co-variates were also entered so that the final F-value represented the main group effect, after co-varying for the effect of confounding factors. Co-variates were only entered into the equation if they were first shown to have a significant effect; in particular, actual age, MADRS score and antidepressant/neuroleptic drug effects were considered. In practice, because the groups were so closely matched, almost all of the necessary adjustment was attributable to depression severity.

The main neuropsychological findings were as follows. Verbal memory was impaired in all treatment groups compared with controls. Global cognitive function, verbal fluency, category production, spatial copying, visual memory, Trial A of the trial-making test and reversed digit span were all comparable with the normal controls in the depressed group. The tests which characterized resistance were category production and perseveration, verbal memory and Trial B of the trial-making test, the first and last of which probably reflect frontal or subcortical/frontal deficit.

These preliminary findings are reported elsewhere (Baldwin and Simpson, 1996), but they add weight to the theory that organic brain changes are not only associated with depressive illness in later life but influence outcome adversely. The finding of residual deficits, especially in frontal test function, is also consistent with the literature. The implication is that the structural change mediates both treatment resistance and poor cognitive function; and that, furthermore, possibly the nuclei in the brainstem thought to mediate neurotransmitter function in depression may be atrophied. This is a fruitful area for further research.

FUTURE CHALLENGES IN AFFECTIVE DISORDERS RESEARCH

The treatment of depression is subdivided into three phases: acute treatment; continuation therapy; and maintenance treatment (prophylaxis). There have been important developments in the conceptualization of terms relevant to these three aspects of the outcome of major depressive disorder. In 1988, in the USA the MacArthur Foundation Research Network on the Psychopathology of Depression convened a task force to examine the ways in which change points in the course of depression could be defined (Frank *et al.*, 1991) (Figure 1). *Remission* is defined as the point after treatment when the individual becomes asymptomatic, in other words no longer meets syndromal criteria for the disorder. A *recovery* is a remission which lasts more than *x* amount of time, *x* being an arbitrary period in months. *Relapse*

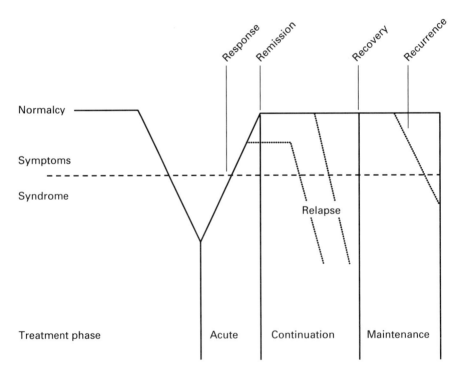

Figure 1. Response, remission, recovery, relapse, recurrence. (Reproduced, with permission, from Frank *et al.*, 1991.)

is a return of symptoms satisfying the full syndrome of the original episode. *Recurrence* refers to a new episode after a period of recovery. Precise times for some of these terms have not been established for older depressed patients.

Hollon *et al.* (1990) have estimated, for younger adults, that the expected length of an episode of major depression averages six to nine months. Data summarized by the National Institutes of Health (NIH) Consensus Development Conference on the Diagnosis and Treatment of Depression in Late Life (Schneider *et al.*, 1994) has established some useful facts regarding depression in older patients. First, they take longer to achieve remission compared with younger patients. Secondly, antidepressants have improved the prognosis of depression in the elderly, but still the response rate, at around 50–60% for a given episode, gives no cause for complacency. Further improvement should be possible, provided of course the disorder is first detected. Before exploring strategies which might improve prognosis at each of these three stages this issue will first be addressed.

Detection of depression

The Liverpool community studies (Green *et al.*, 1992, 1994) and the study of Forsell *et al.* (1994), both already referred to, have shown low rates of antidepressant use. Also in a hospital setting the author's own surveys have confirmed poor detection in both inpatients (Jackson and Baldwin, 1993) and outpatients (Neal and Baldwin, 1994), by both nursing and medical staff. For example, in the latter study physicians only detected 40% of syndromal depression. Lastly, in the study by Koenig *et al.* (1992) referred to, no mention of depression was made by physicians in 44% of cases, nor was it even mentioned in the active problem list in 32% of cases where it was diagnosed. Treatment by or referral to a psychiatrist occurred in only 44% of cases.

Better detection might lead to better treatment, and hence improved outcome. Cole and Yaffe (1996) conducted a survey of literature between 1960 and 1992 to test Goldberg and Huxley's (1980) 'filter' model in over 65-year-olds with depression. Figure 2 illustrates their model. If correct, only 10% of patients with moderate to severe depressions are referred to psychiatric services.

Successful detection in primary care does not guarantee adequacy of treatment (Bridges, 1983). Undertreatment has been reported even when primary care physicians have detected depression in older patients (MacDonald, 1986). Similar findings have been reported among hospital physicians (Koenig *et al.*, 1992; Orrell *et al.*, 1995a). In an interesting study, Jerling (1995), using the results of serum antidepressant assays, demonstrated that physicians were too conservative in the dosages of tricyclic drugs which they

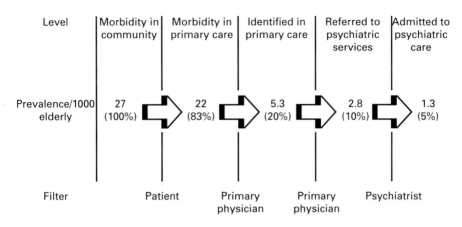

Figure 2. Pathways to psychiatric care. (After Cole and Yaffe, 1996.)

prescribed to older depressed patients. A primary care study (Orrell *et al.*, 1995b) has demonstrated a reluctance to prescribe antidepressants to older people in adequate dosages or to persist with treatment after recovery. Also, presumably poor detection or undertreatment leads to chronicity, and, as already discussed, duration of symptoms predicts poorer outcome. The implication is that earlier referral and energetic treatment might improve it, but this has not been proven.

Improving detection in the primary care setting and better liaison with secondary care services seem obvious ways to improve the twin problems of poor detection and undertreatment. There is then a case in the UK for orientation of old age psychiatric services around general practices rather than the traditional catchment area, and for specific links with geriatric medicine teams. Better liaison with other front-line services, such as social service departments, and with other facilities where rates of depression are high, such as day centres and nursing homes, might also improve detection. The author's own practice is to have three-monthly meetings with the main group practices for whom he is the designated consultant and four- to six-weekly meetings with social service personnel, including the home care organizers. At each meeting our information system is able to generate a list of patients/clients. Further links include a regular joint clinic with a physician and outreach nurses to selected nursing homes and day centres.

Acute treatment

Some general methodological issues should be borne in mind in future studies. These include case selection, which should ideally be representative of patients not only referred to specialists but also those managed by primary care. Measurement of physical morbidity is not standardized, although Burvill *et al.* (1990) have proposed a system of quantification based on a coding matrix, with each system rated separately by first acute and then chronic disease, and then again according to (a) severity and (b) disability, on a four-point scale.

It is unclear how best to measure the clinical outcome in older depressed patients. A 50% reduction in the Hamilton Depression Rating Scale (HDRS) has become a common way to assess positive outcome, especially as it is an easy way of evaluating one drug against another or against placebo. Whether it is a meaningful way to assess clinical outcome is debatable. Clearly a reduction in the HDRS score from 40 to 20 indicates marked improvement but the patient could hardly be described as well. Categorical outcomes are more meaningful to clinicians but tend to be nonstandardized.

Studies which compare one strategy, be it pharmacological or psychological, with another, rather than with a placebo, require very much larger numbers of patients than we have hitherto been used to. The following scenario illustrates the point. The methodology is of a double-blind, parallel group study comparing the effects of antidepressants alone with an antidepressant plus augmentation treatment (e.g. lithium) in the acute phase. It might equally well be a maintenance study in which the effect of lithium prophylaxis is compared with lithium plus a psychotherapeutic intervention. The assumptions are that the non-recovery rate (if an acute study) or the recurrence rate (if a trial of maintenance) is between 30 and 40% and that the additional treatment, there being no placebo arm, would result in a 10% measurable improvement on whatever outcome measure is chose. A significance level of no more than 5% is specified with a power of at least 80%, an allocation ratio of 1:1 (i.e. equal group sizes) and good compliance. The recommended minimum sample sizes (per group) are given in Table 6.

Naturalistic studies with small numbers, such as those reported by Cole (1990) have probably taken us as far as is possible. The implication of Table 6 is that well organized, multi-centre trials will be required in future prognostic studies of depression where an intervention is planned.

Table 6. A power test to illustrate numbers required for a trial of treatment, without a placebo group, in patients with depression. A range of rates of recurrence/relapse is illustrated and the numbers refer to patients per group (i.e. the total sample size would be double).

Relapse/recurrence rate with normal treatment	Sample size to detect 10% reduction
35%	231
30%	165
40%	258

Resistant depression

As suggested earlier, there are relative levels of resistance, but defining the steps appropriate to each level of 'resistance' is unclear. Clinical dogma abound; research to substantiate it is sparse. The issues have been summarized elsewhere (Baldwin, 1996). In brief, when faced with a patient whose depression has not shown worthwhile improvement after six weeks the options are as follows: (1) extend the trial beyond the 'traditional' six-week period, ensuring the dose is optimal, for between three and six more weeks (there is some evidence that this helps up to 50% of patients, provided of course it is not merely adding to personal misery (Georgotas and McCue, 1989)), (2) change to an antidepressant of another class, a popular strategy for which there is remarkably little convincing evidence; (3) use an augmentation strategy.

With regard to (2), a recent study by Flint and Rifat (1996), referred to earlier, is worth further comment. The design was to give a trial of nortriptyline for six weeks and augment with lithium for two weeks if there had been an inadequate response (defined by a score of higher than 10 on the HDRS). If unsuccessful, patients were changed to phenelzine for six weeks and again augmented with lithium for two weeks if there was an inadequate response. If recovery had still not occurred then ECT was offered or, if refused, fluoxetine given with or without lithium. In this way 84 of 89 patients (95%) who completed the study eventually responded, or 84% using the intention-to-treat analysis. Response to phenelzine was not as high as for nortriptyline and response to the latter plus lithium or ECT or fluoxetine was poor, although numbers were small. Longer duration of symptoms and higher baseline anxiety scores predicted non-response.

The main drawback of the study was that it was not conducted blindly. Also, the duration of lithium augmentation may have been too short. Lastly, a number of newer antidepressants have been introduced since it was carried out. Nevertheless, the authors' conclusion that persisting with different physical treatment strategies results in improvement in the majority of patients with major depression is an important message.

With regard to lithium augmentation (LA) in refractory depression there has been little evaluation. Flint (1995) reviewed 25 cases from several reports. He found that 76% of patients had a complete response and 16% a partial one. He was sceptical of drawing firm conclusions because of a lack of standardization regarding what was meant by depression and what was a successful outcome and because often the prior antidepressant trial could be deemed to have been inadequate. Three retrospective case series (Lafferman et al., 1988; Finch and Katona, 1989; van Marwijk et al., 1990) have involved 74 patients with less striking results, only 40% showing a complete response and 26% a partial one.

There have been four prospective studies of LA in elderly patients to date. Zimmer *et al.* (1988) and Flint and Rifat (1994) found response rates of 20% and 23% respectively, much lower than open studies of younger adults. Parker *et al.* (1994) compared a group treated with a single antidepressant (*n* = 23) with a lithium-augmented group (*n* = 21) in a prospective study. The latter group were found to have significantly lower depression severity scores at follow-up and a trend for lower scores on the Geriatric Depression Scale. However, this study did not utilize random allocation or blinded measures, so the results can be viewed only as encouraging, but preliminary.

There have been no double-blind placebo-controlled trials of augmentation therapy in elderly patients.

Compliance with LA is addressed by Katona *et al.* (1995), who found that despite careful monitoring only 16 of 29 LA patients achieved adequate lithium levels. Flint and Rifat (1994) found in their study that half their elderly patients on lithium developed dose-limiting side-effects.

The issue of the optimum dose of lithium in LA has not been settled. For example, Zusky *et al.* (1988) studied 18 patients aged 18–80 using low-dose lithium (dose 100–500 mg; levels 0.1–0.8 mmol/l) and found poor results. Kushnir (1986) reported a series of five physically ill depressed elderly patients and found that low-dose lithium (150–300 mg; levels 0.15–0.25 mmol/l) was effective.

Continuation therapy

This refers to the period after remission during which treatment should be continued in order to minimize the risk of relapse. This period is usually specified as six months in general adult psychiatry but, as has been pointed out from the available evidence, the main risk period in older adults may be as much as two years (Zis *et al.*, 1980; Flint, 1992; Stoudemire *et al.*, 1993).

There are few data specific to elderly people. Georgotas *et al.* (1989) treated 60 patients with either nortriptyline or phenelzine for four or eight months following remission of symptoms. The cumulative probability of remaining well during the continuation phase was over 80% for either drug. This suggests a protective role for antidepressant therapy in the months after recovery.

There is no consensus regarding the optimum period of continuation therapy. In the UK Old Age Depression Interest Group (OADIG) study (see below) most relapses occurred in the first 12 months (OADIG, 1993). One way of settling this would be a double-blind discontinuation study (i.e. discontinuation from antidepressant treatment) at particular times. The author's own practice is to continue for 12 months before reviewing whether to discontinue treatment.

Continuation ECT has not been evaluated properly in elderly depressed patients, but anecdotally is helpful in cases refractory to pharmacological prophylaxis. For example, Mirchandani *et al.* (1994) reported nine such patients. Four who complied with continuation ECT (over 9–12 months) fared well, whereas of the five who stopped prematurely one died, three were rehospitalized and one required continuous inpatient care.

Prophylaxis

In an open study of nortriptyline (mean dosage 50 mg) in maintenance treatment of 27 recovered elderly depressed patients, 85% were relapse-free over 12 months and 81.5% at 18 months (Reynolds *et al.*, 1989).

In a British study, the Old Age Depression Interest Group (OADIG, 1993), of 219 patients with major depression, 69 recovered sufficiently to enter a two-year double-blind placebo-controlled trial of dothiepin. Survival analysis showed that dothiepin (75 mg daily) reduced the relative risk of relapse/recurrence by a factor of 2.5.

As a result of this finding, the double-blind placebo trial may no longer be ethically justified in studies of prevention. However, 30% of those in the actively treated group still experienced a relapse, so scope for further improvement seems possible. For example, the adage coined by the Pittsburgh research group (Frank *et al.*, 1990) that '... the dose that got you well keeps you well' has not been evaluated in elderly depressed patients. Might the OADIG result have been better still if the maintenance dose had always been kept as close to the treatment dose as possible and not maintained at a fixed dose?

Given these findings, plus the high rate of recurrence and relapse among elderly depressed patients, there is an argument for indefinite prophylatic treatment of *any* newly presenting episode of major depression in an older patient. An elderly person in his or her seventies may have an expected lifespan of five years. The potential for preventing six-month morbidity due to a recurrence of depressive illness thus becomes an important gain, and the considerations are therefore different from those that may apply to a patient in his or her thirties.

There are difficulties with the long-term use of tricyclics, notably weight gain and dental decay. Do the newer antidepressants offer prevention against recurrence with fewer side-effects? In a small open-label study (Feighner and Cohn, 1985) patients were continued on fluoxetine or doxepin. Both were equally effective in preventing relapse over 48 weeks. Clearly studies of the benefits of serotonin-specific reuptake inhibitors (SSRIs) and other new antidepressants in prevention of relapse and recurrence of depression in older patients are needed.

A different point of view is that some in the OADIG study who were in the placebo group nevertheless remained well. There would be a risk of overtreatment if there were a blanket policy of prophylaxis, with all the risks of unwanted drug side-effects to which older patients become even more susceptible as they age.

Identifying which patients benefit more from prophylactic medication is an important task for future research. Those with two or more recurrences in the past two years, serious ill health, chronic social difficulties or very severe depression at the outset are the most obvious candidates based on current (limited) knowledge.

Another pressing need is to ascertain the place of lithium prophylaxis in the prevention of recurrence of depression. Preliminary evidence is encouraging. Abou-Saleh and Coppen (1983), having established the effectiveness of lithium prophylaxis in a mixed-aged population, analysed a subgroup of 22 patients aged over 60 years. Their morbidity was assessed by use of an 'Affective Morbidity Index'. The elderly group benefited as much as the main group. Surprisingly, no further prospective studies of the role of lithium prophylaxis have been conducted.

Psychosocial interventions

Although it was pointed out earlier that social measures appear to exert less influence on the course of major depression in later than earlier life, there is nevertheless a need to examine the role of social psychological factors which might influence outcome for the better. While Murphy (1983) did not find that a confidant protected against relapse, Henderson et al. (1986) reported that elderly depressed patients reported no lack of close, supportive relationships but did indicate a marked reduction in more diffuse social relationships. The use of a different instrument to rate intimacy may have accounted for this in part, but it does leave open the question of whether an attempt to improve more diffuse social relationships, as with a day centre, might nevertheless be effective.

In another study, Oxman et al. (1992) examined the effect of social networks and supports on depressive symptoms in people seen three years apart. Using multiple regression analysis, most variance was explained by disability, but there were important social variables too such as loss of spouse, adequacy of emotional support, presence of 'tangible' support and the role of family and confidants. Clearly these are issues which merit further study.

Although many social interventions are most likely to act as a buffer against relapse and/or recurrence they may also help with management of the acute episode. Waterreus et al. (1994) described the positive impact of interventions by a community psychiatric nurse (CPN) to elderly patients with depression in an Inner London study. The group with CPN involvement (n = 47) had significantly lower depression scores at the end of the study than those who were followed up by primary care services (n = 49). The interventions described in this study are informative and included: personal

supportive therapy; behaviour therapy and teaching relaxation; encouragement to seek medical advice regarding physical health problems; family and
marital work; and bereavement counselling. However, the biggest impact in
this study appears to have been via improved medication education.

Ong *et al.* (1987) were able to demonstrate that a support group for
discharged elderly depressives, run by a social worker and a community
psychiatric nurse, resulted in a significant reduction in relapses and readmissions over a one-year period. Formal psychotherapy has not been evaluated
in detail, but Gallagher and Thompson (1982) followed up a group of
patients one year after brief psychotherapy and found that cognitive therapy
led to a more effectively maintained improvement. Steuer *et al.* (1984)
treated 20 patients aged over 55 who had DSM-IIIR major depression. They
were randomly allocated to one of four groups, two psychodynamic and two
run on cognitive behavioural lines. There were significant reductions in
depression scores in all treatment groups over nine months. The large
number of drop-outs and the absence of a control group make it difficult to
draw firm conclusions.

The combination of drug therapy with psychotherapy has been advocated
in the treatment of depression in mixed adult patients. Reynolds *et al.* (1992)
have evaluated the use of interpersonal psychotherapy (IPT; Klerman *et al.*,
1984) in 73 elderly depressed patients. Of 61 patients given adequate trials
of nortriptyline and IPT, 79% achieved complete remission, as judged by an
HDRS score of less than 10 over 16 weeks. Responders were assigned to a
double-blind placebo-controlled trial comprising four treatment cells in all.
The authors reported the first two years' experience of a three-year maintenance trial. Although preliminary, the results showed that those maintained
on nortriptyline had significantly lower relapse rates than those given the
placebo, and that the combination of IPT with nortriptyline was associated
with good response and low attrition from the study. In a further report of
32 elderly patients, Reynolds *et al.* (1994) showed that 80% were successfully
treated to remission after a further relapse using the same combined
approach which had produced recovery in the index episode.

Hinrichsen and Hernandez (1993) have shown that three factors, psychiatric symptoms in the carer, reported difficulties and poorer carer health,
were all associated with poorer outcome at one year from major depression
in a cohort of patients with a mean age of just over 70. Attention to carers
(see above) may thus enhance the prognosis of the designated patients.

Other outcomes

Other aspects of outcome are the use of resources by elderly depressives and
social outcomes. Regarding the former, Murphy and Grundy (1984) demonstrated in a London hospital that, compared with younger depressives, the

elderly accounted for roughly one and a half more bed days. Elderly depressed inpatients often suffer physical ill health as well as depression and often live alone. They cannot therefore be discharged partially recovered, so these findings are not all that surprising.

Wells *et al.* (1989), in a study of adult medical and psychiatric patients, concluded that patients with either depressive symptoms or a depressive syndrome have an impairment in objective and subjective qualities of life that is comparable to or worse than eight common, chronic major medical conditions. Besides symptom control then, quality of life, use of resources, functional level, dependency and social adaptation should be incorporated as measures of outcome. A matrix of outcomes which include not only symptom control but these aspects too would '. . . show the place of depression within the balance of a person's whole life' (Gurland, B.J., quoted in Schneider *et al.*, 1994).

Another measure which has been suggested previously (Baldwin and Jolley, 1986) is to document the amount of time experienced by the patient in either remission/recovery or relapse/recurrence, in relation to the inpatient or outpatient setting. This simple expedient has gained acceptance recently (Gurland, B.J., quoted in Schneider *et al.*, 1994; Burvill *et al.*, 1991).

Whatever measures are chosen, it is clear that modern statistical techniques such as survival analysis (Allgulander and Fisher, 1986) should be a routine part of analysis of outcome in further research. There are methods for capturing multidimensional data which can be incorporated into such analyses. The best known is the LIFE (Longitudinal Interval Follow-Up Evaluation) (Keller *et al.*, 1987). This allows data to be recorded not only on a symptom level of depression but also for illness episodes, inter-episode function, co-morbid health problems, social factors and treatments.

IMPROVING THE PROGNOSIS

There is little doubt that there is room for improvement in the prognosis in elderly psychiatric patients. The three areas which merit attention are: treatment adequacy, aftercare and prophylaxis.

Treatment adequacy

Many of the important issues have been covered and will not be rehearsed. In summary, a sizeable minority of elderly depressed patients do not achieve a full remission. Until it can be established which is the most effective strategy for patients who do not respond to antidepressant monotherapy, all that can be said is that vigorous treatment with antidepressants and/or ECT seem associated with better outcomes, as has been discussed. Although this seems obvious, a review of the literature on prognosis which the author conducted in 1990 found striking variability in the use of antidepressant drugs (45–72%), lithium (5–32%) and ECT (0–67%) (Baldwin, 1991). If one adds to this the evidence from community studies of undertreatment of geriatric depression (MacDonald, 1986; Green *et al.*, 1992, 1994), then it is clear that treatment adequacy cannot then be taken for granted in any studies of outcome of depression. Indeed, there is a striking disparity between studies sponsored by the pharmaceutical industry, in which dosage and type of treatment are rigorously controlled but the setting is far removed from clinical reality, and naturalistic studies which have been reported herein, which correspond more to the real world of clinical practice but hardly ever control for the adequacy of a treatment intervention.

After-care

Without planned after-care patients slip through the net and/or their relapses or recurrences go unnoticed (Sadavoy and Reiman-Sheldon, 1983). Given that the highest risk of return of symptoms is relatively early on, then after-care, either through direct deployment of one of the multidisciplinary team, or under the supervision of a general practitioner, should be continued for a minimum of 12 months and preferably two years.

In studies of younger depressed patients, early intervention in a recurrence resulted in reducing the morbid period for the next episode by four to five months (Kupfer *et al.*, 1989). It is not known what interventions constitute the most effective ingredients of planned after-care for depression. Many practitioners would cite monitoring of symptoms, education regarding drugs, rapid and easy access to the services to report fresh symptoms, improving the patient's social outlets, support for carers, support with episodes of adversity and ongoing support with chronic social problems as key aspects. Perhaps the best way to define 'after-care' is by consensus from what is nowadays regarded as good clinical practice. This could then be incorporated into future outcome studies of depression in older patients as a controlled variable.

After-care includes education of the patient and family, as discussed earlier, and an opportunity to access specialist support easily. Helping the patient and his or her carers to recognize signs of recurrence and giving the telephone number of someone who can respond if such signs and symptoms occur are important objectives in management.

Prophylaxis

This is another aspect of secondary prevention. Again, there is no need to rehearse what has already been said. Clearly though there is an urgent need to evaluate, first, the role of medical interventions to improve outcome, such as lithium and maintenance ECT, and secondly, the role of adjunctive treatment of a psychological nature, such as adaptations of interpersonal psychotherapy and cognitive behavioural therapy. The early evidence, as discussed, is promising for both these strategies.

REFERENCES

Abas, M.A., Sahakian, B.J. and Levy, R. (1980). Neuropsychological deficits and CT scan changes in elderly depressives. *Psychol Med* **20**, 507–520.

Abou-Saleh, M.T. and Coppen, A. (1983). The prognosis of depression in old age: the case for lithium therapy. *Br J Psychiatry* **142**, 527–528.

Alexopoulos, G.S., Young, R.C., Abrams, R.C., Meyers, B. and Shamoian, C.A. (1989). Chronicity and relapse in geriatric depression. *Biol Psychiatry* **26**, 551–564.

Alexopoulos, G.S., Meyers, B.S., Young, R.C., Mattis, S. and Kakuma, T. (1993). The course of geriatric depression with 'reversible dementia': a controlled study. *Am J Psychiatry* **150**, 1693–1699.

Alexopoulos, G.S., Meyers, B.S., Young, R.C. *et al.* (1996). Recovery in geriatric depression. *Arch Gen Psychiatry* **53**, 305–312.

Allgulander, C. and Fisher, L.D. (1986). Survival analysis (or time to an event analysis), and the Cox regression model – methods for longitudinal psychiatric research. *Acta Psychiatr Scand* **74**, 529–535.

American Psychiatric Association (1987). *Diagnosis and Statistical Manual, (3rd edn, revised)*. APA, Washington, DC.

Ames, D. (1990). Depression among elderly residents of local-authority residential homes. *Br J Psychiatry* **156**, 667–675.

Army Individual Test Battery (1944). *Manual of Directions and Scoring*. Adjutant General's Office, War Department, Washington, DC.

Avery, D. and Winokur, G. (1976). Mortality in depressed patients treated with electrconvulsive therapy and antidepressants. *Arch Gen Psychiatry* **33**, 1029–1037.

Babigian, H.M. and Guttmacher, L.B. (1984). Epidemiological considerations in electroconvulsive therapy. *Arch Gen Psychiatry* **41**, 246–253.

Baldwin, R.C. (1988). Delusional and non-delusional depression in late life: evidence for distinct subtypes. *Br J Psychiatry* **152**, 39–44.

Baldwin, R.C. (1991). The outcome of depression in old age. *Int J Geriatr Psychiatry* **6**, 395–400.

Baldwin, R.C. (1993). Late life depression and structural brain changes: a review of recent magnetic resonance imaging research. *Int J Geriatr Psychiatry* **8**, 115–123.

Baldwin, R.C. (1996). Refractory depression in late life: a review of treatment options. *Rev Clin Gerontol* **6** (in press).

Baldwin, R.C. and Jolley, D.J. (1986). The prognosis of depression in old age. *Br J Psychiatry* **149**, 574–583.

Baldwin, R.C. and Tomenson, B. (1995). Depression in later life: a comparison of symptoms and risk factors in early and late onset cases. *Br J Psychiatry* **167**, 649–652.

Baldwin, R.C., Benbow, S.M., Marriott, A. and Tomenson, B. (1993). The prognosis of depression in later life: a reconsideration of cerebral organic factors in relation to outcome. *Br J Psychiatry* **163**, 82–90.

Baldwin, R.C. and Simpson, S. (1996). Outcome studies of depression in the elderly. *Clin Neurosci* (in press).

Ballard, C.G., Eastwood, C., Gahir, M. and Wilcock, G. (1996). Follow-up study of depression in the carers of dementia sufferers. *BMJ* **312**, 947.

Beats, B., Levy, R. and Forst, L. (1991). Ventricular enlargement and caudate hyperdensity. *Biol Psychiatry* **30**, 452–458.

Beats, B.C., Sahakian, B.J. and Levy, R. (1996). Cognitive performance in tests sensitive to frontal lobe dysfunction in the elderly depressed. *Psychol Med* **26**, 591–603.

Blazer, D.G., Hughes, D.C. and George, L.K. (1992). Age and impaired subjective support: predictors of depressive symptoms at one year follow-up. *J Nerv Ment Dis* **180**, 172–180.

Bridges, P.K. (1983). '. . . and a small dose of an antidepressant might help'. *Br J Psychiatry* **142**, 626–628.

Brodaty, H., Harris, L., Peters, K. *et al.* (1993). Prognosis of depression in the elderly: a comparison with younger patients. *Br J Psychiatry* **163**, 589–596.

Burvill, P.W. and Hall, W.D. (1994). Predictors of increased mortality in elderly depressed patients. *Int J Geriatr Psychiatry* **9**, 219–227.

Burvill, P.W., Mowry, B. and Hall, W.D. (1990). Quantification of physical illness in psychiatric research in the elderly. *Int J Geriatr Psychiatry* **5**, 161–170.

Burvill, P.W., Hall, W.D., Stampfer, H.G. and Emmerson, J.P. (1991). The prognosis of depression in old age. *Br J Psychiatry* **158**, 64–71.

Ciompi, L. (1969). Follow-up studies on the evolution of former neurotic and depressive states in old age. *J Geriatr Psychiatry* **3**, 90–106.

Cole, M.G. (1983). Age, age of onset and course of primary depressive illness in the elderly. *Can J Psychiatry* **28**, 102–104.

Cole, M.G. (1985). The course of elderly depressed outpatients. *Can J Psychiatry* **30**, 217–220.

Cole, M.G. (1990). The prognosis of depression in the elderly. *Can Med Assoc* **143**, 633–640.

Cole, M.G. and Yaffe, M.J. (1996). Pathway to psychiatric care of the elderly with depression. *Int J Geriatr Psychiatry* **11**, 157–161.

Copeland, J.R., Kelleher, M.J., Kellet, J.M. *et al.* (1976). A semi-structured clinical interview for the assessment of diagnosis and mental state in the elderly. *Psychol Med* **6**, 439–449.

Curràn, S.M., Murray, C.M., van Beck, M. *et al.* (1993). A single photon emission computerized study of regional brain function in elderly patients with major depression and with Alzheimer-type dementia. *Br J Psychiatry* **163**, 155–165.

Emmerson, J.P., Burvill, P.W. and Finlay-Jones, R. (1989). Life events, life difficulties and confiding relationships in the depressed elderly. *Br J Psychiatry* **155**, 787–792.

Feighner, J.P. and Cohn, J.B. (1985). Double-blind comparative trials of fluoxetine and doxepin in geriatric patients with major depressive disorder. *J Clin Psychiatry* **46**, 20–25.

Finch, E.J.L. and Katona, C.L.E. (1989). Lithium augmentation in the treatment of refractory depression in old age. *Int J Geriatr Depress* **4**, 41–46.

Flint, A.J. (1992). The optimum duration of antidepressant treatment in the elderly. *Int J Geriatr Psychiatry* **7**, 617–619.

Flint, A.J. (1995). Augmentation strategies in geriatric depression. *Int J Geriatr Psychiatry* **10**, 137–146.

Flint, A.J. and Rifat, S.L. (1994). A prospective study of lithium augmentation in antidepressant-resistant geriatric depression. *J Clin Psychopharmacol* **14**, 353–356.

Flint, A.J. and Rifat, S.L. (1996). The effect of sequential antidepressant treatment on geriatric depression. *J Affect Disord* **36**, 95–105.

Folstein, M.F., Folstein, S.E. and McHugh, P.R. (1975). 'Mini-Mental State': a practical method for grading the cognitive state of patients for the clinician. *J Psychiatr Res* **12**, 185–198.

Forsell, Y., Jorm, A.F. and Winblad, B. (1994). Outcome of depression in demented and non-demented elderly: observations from a three-year follow-up in a community-based study. *Int J Geriatr Psychiatry* **9**, 5–10.

Frank, E., Kupfer, D.J., Perel, J.M. *et al.* (1990). Three-year outcomes for maintenance therapies in recurrent depression. *Arch Gen Psychiatry* **47**, 1093–1099.

Frank, E., Prien, R.F., Jarrett, R.B. *et al.* (1991). Conceptualisation and rationale for consensus definitions of terms in major depressive disorder. *Arch Gen Psychiatry* **48**, 851–855.

Freyne, A. and Wrigley, M. (1995). Prognosis of depression in the elderly. *Ir J Psychol Med* **12**, 6–11.

Fujikawa, T., Yamawaski, S. and Touhouda, Y. (1993). Incidence of silent cerebral infarction in patients with major depression. *Stroke* **24**, 1631–1634.

Gallagher, D.E. and Thompson, L.W. (1982). Treatment of major depressive disorder in older adult outpatients with brief psychotherapies. *Psychother Theory Res Pract* **19**, 482–489.

Georgotas, A. and McCue, R. (1989). The additional benefit of extending an antidepressant trial past seven weeks in the depressed elderly. *Int J Geriatr Psychiatry* **4**, 191–195.

Georgotas, A., McCue, R.E. and Cooper, T.B. (1989). A placebo-controlled comparison of nortriptyline and phenelzine in maintenance therapy of elderly depressed patients. *Arch Gen Psychiatry* **46**, 783–786.

Godber, C., Rosenvinge, H., Wilkinson, D. and Smithies, J. (1987). Depression in old age: prognosis after ECT. *Int J Geriatr Psychiatry* **2**, 19–24.

Goldberg, D. and Huxley, P. (1980). *Mental Illness in the Community: The Pathway to Psychiatric Care*, Tavistock, New York.

Gomori, J.M., Steiner, I., Melamed, E. and Cooper, G. (1984). The assessment of changes in brain volume using combined linear measures. *Neuroradiology* **26**, 21–24.

Gordon, W.F. (1981). Elderly depressives: treatment and follow-up. *Can J Psychiatry* **26**, 110–113.

Green, B.H., Copeland, J.R.M., Dewey, M.E. *et al.* (1992). Risk factors for depression in elderly people: a prospective study. *Acta Psychiatr Scand* **86**, 213–217.

Green, B.H., Copeland, J.R.M., Dewey, M.E., Sharma, V. and Davidson, I.A. (1994). Factors associated with recovery and recurrence of depression in older people: a prospective study. *Int J Geriatr Psychiatry* **9**, 789–795.

Henderson, A.S., Grayson, D.A., Scott, R., Wilson, J., Rickwood, D. and Kay, D.W.K. (1986). Social support, dementia and depression among the elderly living in the Hobart community. *Psychol Med* **16**, 379–390.

Hickie, I., Scott, E., Mitchell, P., Wilhelm, K., Austin, M.-P. and Bennett, B. (1995). Subcortical hyperintensities on magnetic resonance imaging: clinical correlates and prognostic significance in patients with severe depression. *Biol Psychiatry* **37**, 151–160.

Hinrichsen, G.A. (1993). Recovery and relapse from major depressive disorder in the elderly. *Am J Psychiatry* **149**, 1574–1579.

Hinrichsen, G.A. and Hernandez, N.A. (1993). Factors associated with recovery from and relapse into major depressive disorder in the elderly. *Am J Psychiatry* **150**, 1820–1825.

Hollon, S.D., Evans, M.D. and DeRubeis, R.J. (1990). Cognitive mediation of relapse prevention following treatment for depression: implications of different risk. In: Ingram, R.E. (Ed.), *Psychological Aspects of Depression*. Plenum Press, New York, pp. 117–136.

Hughes, D.C., DeMalie, D. and Blazer, D.G. (1993). Does age make a difference in the effects of physical health and social support on the outcome of the major depressive episode? *Am J Psychiatry* **150**, 728–733.

Jackson, R.J. and Baldwin, R.C. (1993). Detecting depression in elderly medically-ill patients: the use of the Geriatric Depression Scale compared with medical and nursing observations. *Age Ageing* **22**, 349–353.

Jacoby, R.J., Levy, R. and Bird, J.M. (1981). Computed tomography and the outcome of affective disorder: a follow-up study of elderly patients. *Br J Psychiatry* **139**, 288–292.

Jerling, M. (1995). Dosing of antidepressants – the unknown art. *J Clin Psychopharmacol* **15**, 435–439.

Jorm, A.F., Henderson, A.S., Kay, D.W.K. and Jacomb, P.A. (1991). Mortality in relation to dementia, depression and social integration in an elderly community sample. *Int J Geriatr Psychiatry* **6**, 5–11.

Katona, C.L.E., Abou-Saleh, M.T., Harrison, D.H. *et al.* (1995). Placebo-controlled trial of lithium augmentation of fluoxetine and lofepramine. *Br J Psychiatry* **166**, 80–86.

Kay, D.W.K., Roth, M. and Hopkins, B. (1955). Affective disorders in the senium: their association with organic cerebral degeneration. *J ment Sci* **101**, 302–316.

Keller, M.B., Lavori, P.W., Friedman, B. *et al.* (1987). The longitudinal interval follow-up evaluation. *Arch Gen Psychiatry* **44**, 540–548.

Kivela, S.-L., Pahkala, K. and Laippala, P. (1991). A one-year prognosis of dysthymic disorder and major depression in old age. *Int J Geriatr Psychiatry* **6**, 81–87.

Kivela, S.-L., Kongas-Saviaro, P., Pahkala, K., Kesti, E. and Laippala, P. (1993). Five-year prognosis for dysthymic disorder in old age. *Int J Geriatr Psychiatry* **11**, 939–947.

Klerman, G.L., Weismann, M.M., Rounsaville, B.J. and Chevron, E.S. (1984). *Interpersonal Psychotherapy of Depression*, Basic Books, New York.

Koenig, H.G., Goli, V., Shelp, F., Kudler, H.S., Cohen, H.J. and Blazer, D.G. (1992). Major depression in hospitalised medically ill older men: documentation, management and outcome. *Int J Geriatr Psychiatry* **7**, 25–34.

Kupfer, D.J., Frank, E. and Perel, J.M. (1989). The advantage of early treatment intervention in recurrent depression. *Arch Gen Psychiatry* **46**, 771–775.

Kushnir, S.L. (1986). Lithium-antidepressant combinations in the treatment of depressed, physically ill geriatric patients. *Am J Psychiatry* **143**, 378–379.

Lafferman, J., Soloman, K. and Ruskin, P. (1988). Lithium augmentation for treatment-resistant depression. *J Geriatr Psychiatry Neurology* **1**, 49–52.

Lee, A.S. and Murray, R.M. (1988). The long-term outcome of Maudsley depressives. *Br J Psychiatry* **153**, 741–751.

Lindgren, A., Roijer, A., Rudling, O. *et al.* (1994). Cerebral lesions on magnetic resonance imaging, heart disease, and vascular risk factors in subjects without stroke: a population-based study. *Stroke* **25**, 929–934.

MacDonald, A.J.D. (1986). Do general practitioners 'miss' depression in elderly patients? *BMJ* **292**, 1365–1367.

Magni, G., Palazzolo, O. and Bianchin, G. (1988). The course of depression in elderly outpatients. *Can J Psychiatry* **33**, 21–24.

Manolio, T.A., Kronmal, R.A., Burke, G.L. *et al.* (1994). Magnetic resonance abnormalities and cardiovascular disease in older adults: the cardiovascular health study. *Stroke* **25**, 318–327.

Meats, P., Timol, M. and Jolley, D. (1991). Prognosis of depression in the elderly. *Br J Psychiatry* **159**, 659–663.

Millard, P.H. (1983). Depression in old age. *BMJ* **287**, 375–376.

Mirchandani, I.C., Abrams, R.C., Young, R.C. and Alexopoulos, G.S. (1994). One-year follow-up continuation convulsive therapy prescribed for depressed elderly patients. *Int J Geriatr Psychiatry* **9**, 31–36.

Montgomery, S.A. and Asberg, M. (1979). A new depression scale designed to be sensitive to change. *Br J Psychiatry* **134**, 382–389.

Murphy, E. (1983). The prognosis of depression in old age. *Br J Psychiatry* **142**, 111–119.

Murphy, E. and Grundy, E. (1984). A comparative study of bed usage by younger and older patients with depression. *Psychol Med* **14**, 445–450.

Murphy, E., Smith, R., Lindesay, J. and Slattery, J. (1988). Increased mortality rates in late-life depression. *Br J Psychiatry* **152**, 347–353.

Neal, R.M. and Baldwin, R.C. (1994). Screening for anxiety and depression in elderly medical outpatients. *Age Ageing* **23**, 461–464.

Nelson, H. (1976). A modified card sorting test sensitive to frontal lobe defects. *Cortex* **12**, 313–324.

O'Brien, J.T. and Ames, D. (1994). Why do the depressed elderly die? *Int J Geriatr Psychiatry* **9**, 689–693.

O'Brien, J., Desmond, P., Ames, D., Schweitzer, I., Harriagan, S. and Tress, B. (1996). A magnetic resonance imaging study of white matter lesions in depression and Alzheimer's disease. *Br J Psychiatry* **168**, 477–485.

Old Age Depression Interest Group (1993). How long should the elderly take antidepressants? A double-blind placebo-controlled study of continuation/prophylaxis therapy with dothiepin. *Br J Psychiatry* **162**, 175–182.

Ong, Y.-L., Martineau, F., Lloyd, C. and Robbins, I. (1987). Support group for the depressed elderly. *Int J Geriatr Psychiatry* **2**, 119–123.

Orrell, M.W., Baldwin, B., Collins, E. and Katona, C. (1995a). A UK national survey of the management of depression by geriatricians and old age psychiatrists. *Int J Geriatr Psychiatry* **10**, 457–467.

Orrell, M.W., Collins, E., Shergill, S. and Katona, C. (1995b). The management of depression in the elderly by practitioners. 1: Use of antidepressants. *Fam Pract* **12**, 5–11.

Oxman, T.E., Berkman, L.F., Kasl, S., Freeman, D.H. Jr and Barrett, J. (1992). Social support and depressive symptoms in the elderly. *Am J Epidemiol* **135**, 356–368.

Parker, K.L., Mittmann, N., Shear, N.H. *et al.* (1994). Lithium augmentation in geriatric depressed outpatients: a clinical report. *Int J Geriatr Psychiatry* **9**, 995–1002.

Pearlson, G.D., Rabins, P.V., Kim, W.S. *et al.* (1989). Structural brain CT changes and cognitive deficits in elderly depressives with and without reversible dementia ('pseudodementia'). *Psychol Med* **19**, 573–584.

Post, F. (1962). *The Significance of Affective Symptoms in Old Age*. Maudsley Monographs 10. Oxford University Press, London.

Post, F. (1968). The factor of ageing in affective disorder. In: Coppen, A. and Walk, A. (Eds), *Recent Developments in Affective Disorders*. Royal Medico-Psychological Association Publication No. 2. Headley Bros, Kent, pp. 105–116.

Post, F. (1972). The management and nature of depressive illnesses in late life: a follow-through study. *Br J Psychiatry* **121**, 393–404.

Rabins, P.V., Harvis, K. and Koven, S. (1985). High fatality rates of late-life depression associated with cardiovascular disease. *J Affect Disord* **9**, 165–167.

Reding, M., Haycox, J. and Blass, J. (1985). Depression in patients referred to a dementia clinic. *Arch Neurol* **42**, 894–896.

Rey, A. (1964). *L'Examen Clinique en Psychologie*, Presses Universitaires de France, Paris.

Reynolds, C.F., Perel, J.M., Cornes, C. and Kupfer, D.J. (1989). Open-trial maintenance pharmacotherapy in late-life depression: survival analysis. *Psychiatr Res* **27**, 225–231.

Reynolds, C.F., Frank, E., Perel, J.M. *et al.* (1992). Combined pharmacotherapy and psychotherapy in the acute and continuation treatment of elderly patients with recurrent major depression. *Am J Psychiatry* **149**, 1687–1692.

Reynolds, C.F., Frank, E., Perel, J.M. *et al.* (1994). Treatment of consecutive episodes of major depression in the elderly. *Am J Psychiatry* **151**, 1740–1743.

Robinson, J.R. (1989). The natural history of mental disorder in old age: a long-term study. *Br J Psychiatry* **154**, 783–789.

Sadavoy, J. and Reiman-Sheldon, E. (1983). General hospital geriatric psychiatric treatment: follow-up study. *J Am Geriatr Soc* **31**, 200–205.

Schneider, L.S., Reynolds, C.F., Lebowitz, B.D. and Friedhoff, A.J. (1994). *Diagnosis and Treatment of Depression in Late Life*. American Psychiatric Press, Washington, DC.

Snowden, J. and Lane, F. (1994). Outcome of depression in dementia. *Int J Geriatr Psychiatry* **9**, 589–591.

Steuer, J.L., Mintz, J., Hammen, C.L. *et al.* (1984). Cognitive–behavioural and psychodynamic group psychotherapy in treatment of geriatric depression. *J Consult Clin Psychol* **52**, 180–189.

Stoudemire, A., Hill, C.D., Morris, R., Martino-Saltzman, D. and Lewison, B. (1993). Long-term affective and cognitive outcome in depressed older patients. *Am J Psychiatry* **150**, 896–900.

van Marwijk, D.W.J., Bekker, F.M., Nolen, W.A., Jansen, P.A.F., van Nieuwkerk, J.F. and Hop, W.C.J. (1990). Lithium augmentation in geriatric depression. *J Affect Disord* **20**, 217–223.

Waterreus, A., Blanchard, M. and Mann, A. (1994). Community psychiatric nurses for the elderly: few side-effects and effective in the treatment of depression. *J Clin Nurs* **3**, 299–306.

Wells, K.B., Stewart, A., Hays, R.D. *et al.* (1989). The functioning and well-being of depressed patients: results from the Medical Outcomes Study. *JAMA* **262**, 914–919.

Yesavage, J.A., Brink, T.L., Rose, T.L. *et al.* (1983). Development and validation of a geriatric depression screening scale: a preliminary report. *J Psychiatr Res* **17**, 37–49.

Zimmer, B., Rosen, J., Thornton, J.E., Peral, J.M. and Reynolds, C.F. (1988). Adjunctive low-dose lithium carbonate in treatment-resistant depression: a placebo-controlled study. *J Clin Psychopharmacol* **8**, 120 124.

Zis, A.P., Grof, P., Webster, M. and Goodwin, F.K. (1980). Prediction of relapse in recurrent affective disorder. *Psychopharmacol Bull* **16**, 47–49.

Zusky, P.M., Biederman, J., Rosenbaum, J.F. *et al.* (1988). Adjunct low dose lithium carbonate in treatment-resistant depression: a placebo-controlled study. *J Clin Psychopharmacol* **8**, 120–124.

V

Functional Disorders

Advances in Old Age Psychiatry: Chromosomes to Community Care
Edited by C. Holmes and R. Howard
© 1997 Wrightson Biomedical Publishing Ltd

18

Phobic Disorders and Panic in Old Age

JAMES LINDESAY
Department of Psychiatry for the Elderly, University of Leicester, Leicester, UK

INTRODUCTION

There are still significant obstacles to the effective identification and treat-ment of anxiety disorders in elderly people. Despite the increased attention they have received in recent years, many health professionals, particularly at the primary care level, still do not recognize that at least some of these disor-ders exist to a significant extent in this age group, or that they are clinically important in terms of their frequency, severity, treatability and cost. To some extent clinical awareness is low because elderly patients with anxiety disor-ders tend not to present in clinical settings, such as inpatients, outpatients or casualty departments (Sheehan *et al.*, 1981; Thyer *et al.*, 1985; Schwartz *et al.*, 1987). Even in primary care, where there is a steady accumulation of chronic cases over time, there is a decline in the rate of new consultations with age (Shepherd *et al.*, 1981). However, community surveys show that conditions such as phobic disorders and generalized anxiety occur in the elderly popula-tion at rates not much lower than in younger adults, and that in old age they are among the commonest psychiatric disorders identified (Regier *et al.*, 1988; Lindesay *et al.*, 1989; Flint, 1994; Manela *et al.*, 1996). As Table 1 shows, prevalence rates of these disorders vary significantly according to how they are assessed and defined by the survey methodology. Some diagnostic and case-finding systems, such as DIS/DSM-III and PDS-GAS, identify substan-tially more cases than do others such as GMS/AGECAT. These differences are due principally to different diagnostic hierarchical rules and different severity criteria (Lindesay and Banerjee, 1993), which raises the question of the extent to which the identification of anxiety disorders in clinical practice suffers as the result of applying in hierarchical criteria of modern taxonomies (Lindesay, 1995). So far as the severity of anxiety and fear in old age is concerned, the problem is one of how this judgement is made. Ageist assumptions about what is a 'normal' or 'reasonable' level of anxiety in an elderly patient will result in potentially treatable cases being missed. Elderly

Table 1. Prevalence of anxiety disorders (%) in old age (65+), using different diagnostic systems.

	Phobic disorder	*Panic disorder*	*Generalized anxiety*
DIS/DSM-III			
Regier *et al.* (1988)	4.8	0.1	–
Blazer *et al.* (1991)	–	–	1.9
GMS/AGECAT			
Copeland *et al.* (1987):			
case (3 + 4)	0.0	–	1.1
sub-case (1 + 2)	1.8	–	17.2
PDS-GAS			
Lindesay *et al.* (1989)	10.0	0.0	3.7
Manela *et al.* (1996)	12.0	0.1	4.7

people perceive vulnerability and evaluate risk in terms of the severity of the consequences rather than the likelihood of exposure, and it is factors such as physical disability, social support and integration within local community that are important in this evaluation, not age *per se*. Risk evaluation is also influenced by emotional and cognitive factors, and may be significantly biased by psychiatric disorder. For example, the rates of problematic fear of crime are much higher in elderly individuals with phobic disorders than in nonphobic controls (62% versus 17%) (Lindesay, 1996).

PHOBIC DISORDERS

In the USA Epidemiologic Catchment Area (ECA) study, phobic disorders were found to be the commonest psychiatric disorder in women aged 65 years and older, and the commonest after cognitive impairment in men of that age (Robins and Regier, 1991). Other studies have found comparable rates of phobic disorders in elderly populations (Table 1). The fears reported by elderly people are similar to those in younger age groups, although the relative frequency may differ; the commonest fears expressed by the urban elderly in one study were travelling and using public transport (Lindesay, 1991).

Not all of the subjects identified by community surveys as having a phobic disorder have clinically significant conditions. In one case–control study, half the cases had an Index of Definition (Wing, 1976) of four or more (Lindesay, 1991); in addition, half the cases were agoraphobic, one-third were of late onset, one-third were significantly socially impaired, and one-third were also depressed. These characteristics overlapped extensively, defining a clinically important group of cases with late-onset agoraphobia who were both depressed and socially impaired.

Detailed studies of phobic disorders in old age are few, but they demonstrate some of the significant associated factors. Following Goldberg and Huxley (1992), these may be grouped into those conferring vulnerability to the disorder, those associated with the onset of symptoms (destabilization), and those influencing the evolution and outcome of the episode (restitution).

Vulnerability

Elderly subjects with phobic disorders have higher concurrent and past rates of other anxiety and depressive disorders (Lindesay, 1991). It is not clear whether this increased liability to other disorders confers a specific vulnerability to phobic disorders; more likely, the concurrence of these disorders reflects an underlying common genetic vulnerability. Studies have demonstrated that, while there is a significant genetic contribution to neurotic vulnerability, it is not specific to particular disorders (Andrews et al., 1990; Kendler et al., 1992).

Chronic physical disability due to conditions such as arthritis and sensory impairment is associated with high rates of subjective anxiety and avoidance (Kay et al., 1987; Lindesay, 1990), perhaps because it heightens the individual's sense of vulnerability to and gravity of the consequences of possible future adverse events. An intense fear of falling in the absence of visual supports ('space phobia') has been described in association with disturbed vestibulo-ocular and righting reflexes (Marks, 1981).

Social adversity does not emerge strongly as a risk factor for phobic disorders in old age. In the ECA study, and in a study of elderly women in New Zealand (Walton et al., 1990) there was an association with urban domicile, but this may be a reflection of poor social networks rather than poverty (Blazer et al., 1985). A number of studies have found an association between phobic disorders and early parental loss in both patients and general adult populations (Tweed et al., 1989). Lindesay (1991) found that phobic disorders in elderly subjects were associated with loss of a parent, particularly the father, before the age of 18 years. This adverse early experience may contribute to the development of an avoidant cognitive 'defence style' (Pollock and Andrews, 1989) that in turn predisposes to the acquisition of phobic disorders both in early adulthood and in later life.

Destabilization

The commonest factor precipitating the onset of agoraphobia after the age of 65 years appears to be an acute physical health event, such as myocardial infarct, a stroke or admission to hospital for surgery (Lindesay, 1991; Burvill et al., 1995). Other traumatic events such as muggings are also reported as the causal event in a proportion of cases. Notable for its rarity as a cause of late-onset agoraphobia is panic; although cases have been described (e.g. Frances and Flaherty, 1989), it was not identified as a cause in any of the subjects studied by Lindesay (1991) or Burvill et al. (1995).

Restitution

The behavioural avoidance in phobic disorders may be regarded as a maladaptive restitution, whereby the subject mitigates their anxiety by avoiding the threatening stimuli (Goldberg and Huxley, 1992). In elderly people, this may be reinforced by well-meaning but misguided support from family, friends and domiciliary services, which enables the individual to remain housebound without undue inconvenience (Lindesay, 1991). However, the finding of Burvill et al. (1995) that two-thirds of cases of poststroke agoraphobia had spontaneously recovered at one-year follow-up suggests that the fear and loss of confidence associated with a sudden episode of illness do abate with time, at least in this disorder. Specific factors associated with spontaneous resolution are not known.

Treatments are an important class of restitution factor for any disorder. There are few reports of cognitive-behaviour therapies for elderly people with phobic disorders, but the evidence from single-case studies and small patient series suggests that they are just as effective for phobias, generalized anxiety and panic in old age as they are in younger adulthood (Woods, 1995). Unfortunately, very few of those who might benefit from this treatment actually receive it (Lindesay, 1991).

PANIC

Very little is known about panic in old age. In marked contrast to phobic disorders and generalized anxiety in this age group, the prevalence rates reported by epidemiological studies suggest that it is rare (q.v. Table 1), although cross-sectional surveys will inevitably underestimate the true prevalence rate of a chronic episodic disorder (Von Korrf and Eaton, 1989). However, incidence data from the ECA study also show that it is much less common in old age than in earlier life (Eaton et al., 1989). This study also found some evidence of differences between ethnic groups, with increasing rates of panic with age in Hispanic women (Robins and Regier, 1991).

Most of our information about panic in old age is derived from case-studies (Frances and Flaherty, 1989; Luchins and Rose, 1989), volunteer samples (Sheikh et al., 1991) and nonpsychiatric patient populations (Katon, 1984; Beitman et al., 1991). As has been noted, panic rarely causes late-onset agoraphobia and so tends not to present to psychiatric services unless it occurs in the context of depression. Instead, patients appear to be referred to cardiologists, gastroenterologists and neurologists; in one study of cardiology patients with chest pain and no evidence of coronary artery disease, one-third of those aged 65 years and over met diagnostic criteria for panic disorder (Beitman *et al.*, 1991). The evidence from these admittedly unrepresentative samples suggests that panic in old age is commoner in women and in the widowed, and that it is symptomatically less severe than that occurring earlier in adult life (Sheikh *et al.*, 1991). There is a suggestion that it may be associated with childhood sexual abuse (Sheikh *et al.*, 1994).

Flint *et al.* (1996) have reviewed the possible reasons why panic is rarely identified in elderly populations. One possibility is that cases are misdiagnosed, either as another psychiatric disorder, or as physical illness; Katon (1984) found that panic disorder in patients of all ages was commonly misdiagnosed by general practitioners as somatization disorder. Secondly, if panic is a less severe disorder in old age (not all studies show this), then cases may fall short of the requirements of classifications such as DSM-IV. However, there was no difference in the panic syndrome/subsyndrome ratio with age in the ECA study. Thirdly, institutionalized cases will not have been identified by community surveys. However, nursing home studies do not reveal significantly higher levels of panic in institutionalized populations that would elevate the total rates in old age to those found in younger adults (Parmalee *et al.*, 1993; Cheok *et al.*, 1996). Fourthly, it may be that individuals with panic disorder are vulnerable to excess mortality from suicide, alcohol abuse and smoking-related diseases, and so are removed from elderly cohorts. There is some evidence that this occurs, particularly in men (Coryell, 1984), but it does not completely account for the lower rates of panic seen in old age. A fifth possibility is that specific cohort effects are operating, such as have been proposed to account for the increased rates of depression and substance abuse seen in younger adults (Klerman, 1988). However, there is no evidence for generational effects in panic. Finally, it may be that biological changes with age in the neuronal systems thought to be dysfunctional in panic, such as the noradrenergic, serotonergic (5-HT) and cholecystokinin (CCK) systems, may place elderly people at lower risk of developing the disorder. For example, there is lowered noradrenergic activity, and cell loss in the locus ceruleus with ageing, and similar changes may also occur with 5-HT and CCK.

CONCLUSIONS

Although the occurrence of panic falls with age, this is not associated with an equivalent fall in the rates of phobic disorder. This is because other events, such as physical illness, assume the role of the panic attack in precipitating phobic avoidance in old age. Although there is some suggestion that late-onset agoraphobia may be less liable to become chronic than cases beginning earlier in adult life, it is nevertheless distressing and disabling, and health services should be aiming to improve on the current low rates of detection and treatment.

REFERENCES

Andrews, G., Stewart, G., Allen, R. and Henderson, A.S. (1990). The genetics of six neurotic disorders: a twin study. *J Affect Disord* **19**, 23–29.

Beitman, B.D., Kushner, M. and Grossberg, G.T. (1991). Late onset panic disorder: evidence from a study of patients with chest pain and normal cardiac evaluations. *Int J Psychiatry Med* **21**, 29–35.

Blazer, D.G., George, L.K., Landermann, R. *et al.* (1985). Psychiatric disorders: a rural/urban comparison. *Arch Gen Psychiatry* **42**, 651–656.

Blazer, D.G., George, L.K. and Hughes, D. (1991). The epidemiology of anxiety disorders: an age comparison. In: Salzman, C. and Lebowitz, B.D. (Eds), *Anxiety in the Elderly*, Springer, New York, pp. 17–30.

Burvill, P., Johnson, G.A., Jamrozik, K.D., Anderson, C.S., Stewart-Wynne, E.G. and Chakera, T.M.H. (1995). Anxiety disorders after stroke: results from the Perth community stroke study. *Br J Psychiatry* **166**, 328–332.

Cheok, A., Snowdon, J., Miller, R. and Vaughn, R. (1996) The prevalence of anxiety disorders in nursing homes. *Int J Geriatr Psychiatry* **11**, 405–410.

Copeland, J.R.M., Dewey, M.E., Wood, N., Searle, R., Davidson, I.A. and McWilliam, C. (1987). Range of mental illness among the elderly in the community: prevalence in Liverpool using the GMS-AGECAT package. *Br J Psychiatry* **150**, 815–823.

Coryell, W. (1984). Mortality after thirty to forty years. Panic disorder compared with other psychiatric illnesses. In: Grinspoon, L. (Ed.), *Psychiatry Update*. American Psychiatric Association, Washington, DC, pp. 460–467.

Eaton, W.W., Kramer, M., Anthony, J.C., Dryman, A., Shapiro, S. and Locke, B.Z. (1989). The incidence of specific DIS/DSM-III mental disorders: data from the NIMH Epidemiologic Catchment Area program. *Acta Psychiatr Scand* **79**, 163–178.

Flint, A.J. (1994). Epidemiology and comorbidity of anxiety disorders in the elderly. *Am J Psychiatry* **151**, 640–649.

Flint, A.J., Cook, J.M. and Rabins, P.V. (1996). Why is panic disorder less frequent in late life? *Am J Geriatr Psychiatry* **4**, 96–109.

Frances, A. and Flaherty, J.A. (1989). Elderly widow develops panic attacks, followed by depression. *Hosp Community Psychiatry* **40**, 19–23.

Goldberg, D. and Huxley, P. (1992). *Common Mental Disorders: A Bio-social Model*. Tavistock/Routledge, London.

Katon, W.J. (1984). Chest pain, cardiac disease and panic disorder. *J Clin Psychiatry* **51**, 27–30.

Kay, D.W.K., Holding, T.A., Jones, B. and Littler, S. (1987). Psychiatric morbidity in Hobart's dependent aged. *Aust NZ J Psychiatry* **21**, 463–468.

Kendler, K.S., Kessler, R.C., Heath, A.C. and Eaves, L.J. (1992). Major depression and generalized anxiety disorder. Same genes, (partly) different environments? *Arch Gen Psychiatry* **49**, 716–722.

Klerman, G. (1988). The current age of youthful melancholia: evidence for increase in depression among adolescents and young adults. *Br J Psychiatry* **152**, 4–14.

Lindesay, J. (1990). The Guy's/Age Concern Survey: physical health and psychiatric disorder in an urban elderly community. *Int J Geriatr Psychiatry* **5**, 171–178.

Lindesay, J. (1991). Phobic disorders in the elderly. *Br J Psychiatry* **159**, 531–541.

Lindesay, J. (1995). Introduction: the concept of neurosis. In: Lindesay, J. (Ed.), *Neurotic Disorders in the Elderly*. Oxford University Press, Oxford, pp. 1–11.

Lindesay, J. (1996). Phobic disorders and fear of crime in the elderly. *Aging Ment Health* (in press).

Lindesay, J. and Banerjee, S. (1993). Phobic disorders in the elderly: a comparison of three diagnostic systems. *Int J Geriatr Psychiatry* **8**, 387–393.

Lindesay, J., Briggs, K. and Murphy, E. (1989). The Guy's/Age Concern Survey: prevalence rates of cognitive impairment, depression and anxiety in an urban elderly community. *Br J Psychiatry* **155**, 317–329.

Luchins, D.J. and Rose, R.P. (1989). Late-life onset of panic disorder with agoraphobia in three patients. *Am J Psychiatry* **146**, 920–921.

Manela, M., Katona, C. and Livingston, G. (1996). How common are the anxiety disorders in old age? *Int J Geriatr Psychiatry* **6**, 65–70.

Marks, I.M. (1981). Space phobia: a pseudo-agoraphobic syndrome. *J Neurol Neurosurg Psychiatry* **44**, 387–391.

Parmalee, P.A., Katz, I.R. and Lawton, M.P. (1993). Anxiety and its association with depression among institutionalized elderly. *Am J Geriatr Psychiatry* **1**, 46–58.

Pollock, C. and Andrews, G. (1989). The defense style associated with specific anxiety disorders. *Am J Psychiatry* **146**, 455–460.

Regier, D.A., Boyd, J.H., Burke, J.D. *et al.* (1988). One-month prevalence of mental disorders in the United States. *Arch Gen Psychiatry* **45**, 977–986.

Robins, L. and Regier, D. (Eds) (1991). *Psychiatric Disorders in America*. The Free Press, New York.

Schwartz, G.M., Braverman, B.G. and Roth, B. (1987). Anxiety disorders and psychiatric referral in the general medical emergency room. *Gen Hosp Psychiatry* **9**, 87–93.

Sheehan, D.V., Sheehan, K.E. and Minichiello, W.E. (1981). Age of onset of phobic disorders: a re-evaluation. *Compr Psychiatry* **22**, 544–553.

Sheikh, J.I., King, R.J. and Barr Taylor, C. (1991). Comparative phenomenology of early-onset versus late-onset panic attacks: a pilot survey. *Am J Psychiatry* **148**, 1231–1233.

Sheikh, J.I., Swales, P.J., Kravitz, J., Bail, G. and Barr Taylor, C. (1994). Childhood abuse history in older women with panic disorder. *Am J Geriatr Psychiatry* **2**, 75–77.

Shepherd, M., Cooper, B., Brown, A.C. and Kalton, G. (1981). *Psychiatric Illness in General Practice*. Oxford University Press, London.

Thyer, B.A., Parrish, R.T., Curtis, G.C., Nesse, R.M. and Cameron, O.G. (1985). Ages of onset of DSM-III anxiety disorders. *Compr Psychiatry* **26**, 113–122.

Tweed, J.L., Schoenbach, V.J., George, L.K. and Blazer, D.G. (1989). The effects of childhood parental death and divorce on six-month history of anxiety disorders. *Br J Psychiatry* **154**, 823–828.

Von Korff, M.R. and Eaton, W.W. (1989). Epidemiologic findings on panic. In: Baker, R. (Ed.), *Panic Disorder: Theory, Research and Therapy*. John Wiley and Sons, Chichester, pp. 35–50.

Walton, V.A., Romans-Clarkson, S.E., Mullen, P.E. and Herbison, G.P. (1990). The mental health of elderly women in the community. *Int J Geriatr Psychiatry* **5**, 257–263.

Wing, J.K. (1976). A technique for studying psychiatric morbidity in in-patient and out-patient series and in general population samples. *Psychol Med* **6**, 665–671.

Woods, R.T. (1995). Psychological treatments I: behavioural and cognitive approaches. In: Lindesay, J. (Ed.), *Neurotic Disorders in the Elderly*. Oxford University Press, Oxford, pp. 97–113.

Advances in Old Age Psychiatry: Chromosomes to Community Care
Edited by C. Holmes and R. Howard
© 1997 Wrightson Biomedical Publishing Ltd

19

Functional Disorders in Ethnic Minority Elders

MELANIE ABAS

Section of Old Age Psychiatry, Institute of Psychiatry, London, UK

This chapter will focus on common nonpsychotic disorders such as depression and anxiety, but will first discuss some general aspects such as demography, UK Government health strategy and physical health, with respect to ethnic minority adults living in the UK.

DEMOGRAPHY

The Office of Population Censuses and Surveys (OPCS, 1992) estimates the Black and ethnic minority population of Great Britain, for 1987–89, to be 4.7% of the total population, i.e. around 2.6 million. The OPCS figures show that the largest non-White ethnic minority groups are Indian, Black Caribbean, Pakistani, Black African, Bangladeshi and Chinese. At present, those aged 65 and over form only around 3–4% of the ethnic minority population compared with 16% of the White population. It is possible that numbers of ethnic elders have been underestimated, because of a tendency to give younger ages on entry to the UK (Ebrahim and Hillier, 1991). However, despite probable inaccuracies, the census data do show that, given the large numbers in the preretirement age bands, there will be at least a fourfold increase in those Black and ethnic minority people aged over 65 by the year 2016.

Many of the ethnic minority population live in inner city areas, especially within Greater London and the Midlands. In several of the electoral wards of London and Birmingham, ethnic 'minorities' now make up the majority of the resident population with, for example, minority groups comprising 71% of the population in Soho, Birmingham, and 90% of the residents in Northcote, Ealing, London (OPCS, 1992). Many inner city areas in the UK are characterized by social deprivation, poverty and poor housing, which adversely affect the health of those living within them (Tonks, 1992). Only around 5% of older Black and ethnic minority people own their own homes versus over 50% of all people of pensionable age. Most older Black and Asian people had jobs in the semiskilled, skilled manual or unskilled sectors whereas young Black and Asian people are heavily represented in the non manual and skilled manual sectors (Blakemore and Boneham, 1994). As a whole, more Black and Asian elders are economically disadvantaged relative to White working class elders and, for example, most older Asian women have never been in paid work (AFFOR, 1981; Blakemore and Boneham, 1994).

GOVERNMENT HEALTH STRATEGY

Prior to 1980, areas of concern in terms of health provision for ethnic minorities were mainly limited to such issues as barriers to communication and the need for interpreters. In 1988, Black and ethnic minority health was included in the Department of Health management review of Health Service performance. As a result of this, it became apparent that better health authority planning was required and this led the Department of Health to take initiatives to improve Black and ethnic minority health (Bahl, 1993). The key themes in the development of these health policies are:

1. Elimination of racial discrimination
2. Promotion of availability of data on Black and ethnic minority groups
3. Delivery of appropriate quality services
4. Training of health professionals
5. Making available information for Black and ethnic minority groups on health and health services
6. Recognition of differing patterns of health and disease

PHYSICAL HEALTH

Relative to the indigenous population, potential types of inequalities faced by minority elders include income inequalities, inequalities in life expectancy and disease, social support inequalities, and inequalities in life satisfaction, morale and psychological well-being. The issue of 'double jeopardy' has particularly emerged from studies in the USA which commonly find that older Blacks are doubly disadvantaged in income and physical health but not in terms of mental health (Jackson *et al.*, 1982). In the USA, inequalities in income, housing and urban environment widen with age between Black and White. However, Black elders have not been found to be especially disadvantaged in terms of social support and life satisfaction. Dowd and Bengston (1978), again writing from the USA, found that poorer physical health remained associated with ethnicity even when social class, sex and income were controlled for.

In the UK there have been relatively fewer studies of health in older ethnic minority adults but those that have been carried out appear to present a picture of lower mortality from certain illnesses, especially certain forms of cancer, but higher rates of death in Asians from coronary heart disease, diabetes, tuberculosis and liver cancer, and in Caribbeans from stroke, cardiovascular disease, liver cancer, diabetic complications and accidents (Whitehead, 1988; Balarajan and Yuen, 1984). Ebrahim *et al.* (1991), studying Gujaratis in north London, concluded that common chronic diseases affected Asians more frequently than the indigenous population but that certain problems of old age including falls, incontinence and depression were less frequent. Afro-Caribbean women have been shown to have especially high rates of hospitalization for physical illness. Overall, therefore, there is no simple generalization to describe health in older ethnic minority adults, but instead a rather complex pattern.

PRIMARY CARE

In terms of overall general practitioner (GP) consultation rates, men and women of Pakistani origin and men of Asian and African Caribbean origin are more likely to consult their GPs than the general population (Balarajan *et al.*, 1989). Other studies have largely confirmed these findings. However, when it comes to consultation rates for psychosocial problems, the picture is almost reversed. White women form the group most likely to be diagnosed by the GP as having psychological disorder, with women of African Caribbean and Asian origin the least likely to be identified as having significant psychological problems (Gillam *et al.*, 1989). It is not clear whether these findings are due to lower prevalence of minor psychological disorders in ethnic minorities or if such observations are an artefact, possibly a result of misdiagnosis by GPs (Lloyd, 1993). GPs have certainly stressed that the assessment of mental health problems in ethnic minorities is difficult and have called for further training in this area (Pharaoh, 1994).

MENTAL HEALTH: OVERALL PATTERN OF MENTAL DISORDERS IN ALL AGES

Methodological problems, inherent in National Health Service (NHS) statistics relating to ethnicity, include the following:

1. Only data based on 'country of birth', not ethnicity, have been available until very recently.

2. Statistical returns in the NHS have hitherto been of a very low standard. For example, in 1981 only 70% of mental hospital inpatient record returns provided information on country of birth (Cochrane and Sashidharan, 1996). Virtually no statistics at all are available for outpatients or other forms of psychiatric care.

3. Schemes for recording diagnosis vary from region to region and hospital to hospital, giving rise to regional variations in case definition and making the interpretation of trends over time difficult as diagnostic criteria change.

Taking these limitations into account, the most recent comprehensive survey covered admissions in 1981, for all ages, by country of birth as represented in the NHS returns (168 000 admissions) (Cochrane and Bal, 1989). Rates were calculated based upon population data drawn from the Census which occurred in that year. All diagnostic categories and readmissions as well as first admissions were included. The main findings include:

1. An excess of diagnosed schizophrenia in people born in the Caribbean. Males had 4.3 times the native English-born rate and females 3.9 times the native rate of first admissions for schizophrenia.

2. For all diagnoses combined, the admission rate of the Caribbean-born was substantially below that for the native-born – especially for neurotic conditions, personality disorders and alcohol abuse.

3. For migrants from South Asia (India, Pakistan, Bangladesh and Hong Kong) overall admission rates were lower than those for people born in England. Other than a high rate for alcohol-related disorders among Indian-born men, rates for disorders other than schizophrenia were substantially below those of the native-born.

Why should rates of inpatient admissions, for diagnoses other than schizophrenia, be lower among adults from ethnic minorities? As discussed by Cochrane and Sashidharan (1996), three possibilities exist.

1. Black and Asian people may have a lower prevalence of nonpsychotic conditions.

2. Black and Asian people may have a similar prevalence of these disorders to White people but receive alternative forms of care.

3. Black and Asian people may suffer these disorders at a similar rate to White people but do not gain access to services because either they find existing facilities inappropriate and/or they are not offered similar access to systems of care.

So far, for the main disorders, there is a lack of adequate data from which to form conclusions regarding these three possibilities, although data should emerge soon from several surveys in different parts of the UK.

DEPRESSION AND ANXIETY IN ETHNIC MINORITY ELDERS

A small number of reports suggest that ethnic minority elders are under-represented among patients in touch with community or hospital mental health facilities (Bahl, 1993; Pharaoh, 1994; Blakemore and Boneham, 1994; Bethlem and Maudsley NHS Trust Information Office, 1992, personal communication). Impressions, and the limited data available, suggest a 'splintering off' with people preferring to use culture-specific voluntary and other services (Pharaoh, 1994). As yet, there is no clear picture with respect to prevalence. Blazer (1980) and Gibson (1988), have reported lower rates of mental ill health among older Black adults in the USA, relative to White Americans. However, at least one review has concluded that there are no consistent findings with regard to the association between mental health problems and ethnicity (Krause, 1988). There are two main reasons for this. First, variables such as race or ethnicity are, in many cases, no more than a crude proxy for increased life stress, increased physical illness and financial difficulties. The other problem is that research has continued to confront formidable problems in the measurement of psychiatric disorder including problems in obtaining a representative sample, in defining ethnicity, and in the need to develop appropriate psychiatric instruments.

One of the targets of the *Health of the Nation* (Department of Health, 1992) is to improve the detection and management of depression in the general population. Although GPs are increasingly likely to be aware of depression in their older patients, such patients are rarely offered treatment. Potential problems for GPs in recognizing depression and anxiety in ethnic minority elders include genuine language problems in some situations, producing a need for interpreters, and different presentations of the disorders. A more 'somatic' presentation is commonly cited but many White elders also present somatically.

The general impression is that both somatic and psychological symptoms are commonly presented by depressed ethnic minority elders; that there may be a different emphasis in the psychological terms used, for example, terms such as 'fed-up', 'bad', or 'low' rather than 'depressed' or 'suicidal' (Abas *et al.*, 1996) and/or that the psychological symptoms may have to be enquired about more carefully (Mumford *et al.*, 1991).

SCREENING FOR DEPRESSION AND ANXIETY

The Department of Health recommends that the Geriatric Depression Scale (GDS) (Yesavage, 1988) be used for screening in the elderly. However, there are no data on the validity of the GDS among the main ethnic minority populations in the UK. This leads us to one of the main issues in cross-cultural psychiatry, namely, is it valid to use screening instruments such as the GDS, and even standardized diagnostic interviews such as the Geriatric Mental State (GMS) (Copeland *et al.*, 1986), without modification, in people of different cultures?

Much cross-cultural research has assumed that disorders such as depression have universal validity, an assumption which has been the focus of increasing debate in recent years (Littlewood, 1990). While there is evidence to support the existence of broad similarities in the pattern of depression across cultures (Marsella *et al.*, 1985) there are also differences, particularly in expression and experience of the commoner, less severe, forms of depression and anxiety (Kleinman, 1987; Beiser, 1985). Older Caribbean people rarely use the terms 'sad' or 'unhappy' (Abas *et al.*, 1996). They do, however, speak of being low-spirited, fed up, and weighed down. Is it therefore possible that a range of culture-specific screening tools will be required or will international screens such as the GDS have adequate sensitivity and specificity?

In order to answer this question, among predominantly Jamaican-born elderly people in Brixton, south-east London, the author and co-workers have devised a culture-specific screen for emotional distress and are in the process of comparing its properties with the GDS.

DEVELOPMENT OF A CULTURE-SPECIFIC SCREEN FOR EMOTIONAL DISTRESS FOR USE WITH BLACK CARIBBEAN ELDERS

A combination of semistructured interviews with nonpsychiatrically trained carers for elderly Black Caribbean people (including church ministers, voluntary workers, practice nurses and home care organizers), and with elders identified by those workers as emotionally distressed, was used to generate a lay Caribbean classification of mental illness categories. Techniques used were adapted from a range of anthropological and psychiatric studies (Wig *et al.*, 1980; Kleinman, 1980; Manson *et al.*, 1985; Khan and Manderson, 1992). Many of those interviewed held a unitary view of mental disorder and 'stress' as the end result of a variety of insults. Severe insults and/or 'inability to cope with stress' would lead to 'a stressful condition'/'depression of the spirit'/'depression' and this could deteriorate to states of 'confusion' and of 'not making sense' (Abas *et al.*, 1996).

Over 100 idioms, apparently linked to nonpsychotic emotional distress, were collected. The word 'depression' was mentioned by only 9% of respondents and suicidal ideation or intent by none. A consensus approach was used to group the idioms into domains, 13 domains emerging as particularly dominant, e.g 'worrying/fretting', 'feeling low or down', 'feeling pressured', 'feeling empty inside', 'being weighed down', 'feeling cut-off or alone', an idiom from one of these having been mentioned by 15–63% of respondents (Table 1). Idioms from these 13 key domains were chosen to create a preliminary Caribbean culture-specific screen (Table 2).

Table 1. Some terms for emotional distress volunteered by older Jamaican adults.

Weighed down	
Being weighed down	Being pulled down
Weighed down	Heavy
Just pulling along	Laden down
Empty/spiritless inside	
Empty	Thrill has gone
Spiritless	No spirit in me
Dead inside	Nothing
No excitement in my life	No emotional energy
Stomach discomfort	
Belly pain	Pain in the pit of my stomach
Empty stomach	Upset stomach
Gas in stomach	Gas
Twisting guts	Pain-filled guts
Gas bubbling	
Worrying too much/fretting	
Worry too much	Worries me
In bed worrying	Me fret
Fretting	Mind worried
Thinking too much	

Source: From Abas, 1996.

Table 2. Items included in the preliminary 'Culture-specific screen' for emotional distress in Caribbean elders.

In the past month:
1. Have you been worrying too much or fretting?
2. Have you felt pressured, like pressure is rising in your head?
3. Have you had lots of pain or gas in the belly or the pit of your stomach?
4. What about pain or aching all over the body?
5. Have you felt weak or tired a lot of the time?
6. Have you slept well most of the time?
7. Have you been feeling down or low-spirited or like you're crying inside?
8. Have you felt palpitations or fear around the heart?
9. Have you felt fed up with yourself or even with others, like you want to curse or scream?
10. Have you felt cut off or alone, like people don't appreciate you?
11. Or been feeling empty or spiritless inside?
12. Do you feel weighed down by life?
13. Do you still feel hopeful?

Source: From Abas, 1996.

Compared with screening scales in common use (Bird *et al.*, 1987; Yesavage, 1988) there is an overlap in symptoms concerning poor sleep, worry and lack of energy/tiredness. However there are also some differences. The Caribbean term of feeling 'cut-off' may reflect heightened feelings of social or family alienation (Sokolovsky, 1990) or of loss of a homeland (Manthorpe and Hettiaratchy, 1993) but neither that term nor the common expression of 'feeling fed up' feature on the other 'standard' scales. Whereas the question on 'emptiness' in the Geriatric Depression Scale is connected with life being empty, those questioned here emphasized emptiness or 'spirit-lessness' as emerging from inside themselves. A tendency for people of Caribbean origin to feel 'low' rather than depressed or sad, and to complain of tiredness and diffuse pain when depressed, has also been described in older African Americans in Baltimore (Baker *et al.*, 1995). Other features of the new screen include items possibly linked to anxiety and tension, such as feeling pressured and having a sensation of gas bubbling in the stomach.

Pilot validation has been carried out in Caribbean elders from a community and a clinical sample, most of whom were born in Jamaica. The screen performed well in discriminating between 'depressed cases' and 'nonde-pressed cases', with a sensitivity and specificity above 80% at a cut-off of 4/5. However, the criteria for 'caseness' were based on a medical psychiatric assessment and, as Helman (1990) has outlined, mental disorder should be defined within parameters agreed as abnormal by key people from one's own culture. A full-scale validation of the Caribbean culture-specific screen and the GDS is under way, involving two sets of validating criteria, one being a standardized psychiatric interview (Copeland *et al.*, 1986) and the other a 'culture-specific diagnosis' of emotional disorder (Beiser, 1985; Leff, 1990; Helman, 1990). The latter will be based on a consensus between a Black Caribbean psychiatric social worker and a Black Caribbean church minister, both with extensive experience of working with elderly people from the Caribbean region. Statistical modelling can be used to examine the relationship between the two screens and the two sets of validating criteria and to determine the most sensitive and specific screening items (Dunn,1989).

UNMET NEED AND THE PROVISION OF APPROPRIATE SERVICES

In a recent pilot survey (Richards *et al.*, 1995), all depressed elderly Caribbean people found by screening in the community had unmet needs (e.g. assistance with caring for a demented spouse, assessment of physical illness, prescription of antidepressants). Many of these needs were subsequently addressed through existing health and social care provision, but some services offered were seen by elders and their families as inappropriate. If services are to be made more accessible and appropriate, it will be vital to study attitudes towards depression and dementia and towards acceptable service provision.

The explanatory model approach (Kleinman, 1980; Helman, 1990; Weiss *et al.*, 1992) can be used which explores the person's own notions about an episode of sickness and its appropriate treatment and also gathers information about cultural background and experience in the host culture. In one study (Abas, 1996), this has been extended for the elderly Caribbean person and their carer to define their own main needs, the extent to which these are being met, their satisfaction with the help received and the ways in which they would like services to be provided. A systematic enquiry can then be carried out into preferred modes of delivery of a range of mental health services, including psychiatric assessment, counselling, psychotropic medication, measures to improve isolation and assistance with activities of daily living, and how and by whom they should be delivered. Preferences may not all involve great financial costs. Although specific services, e.g. counselling provided by Black staff, may be preferable, preliminary findings suggest that a sense of being genuinely 'listened to' would help to overcome perceived barriers. Initial interviews have also indicated the need for awareness of and a nonjudgemental attitude to cultural differences, such as variations in family structures, the tendency for older Caribbean people to bring up young grandchildren, and their discomfort in accepting help from outside agencies. A professional's readiness to acknowledge and discuss factors operating for the patient such as racism and deprivation is fundamental, and referral to voluntary, religious, community health and local authority services welcomed. The very term 'depression', for example, seems associated with much stigma and simply using it as justification for prescribing without elaboration or assistance for associated stressors will be unlikely to result in compliance. Also, and fundamentally, pilot interviews suggest that lay theories of mental disorders in older people from some ethnic groups strongly focus on a 'reactive' aetiology (including physical, social and spiritual causation); hence it would be culturally offensive to focus on the diagnosis of 'mental illness' without an exploration of wider requirements for care.

Among others, the issues shown in Table 3 require attention when carrying out an assessment and making management plans.

In conclusion, mood disorders are clearly found in ethnic minority elders. It seems likely that there is a considerable overlap in symptoms relative to the White UK population although there is also some variation in presentation and in the psychological terminology expressed. There are also some differences in the approach required to service delivery. Some ethnic minority elders may prefer to use alternative services. However, our emphasis should be on improving recognition of these disorders, being involved in training of primary care and psychiatric personnel, and on being pragmatic,

Table 3. Issues in assessment and management.

Showing courtesy and respect
Showing interest in ethnicity and country of origin
Being prepared to be flexible about 'standard' professional boundaries, e.g. giving away limited information about oneself, so allowing patients to make a 'connection' such as through sharing a locality of residence, thus facilitating their ease in accepting help
Being prepared to listen and show warmth
Offering no false promises
Offering a copy of written material
Acknowledging their losses, both recent and chronic, including racism
Acknowledging gender-specific needs
Exploring family expectations
Discussing the interrelation of drugs and traditional medicines/remedies
Ensuring understanding of service procedures and of terms like 'support' and 'keeping in touch'
Informing re available services
Asking how they and the family would prefer services to be arranged and delivered
Delivering appropriate food/beverages
Allowing observance of religious practices
Reducing isolation

focusing on needs-based assessment and ensuring that mainstream services can be flexible enough to take in the needs of an ethnically diverse population.

REFERENCES

Abas, M.A. (1996). Depression and anxiety among older Caribbean people in the UK: screening, unmet need and the provision of appropriate services. *Int J Geriatr Psychiatry* **11**, 377–382.

Abas, M.A., Phillips, C., Richards, M., Carter, J. and Levy, R. (1996). Initial development of the new culture-specific screen for emotional distress in older Caribbean people. *Int J Geriatr Psychiatry* (in press).

AFFOR (All Faiths for One Race) (1981). Unpublished data from survey of elders of minority ethnic groups, Birmingham.

Bahl, V. (1993). Access to health care for black and ethnic minority elderly people: general principles. In; Hopkins, A. and Bahl, V. (Eds), *Access to Health Care for People from Black and Ethnic Minorities*. Royal College of Physicians of London, London, pp. 93–96.

Baker, F.M., Parker, D.A., Wiley, C., Velli, S.A. and Johnson, J.T. (1995). Depressive symptoms in African American medical patients. *Int J Geriatr Psychiatry* **10**, 9–14.

Balarajan, R. and Yuen, P. (1984). Patterns of mortality among immigrants in England and Wales. *BMJ* **289**, 237–239.

Balarajan, R., Yuen, P. and Soni-Raleigh, V. (1989). Ethnic differences in general practitioner consultation. *BMJ* **299**, 958–968.

Beiser, M. (1985). A study of depression among traditional Africans, urban North Americans, and Southeast Asian refugees. In: Kleinman, A. and Good, B. (Eds), *Culture and Depression*. University of California Press, Berkeley, CA, pp. 272–298.

Bird, A.S., MacDonald, A.J.D., Mann, A.H. and Philpot, M.P. (1987). Preliminary experience with the SELFCARE (D): a self-rating depression questionnaire for use in elderly, non-institutionalised subjects. *Int J Geriatr Psychiatry* **2**, 31–38.

Blakemore, K. and Boneham, M. (1994). *Age, Race and Ethnicity: A Comparative Approach*. Open University Press, Buckingham.

Blazer, D.G. (1980). Life events, mental health functioning and the use of healthcare services by the elderly. *Am J Public Health* **10**, 1174–1179.

Cochrane, R. and Sashidharan, S.P. (1996). Mental health and ethnic minorities: a review of the literature and implications for services. In: *Ethnicity and Health: Reviews of Literature and Guidance for Purchasers in the Areas of Cardio-vascular Disease, Mental Health and Haemoglobinopathies*. NHS Centre for Reviews and Dissemination, University of York, York.

Cochrane, R. and Bal, S.S. (1987). Migration and schizophrenia: an examination of five hypotheses. *Soc Psychiatry* **22**, 181–191.

Cochrane, R. and Bal, S.S. (1989). Mental hospital admission rates of immigrants to England: a comparison of 1971 and 1981. *Soc Psychiatry Psychiatr Epidemiol* **24**, 2–12.

Copeland, J.R., Dewey, M.E. and Griffiths-Jones, H.M. (1986). A computerised psychiatric diagnostic system and case nomenclature for elderly subjects: GMS and AGECAT. *Psychol Med* **16**, 89–99

Department of Health (1992). *The Health of the Nation – A Strategy for Health in England*, HMSO, London.

Dowd, J.J. and Bengston, V.L. (1978). Aging in minority populations – an examination of the double jeopardy hypothesis. *J Gerontol* **33**, 427–436.

Dunn, G. (1989). *Design and Analysis of Reliability Studies: Statistical Evaluation of Measurement Errors*. Edward Arnold, London.

Ebrahim, S. and Hillier, S. (1991). Ethnic minority needs. *Rev Clin Gerontol* **1**, 195–199.

Ebrahim, S., Patel, N., Coates M. *et al.* (1991). Prevalence and severity of morbidity among Gujarati Asian elders. *Fam Pract* **8**, 57–62.

Gibson, R.C. (1988). Aging in Black America: the effects of an aging society. In: Gort, E. (Ed.), *Aging in Cross-Cultural Perspective* Phelps-Stokes Fund, New York, pp. 105–129.

Gillam, S., Jarman, B. and White, P.L. (1989). Ethnic differences in consultation rates in urban general practice. *BMJ* **229**, 953–957.

Helman, C.G. (1990). *Culture, Health and Illness. (2nd edn)*. Wright, Bristol.

Jackson, M., Kolody, B. and Wood, J.L. (1982). To be old and black: the case for double jeopardy on income and health. In: Manuel, R.C. (Ed.) *Minority Aging*. Greenwood Press, Westport, CT.

Khan, M.E. and Manderson, L. (1992). Focus groups in tropical diseases research. *Health Policy Planning* **7**, 56–66.

Kleinman, A. (1980). *Patients and Healers in the Context of Culture*. University of California Press, London.

Kleinman, A. (1987). Anthropology and psychiatry. *Br J Psychiatry* **151**, 447–454.

Krause, N. (1988). Gender and ethnicity differences in psychological well being. *Ann Rev Gerontol Geriatr* **8**, 156–186.

Leff, J. (1990). The 'new cross-cultural psychiatry'. A case of the baby and the bathwater. *Br J Psychiatry* **156**, 305–307.

Littlewood, R. (1990). From categories to contexts: a decade of the 'new cross-cultural psychiatry'. *Br J Psychiatry* **156**, 308–327.

Lloyd, K. (1993). Depression and anxiety among Afro-Caribbean general practice attenders in Britain. *Int J Soc Psychiatry* **39**, 1–9.

Manson, S.M., Shore, J.H. and Bloom, J.D. (1985). The depressive experience in American Indian communities: a challenge for psychiatric theory and diagnosis. In: Kleinman, A. and Good, B. (Eds), *Culture and Depression.* University of California Press, Berkeley, CA, pp. 331–368.

Manthorpe, E.J. and Hettiaratchy, P. (1993). Ethnic minority elders in the UK. *Int Rev Psychiatry* **5**, 171–178.

Marsella, A.J., Sartorius, N., Jablensky, A. and Fenton, F.R. (1985). Cross-cultural studies of depression. In: Kleinman, A. and Good, B. (Eds), *Culture and Depression.* University of California Press, Berkeley, CA, pp. 299–324.

Mumford, D.B., Bavington, J.T., Bhatnagar, K.S. and Hussain, Y. (1991). The Bradford Somatic Inventory: a multi-ethnic inventory of somatic symptoms. *Br J Psychiatry*, **158**, 379–386.

Office of Population Censuses and Surveys. (1992). OPCS National Monitor: 1991 Census Great Britain. London: HMSO.

Pharaoh, C. (1994). *The Provision of Primary Health Care for Elderly People from Black and Minority Ethnic Communities.* Age Concern, Institute of Gerontology, King's College, London.

Richards, M., Brayne, C., Forde, C., Abas, M. and Levy, R. (1995). Surveying African-Caribbean elders in the community: implications for research on health and health service use. *Int J Psychogeriatr* **11**, 4.

Sokolovsky, J. (1990). *The Cultural Context of Ageing.* Bergin and Garvey, New York.

Tonks, A. (1992). Fifteen years of deprivation: Britain's inner cities. *BMJ* **305**, 138.

Weiss, M.G., Doongaji, D.R., Siddhartha, S. *et al.* (1992). The explanatory model interview catalogue (EMIC). Contribution to cross-cultural research methods from a study of leprosy and mental health. *Br J Psychiatry* **160**, 819–830.

Whitehead, M. (1988). Inequalities in health. In: Townsend, P. and Davidson, N. (Eds), *The Black Report and The Health Defied.* Penguin, London.

Wig, N.N., Suleiman, M.A., Routledge, R. *et al.* (1980). Community reactions to mental disorders: a key informant study in three developing countries. *Acta Psychiatr Scand* **61**, 111–126.

Yesavage, G.A. (1988). Geriatric depression scale. *Psychopharmacol Bull* **24**, 709–710.

Advances in Old Age Psychiatry: Chromosomes to Community Care
Edited by C. Holmes and R. Howard
© 1997 Wrightson Biomedical Publishing Ltd

20

Diogenes Syndrome: The Role of the Psychiatrist

COLM COONEY

Department of Old Age Psychiatry, St Vincent's Hospital, Dublin, Republic of Ireland

INTRODUCTION

Almost all practising psychiatrists in old age psychiatry will have experience in assessing elderly people living in conditions of extreme squalor. The referral request may come from an exasperated district nurse, public health doctor or general practitioner, the assumption being that the older person is suffering from mental illness. The scene encountered is typically that of a reclusive elderly person living in a dilapidated filthy house with piles of apparently useless items cluttered all round, and decomposing food and excrement strewn around the floors. The stench emanating from the house is unbearable to all but the occupant who is usually blissfully unconcerned by the situation. In the literature, the term most often used to describe this situation is Diogenes syndrome (Clarke *et al.*, 1975) although it has been variously referred to in the literature as senile breakdown (Macmillan and Shaw, 1966), social breakdown (Radebaugh *et al.*, 1987) and senile squalor syndrome (Shah, 1990). It is characterized by extreme self-neglect, domestic squalor, excessive hoarding (syllogomania) and lack of concern about one's living conditions. Although it refers to elderly people it has been described in younger adults both in the psychiatric literature (Berlyne, 1975; Snowdon, 1987; Vostanis and Dean 1992) and the popular press. One such case was reported in the *Daily Mail* (4 March 1995) of an unemployed man in his thirties living in squalor described by environmental health officers who visited him as the worst they had ever seen. They discovered he had been breeding 'giant mutant rats' in breeding cages stacked to ceiling height in each room and in one room rat droppings had accumulated to the window level.

It is estimated that the annual incidence is five new cases per 10 000 (Macmillan and Shaw, 1966; Wrigley and Cooney, 1992), about one-third to a half of whom will have dementia or some form of mental illness (Macmillan and Shaw, 1966; Shah, 1990; Clarke et al., 1975; Wrigley and Cooney, 1992).

Diogenes of Sinope was a Greek philosopher of the fourth century BC who became known for his disregard for domestic comforts and social niceties and who advanced the principles of self-sufficiency and contentment unrelated to material possessions. Clinical experience would suggest that those elderly people who fulfil criteria for the syndrome are not motivated by such lofty ideals but rather by a rejection and suspicion of the outside world. It is on this basis that alternative terms for the syndrome have been proposed including Havisham's and Plyushkin's syndromes, based on more appropriate literary figures (Cybulska and Rucinski, 1986). However, the current eponym of the syndrome is the most widely used in the literature and has undoubtedly helped to increase medical awareness of the condition.

CLINICAL FEATURES AND AETIOLOGY

There are a number of difficulties in making generalizations about Diogenes syndrome from published research as all the major studies have recruited cases in contact with health services. These cases may not be truly representative of the group in general. It has been difficult to gather data about the natural evolution of the condition and which life-events play an important role in its development. However, despite these limitations a core body of knowledge has emerged about the condition and the major case series have been notable more for their similarities than their differences. Thirty years ago Macmillan and Shaw (1966) described the first major series of cases and indeed the most comprehensive to date. It was a three-year prospective community study of all cases of senile squalor which were reported by general practitioners, geriatricians, social workers and clergy. They called it senile breakdown, considered it to be a distinct syndrome and reported no evidence of psychosis in 34 (47%) of the 72 cases encountered. They viewed it as an active 'expression of a hostile attitude to and a rejection of the outside community' and characterized those who manifested the disorder as 'old people of the independent and domineering type living alone, with poor or non-existent links with their local community'.

Clarke et al. (1975) studied 30 cases of senile squalor admitted to an inpatient unit over a 10-month period. In addition to replicating the Macmillan and Shaw (1966) finding of almost half the cases having no mental illness, Clarke et al. (1975) highlighted the high levels of morbidity and nutritional deficiencies in this population. They suggested the term Diogenes syndrome and reported that half the cases had no evidence of psychiatric disorder, although there was no attempt formally to diagnose psychiatric disorders in this group.

In a study of 29 cases presenting to an old age psychiatry service, Wrigley and Cooney (1992) found that about one-third of cases had no psychiatric disorder. There is thus a consensus from the literature that a significant proportion of cases of senile squalor have no evidence of a psychiatric disorder. The usual psychiatric disorders encountered include dementia, affective disorders, alcohol abuse and schizophrenia.

Although the majority of cases in all three studies were living alone, Macmillan and Shaw (1966) and Wrigley and Cooney (1992) described five and four cases respectively in which two co-habitees fulfilled criteria for the syndrome. The similarity with 'Folie à deux' has been noted (Macmillan and Shaw, 1966; Cole and Gillett, 1992). Diogenes syndrome by proxy (O'Mahoney and Grimley Evans, 1994) has recently been described as manifesting as a form of elder abuse and could be an explanation for some cases of 'Diogenes à deux'. To date all studies have concentrated exclusively on persons in private dwellings who exhibit the syndrome although there is no doubt that it occurs among homeless elderly people.

AETIOLOGY

It is not easy to understand why a gross deterioration in standards of personal and domestic hygiene should develop in persons who manifest no frank mental illness. While it might be suggested that these patients have inadequate material resources for self-care or a lack of social supports, there is no supporting evidence for this view in the majority of cases (Wrigley and Cooney, 1992; Macmillan and Shaw, 1966; Clarke et al., 1975)

A number of hypotheses have been suggested. It has been argued that it represents the 'end stage of a personality disorder' (Post, 1982). Using Cattell's scale for personality assessment Clarke et al. (1975) found sufferers to be more aloof, detached, shrewd, suspicious and less well integrated, while Macmillan and Shaw (1966), using informant reports of premorbid personality, noted that their cases were of the domineering, quarrelsome and independent type. Clinical experience supports these findings. These personality traits fulfil some of the criteria for a schizoid or paranoid personality disorder but whether they justify a diagnosis of personality disorder is debatable and would require more rigorous analysis. The hypothesis of Orrell and Sahakian (1991) that Diogenes syndrome is really a manifestation of a frontal-lobe dementia is intriguing but there is little evidence. Frontal-lobe pathology may share symptoms in common with Diogenes syndrome including irritability, aggression, reduced motivation and lack of insight, while syllogomania could represent a form of perseveration. However, the age distributions of the two disorders do not match, with frontal-lobe dementia occurring on average 10 years earlier. Neuro-imaging or neuropathological studies of the condition would help resolve this issue but would be difficult to conduct because of poor co-operation on the part of those affected. Obsessive compulsive disorder may explain some cases of the condition but the hoarding of useless objects which is so often a feature does not have the classic element of a compulsive ritual, in that patients are neither distressed by it nor try to resist it.

Overall it seems that no single model satisfactorily explains the development of Diogenes syndrome. The most convincing hypothesis is that proposed by Clarke *et al.* (1975) who argued that the development of the condition depends on the interaction between a vulnerable personality and significant medical or social life changes including the development of dementia and bereavement. This conceptualization of Diogenes syndrome is supported by the work of Radebaugh *et al.* (1987) who viewed it as the 'net result of dementing disorders and debilitating physical conditions, and perhaps certain personality configurations of hostility and withdrawal, the interactions of these conditions and afflictions'.

ILLUSTRATIVE CASES

The following cases are illustrative of some of the problems of assessing and managing persons with Diogenes syndrome.

Case 1

A 79-year-old single French man was referred to the Old Age Psychiatry service by the local district health nurse who had been attending him for the management of infected varicose ulcers on both legs. She had become exasperated by his hostility and lack of co-operation, and was concerned that he had become increasingly immobile, was spending most of the day in bed, and had become doubly incontinent. He was the owner of the basement flat of an old period building and was friendly with an upstairs neighbour who managed his shopping. He was assessed by the old age psychiatry service and was found to be quarrelsome and unco-operative with the interview formalities. He had evidence of short-term working memory impairment on cognitive assessment and an equivocal history from his neighbour of deterioration of memory over the previous six months, but a full cognitive examination was difficult due to noncompliance.

He was admitted compulsorily to the old age psychiatry department under the Mental Health Act, 1983. He settled quite quickly and from early on during his admission he expressed the determined wish to return home. An individualized care plan was devised to achieve this aim. He had mild memory impairment which did not progress during his stay in hospital. He admitted to a long-term problem with constipation which he had managed for many years by self-digital rectal evacuation. He was encouraged to adopt more appropriate and hygienic toileting practices and his constipation was treated with a combination of a higher-fibre diet and weekly enemas. He began to mobilize with regular physiotherapy and, following successful home leave, he was discharged home with community supports including home helps, district health nurse support and meals-on-wheels service.

Case 2

A 73-year-old lady was referred by her general practitioner because of gross self-neglect and behavioural problems. She believed that her neighbours were coming into her flat at night-time through the walls (partition delusions) to spray noxious gases on her and steal all her possessions. To protect herself and her possessions from this unwanted company she kept her possessions in plastic bags tied around her waist, keeping the blinds drawn and door locked and stuffing the keyholes with paper to prevent access to her persecutors. Her flat was in a terrible condition, with accumulated rubbish, some of which was kept in a pile of suitcases stacked against the wall to ceiling height, and her flat was infested with a range of insects that would keep an entomologist happy for a year!

She was of dishevelled appearance, dressed in a black raincoat held together by safety pins under which she was naked. Around her waist were tied a number of plastic bags containing rubbish. She was barefoot. On mental state examination she had well systematized persecutory delusions and tactile hallucinations. Cognitive function was grossly intact. She had very poor insight into her problems.

She was diagnosed as suffering from paranoid schizophrenia, refused to co-operate with treatment and was admitted under a compulsory order to the psychiatric unit. Throughout her inpatient admission she continued to harbour marked persecutory delusions towards fellow patients, accusing them of trying to steal her belongings. Her delusions persisted despite treatment with adequate doses of neuroleptic medication and she required extended care.

MANAGEMENT

Most clinicians who have experience of dealing with sufferers from this condition will readily attest to the difficulties of managing these patients. Although many are known to community health services they are notoriously reluctant to access services and often reject offers of help. They often present in crisis. Referrals are usually prompted by exasperated neighbours as the degree of squalor or self-neglect often constitutes a public health risk. Certain hazards, such as the fire risk associated with hoarding, may prompt urgent action. Some present acutely to medical services following a collapse or fall and require urgent admission to hospital. The outcome of this group is uncertain, with half of one series dying within days of admission (Clarke *et al.*, 1975) whereas another study reported a much more favourable outcome where, over a five-year period, only three of 25 patients died within three weeks of admission (Roe, 1977). Poor outcome has also been recorded for those who were electively admitted (Macmillan and Shaw, 1966).

The greatest challenge in these cases is to engage with the person and develop a therapeutic relationship with them as sufferers are often reluctant to seek help and resist it when offered. Assessments are necessarily and more appropriately carried out in the person's home. The Diogenes sufferer will often refuse access and a certain creativity is usually required. A joint visit with the general practitioner or a concerned relative often helps to overcome this difficulty. A comprehensive multidisciplinary assessment of need is the cornerstone of good practice in these cases. The difficulty of carrying out adequate mental state assessments has been understated. Cognitive examination poses particular problems as, in addition to their unco-operativeness, many of these patients are poorly motivated and their cognitive test scores may underestimate their true ability. Repeated assessments are often necessary to formulate an informed management plan.

Following initial assessment a key worker may be assigned to the case who would adopt a nonintrusive and persistent approach with the strategy of implementing an individually tailored and flexible care programme. The key principle would be that any gains made, however small, may have a significant impact on the person's quality of life and allow the person to stay at home for as long as possible. This strategy may also assuage the fear of neighbours that nothing is being done.

There are complex ethical and medico-legal issues involved in the management of such cases. A balance needs to be struck between the need to respect the individual rights and wishes of patients and the need to meet their health care needs. Compulsory treatment should be a last resort. As between a half to one-third of cases have a mental illness the use of mental health legislation may be justified where serious self-neglect or substantial risk to others exists. The use of Section 47 of the National Assistance Act, 1948, has been advocated to deal with some cases (MacAnespie, 1975). This allows a local authority to apply to a magistrate, on the recommendation of a public health doctor, for an individual 'who is suffering from grave, chronic disease or, being aged, infirm or physically incapacitated is living in unsanitary conditions and is unable to devote to himself and is not receiving from any other person proper care and attention' to be removed to a hospital or other place to secure necessary care and attention. However, the Section is open to criticism for a number of reasons including the danger of infringing an elderly person's right to live as he or she pleases (Muir Gray 1980; Norman, 1980), the lack of an appeal procedure once the order is made, and the removal conditions, which are extraordinarily vague.

In some cases the use of environmental health legislation may be justified, including Section 83 of the Public Health Act, 1936 (amended by Section 35 of the 1961 Act), which requires the owners of 'filthy and verminous premises' to clean them and, if not complied with, allows the Environmental Health Department to do so. The Pest Act, 1949 (Section 4) requires the owners of rodent-infested properties to attend to the situation and again, if not complied with, the Environmental Health Department is empowered to deal with the situation.

Clinical experience suggests that there is often confusion between old age psychiatrists, geriatricians, public health doctors and social services about who should manage these patients. One way forward may be to develop guidelines at local level to deal with such cases, with the emphasis on responding to need rather than adopting overly restrictive policies. There is a need for future research to clarify which interventions are the most appropriate and what is the longer-term outcome of this condition.

REFERENCES

Berlyne, N. (1975). Diogenes syndrome. *Lancet* **i**, 515.

Clarke, A.N.G., Manikar, G.O. and Gray, I. (1975). Diogenes syndrome: a clinical study of gross neglect in old age. *Lancet* **i**, 366–368.

Cole, A.J. and Gillett, T.P. (1992). A case of senile self-neglect in a married couple: 'Diogenes à deux'. *Int J Geriatr Psychiatry* **7**, 839–841.

Cybulska, E. and Rucinski, J. (1986). Gross self-neglect in old age. *Br J Hosp Med* **36**, 21–24.

MacAnespie, H. (1975). Diogenes syndrome. *Lancet* **i**, 750.

Macmillan, D. and Shaw, P. (1966). Senile breakdown in standards of personal and environmental cleanliness. *BMJ* **2**, 1032–1037.

Muir Gray, J.A. (1980). Section 47. *Age Ageing* **9**, 205–209.

Norman, A.J. (1980). *Rights and Risks: A Discussion Document on Civil Liberty in Old Age*, Centre for Policy on Ageing, London

O'Mahoney, D. and Grimley Evans, J. (1994). Diogenes syndrome by proxy. *Br J Psychiatry* **164**, 705–706.

Orrell, M. and Sahakian, B. (1991). Dementia of frontal lobe type. *Psychol Med* **21**, 553–556.

Post, F. (1982). Functional disorders: description, incidence and recognition. In: Post, F. and Levy, R. (Eds.), *The Psychiatry of Later Life*. Blackwell, Oxford, pp. 180–181.

Radebaugh, T.S., Hooper, F.J. and Gruenberg, E.M. (1987). The social breakdown syndrome in the elderly population living in the community: the helping study. *Br J Psychiatry* **151**, 341–346.

Roe, P.F. (1977). Self-neglect. *Age Ageing* **6**, 192–194.

Shah, A.K. (1990). Senile squalor syndrome: what to expect and how to treat it. *Geriatr Med* **20**, 10–26.

Snowdon, J. (1987). Uncleanliness among persons seen by community health workers. *Hosp Community Psychiatry* **38**, 491-494.

Vostanis, P. and Dean, C. (1992). Self-neglect in adult life. *Br J Psychiatry* **161**, 265–267.

Wrigley, M. and Cooney, C. (1992). Diogenes syndrome – an Irish series. *Ir J Psychol Med* **9**, 37–41.

Advances in Old Age Psychiatry: Chromosomes to Community Care
Edited by C. Holmes and R. Howard
© 1997 Wrightson Biomedical Publishing Ltd

21

Drug Treatments in Paranoid States of the Elderly

ROBERT HOWARD
Section of Old Age Psychiatry, Institute of Psychiatry, London, UK

INTRODUCTION

Although the rising tide of cases of dementia gains much of the attention of old-age psychiatrists it is important to remember that as people live longer an increasing proportion of patients with schizophrenia and delusional disorder will be elderly. Little has been published on treatment response, effective treatment strategies or the use of atypical neuroleptics in this group of patients and this chapter examines issues such as response rate, route and dosage of neuroleptics and the use of novel drugs. Despite great variation in the neuroleptic dose ranges employed, late-onset patients often continue to experience psychotic symptoms. Compliance with treatment is the most important determinant of outcome, while atypical neuroleptics are specifically indicated for patients with visual hallucinations or extrapyramidal symptoms. Elderly psychotic patients should be treated as vigorously and with as wide a range of neuroleptics as their younger counterparts and physicians should not restrict drug doses to modest levels in all cases so long as patients are monitored frequently for the emergence of side-effects.

TREATMENT RESPONSIVENESS

The efficacy of neuroleptic treatment of elderly patients was initially so striking that no controlled double-blind trials were ever thought neccessary (Post, 1980). Clinicians accept that treatment will lead to a remission or reduction in symptoms together with earlier discharge from hospital in most cases (Tran-Johnson *et al.*,1994), but there is no agreement as to exactly how much improvement can be expected or in what proportion of patients it will be seen.

Table 1. Treatment studies in early-onset patients who have grown old.

Author	Patients	Design	Results
Honigfeld et al. (1965)	308 male schizo-phrenics; mean age 66 years	24-week, double-blind, placebo-controlled study of acetophenazine and trifluoperazine	Drugs significantly superior to placebo. Acetophenazine superior to trifluoperazine in reduction of excitement and irritability
Tsuang et al. (1971)	50 chronic schizo-phrenics over age 60 years	12-week, double-blind comparison of halo-peridol and thioridazine	Anxiety, irritability, hallucinations and suspiciousness improved with both drugs
Branchey et al. (1978a)	30 chronic schizo-phrenics; mean age 67 years	Double-blind, crossover comparison of fluphena-zine and thioridazine following non-drug washout period	BPRS and global clinical impression scores improved on both drugs
Branchey et al. (1978b)	14 chronic schizophrenics	12-week open trial of loxapine preceded by four-week non-drug washout period	Significant improvement on BPRS scores
Altamura et al. (1990)	20 chronic schizo-phrenics; mean age 63 years	Prospective open study of fluphenazine decanoate for six months	Significant improvements in emotional withdrawal, suspiciousness and thought disturbances
Jeste et al. (1993)	39 chronic schizo-phrenics over age 45 years	Cross-sectional open study. Most common drug haloperidol	Required dose significantly correlated with negative symptom scores and performance on neuropsychological testing

Published studies of the results of drug treatments of elderly patients with schizophrenia and delusional disorder are summarized in Tables 1 and 2. Because there are clear phenomenological (Howard et al., 1993), demographic (Castle and Murray, 1991; Howard et al., 1994a) and aetiolog-ical (Castle and Howard, 1992) differences between cases with late and early onset, and since early-onset patients who have grown old may have been receiving treatment for several decades prior to the period of study, these categories of patients are considered separately. Some authors have suggested a direct extrapolation of neuroleptic efficacy and response rates to the elderly from younger populations of early-onset schizophrenic patients (Jeste et al., 1993; Makanjuloa, 1985; Rabins et al., 1984). Most studies of late-onset schizophrenic or delusional disorder patients, however, are limited by a lack of double-blind case design and are, in fact, mostly open trials and cross-sectional or retrospective case-note evaluations. One advantage of the

Table 2. Treatment studies in late-onset patients.

Author	Patients	Design	Results
Post (1966)	65 patients with 'persistent persecutory states'	Retrospective case-note study	Treatment reduced psychotic symptoms and time in hospital
Raskind et al. (1979)	26 late paraphrenics	Open trial of flu-phenazine enanthate versus haloperidol	11/13 patients on depot and 3/13 patients on haloperidol improved
Rabins et al. (1984)	35 late-onset schizo-phrenics (16: onset after 44 years; 19: after 60 years)	Mixed prospective open and retrospective case-note study	57% symptom-free; 28.5% symptomatic but improved
Craig and Bregman (1988)	65 patients with schizo-phrenia or paranoid disorders with onset after 45 years	Retrospective case-note review	53.1% improved
Pearlson et al. (1989)	54 late-onset schizophrenics	Retrospective case-note review	48.1% complete and 27.8% partial response
Phanjoo and Link (1990)	18 psychotic patients; mean age 78 years	Six-week, double-blind study of remoxipride versus thioridazine	BPRS scores reduced in both groups
Howard and Levy (1992)	64 late paraphrenics; mean age 79.8 years	Cross-sectional open study	26.6% complete and 31.3% partial response
Jeste et al. (1993)	25 late-onset schizophrenics	Cross-sectional open study	Required dose significantly correlated with negative symptom scores and performance on neuropsychological testing

methodologically weaker studies in late-onset patients, however, is that they have generally been able to report treatment success rates under essentially best clinical practice conditions. The most pessimistic and most optimistic estimations of the proportion of such patients who continue to experience psychotic symptoms, despite treatment, range from 73% (Howard and Levy, 1992) and 66% (Post, 1966) to 52% (Pearlson et al., 1989) and 48% (Rabins et al., 1984). In early-onset schizophrenic patients, however, such inability to achieve complete symptomatic remission is less common, with figures of 25% (Davis and Casper, 1977) to 50% (Johnstone et al., 1991) typically quoted.

DOSAGE CONSIDERATIONS

Age-related pharmacokinetic changes in drug disposition may result in higher plasma levels in elderly patients receiving the same dose as younger subjects (Jeste *et al.*, 1982; Movin *et al.*, 1990; Yesavage *et al.*, 1982). Further, pharmacodynamic changes with ageing result in a greater sensitivity of response to both the wanted and unwanted effects of neuroleptics (Tran-Johnson *et al.*, 1992).

Although the British National Formulary recommends that doses of neuroleptics in the elderly should be 25–50% of those given to young adults, elderly psychotic patients can often be effectively treated using neuroleptic doses which are much lower than this. In four North American clinical centres, the mean daily dose prescribed to late-onset schizophrenic patients whose mean age was 61 years, was 192 chlorpromazine milligram equivalents (CpmgEq) compared with 1437 CpmgEq in a group of young early-onset schizophrenics (Jeste *et al.*, 1988). In two groups of late paraphrenic patients, treatment was prescribed at mean daily doses of 178 CpmgEq (Hymas *et al.*, 1989) and 107 CpmgEq (Howard and Levy, 1992). The apparently low dose seen in Howard and Levy's (1992) group of 64 late paraphrenics was probably related both to the high mean age of patients (79.8 years) and the chronicity of illness in this group whose mean duration of symptoms was 74 months.

There is some evidence that patients with chronic schizophrenia who have 'graduated' into old age are given higher doses of treatment than cases with onset in late life. Although late-onset patients may often be older than early-onset cases who have themselves grown old, such variation in age does not account for the differences in prescribed dose seen between these two patient populations. Jeste *et al.* (1993) have suggested that late-onset schizophrenia is actually 'better prognosis schizophrenia' (Castle and Murray, 1991; Harris and Jeste, 1988) and that larger doses of medication are thus needed to achieve remission in early-onset chronic patients who have a more malignant illness. Certainly, in studies which have involved mixed late-onset and early-onset-grown-old schizophrenics, higher mean daily doses are reported than from the late-onset or late paraphrenic studies. Jeste *et al.* (1993) reviewed a group containing 25 late-onset schizophrenic and 39 early-onset-grown-old patients whose mean age was 59 years. These patients had been treated in an 'individualized, clinically optimal manner' and received on average 443 CpmgEq per day. Prescribed medication dose was significantly higher in the early-onset group and correlated significantly with current age and age at onset. In a group of 14 chronic early-onset schizophrenics with a mean age of 72 years, the therapeutic dose range of loxapine was 10–80 mg daily (100–800 CpmgEq per day) (Branchey *et al.*, 1978b). An exception to the general rule that chronic patients require greater doses than equivalent aged but late-onset cases is provided by Altamura *et al.* (1990) who treated a group of chronic patients whose mean age was 63 years with only 12.5 mg of fluphenazine decanoate every three weeks for six months. Although patients showed general improvements on measures such as the Brief Psychiatric Rating Scale (BPRS), the treatment had no effect on hallucinations. If this had not been a fixed-dose trial it is probable that higher doses would have been used in order to try and control hallucinosis.

Despite concern about enhanced sensitivity to unwanted side-effects of neuroleptics induced in the elderly, few studies have investigated how these might limit effective treatment regimens. In a comparison of the relative efficacy and acceptability of what the authors chose to term a 'high potency' and a 'low potency' neuroleptic in a group of 30 chronic schizophrenics with a mean age of 67, the main differences in outcome related to adverse side-effects (Branchey et al., 1978a). Effective treatment was provided by 285 mg of thioridazine or 5 mg of fluphenazine hydrochloride per week. Rigidity and tremor were significantly more common in the fluphenazine group, but 90% of the thioridazine-treated patients had a reduction in standing systolic and diastolic blood pressure together with electrocardiogram (ECG) changes.

ESTABLISHING AND MAINTAINING TREATMENT COMPLIANCE

In practical terms, the most important factor determining treatment response is compliance. Since patients are often socially isolated and typically insight-less, adequate compliance with medication can often only be assured after hospital admission (Raskind and Risse, 1986). Post (1980) predicted that the introduction of depot preparations of neuroleptics would make treatment failures rare by ensuring compliance. There is good evidence that, certainly in outpatient populations, use of a depot preparation rather than the oral route is associated with superior treatment response (Howard and Levy, 1992; Raskind et al., 1979). Of course, it is possible that an initial positive response to oral medication may encourage and motivate both the patient and clinician to proceed to a regular injection, and so prescription of depot medication may be an effect rather than a cause of good response. In Howard and Levy's (1992) retrospective study of late paraphrenic patients, allocation of a community psychiatric nurse was also associated with a better response to treatment. While the same cause and effect argument may operate here also, the treatment effects of an established relationship with a community worker should not be underestimated.

THE PLACE OF DEPOT INJECTIONS

Although the use of long-acting depot neuroleptic preparations overcomes some compliance problems (assuming that patients make themselves acces-sible for injections and continue to consent to receive them), theoretically they may be associated with an increased risk of unwanted side-effects (Altamura et al., 1990). The evidence suggests, however, that if low doses of depot medication are used and regular reviews for side-effects are carried out, then patients so treated may receive less total neuroleptic and experience fewer adverse events than if they had been treated with oral medication. In a study of the treatment of 20 chronic schizophrenic patients (mean age 63 years) with 12.5 mg of fluphenazine decanoate every 21 days for six months, Altamura et al. (1990) presented an analysis of risk/benefit considerations. After 18 weeks of treatment, patients' total BPRS scores were reduced by 31.3% although there was no improvement in hallucinations. The authors attributed the modest nature of symptomatic improvement to a combination of the chosen low dose and the chronicity of symptoms in the studied group, who had a mean illness duration of 33.8 years. At entry to the study, extrapyramidal side-effects from previously prescribed oral medication were more common than would have been expected in younger patients (Johnson, 1973; Rifkin et al., 1977), with some degree of rigidity present in 90%, akathisia and tremor in 50% and dysarthria in 35%. During the course of the study there were actually slight reductions in rigidity, tremor and dysarthria and the number of patients affected by akathisia fell to 20%. Extrapyramidal side-effects reached a maximal peak 36 hours after each of the first four injections, presumably reflecting early peak plasma concentrations (Altamura et al., 1985), but these were less prominent after the fifth dose, suggesting the development of tolerance. Reductions in measured supine and standing blood pressure were maximal in the first few days after each injection although this was not clinically significant. The authors concluded that prescription of such low doses of depot medication had advantages over the oral medication regimens that these patients had received previously in terms of improvements in both efficacy and unwanted side-effects and a general reduction in the amount of neuroleptic administered. Howard and Levy (1992) also reported use of lower total neuroleptic dose with depot rather than oral treatment. Late paraphrenic patients prescribed oral medication received on average a daily dose of 115 CpmgEq compared with 90 CpmgEq in those receiving a depot. Depot-treated patients also had lower total Abnormal Involuntary Movement Scale scores (Schooler, 1988) than those receiving oral treatment.

USE OF ATYPICAL NEUROLEPTICS

Because of its anticholinergic activity and relatively weak blockade of striatal dopamine D_2 receptors, low-dose clozapine may prove useful in the treatment of elderly psychotic patients who have individual sensitivity to extrapyramidal symptoms caused by typical neuroleptics (Jeste et al., 1993). Potentially confusing anticholinergic, together with hypotensive and sedating effects may, however, discourage widespread prescribing in this age group.

It is also difficult to see how a drug which has been shown to impair memory function in young patients (Goldberg and Weinberger, 1994) will find favour with those who regularly prescribe for the elderly. A few case-reports of individual elderly patients with functional psychoses who have been treated with clozapine are, however, generally positive. Within a group of (mostly demented) elderly subjects which contained a patient with schizophrenia and another with schizoaffective psychosis, treated with a mean daily clozapine dose of 53.2 mg, Oberholzer et al. (1992) reported improvements in noncognitive symptomatology. Bajulaiye and Addonizio (1992) succesfully treated an 82-year-old woman with a four-year history of paranoid schizophrenia and tardive dyskinesia with 125 mg/day of clozapine.

Risperidone is a benzisoxazole derivative with extremely strong binding affinity for serotonin 5-HT$_2$ receptors, strong affinity for dopamine D$_2$ receptors and alpha-1 and alpha-2 adrenergic and histamine H$_1$ receptors (Cohen, 1994; Livingstone, 1994). Although clinical experience with risperidone in this patient group is extremely limited, activity at 5-HT$_2$ receptors appears to be important in the treatment of complex visual hallucinations (Howard et al., 1994b; Sadzot et al., 1989), which are traditionally regarded as treatment-resistant (Howard and Levy, 1994; Phanjoo, 1995; Post, 1965). Risperidone appears to be effective against hallucinations and delusions in elderly patients at very low doses (typically 0.5–2.0 mg/day (Heylen et al., 1988; Howard et al., 1994b)). Hypersalivation is sometimes the only troublesome side-effect at such dosages although cases of the neuroleptic malignant syndrome have been reported (Webster and Wijeratne, 1994).

Negative symptoms are not prominent in late-onset schizophrenia (Almeida et al., 1995; Howard et al., 1993; Howard et al., 1994a), but typically affect early-onset patients who have grown old. Since both clozapine (Kane et al., 1988) and risperidone (Hoyberg et al., 1993; Marder and Meibach, 1994) are effective in the treatment of negative symptoms, they may be indicated for the treatment of such patients.

In the absence of many reported studies involving elderly schizophrenic or delusional disorder patients, the treatment of drug-induced psychotic phenomena in Parkinson's disease (PD) with novel antipsychotics indicates that these drugs are tolerated by patients in this age group. Hallucinations and delusions appearing as side-effects of levodopa treatment in PD may be due to dopamine receptor hypersensitivity (Cummings, 1992) or overstimulation of serotonin receptors (Zoldan et al., 1993). Clozapine in doses of 25–150 mg/day is an effective treatment for psychosis in PD (Quinn, 1995; Scholz and Dichgans, 1985; Wolk and Douglas, 1992; Wolters et al., 1990) although delirium is commonly induced at higher doses (Wolters et al., 1990). Risperidone in very small doses (0.25–1.25 mg/day) improved hallucinosis in all of a group of six PD patients without worsening motor symptoms (Meco et al., 1994).

CONCLUSIONS

With the exception of clozapine and risperidone, which may have a part to play in the treatment of otherwise resistant symptoms, there is no real evidence that any particular drug is more effective in this group of patients. Choice of drug for each individual patient should thus be based on considerations of concomitant physical illness and other treatments received, together with the specific side-effect profile of the drug (Tran-Johnson et al., 1994). While there is an argument that all patients should be commenced on depot medication (Raskind and Risse, 1986), treatment will usually be commenced at a low dose of an oral preparation which can be increased until a therapeutic effect is reached or side-effects develop. Patients who do not respond to oral treatment (whether due to poor compliance or genuine treatment resistance) can be treated with a depot. Treatment of late-onset patients can often be at very modest doses. For example, the mean dose of prescribed depot in Howard and Levy's (1992) study was 14.4 mg of flupenthixol decanoate or 9 mg of fluphenazine decanoate every fortnight. Early-onset-grown-old patients do need bigger doses to control positive symptoms and there seems to be a wide variation between individual patients in the effective dose and tolerance of adverse side-effects. Certainly, within the author's own practice, there are handful of chronic graduate schizophrenics who need what are effectively young adult doses of neuroleptic to prevent relapse. This must certainly represent a group who are at particular risk of developing tardive dyskinesia (Jeste et al., 1993) and who should be reviewed every few months by the prescribing psychiatrist rather than by a nonmedical team member.

In those patients who continue to experience psychotic symptoms after receiving depot for several weeks, the dose can be increased by 10% every two to three weeks until a response is seen or side-effects emerge. If this strategy is unsuccessful, and if compliance with oral medication (and regular venepuncture in the case of clozapine) can be assured, then use of one of the atypical antipsychotics may be indicated.

REFERENCES

Almeida, O., Howard, R., Levy, R. and David, A. (1995). Psychotic states arising in late life (late paraphrenia): psychopathology and nosology. *Br J Psychiatry* **166**, 205–214.

Altamura, A.C., Curry, S.H., Montgomery, S. and Wiles, D.H. (1985). Early unwanted effects of fluphenazine esters related to plasma fluphenazine concentrations in schizophrenic patients. *Psychopharmacology* **87**, 30–33.

Altamura, A.C., Mauri, M.C., Girardi, T. and Panetta, B. (1990). Clinical and toxicological profile of fluphenazine decanoate in elderly chronic schizophrenia. *Int J Clin Pharmacol Res* **10**, 223–228.

Bajulaiye, R. and Addonizio, G. (1992). Clozapine in the treatment of psychosis in an 82-year-old woman. *J Clin Psychopharmacol* **12**, 364–365.

Branchey, M.H., Lee, J.H., Ramesh, A. and Simpson, G.M. (1978a). High- and low-potency neuroleptics in elderly psychiatric patients. *JAMA* **239**, 1860–1862.

Branchey, M.H., Lee, J.H., Simpson, G.M., Elgart, B. and Vicencio, A. (1978b). Loxapine succinate as a neuroleptic agent: evaluation in two populations of elderly psychiatric patients. *J Am Geriatr Soc* **26**, 263–267.

Castle, D.J. and Murray, R.M. (1991). The neurodevelopmental basis of sex differences in schizophrenia. *Psychol Med* **21**, 565–575.

Castle, D.J. and Howard, R. (1992). What do we know about the aetiology of late-onset schizophrenia? *Eur Psychiatry* **7**, 99–108.

Cohen, L.J. (1994). Risperidone. *Pharmacotherapy* **14**, 253–265.

Craig, T.J. and Bregman, Z. (1988). Late onset schizophrenia-like illness. *J Am Geriatr Soc* **36**, 104–107.

Cummings, J.L. (1992). Psychosis in neurologic disease: neurobiology and pathogenesis. *Neuropsychiatry Neuropsychol Behav Neurol* **5**, 144–150.

Davis, J.M. and Casper, R. (1977). Antipsychotic drugs: clinical pharmacology and therapeutic use. *Drugs* **14**, 260–282.

Goldberg, T.E. and Weinberger, D.R. (1994). The effects of clozapine on neurocognition: an overview. *J Clin Psychiatry* **55**(Suppl B,) 88–90.

Harris, M.J. and Jeste, D.V. (1988). Late-onset schizophrenia: an overview. *Schizophr Bull* **14**, 39–55.

Heylen, S.L., Gelders, Y.G. and Vanden Bussche, G. (1988). Risperidone (R 64 766) in the treatment of behavioural symptoms in psychogeriatric patients: pilot clinical investigation. Paper presented at the International Symposium of Psychogeriatrics, Lausanne, Switzerland, 28 April.

Honigfeld, G., Rosenbaum, M.P., Blumenthal, I.J., Lambert, H.L. and Roberts, A.J. (1965). Behavioral improvement in the older schizophrenic patient: drug and social therapies. *J Am Geriatr Soc* **13**, 57–71.

Howard, R. and Levy, R. (1992). Which factors affect treatment response in late paraphrenia? *Int J Geriatr Psychiatry* **7**, 667–672.

Howard, R. and Levy, R. (1994). Charles Bonnet syndrome plus: complex visual hallucinations of Charles Bonnet type in late paraphrenia. *Int J Geriatr Psychiatry* **9**, 399–404.

Howard, R., Castle, D., Wessely, S. and Murray, R. (1993). A comparative study of 470 cases of early- and late-onset schizophrenia. *Br J Psychiatry* **163**, 352–357.

Howard, R., Almeida, O. and Levy, R. (1994a). Phenomenology, demography and diagnosis in late paraphrenia. *Psychol Med* **24**, 397–410.

Howard, R., Meehan, O., Powell, R. and Mellers, J. (1994b). Successful treatment of Charles Bonnet syndrome type visual hallucinosis with low-dose risperidone. *Int J Geriatr Psychiatry* **9**, 677–678.

Hoyberg, O.J., Fensbo, C., Remvig, J., Lingjaerde, O., Sloth-Nielsen, M. and Salvesen, I. (1993). Risperidone versus perphenazine in the treatment of chronic schizophrenic patients with acute exacerbations. *Acta Psychiatr Scand* **88**, 395–402.

Hymas, N., Naguib, M. and Levy, R. (1989). Late paraphrenia: a follow-up study. *Int J Geriatr Psychiatry* **4**, 23–29.

Jeste, D.V., Linnoila, M., Wagner, R.L. and Wyatt, R.J. (1982). Serum neuroleptic concentrations and tardive dyskinesia. *Psychopharmacology* **76**, 377–380.

Jeste, D.V., Harris, M.J., Pearlson, G.D *et al.* (1988). Late-onset schizophrenia: studying clinical validity. *Psychiatr Clin North Am* **11**, 1–14.

Jeste, D.V., Lacro, J.P., Gilbert, P.L., Kline, J. and Kline, N. (1993). Treatment of late-life schizophrenia with neuroleptics. *Schizophr Bull* **19**, 817–830.

Johnson, D.A. (1973). The side-effects of fluphenazine decanoate. *Br J Psychiatry* **123**, 519–522.

Johnstone, E.C., Owens, D.G.C., Frith, C.D. and Leary, J. (1991). Disabilities and circumstances of schizophrenic patients: a follow-up study. III. Clinical findings. Abnormalities of the mental state and movement disorders and their correlates. *Br J Psychiatry* **159**(Suppl 13), 21–25.

Kane, J., Honigfeld, G., Singer, J. and Meltzer, H. (1988). Clozapine for the treatment-resistant schizophrenic. A double-blind comparison with chlorpromazine. *Arch Gen Psychiatry* **45**, 789–796.

Livingstone, M.G. (1994). Risperidone. *Lancet* **343**, 457–460.

Makanjuloa, R.O. (1985). Psychiatric disorders in elderly Nigerians. *Trop Geogr Med* **37**, 348–351.

Marder, S.R. and Meibach, R.C. (1994). Risperidone in the treatment of schizophrenia. *Am J Psychiatry* **151**, 825–835.

Meco, G., Alessandria, A., Bonifati, V. and Giustini, P. (1994). Risperidone for hallucinations in levodopa-treated Parkinson's disease patients. *Lancet* **343**, 1370–1371.

Movin, G., Gustafson, L., Franzen, G. *et al.* (1990). Pharmacokinetics of remoxipride in elderly psychotic patients. *Acta Psychiatr Scand* **358**, 176–180.

Oberholzer, A.F., Hendriksen, C., Monsch, A.U., Heierli, B. and Stahelin, H.B. (1992). Safety and effectiveness of low-dose clozapine in psychogeriatric patients: a preliminary study. *Int Psychogeriatr* **4**, 187–195.

Pearlson, G., Kreger, L., Rabins, P. *et al.* (1989). A chart review study of late-onset and early-onset schizophrenia. *Am J Psychiatry* **146**, 1568–1574.

Phanjoo, A.L. (1995). Novel antipsychotics in the elderly. In: Levy, R. and Howard, R. (Eds), *Developments in Dementia and Functional Disorders in the Elderly.* Wrightson Biomedical, Petersfield, Hants, pp. 151–166.

Phanjoo, A.L. and Link, C. (1990). Remoxipride versus thioridazine in elderly psychotic patients. *Acta Psychiatr Scand Suppl* **358**, 181–185.

Post, F. (1965). *The Clinical Psychiatry of Late Life.* Pergamon, Oxford.

Post, F. (1966). *Persistent Persecutory States of the Elderly.* Pergamon, Oxford.

Post, F. (1980). Paranoid, schizophrenia-like and schizophrenic states in the aged. In: Brien, E. and Sloane, R.B. (Eds), *Handbook of Mental Health and Aging.*Prentice Hall, Englewood Cliffs, NJ, pp. 151–180.

Quinn, N. (1995). Drug treatment of Parkinson's disease. *BMJ* **310**, 575–579.

Rabins, P.V., Pauker, S. and Thomas, J. (1984). Can schizophrenia begin after age 44? *Compr Psychiatry* **25**, 290–293.

Raskind, M.A. and Risse, S.C. (1986). Antipsychotic drugs and the elderly. *J Clin Psychiatry* **47**(Suppl 5), 17–22.

Raskind, M., Alvarez, C. and Herlin, S. (1979). Fluphenazine enanthate in the outpatient treatment of late paraphrenia. *J Am Geriatr Soc* **27**, 459–463.

Rifkin, A., Quitkin, R. and Rabiner, C. (1977). Fluphenazine decanoate and fluphenazine hydrochloride given orally and placebo in remitted schizophrenics. *Arch Gen Psychiatry* **34**, 43–47.

Sadzot, B., Baraban, J.M., Glennon, R.A. *et al.* (1989). Hallucinogenic drug interactions at human brain 5-HT$_2$ receptors: implications for treating LSD-induced hallucinogenesis. *Psychopharmacology* **98**, 495–499.

Scholz, E. and Dichgans, J. (1985). Treatment of drug-induced exogenous psychosis in Parkinsonism with clozapine and fluperlapine. *Eur Arch Psychiatry Neurol Sci* **235**, 60–64.

Schooler, N.R. (1988). Evaluation of drug-related movement disorders in the aged. *Psychopharmacol Bull* **24**, 603–607.

Tran-Johnson, T.K., Krull, A.J. and Jeste, D.V. (1992). Late life schizophrenia and its treatment: the pharmacologic issues in older schizophrenic patients. In: Alexopoulos, G.S. (Ed.), *Clinics in Geriatric Medicine.* W.B. Saunders, Philadelphia.

Tran-Johnson, T.K., Harris, M.J. and Jeste, D.V. (1994). Pharmacological treatment of schizophrenia and delusional disorder of late life. In: Copeland, J.R.M., Abou-Saleh, M.T. and Blazer, D.G. (Eds), *Principles and Practice of Geriatric Psychiatry.* Wiley, New York, pp. 685–692.

Tsuang, M.M., Lu, L.M., Stotsky, B.A. and Cole, J.O. (1971). Haloperidol versus thioridazine for hospitalised psychogeriatric patients: double-blind study. *J Am Geriatr Soc* **19**, 593–600.

Webster, P. and Wijeratne, C. (1994). Risperidone-induced neuroleptic malignant syndrome. *Lancet* **344**, 370–371.

Wolk, S.I. and Douglas, C.J. (1992). Clozapine treatment of psychosis in Parkinson's disease: a report of 5 consecutive cases. *J Clin Psychiatry* **53**, 373–376.

Wolters, E.C., Hurwitz, T.A., Mak, E. *et al.* (1990). Clozapine in the treatment of parkinsonian patients with dopaminomimetic psychosis. *Neurology* **40**, 832–840.

Yesavage, J.A., Becker, J., Werner, P.D., Mills, M.J., Holman, C.A. and Cohn, R. (1982). Serum level monitoring of thiothixene in schizophrenia: acute single-dose levels at fixed doses. *Am J Psychiatry* **139**, 174–178.

Zoldan, J., Friedberg, G., Goldberg-Stern, H. and Melamed, E. (1993). Ondansetron for hallucinosis in advanced Parkinson's disease. *Lancet* **341**, 562–563.

Advances in Old Age Psychiatry: Chromosomes to Community Care
Edited by C. Holmes and R. Howard
© 1997 Wrightson Biomedical Publishing Ltd

22

Psychotherapy and the Elderly

MARK ARDERN

Department of Psychiatry of Old Age, St Charles' Hospital, London, UK

INTRODUCTION

This chapter debates the contribution of psychodynamic theory to psychiatric practice with the elderly. Using clinical vignettes, various aspects are covered, both in relation to direct psychotherapy with patients and to potential benefits for staff involved in services. While supportive psychotherapy is included, using psychodynamic principles, the emphasis lies with psychoanalytic approaches which might be considered of value by old age psychiatrists in their everyday work. The author writes as a consultant psychiatrist with an interest in this subject, having undertaken a personal analysis and enjoyed clinical collaboration with a psychoanalyst and consultant psychotherapist, Dr Brian Martindale, Parkside Clinic, London.

HISTORICAL PERSPECTIVE

From his writings Freud revealed his contempt for the analysis of older people. At the age of 49 he declared that from 'near or above the age of fifty ... old people are not educable' (Freud, 1905). Some contemporary analysts have noted how fearful he was of his own ageing and how, during his protracted terminal illness, he suffered. Linking Freud's fear of death with that of castration, Woodward suggests that Freud was preoccupied with oedipal anxieties of outliving his father's age of death (Woodward, 1991). For reasons not altogether clear, the Institute of Psychoanalysis usually declines applications from prospective trainees who have entered their forties.

Karl Abraham hesitantly began to undertake therapy with neurotic patients up to the age of 50. In 1919 he wrote, 'To my surprise a considerable number of them reacted very favourably to the treatment. I might add that I count some of those cases among my most successful results (Abraham, 1919).

More recently, case-reports have been published by psychoanalysts who have taken on elderly clients (King, 1974; Sandler, 1978; Segal, 1981). Peter Hildebrand is renowned for his therapy with even the very old, usually for 15 sessions with annual follow-up (Hildebrand, 1986). The dismal view of older people being unworthy of psychoanalytic interventions is therefore being challenged. Nevertheless, a survey of psychotherapists in the USA was presented at a Maudsley Hospital Journal Club in 1995. One hundred and sixty-five therapists responding to a questionnaire indicated a preference for treating young over middle-aged, and these over older clients. This finding appeared to be largely related to the respondents' negative perceptions about the prognosis for the elderly (Zivian *et al.*, 1992). Are they right? Can old dogs not be taught new tricks? Unfortunately, as yet we are remarkably ignorant. However, at least we are developing some curiosity, which is a start.

DEVELOPMENTAL ISSUES FOR THE OLDER PERSON

Throughout life, various developmental challenges face us. Erikson delineated eight stages. In his final stage, man approaches death either with what Erikson termed integrity or despair (Erikson, 1966). Elliot Jaques described the 'mid-life crisis' in which the finiteness of time confronts people who in young adulthood hold on to the fantasy of immortality and unlimited prospects for their ambitions (Jaques, 1965). Recognition of this milestone, which can be postponed until retirement, may provide therapeutic opportunities.

Old age psychiatrists are daily faced with patients whose 'false selves' can be threatened by sudden role changes. Carol Martin draws attention to dangers for older people of either sex who slavishly try and adhere to their traditional gender roles. In parallel with a biological shift towards a relatively androgynous state, external events (such as death of a partner) bring new challenges. Crudely put, an elderly man will need to embrace his more feminine aspects, and an older woman her masculinity (Martin, 1992).

Unsuccessful adaptation may result in clinical depression, which psychiatrists treat with confidence and effectiveness. What may not be so easy for a psychiatrist who has little training in helping patients from a psychodynamic perspective is to grasp an understanding of the factors predisposing to and maintaining the current breakdown. The results of the psychiatrist's pressure to discharge patients as quickly as possible may also come to haunt him through a revolving hospital door.

There are a series of life events which face the older person, well described in sociological literature. From her psychoanalytic stance, Pearl King has identified some of these which she summarizes as loss or threat of loss (King, 1980). These losses can usefully be categorized as concrete or conceptual. Concrete losses include a decline in physical health (and for men, sexual potency); reduction in mobility and financial capacity; loss of partners, relatives and companions; loss of home and mental faculties. Conceptual losses include those of status, role, independence, purpose and youth. These lists are by no means exhaustive and their overlapping nature is evident.

The potential gains of old age such as wisdom, an enhanced capacity to observe and reflect rather than act, the enjoyment of past achievements and new leisure possibilities may become obscured by preoccupation with loss. Looking backwards in nostalgic reminiscence is a pleasurable pastime for the healthy older person, since this acknowledges the fact that the past no longer exists in reality. But many of those who present to psychiatric services have found their experience of loss intolerable, and continue to ruminate over missed opportunities and bitter regrets. These troubled individuals often have the fantasy that ageing itself is reversible or curable, if only their doctor were more competent.

MANAGING LOSS

Bereavement, at least that in relation to people losing partners, has been well studied. The process of grieving is one with which psychiatrists are familiar. Usually we do not assume a therapeutic role, since this is a healthy phenomenon. It is the inability to grieve which is serious and may be bound up with excessive denial, anger and self-reproach. The difference between Mourning and Melancholia originally described by Freud (Freud, 1915) has recently been illuminated in two detailed observational case studies of patients in their eighties (McKenzie-Smith, 1992).

The fact that most people manage to negotiate their current loss satisfactorily does nothing to explain why for others all goes wrong. A detailed life history from the patient should help. Childhood loss or other difficulty in early attachment is likely to sensitize a patient into adopting a life which seeks to avoid a repeat experience; something along the lines of 'once bitten, twice shy'. More mysterious for the psychiatrist is when their patient has repressed early trauma and erected partially successful defences for ego survival. Thus the inexperienced professional may be fooled into assuming that their patient has, by any reasonable measure, lived an integrated life. They may be perplexed as to why the patient is depressed now. Under such circumstances a biological explanation is a tempting refuge.

The author has met several patients who, although severely traumatized in the Holocaust, survived young adulthood and middle age apparently psychologically intact. Even in later years they continued to thrive economically and socially. When one lady developed a stroke, lost her home and several companions died, only then did the full impact of her earlier devastation surface. It became clear that behind her coping façade, life had been a relative void, plugged with space-occupying activity. These manic defences had served her well until now. For her, aloneness and contemplation were not welcomed but a dreaded rekindling of her earlier abandonment. Depression, therefore, was just waiting to happen.

Therapeutic possibilities with the depressed patient

For the depressed patient a psychotherapeutic task is to unravel, where possible together with the patient, the meaning of their current despair in relation to past losses. By acknowledging these losses the patient will be helped to relinquish their present maladaptive response and healthily mourn. A convenient focus might entail mourning the anticipated loss of the therapist. The therapeutic objective, at least in brief therapy, will therefore be no different from that with younger patients. But the themes have a different emphasis and, as will be elaborated later, the technique may need to be modified.

A patient's current relationships are likely to be under strain, this being either a cause or result of the psychological upset. The depressed, narcissistic patient, being unable to identify with the needs of the family, wonders why cries for attention are responded to by their flight. Relatives themselves, guilty in their retreat, commonly project this guilt onto the psychiatric service, unreasonably criticizing hapless professionals. These vicious spirals may be helped by psychoanalytic understanding and perhaps warrant more specialist input from a family therapist.

Direct psychotherapeutic work may well not be achievable when the patient is severely depressed. More crucially it may be contraindicated since it can fuel the patient's guilt and self-destructive impulses. When *not* to intervene is at least as important as when to intervene. Once more active treatments have succeeded and the patient's ego strength has been restored, there remains the possibility of engaging the patient at a later date. The purpose here would be to see if the patient can learn about their illness and its causation at a conscious level. Unconsciously, if internal objects and the harshness of a punitive superego can be modified, one might hope that future relapse can be avoided.

At least one study (Weissman, 1994) of 'inter-personal therapy' in the maintenance treatment of depression has shown promising results. It has to be said that the less psychologically inclined patient is likely to refuse follow-up which is insight-orientated. For some, the relinquishing of personal responsibility permitted by the illness model protects the patient from painful self-discovery. In such cases patients are probably right to avoid the unpicking of old wounds.

Even if the patient does not wish or is unable to pursue insight, there is no reason why a psychiatrist should not attempt a psychodynamic formulation for all patients. Indeed the Royal College of Psychiatrists has emphasized that candidates in the Membership examination should expect to be asked for one. In the clinical setting, a psychodynamic formulation can provide the psychiatric team with a better sense of the patient's predicament and obstacles which may be hindering progress.

Practical considerations

In any psychological undertaking the therapist will need to recognize some limitations imposed on their work by an elderly patient. Practical considerations include deciding whether the patient can make his or her own way to the sessions independently; checking that the patient can hear what is going on, or acknowledging whether because of physical frailty the patient needs a literal helping hand. It follows that the therapist will sometimes have to modify technical aspects of their work, which theoretically might threaten the nurturing of the transference.

In a group which the author ran with Brian Martindale, a patient repeatedly complained that we did not provide welcoming cups of coffee as a sign of our friendliness. While we believe it was correct of us to refuse and use this as interpretative material, the fact that some of our patients determinedly met for coffee outside the group proved a more thorny issue. We had strongly discouraged this for the usual reasons of avoiding splitting, subgrouping and stimulating jealousies. There was also the matter of preserving confidentiality and of trying to persuade patients to use the designated space we had provided. In the face of our patients' tenacity, it eventually dawned on us that we had seriously undervalued the *social* aspects of the group. For these patients, who led especially isolated lives, we had been stifling their opportunity for human contact.

In the same group a somewhat different problem emerged one Christmas. A female member eagerly handed round boxes of chocolates, both to the other patients and to the therapists. The author's reluctance to accept, and preference to interpret, blew a chill wind round the group. The patient herself experienced such a rejection that she stopped attending for several weeks. Of course, this might have been the consequence in a group of younger patients not particularly psychologically minded. Perhaps though it demonstrated the shock older members experience when confronted with a more traditional psychoanalytic approach.

The distinction between patients' real and imagined needs can become blurred. The 'chocolates' lady felt a blow as real as if the author had kicked a walking-stick away from her. Supposing she had asked for a high-backed chair or that, because of increasing arthritis, the author arrange transport to the sessions; would the author's agreement be collusion or a perfectly reasonable concession to the realities of her situation? Such questions are more likely to arise with this age group.

The other issue, hinted at above, the zealous compulsion of younger therapists to interpret, is discussed later in relation to the counter-transference.

IMPENDING DEATH AND DEPENDENCE

Most of us, despite death getting steadily nearer, do not seriously wish to be young again; or rather we may wish to be chronologically younger but retain the wisdom of our ways – a paradox indeed! No doubt we are conscious of when our parents died and, assuming they did so in old age, reckon we have time enough. For the young, death seems far away and risks, even dangerous ones, are taken readily. The state of being old is constantly readjusted upwards as we age. Even people who are truly old seem to regard their contemporaries as different. An 80-year-old lady once protested to me that she did not want to go to 'a ward full of old people' (where most were considerably younger).

Though the meaning of death is an individual one, we hear recurring fantasies. Death may be embraced as a final sleep, the logical end to a satisfactory life. Belief in an afterlife can provide a comforting potential for rejoining lost partners. Benign though this may seem, this can denote unresolved grief, as I illustrate. A Roman Catholic lady had been a controlling and possessive mother to her unmarried middle-aged son who had died some years before. While she was depressed she was intently suicidal, having stopped eating, and unconsciously determined to chase after him in death. When the author reflected this observation to her she reluctantly conceded that this might be correct and she began to trust the staff sufficiently to agree to a course of ECT. Once better, she acknowledged that she now had a life of her own, and began to let go of her dead son, at least temporarily.

For some, death is seen as persecuting, where life is being snatched away or becomes a place of punishment for past sins. It can also be the ultimate abandonment, where the person imagines he will be left rotting and forgotten. The author believes that the usual wish is that we all would like to remain alive in others' minds, once dead. A man he saw individually every week for several years, while desperately awaiting a heart transplant he never received, seemed to have a quite complex view of death. He repeatedly conveyed his wish that his funeral be overflowing with mourners. As it turned out, a handful of us attended his cremation and discovered that he had left behind strict instructions that there were to be no flowers, no music and no words spoken. We were awkward and angry in our silence, at the receiving end of his punitive triumph. Some weeks later the author received a gift of an antique plate. Attached to it was a note which the patient had written three years earlier, drawing attention to how the plate was 'a special edition, of interest to collectors'.

The prodrome to death brings with it the more pressing prospect of dependence, a state which can exist for years; considerably longer than the previous dependence of infancy. While most of us will be apprehensive of a return to this state, it follows that those patients who enjoyed a good experience of having been cared for unconditionally will accept dependence again with relative ease. This question of dependence/independence is central to psychodynamic work with older people. In old age psychiatry we meet patients and their carers who struggle with increasing physical and mental frailty which necessitates help from others. This may involve extra input at home, hospital attendances and, for some, institutional care. The counter-dependence of those who have waged a lifetime's fight against reliance upon others will always provide problems in initially building in this help. If accepted, the attachment by the older person to his helper can have a desperate, clinging quality and come as an unwelcome shock. Staff can feel overwhelmed and easily resort to retaliation when confronted with so greedy a demand.

Another patient in our group, who was pampered as a child, had become highly anxious following impotence induced by a prostatectomy. He longed to be looked after in an idealized hotel where every need would be catered for without question. He constantly berated the therapists for not providing the magic pill to cure his symptoms, and outside went from doctor to doctor in his futile search for his replacement mother. The hostile feelings produced in the therapists and others in the group had to be fully understood if he were not to have the reverse of his wishes come true; that is, to be discharged precipitously.

TRANSFERENCE AND COUNTER-TRANSFERENCE

The story above illustrates a common problem when working with the elderly; that of wanting to rid oneself of the patient under the guise of the patient becoming too dependent for his own good. An important difference from work with younger adults is that the therapists are usually young enough to be their patients' children. While transference reactions will still result in patients seeing their therapists varyingly as surrogate partners, parents, children or even grandchildren, the patient is likely to be envious of their youth and prowess, while simultaneously denigrating the therapist for being too inexperienced. This can come as a hurtful blow to the eager therapist. Some patients may be aware of their own envious attacks and protect their younger therapists by being over-accommodating of their perceived failings; a kind of letting them off the hook.

The younger therapists, in full flight of mid-career, are usually striving towards ever-greater autonomy. They may mistakenly assume that this is what is wished for by their older patients for themselves. In fact, their patients will be edging towards dependence rather than independence. Thus the patient and therapist are at risk of working towards opposite goals; the therapist trying to rid himself of his elderly patient, but with the patient grimly hanging on. Brian Martindale describes these processes in a paper which marked a watershed in the understanding of this crucial area (Martindale, 1989).

These phenomena need not happen just between an individual patient and therapist in the psychotherapeutic setting, but are universal and usually unrecognized problems between older people and organizations set up to help them. Patients' hopes and fears sometimes seem to be towards the institutions themselves, where even the bricks and mortar become objects of transference projections.

To illuminate the potential pitfalls within a psychiatric service, a familiar saga is described. A wary patient is referred to the day hospital. After the initial resistance of the patient has been overcome the patient is more trusting and begins to invest their hopes in the staff. Previously concealed dependent characteristics of the patient may then be unleashed on an unsuspecting professional, who by now has assumed the dubious title of 'key worker'. Case conferences are held with increasing urgency, principally concerned with how the patient needs to be 'moved on', for example to a day centre or to Social Services; at any rate, somewhere else (as long as not here). The patient's protests are wrestled with and rationalized, sometimes in derogatory terms. Thus the staff's own problems, perhaps terror of their own ageing, become located in a convenient receptor. In this example the patient can end up in a worse state, having had a brief and cruel taste of what might have been. A recent analytical paper, highly critical of the National Health Service (NHS) reforms, highlights a shift in the climate away from the 'Nanny State' towards a culture where independence is prized and dependence becomes the focus of society's contempt (Bell, 1996).

It is not suggested that psychiatric services for the elderly can or should take on the problems of patients' dependence with blind omnipotence. There is, however, an urgent need to determine which groups of patients require life-long maintenance therapy and which patients benefit from more short-term interventions. Even with the briefest contact between patient and the service, staff should be alert to their patients' internal battle with dependence. The more disturbed a patient's past deprivations, the more conflicting will be his feelings about accepting help. Of paramount concern will be whether he feels safe enough to be dependent or whether he perceives a likelihood of humiliation, neglect or other abuse in store. At this point it is important to point out that elderly patients' fears are not necessarily neurotic ones, as Paul

Terry describes. In a disarmingly candid manner he has related his experiences as a clinical psychologist attempting to run groups for patients and staff in long-stay medical wards. Some of the patients were confused, and all were severely physically disabled. He drew attention to the persecutory atmosphere on the wards, and the staff's defences against their own despair. The resistance to exposing depressive anxieties he so vividly observed must be familiar to anyone who spends time in such an institutional setting (Terry, 1996).

In order to avoid this despair, staff may be helped to assess their own developmental phase in the 'life cycle'. Within institutions for elderly people the countertransference reactions of staff are likely to be a factor in facilitating patients' own adaptations to the worst consequences of old age. Ambivalent attitudes towards our own parents and our elderly patients are normal, but, as Terry reminds us, the digestion of all of this is not easy. Such impenetrable staff defences can be necessary just to maintain the survival of the institution.

SUPERVISION

This conveniently raises the question of supervision. Dealing with disturbed elderly people is a stressful business. It is also quite a strange undertaking. Given our collective discomfort with old age in the Western world it is not surprising that mental health services for the elderly have been slow to get started. As Woodward puts it: 'old age is one of the discontents of our civilisation' (Woodward, 1991). There are many reasons, good and bad, why some of us choose to work with older people. Psychoanalytic therapists will not accept a chance explanation. Many of us get through our work despite relative ignorance of our motivation, and some stones are probably better left unturned! The elderly who present to psychiatric services are often those who do so because of their demanding or distasteful behaviour. Gratitude may be in short supply for staff under pressure. Naturally, many staff will neither have the time nor the inclination to work psychodynamically, whatever supervision opportunities exist.

Supervision by an experienced therapist can, however, provide a setting in which these complex dynamics are explored safely. If staff are prone to act out personal grievances on patients then they may appreciate help in revealing their unconscious communications. Identification of those patients who should not have their defences dismantled requires expert knowledge of selection criteria. These criteria in regard to the elderly remain unstudied.

Most elderly patients referred to NHS psychiatric services do not have discrete neuroses, and many are frankly psychotic. Supervision, however, may help elicit the relevance of particular delusional manifestations, and facilitate the patients' overall management.

DEMENTIA

If the elderly in general have received relatively little attention from psycho-dynamic theorists, those with dementia have, as yet, been almost excluded. Joan Hunter has published her experiences as an analytical psychotherapist undertaking work with confused older people, both individually and in groups (Hunter, 1989). Ruth Porter illustrates how psychodynamic therapy with demented patients can throw light on superficially meaningless state-ments, and demonstrates the calming effect of her interpretations on the patient's anxiety (Porter, 1996). Where a full life-history is available, the bizarre behaviour of even severely demented patients can make more sense. Therefore patients are more likely to be seen by staff as individuals again.

OUTCOME

Demonstrating the benefits of psychodynamic therapy is notoriously problematic. An annotated bibliography, *Presenting the Case for Psychoanalytic Psychotherapy Services* compiling up-to-date studies on this matter, makes informative reading (Milton, 1996). Within it are synopses of all the major clinical works examining the effectiveness of various psycho-logical therapies.

Outcome can be measured in several ways. Symptom relief is a relatively straightforward theoretical possibility, but psychodynamic therapies usually aim to produce more fundamental changes in personality structure and less tangible satisfaction with life's vicissitudes. Furthermore, *when* to measure outcome is a relevant question, since the process of intrapsychic change and subsequent benefits might continue to occur years after therapy has finished, but while the patient's self-scrutiny continues. Matching patients with controls is also no easy task.

In a controlled study of recently bereaved mid- and late-life individuals recruited prophylactically to group therapy, Lieberman and Yalom failed to demonstrate clinically statistically significant advantages. Both treatment and control patients improved equally during a one-year follow-up, although the treatment patients self-reported the high value they placed on the group (Lieberman and Yalom, 1992).

Another indicator of success for the recurrently ill would be the demon-stration of a reduction of relapse and readmission rates. One study has appar-ently shown benefits for supportive group therapy in reducing readmission of elderly patients to a psychiatric unit (Ong *et al.*, 1987). Mumford, in a meta-analysis of 58 controlled studies, showed that patients receiving low-cost psychological interventions (counselling) were less likely to use medical inpatient care than those without, and this effect appeared larger for persons over 55 years of age (Mumford *et al.*, 1984).

The paucity of studies of psychotherapy with the elderly, and the diversity of methods used, makes comparisons between studies impossible at present.

As in the early days of psychiatry, individual case material provides some optimism for the usefulness of psychotherapy in this age group. Evidence of change as a result of interventions such as interpretation, ego support and containment is persuasively argued by individual clinicians, but as yet we do not know whether patients improved by chance, time, or some other factor, such as the therapist's enthusiasm.

Finally, an outcome measure worthy of study would be rates of staff turnover in a service for the elderly. Although, to the author's knowledge, there is no evidence to show that frequent staff changes are detrimental to patients' states of mind, it seems reasonable to assume so. On this basis, if the presence of a psychotherapist supporting nursing staff showed a reduction in their sick leave or moves elsewhere, this would provide substantial evidence for the cost-benefit of employing a psychotherapist, whose presence indirectly benefited patients.

CONCLUSION

Psychotherapy with the elderly is therefore in its infancy. There has been a considerable resistance to considering the application of psychodynamic principles to older people. Recently a few psychotherapists have chosen to work in this field. Until now psychiatrists have received little training, either in the normal and pathological mental processes which accompany ageing, or with regard to their unconscious reactions to these processes. While there is no proof that psychotherapy is especially of benefit to the older patient, there is a growing body of what can be termed 'accumulating wisdom'. Increased awareness of intrapsychic and interpersonal dynamics provides a deeper understanding of the universal and particular anxieties of our patients. Since the best services are likely to be those flexible enough to combine diverse models of treatment, there remain good reasons why practitioners might wish to research this area further.

REFERENCES

Abraham, K. (1919). The applicability of psycho-analytic treatment to patients at an advanced age. In: Bryan, D. and Strachey, A. (Eds.), *Selected Papers on Psychoanalysis*. Karnac, London, pp. 312–317.
Bell, D. (1996). Primitive mind of state. *Psychoanal Psychother* **10**, 45–57.
Erikson, E. (1966). Eight ages of man. *Int J Psychoanal* **2**, 281–300.
Freud, S. (1905). *On Psychotherapy*, standard edition 7. Hogarth, London.

Freud, S. (1915). *Mourning and Melancholia*. standard edition 14. Hogarth, London.

Hildebrand, P. (1986). Dynamic psychotherapy with the elderly. In: Hanley, I. and Gilhooly, M. (Eds), *Psychological Therapies for the Elderly*. Croom Helm, London, pp. 22–40.

Hunter, J. (1989). Reflections on psychotherapy with ageing people, individually and in groups. *Br J Psychiatry* **154**, 250–252.

Jaques, E. (1965). Death and the mid-life crisis. *Int J Psychoanal* **46**, 502–514.

King, P.H.M. (1974). Notes on the psychoanalysis of older patients. *J Anal Psychol* **19**, 22–37.

King, P.H.M. (1980). The life cycle as indicated by the nature of the transference of the middle aged and elderly. *Int J Psychoanal* **61**, 153–160.

Lieberman, M.A. and Yalom, I. (1992). Brief group psychotherapy for the spousally bereaved: a controlled study. *Int J Group Psychother* **42**, 117–132.

Martin, C. (1992). The elder and the other. *Free Assoc Psychoanal Groups Politics Culture* **3**, 341–354.

Martindale, B.V. (1989). Becoming dependent again: the fears of some elderly patients and their younger therapists. *Psychoanal Psychother* **4**, 67–75.

McKenzie-Smith, S. (1992). A psychoanalytical observational study of the elderly. *Free Assoc: Psychoanal Groups Politics Culture* **3**, 355–390.

Milton, J. (1996). *Presenting the Case for Psychoanalytic Psychotherapy Services: an Annotated Bibliography*. Tavistock Centre, London.

Mumford, E., Schlesinger, H.J., Glass, G.V., Patrick, P. and Cuerdon, B.A. (1984). A new look at evidence about reduced cost of medical utilization following mental health treatment. *Am J Psychiatry* **141**, 1145–1158.

Ong, Y.-L., Martineau, F., Lloyd, C. and Robbins, I. (1987). A support group for the depressed elderly. *Int J Geriatr Psychiatry* **2**, 119–123.

Porter, R. (1996). The psychoanalytic psychotherapist and the old age psychiatry team. In: Jacoby, R. and Oppenheimer, C. (Eds), *Old Age Psychiatry and the Elderly*. Oxford University Press, Oxford, pp. 257–268.

Sandler, A.M. (1978). Problems in the psychoanalysis of an ageing narcissistic patient. *J Geriatr Psychiatry* **11**, 5–36.

Segal, H. (Ed.) (1981). Fear of death – notes on the analysis of an old man. In: *The work of Hanna Segal*. Aronson, New York.

Terry, P. (1996). *Counselling the Elderly and their Carers*. Macmillan, London.

Weissman, M.M. (1994). Psychotherapy in the maintenance treatment of depression. *Br J Psychiatry* **165**(suppl 26), 42–50.

Woodward, K. (1991). *Aging and its Discontents - Freud and other Fictions*. Indiana University Press, Indiana.

Zivian, M.T., Larsen, W., Knox, V.J., Gekoski, W.L. and Hatchette, V. (1992). Psychotherapy for the elderly: psychotherapists' preferences. *Psychotherapy* **29**, 668–674.

Index